REAL ESTATE BROKERAGE
A MANAGEMENT GUIDE

Laurel D. McAdams and Joan m. Sobeck

President: Dr. Andrew Temte
Chief Learning Officer: Dr. Tim Smaby
Vice President, Real Estate Education: Asha Alsobrooks
Development Editor: Evonna Burr

REAL ESTATE BROKERAGE: A MANAGEMENT GUIDE, 8TH EDITION

Published by DF Institute, Inc., d/b/a Dearborn Real Estate Education
332 Front St. S., Suite 501
La Crosse, WI 54601

Printed in the United States of America
13 14 15 10 9 8 7 6 5 4 3 2 1
ISBN: 978-1-4277-4374-9 / 1-4277-4374-6
PPN: 1965-0108

CONTENTS

INTRODUCTION

Welcome to the world of business management—better yet, management in a real estate brokerage company.

Every industry considers itself unique. But the reality is business is business, with the objective to deliver products or services that appeal to the marketplace. Every business enterprise has stakeholders, owners, and investors who want to make money in those endeavors. Every manager plays a role in planning, organizing, and directing the systems, processes, and, most of all, the people that make companies work to achieve their stakeholders' objectives.

The fundamental principles of managing a business are universal, regardless of the industry, product or service, or individual company. So why devote a book to management in a real estate brokerage company?

By the very nature of our industry's licensing procedures, the typical training ground for company owners and managers is real estate sales. Salespeople presumably know their part of the business but generally don't have the training or experience to manage a company, unless they've acquired that in collegiate courses of study or prior business endeavors. And as much as business management principles are universally applicable, the how-to has to follow the lead of numerous industry laws and regulations.

In many states, a course in brokerage management (by whatever title) is required for a broker license. Generally, the course is expected to explore such fundamental issues as business planning, financial management, marketing and advertising, and professional ethics as well as law of agency, antitrust, and other laws (including the state regulators') that serve to protect the public.

A well-run, well-managed company is not only a credit to the industry but best serves the company's other stakeholders—the clients to whom the company is accountable. *Real Estate Brokerage: A Management Guide* suits the purpose of those courses but, most importantly, explores the fundamental principles of managing that well-run company.

As the name implies, the book is a guide. Each company has its own business philosophy, organizational structure, and work culture. Companies are an amalgamation of systems, processes, and people lead by managers who have individual styles and personalities as well. The purpose of a guide is to help you analyze situations and make decisions that suit your company, the prevailing marketplace, and the laws that apply in your circumstances.

The first chapter opens with a statement about there being no magic answers, only some that are better than others in a given situation. Keep that in mind as you open the pages about being a manager and the multitude of activities involved in planning, organizing, staffing, directing, and controlling a business enterprise. Think about how you can inspire people to grow professionally and make your organization a worthy model for success.

Real Estate Brokerage: A Management Guide is now in its eighth edition. Users of previous editions have observed that one of its greatest strengths is its futuristic yet timeless value in a wide range of applications. You should also find this helpful for gathering the tools of today's management trade and seizing new opportunities. We wish you much success!

CHAPTER ONE 1

THE CHALLENGE OF CHANGE

What did you learn about doing business in the recent economic environment?

What will the real estate business look like in the future?

There are no magic answers in business—only some that are better than others, depending on the situation. Guarantees are few. But change is certain.

If you don't like the headlines today, wait. On the other hand, if you do like today's news, that can change, too.

Business management is as much about the situations as it is about the money. The money is the end result of making wise decisions that suit the circumstances, not just today's but those we assume for the future. Any business, a real estate company included, is at the mercy of a number of forces over which it has little control. What separates those that succeed from those that don't is the ability to deal with the realities of change.

The "Challenge of Change" sets the stage for the pages that follow with some poignant lessons about doing business in that environment. Think about what were, what are, and what will be the events framed in the big picture that create opportunities and challenges for business owners and their companies.

■ THE BIG PICTURE

> Our nation continues its struggle to secure peaceful coexistence among differing cultures. The stock market loses value, corporate profits diminish, and older workers are forced to rethink retirement plans for their golden years. Corporate leaders are forced to explain their deception that cost investors mighty amounts of money.

Does this sound like life after 2007?

Actually, these words are extracted from commentary written in 2003 for the 6th edition of this book when our nation was struggling to regain its footing after 9/11, investors were trying to repair the damage after the "tech bubble" burst, and corporate executives were making headlines for appearances in court and jail sentences for fraud.

The sequel to that story is low interest rates played a major role in fueling consumer spending and corporate growth. The stock market regained its stride and reached unprecedented highs, and an exceedingly robust housing market reached new heights, too. Until subprime mortgages made headlines in 2006, and then life changed once again.

We were sitting on a dangerous precipice in 2007 when the 7th edition was written. The editors cringed over commentary (that was eventually stricken) about the brink of a depression or at least major turmoil that would upset multiple sectors of the marketplace worldwide. The words were too pessimistic to print. But we wouldn't have been wrong.

As the magnitude of the subprime mortgage problem came to light, the stock market plunged, Lehman Brothers collapsed, credit markets seized, and thousands of people lost their jobs. The investment market was in shambles, having worldwide implications. Consumers dramatically curtailed their spending. Housing prices dropped 30 percent and wiped out over seven trillion dollars of homeowners' equity. The economy did plunge close to a bottom that hadn't been touched since the 1930s.

Few people are still alive to share first-hand stories about the Great Depression that began on Black Tuesday in October 1929 and left thousands of people destitute and homeless. But people are alive who grew up under the influence of parents who endured those times and remained ever wary that history could repeat itself. They can tell about rationing during World War II and the scarcity of goods that are so easily taken for granted. But that war also mobilized a huge amount of material and manpower that solidified the recovery from the Depression and set us on a path of growth after the war years.

Out of that Great Depression came banking regulations and amortized mortgage loans to protect depositors from bank failures and families from losing their homes. Out of the war came prosperity that fueled great optimism and instilled a rosy, almost fearless view of the future, despite economic ups and downs along the way. In fact, today's younger generations have never had any view but that rosy one.

How easy it was to expect that the real estate market, which drove the economy to record heights into the middle of this century's first decade, couldn't possibly lose steam, let alone plunge to such miserable lows. Or that the mortgage loans that provided financial wherewithal for thousands of homeowners would be the undoing of their American dream. We took credit for granted because it was always there, and saving was something we'd get around to after we lived for today.

Optimism fuels our strength and determination. It also causes us to lose perspective and fail to prepare for the inevitable change along the economic seine waves. There's also an element of greed that craves more in the good times and drives desperation in the bad, not always with praiseworthy results.

These words can be written for any business enterprise or industry. It just so happens that banks, investment houses, and mortgage companies were front and center in the drama that played through what came to be known as the Great Recession.

Profit motives do interesting things. When the economy is good, the real estate market is thriving, and everyone is making money. The banks fuel the market with more money and make loans easier for borrowers to get. Buyers purchase more houses and more expensive ones than they could afford in stricter lending times. Sellers make more money and move up into even more expensive homes. Real estate companies sell more properties, make more money, and salespeople earn better livings. The market is on a roll, real estate prices (values?) rise, and there's no way but up—until it falls down.

The real estate market crumpled, but no one said yes, that was always a possibility. The banking and real estate industries rode the wave but when it was over, few owned up to the part they played in buyers sitting with houses in foreclosure and mortgages that were upside down. Everyone took a risk but not everyone knew how much risk they were taking.

Waves always break.

The Next Wave

Then new waves come along, and we climb on another one.

The current wave is a recovery one. It has more momentum in some sectors of the economy, and there's still debris from the last wave. The government's bailouts for the banks and auto industry still have their critics, as does the nation's debt, which has more causes than just the spending to rescue the economy. Tax policies are in flux (there are always elections to fuel that discussion), and employers are rehiring, but not yet at the pace needed for a really strong economy.

Some real estate markets in the country (some of which weren't as severely affected as others) are regaining their stride. But there are still many foreclosed properties lying in wait, with banks under pressure to work out their differences so borrowers can get on with their lives.

The stock market that has always cycled on the feet of the bulls and the bears is cautiously bullish, though still very volatile. The whys and wherefores of those animals' treks are too complex for many to understand. And even the most respected analysts have difficulty predicting, much less agreeing on, the bulls' and the bears' next moves. But on some days, investors can be happy in positive territory.

The global terrain is rockier than it's been in recent decades. Although our economic woes had global consequences, those pale in comparison to the brink of bankruptcy some countries face and the diminishing number of strong ones that can rescue their debt. The myopic view says we can't make that our problem but with global capital at risk, the problem can easily become a domestic one, as the stock market indicates with drops on each headline of bad news.

The geopolitical environment is as unstable as it was (if not more than) in the first year or so after 9/11. The off-shore venues have changed and political powers have shifted, but threats rooted in cultural differences still persist. This has also changed the tenor of immigration and energy policies, both serving our nation's domestic and global agenda.

These are fragile times but we're working out of the recession with consumers carrying less debt, payoff having been a necessity to weather the times, and with leaner businesses, poised to work smarter and grow more profitable. So, there's an upside to everything.

Only time will tell whether the legislative frenzy to protect consumers and investors will unduly restrain our free enterprise system. Of course, ideologies in power may change and shift the current course. But we know at the moment that mortgage lending, appraising, and settlement procedures live under a critical eye that views practices through the prism of subprime mortgages.

In fact, only time will tell how well or fast the economy grows out of the Great Recession. You, our reader, can add the sequel, hopefully one about optimistic signs that quickly turned into robust economic growth.

THE FUTURE PICTURE

Once we think about the then-and-now, we can appreciate the significance of the decisions that come next. The challenge, of course, is that the barometer on current events changes daily and little about the economic and political climate is the same for very long. But one thing is timeless—the fundamental theories of management or the framework that gives business managers the tools to manage in any climate.

One of the axioms in business management (of several you'll read in this book) is—*companies can't continue to do the same things the same way and expect different results*—especially when the world around them is different.

The smartest thing we can do is challenge our thinking, with no "sacred cow" or "way we always do it" being off limits, and see what surfaces as the best way to do business in the future, regardless of the ups and downs in the economy. Sometimes we have to think way outside the box to decide if we're building the right box. There's no risk in asking the questions.

What Will a Real Estate Company Be Doing?

The fundamental business since its inception has been to bring together real estate properties and users. Those could be properties for sale or rent and users to purchase or lease, and then we dressed this up (or complicated it) with agency representation and fiduciary duties. Unlike other business enterprises, real estate companies don't make any products or have any control over the products they sell. So, companies claimed rights to products with listings and vigorously controlled that information.

How relevant is that model today? The real estate industry organized early in the 1900s when brokers banded together in pursuit of professional business practices. Out of that came a unique alliance of competitors who work together to help one another. In the earliest days, that business alliance was the only way brokers had to share information about their properties for sale. The alliance evolved into a formal structure that came to be known as a multiple listing service (MLS). Before long, numerous such services formed in many geographic areas. MLSs became a controlled conduit for the broker-members' property information.

More than 100 years later, technology gave us the Internet. There's still a need to bring properties and users together, and there's still a need to circulate property information. But gone are the days when brokers relied on the MLS's weekly delivery of paper listing sheets. Technology gave us a far more efficient way to distribute that information, but even that pales in comparison with what the Internet has done for consumers, who now have direct access to information and the ability to drive their own real estate transactions. *What role should the real estate company play?*

Businesses operate on traditions, which are perpetuated by generations of business owners and their models for work. The great divide in today's companies is just that, the generations. The majority of real estate companies are run by the over-age-50 crowd, which is confronted by the Gen Ys who are the ages of their children and grandchildren. They are less steeped in tradition and often frustrated by the "old" that seems irrelevant today. *How will the company deal with tradition versus change?*

What Is the Role for MLS?

Information has become the hot commodity in the marketplace. It can be warehoused, delivered, and exchanged for something of value in return, which has moved the real estate industry into the information business, more than a brick and mortar one. The industry's hot commodity, of course, is property listings—an asset brokers have considered proprietary information, to be shared only among MLS members (as permitted by the property owners).

Information is power—the MLS has the power and those desiring the information must join the fraternity of members. The introduction of the Internet challenged the MLS's information-management model. As MLS members posted their own listings on their Web sites, consumers demanded access to more listings. The MLSs formed Internet Data Exchanges (IDXs) which gave consumers access to an MLS's entire database through a member-company's site (within the limits of MLS policies).

The IDX model provided landing places for consumers and served the purpose of promoting listings. But this was purely an informational model and did not provide an interactive business setting for the consumer and broker. That led to the development of Virtual Office Web sites (VOWs), which added an e-commerce component to the IDX model, again administered according to MLS's policies.

In the information-is-a-hot-commodity scheme of things, a number of Internet-based companies formed to distribute real estate information, listings included. The growing power of Web-based sites such as Zillow makes them attractive venues for real estate companies to promote their listings as well. The RETS (Real Estate Transaction Specification), which is a standardized digital format, makes it easy for companies to update that listing information.

One lesson the Internet teaches, though, is that once information is cast in digital form, there's very little way to control where data circulate and how it's used. This has resurrected the debate over ownership of information, especially when third-party Internet companies sell leads to real estate companies that were generated by the companies own listings. In the process, the number of skirmishes (and litigation) over MLS rules has increased.

MLSs generate revenue (often for local REALTOR® Associations) but that revenue is threatened by the increasing challenges to their business models. The conversation has already begun about MLSs consolidating (perhaps statewide), especially because the real estate business is no longer defined by narrow geographic boundaries. Decisions will ultimately have to be driven by what's in the best interest of the owners whose properties are for sale.

What Will Consumers Want?

For decades company businesses were based on a supplier model—the supplier controls the selection of products and services offered in the marketplace, essentially a take-it-or-leave-it model. But today's companies serve the marketplace with a consumer-driven model, which creates products and services tailored to suit consumer demand, essentially answering the question about what consumers want.

Their wants today are rooted in the cyber economy that gives consumers access to most any product, service, or sliver of information with the stroke of a finger on a tablet, laptop, or smart phone. This means delivering products and services in a "one-stop shop" in front of their devices and with vendors who can link them with other services.

A once geocentric business has no geographic boundaries and serves a very culturally-diverse population. The domestic Hispanic and Asian populations are growing at three times the rate of the overall population, with Hispanics now being the "majority minority." And the global population is increasingly more mobile. The multicultural market has huge buying power, which represents a host of opportunities to tailor products and services to capture that diverse clientele.

For real estate, the meaning of *core services* has expanded beyond brokerage in many companies to include an array of services that seamlessly take buyers and sellers from doorstep to settlement. In some companies, that includes linking consumers with job placement for a spouse, day care for a child or elderly parent, or housecleaning, yard care, or handyman services.

The industry has also provided alternatives to the one-stop-shop and one-size-fits-all service models to appeal to more selective consumers who want to purchase and pay for only selected services from a real estate company. This has pressured companies to unbundle their services, shed transaction-based fee structures in favor of alternative pricing models, and offer a menu of options from which consumers can choose and then pay only for the services they use.

Consumer wants also represent their diverse ages as well. The over-65 age group, which currently outnumbers the 18-to-24 year-olds, will continue to be a huge force in the marketplace as people live longer. This will add to the need for alternatives to the one-size-fits-all service model.

Because more business is done with little personal interface today, some wonder why any commodity can't be traded the same way a sizable investment portfolio can—online without intervention of a person and without paper, too. A few Web sites already give buyers the ability to make offers online. *Will the day come that real estate will be fully traded online that way too?*

Where Will the Real Estate Office Be?

The traditional measure of market share has been tied to brand recognition in geographic or physical locations, with location also being the draw for foot traffic. The industry began in single real estate offices comprised of the broker and perhaps several associates. Then companies grew market share by growing into multiple-office organizations, some staffed by hundreds of personnel who offer a wide range of services.

Large companies got bigger, often by assimilating midsized companies for their command of an appealing share of the market. Megabrokers merged with other megabrokers to further strengthen their presence. They also formed brainstorming groups, such as the Realty Alliance, to enhance their competitiveness as independent companies. Outsiders entered the business, becoming parent companies of organizations such as Coldwell Banker and franchises such as Century 21 and ERA.

Despite the trend of "bigness," the majority of our nation's businesses are small enterprises. There's still a place for small real estate companies, their appeal often being their smallness and more personalized or specialized services. Internet-based companies are also proving there's a place in the market for small, independent enterprises.

In the world of e-commerce, companies (not just real estate ones) are learning that cyberspace is more important than office space. The physical site plays a supporting, rather than starring, role in the great multi-act play of today's business enterprises. There will always be a supporting role for a company's headquarters, and for branch or satellite offices, as long as state regulators hold on to requirements for fixed office locations. But consumers are much more interested in what they consume than in where they consume it. The same can be said for how the sales force works.

What Will a Real Estate Company Look Like?

Real estate companies have merged, divested themselves of previous affiliations, and forged new alliances with other real estate enterprises or enterprises offering complementary products and services. Some have been drawn under a single corporate umbrella along with a number of diverse or even non-real estate-related corporate units. The companies restructure in the same ways our nation's major corporations restructure theirs and do so for the same reason—to achieve more profitable operations.

Downsizing and *reengineering* are terms commonly heard in corporate boardrooms as companies strive to work smarter as the cost of operation increases. Companies often suffer from misaligned structures and bloated workforces as a result of mergers or acquisitions, or changes in the work they do. Real estate companies already function on narrow profit margins and cost of operations must be managed very carefully. Costs that diminish bottom lines are often the very expenditures that help an organization work more efficiently and productively.

Rightsizing is the more accurate term for what companies do to realign their operations. The major part of that involves the workforce. Often, realignment (by whatever term is used) is associated with job loss. Although there may be fewer personnel positions in the short term, especially if adjustments are dictated by a downturn in the economy, the long-term result is new jobs are created with different or refined skill requirements.

Real estate companies can become more effective by downsizing the sales staff, employing a smaller number of people but ones who are highly productive. Companies that still subscribe to the practice of hiring large sales staffs (with the expectation that larger staffs will produce comparably larger revenue) are more closely scrutinizing this strategy because of the cost to attract and retain top producers while also carrying a large number of marginally productive salespeople.

Companies can also work smarter by hiring salespeople as employees rather than as independent contractors. The appeal is that companies can exercise greater control over sales activities and, ultimately, revenue production. While employee costs are higher, the expectation is that those expenditures can be offset with higher revenue. Although this strategy has not yet been widely embraced by residential sales companies, it is prevalent in nonresidential ones.

Certainly, the number of available licensees plays a role in staffing decisions, including the effect of portable licensing that allows practice across regulatory jurisdictions. That number tends to peak and wane as the real estate market rises and falls. The catch is that companies tend to trim staff or not replace loss by attrition when business trails off and are then caught short-handed when business flourishes again. Such is the challenge for a cyclical business like real estate, but that means anticipating shifting trends is all more important.

There is no *one* suitable model for a real estate company, only the one that supports the work the company needs to do in the contemporary environment and do it profitably. *How many people will that take? And what will they be doing?*

Who Will Be Leading the Company in the Next Ten Years?

The logical answer is the next generation, the Gen Ys. But that's not a realistic answer if the parent-and-grandparent-age owners and managers don't inspire youth to enter the business and give that talent a chance to flourish.

Although there are no employment guarantees, today's workforce is more resilient, less intimidated by change, than workers of decades ago. There are few 35-year-service "gold watch" retirements any longer. Today, people go where the jobs are, often skipping from job to job and even switching careers. That mobility brings new blood with fresh perspectives into a company's workforce.

Today's workforce is a melting pot of cultures and generations, especially as people work longer. This gives a company the energy of youth, the voice of experience, and varied perspectives for competing in the global marketplace. Companies fall short, though (our nation's large corporations included), in senior management and executive positions where culturally diverse viewpoints would aid decision making in the contemporary environment.

Unless companies promote younger workers, they will move on and leave the organization with a huge void in leadership as people retire. How will the company appeal to the next generation of buyers and sellers without that next generation of business leaders? Or will those leaders shun established companies and start up their own?

What's the Next Generation's American Dream?

The real estate industry has stumped in favor of homeownership for years. Clearly, the industry has a strong business reason for its advocacy, but homeownership also supports the construct of our nation's social, political, and financial agenda.

Homeownership peaked at 69 percent in 2006, according to the U.S. Census bureau, but that record high was short lived and by the first quarter of 2012, reached a 15-year low as more people turned to rentals. Despite low interest rates and attractive housing prices, people sat on the sidelines, underemployed and with damaged credit, thanks to the Great Recession. The reality is that people haven't really owned, but have borrowed, the American Dream for at least the past three decades.

The rental trend isn't limited to housing. A growing segment of the population is choosing the flexibility of enjoyment for everything from cars to clothing over the permanence of ownership. This appeals to an increasingly mobile population but also serves a cost-efficient mindset—renting even high-end is cheaper than purchasing, even at the low end. And there aren't the continuing costs of maintenance and repair, either.

The rental rationale doesn't suit the mindset that values the economic accomplishment of ownership or investment with the potential for appreciation, which is the premise of homeownership. Buying a home has also been a way to pivot from one stage in life to another, especially noted by single women who were 22 percent of the homebuyers in 2006, as opposed to 11 percent in 1981. Perhaps differences in mindsets are generational ones, but no question there are financial realities that affect choices to rent instead of own.

Add the fact that college students are graduating with record student-loan debt and working to pay off their past, not save for the future. And only 40 percent of them expect their lives to be better than their parents' lives.

One of the few bright lights in the Great Recession has been an increase in building, not single-family homes but multifamily buildings, spawned by demand for rentals. But that building boom is also a normal cycle, the hot segment being attractive until the next segment gets hot. Rental demand also attracted investors to foreclosed properties, which also absorbed overstocked single-family houses from the marketplace. *How long will it take for people to become homebuyer worthy? Or will renting be the new American Dream?*

What Will Professional Associations Be Doing?

These organizations provided a way for people with like-minded interests to learn, socialize, and affect public policy. The professional groups served purposes their members couldn't accomplish by themselves (or elsewhere) and performed self-regulating functions, particularly important when few laws guided professional activities or protected consumers. Real estate brokers, homebuilders, appraisers, virtually every business has organized a place to belong. No question that the organizations are visiting the same questions we are but the answers will come from—*Do the members need what the organizations offer? Or will a new association model emerge?*

What Will Industry Regulations Look Like?

Once was the day that the real estate industry had no oversight other than its own professional associations, especially the National Association of REALTORS®. Not until the 1920s and 1930s did the states pass licensing laws, and still many more years until the laws included education requirements. That's a long way from then to now, with real estate being one of the most highly regulated businesses.

Along the way, the business world (real estate included) encountered a variety of laws that grew out of movements to protect the consumer. And some legislation was borne out of the excesses of business. Those legislative trends continue and temper the creativity of business leaders.

We know after the headlined scandals on Wall Street that company executives are more closely scrutinized, investors are more critical, and the public is more wary of the way companies do business. Establishing credibility and trustworthiness, even for companies that aren't publicly traded (those that don't fall under Securities Exchange Commission and Sarbanes-Oxley accounting rules), is crucial to survival, let alone success. That's particularly significant for sales businesses, which have traditionally been suspect in the public's mind anyway.

The Department of Justice (DOJ), the enforcer of the antitrust laws, has been especially vigilant since the 1970s when it first cited MLSs and other professional groups (including REALTOR® boards, as they were known at the time) for setting commission rates, among other antitrust violations. The best-case outcome was allegations could be resolved by consent decree and agreements to adopt affirmative antitrust practices. In the worst case, brokers served jail time. But in all cases, the defendants incurred huge legal bills.

The DOJ continues to pursue an aggressive antitrust agenda, and the industry continues to defend. One recent case asserted that the industry's traditional policies and procedures inhibited the providers of innovative alternatives, particularly those whose business is primarily Internet-based. Therefore, consumers were denied access to property information and other services at a lower cost.

Another case alleged that policies of an MLS controlled the marketplace and restrained competition, affecting practices of non-members as well as choices for the consumer. A consent order precluded enforcing certain MLS policies, including the use of pre-printed language in listing contracts that was deemed anticompetitive.

The industry is already in transition from a singular, long-standing business model into the world of numerous creative alternatives, supported in large part by the Internet. But the question remains how significantly business models will change over time. Regulatory law is typically reactive rather than proactive to foster innovation and creative free enterprise. And laws take time to change.

One last question—can you answer the other questions objectively without stumbling on the "big elephant in the room?" *The money*. We know how we make money now (usually), but it's hard to be candid if the answer would diminish or eliminate a current revenue stream. The fundamental principle of the real estate business is rooted in the long-held belief that consumers need real estate people to help navigate the complexities of a transaction. But what do consumers need in the 21st century? Is there something new a company can do that is just as good or perhaps even better?

The point is to ponder the questions to be sure that the company does make money in the future. The goal is to establish a vibrant, relevant enterprise. If it can't be vibrant or isn't relevant, then it needs to be doing something differently. This is the ultimate challenge of change. It may well be that not much needs to change. But it doesn't cost anything to ask the questions, especially if the answers prevent the company from becoming a victim of progress.

■ A FINAL THOUGHT

Some observers say that fundamentally nothing has changed about the real estate industry. In a sense, there's an element of truth in that—the industry is still about real estate. But *the way* the industry does business definitely has changed, and that will continue in the future. In the triteness of "the future is closer than you think," there's another element of truth. The future any real estate company has to prepare for is not decades from now, but next year and the next.

All business organizations face similar challenges for similar reasons. Bottom line pressures, economic downturns, abundant regulations, and aggressive competition are but a few of the realities of life. The latest challenge is the competitive forces brought about by the Internet. The real estate business isn't any different in these respects.

Many valuable lessons can be learned from the corporate world. But this means stepping outside the real estate industry and learning how business organizations, in general, function. The processes that are explored in later chapters are similar to those that any business organization goes through. That is, business management.

■ CONCLUSION

The fitting conclusion to this chapter is really a beginning. Having opened some lines of thinking from a global perspective, now you can take the next step. Look at your local business environment and your own organization. Some situations may be similar or you may identify other forces that impact your business. The point is that change is inescapable. Astute businesspeople see change as an opportunity. Be open-minded and innovative, especially when you look into the future. No old way is so good that it can't be improved on. Keep this in mind as you work through the management functions explored in this book.

■ DISCUSSION EXERCISES

What is your candid assessment of the current housing market in your area? The current economic climate? What do you expect to be different during the next few years?

What has changed about the demographic profile of your consumers and your company's workforce in recent years? What do you expect in the future?

What effect has recent litigation or regulatory changes had on real estate practices in your area? What issues are pending that could affect future practices?

Considering the financial pressures on today's organizations and the consumers' attitudes about the cost of real estate services, how do you think fees for real estate services and costs for transactions should be structured?

UNIT I
THE MANAGER

The logical place to begin a business management discussion is with the manager. A company is an organization of systems and processes, but the driving force behind them is the manager. In fact, many contemporary business writers take readers through organizational functions solely through the viewpoint of a manager. Regardless of how the functions are discussed, however, the fact remains that organizations are administered by the actions of their managers.

A business organization is nothing more than an aggregation of people. All the other systems are simply ways to organize the collected people so they can work effectively and efficiently, and make money for the organization. Someone needs to lead the group and that someone is the manager. In a real estate company, a manager can have such titles as broker/owner, sales manager, or department manager.

The manager's success in leading the group of people depends on a number of factors that have less to do with the formal organization and much more to do with the person. Because there is a human element in everything a manager does, a manager's effectiveness is directly related to his or her people skills. Peter Drucker, a respected management theorist, described management's job as being all about human beings.

The emphasis on people skills arises from an evolution of management thinking that began in the 1930s when theorists began studying human relationships in business organizations. The recognition that people are an organization's most valuable resource led to studies about the psychology of work and workplace motivations; in essence, why people work.

Theorists learned that organizations benefited when they invested in the workers' professional growth and engaged them in the organization's processes. The outgrowth of these discoveries is the job enrichment and participatory environments that are common in the workplace today.

This first unit is a journey through some discussions to help you command a leadership position in an organization and manage the interdependent relationships of its people. Unlike the one-two-three-step formulas commonly learned in sales, management development is an evolving process. It begins with understanding how personal traits, strengths, and weaknesses affect relationships (positively or negatively) in an organization and continues as the manager fine tunes the skills needed to be effective in the job. To help meet the personal challenges of management, we explore

- leadership and the characteristics in leaders that inspire people to follow,
- management, the connection between management and leadership, and the skills managers use to lead people in the workplace, and
- communications in the business setting and quality decision making.

Entire publications by notable authors are devoted exclusively to leadership development, management skills, business writing, and other personal skills managers need to be successful. These books are useful regardless of whether you are the broker/owner of the company or hold another management position in the organization.

2

CHAPTER TWO

LEADERSHIP

Whom do you admire as an effective leader? Why?

What do you know about yourself that would help—or hinder—you, as a leader?

Why do we need a leader? The provocative answer is we don't—if we're willing to live in chaos. But world history paints ugly pictures of civil, economic, and political turmoil when leaders lose their following.

Will any leader do? Another provocative answer is yes—if we're willing to live with the consequences. History also shows how brutal those consequences can be with Adolf Hitler, Muammar Gaddafi, and other oppressive heads of state who ruled by purging the dissenters and the disfavored.

Why do people want to be president, chief, or chair? Power and influence are acceptable answers—if we can trust them to use their power and influence responsibly.

How do we choose the right person for the position?

It's primary election season, a number of candidates are vying for their party's nomination to run against an incumbent president, and the campaign discourse is all about how each person would lead us in the right direction. Not surprisingly, each "right" is different. Also no surprise is that values, integrity, truthfulness, and assorted other personal issues are part of the discourse as well. The passion is obvious, the private motives behind the public words are less so.

The good and bad behind the other questions tell us what we need to know about choosing the right person.

- We see a mission or purpose for where the leader wants to go and how to get there. And that's what we want, too.
- We see strength of conviction, passion, and commitment to certain ideals that tell us the leader is worthy of our allegiance.
- We have faith that the leader has our best interests at heart and that following is the right thing to do.
- We trust the leader to use the power and influence responsibly and not cause us harm.
- We believe the leader is telling the truth and will deliver on the promises the person makes.

The essence of leadership—the ability to influence other people and persuade them to follow—explains why some people are formally elected or appointed to a position and others command a following regardless of a formal title. We are inspired by what we see in the person and what the person stands for. Then we are willing to follow.

■ CHARACTER OF A LEADER

One of the most powerful lessons from history is the risk of aligning with someone who can profoundly affect our lives. We are willing to take that risk when we see admirable character traits and have confidence the person will use the position responsibly. The most revered traits include

- **Integrity.** Webster's dictionary says integrity is *a firm adherence to a code of especially moral or artistic values, implying trustworthiness and incorruptibility.*
- **Honesty.** Citing Webster again, honesty is found to *imply a refusal to lie, steal, or in any way deceive, an unswerving fidelity to the truth.*
- **Trustworthiness.** The essential element is *confidence that a person can be trusted, the faith others have that a person will use the position of trust responsibly and no harm will come to them.*
- **Loyalty.** Webster says loyalty implies a *faithfulness that is steadfast in the face of any temptation to betray.*
- **Respect.** This is the *high regard for the welfare and rights of others* and when mutual, others highly regard that person.

Webster's definitions reveal how interrelated the traits are. Honesty and integrity are frequently associated because with integrity also comes the expectation that a person does not lie, cheat, steal, or deceive. A person can use knowledge for truthful and honorable purposes, or for manipulation or self-serving gain. Once the latter happens, we no longer feel we can trust a person.

Trusting one another is risky, but we'll take that risk when we feel people will use our trust wisely. Some people are so successful at engendering trust that they can persuade others to believe in them despite their gross failings—Adolf Hitler, for example. Blind trust is often misplaced trust. Trust abused is trust violated.

Loyalty arises from our belief that pledging allegiance to a person or a cause is beneficial. People are faithful when they feel their personal needs are being met. Once our devotion no longer reaps those benefits or we discover that our allegiance was misplaced, we are no longer loyal.

Respect is essentially the culmination of all we learn about a person's character. We may not necessarily love, like, or even feel any particular kinship with another. Yet, we respect a person because he or she is worthy of the regard.

Values and Ethics

Why is it, then, that we elect or appoint heads of state, corporate executives, and even managers that seem to have flawed characters? Maybe their characters aren't flawed. If their values, ethics, and moral codes align with our own, we see nothing wrong with the way those people behave. On the other hand, if their systems and codes are different than ours, we are offended, even outraged, by their behavior.

Why the difference?—because there is no one universal set of values, ethics, and moral codes. Each of us has a personal set of values (money, health, other people, power, prestige, a job, etc.) and codes for ethical and moral behavior, all of which are influenced by family, culture, religion, and society. Values and the like that are acceptable (or tolerated) in one arena are not necessarily accepted in another.

We set the highest standards for our leaders, expecting that their value systems, ethics, and moral codes are especially honorable and models for us to emulate.

We face a dilemma when our values or standards and those of other people are misaligned. One of the best examples involves money. Is money valued at all cost, regardless of how it is gotten? Or is money valued only when gotten honorably? When a person functions with the money-at-all-cost notion while the organization functions on the honorable notion (or vice versa), the holder of the honorable notion feels that a fundamental code has been violated. Eventually, the moral compromise becomes intolerable.

Power

Another lesson from history shows us what a leader can do with power. We expect that the person has the integrity to use power to positively affect our lives. But we often hear that power corrupts. Power in the hands of a corruptible person does just that.

When a person uses power to coerce, we obey out of fear rather than respect. Once we become suspicious of our leader's motives or feel we've surrendered too much control to someone else, coercion no longer works. That is, unless we are threatened with brutal consequences. Clearly, that's the ultimate abuse of power.

Just as we need to respect the leader, we need to feel that the person respects us, treating us fairly and with dignity. We may not always like the leader's decisions, but we can respect those that ultimately benefit the whole of our group, be it a country or a company. We judge the leader unworthy of the power if our personal values or ethics are compromised, or the leader is willing to compromise those of the organization for personal gain.

Even in organizations with highly structured ranks (like the military) and serious consequences for failing to acquiesce to superiors, there are always subordinates that don't fall into line. In fact, a person may choose the negative consequences rather than abide a superior who is not deemed worthy of allegiance.

■ LEADERSHIP QUALITIES

We need to see that our leaders have a clear direction and certain qualities that show they can do an admirable job of guiding us. A leadership position is a conspicuous (and vulnerable) place to be, which requires courage and often personal sacrifice as well.

Vision

Leaders are long-range, independent thinkers who look for new, more inspired ways to do things. They are the risk takers, the trail blazers, the entrepreneurs who "think outside the box" rather than within the parameters of established systems. Leaders inspire us by their passion and enthusiasm for the work they do or the course they want to take.

Ego and Empathy

Ego is about self-esteem. Ego is not about boisterousness or inflated self-importance but the quiet dignity that shows us people respect and believe in themselves. When people are self-assured or self-confident, they engender our confidence in them.

Empathy is all about the followers, acknowledging their worth or value and respecting their thoughts, feelings, and abilities (and shortcomings). The people matter. Ego and empathy are linked, expecting that a self-assured leader will support us and not sacrifice our interests to make that person look good. We want leaders who are self*less* rather than self*ish*.

Team Building

Leaders are effective because they draw people together, build coalitions, or team build. The coalition may be an in-house circle of a few trusted advisors or as broad as a group of people from other companies or countries. Those relationships serve to

- stimulate creative thinking or problem solving.
- build consensus.
- resolve or manage conflict.
- achieve support for a policy, position, or course of action.

Coalitions build a core following that demonstrates to others the merits of following the leader. The group-think or participatory (inclusive rather than exclusive) process is more evidence that the people matter.

Of course, if the leader is less than admirable, the coalition is as well. This is how tyrannical leaders get away with their ruthless ways. They build an inner circle of like-minded loyalists who will help further their agenda. That agenda, for any leader, is often revealed by the people with whom he or she associates.

Decisiveness

We expect leaders to take charge and provide direction. Their decisiveness gives us the assurance that they have a clear vision of where we're going. Ambiguity muddles perceptions about who is in charge and causes the followers to fall by the wayside. Lacking direction from elsewhere, people chart their own courses, which may not necessarily be the path the leader wants them to take.

Decisiveness is not as much about decision-making processes as it is about the ability to frame definitive courses of action. Some people are naturally decisive, while others have to learn how to form direction for themselves and for others. Formal decision-making processes vary, but the important point is we expect a leader to provide the guidance that people need.

When people assume responsibility, they also become responsible or accountable for the outcomes.

Accountability

Accountability is easy to handle when actions produce the desired results or exceed expectations. But accountability also means taking the blame for failing to act or for actions that went astray. A leader stands up and says, "it's my fault, I made a mistake," and doesn't blame other people, unrealistic policy, or flawed laws or procedures for undesirable outcomes. The "buck stops here"—that is, with the leader.

In real estate companies, this stops with the brokers because licensing laws hold them responsible for the activities of the licensees who work for them. Regulators do not excuse a salesperson's ineptitude or a broker's inability to know all that the licensees are doing as a defense for violations of the law.

Accountability extends to all that happens under the leader's domain. That domain gets larger with higher positions in the organization, which means being accountable for activities for which other people are also responsible. Leaders are willing to share credit (and blame) for the actions (or inaction) of others.

Delegation

The sequel to accountability is delegation. This assigns responsibility for certain activities to another person and, most importantly, confers *authority* or the right to direct the job that is to be done. Delegating means giving up control and trusting someone else to do a job for which the delegator is ultimately accountable.

Delegation helps people make meaningful contributions and feel good. But the delegated tasks have to be significant, or people will feel insulted. Delegation works when

- the right people are identified for the specific work. They must have the experience, knowledge, or skill to carry out the assignment. They also must be willing to accept the responsibility and be accountable for the work and achieving the desired outcomes.
- the delegator lets go. People must be given the authority to perform the work without interference. Once a job is delegated, the person to whom it is assigned must be given the opportunity to decide how to do it and to get it done.

Some people delegate but don't confer the authority to make commitments, use resources, or take other steps that are needed to do the job. This is a failure of trust and confidence—trust that someone else can do a job at least as well (even if not the same way) as the delegator would do, and confidence that the delegator's stature will not be diminished if someone else does the job or does it better.

■ LEADERS VERSUS MANAGERS

We learn more about leadership when we look at how leaders and managers see their functions in a business setting. Some business management theorists contend that these are two separate roles while others contend that a person has to be a good leader to be a good manager. You be the judge.

- Managers are work focused. They administer or make the organization run, doing things that keep business on course. Managers manage work—systems, processes, and people—with an eye on short-term objectives and bottom-line dollars to achieve or preserve stability. Managers are more reactive than proactive and see their job as one that ensures the organization operates effectively and efficiently.
- Leaders are people focused. They have followers (managers have subordinates). Leaders are the coaches, counselors, mentors, and teachers that strive to develop the talents of others. Leaders are proactive rather than reactive and design systems and processes to support the people (managers use people to support the systems and processes). As people achieve, the company will gain maximum benefit.

Managers use formal authority to direct work. Leaders inspire people to work. Managers protect the organization's hierarchy and lines of authority but leaders engage talent and build trust, regardless of formal positions. Managers take the credit while leaders give credit where it is due; managers blame others while leaders blame themselves.

Organizations do need management but do we want a manager or a leader at the helm of a department, division, or boardroom? The two-role theorists don't see an overlap except in very senior or influential positions within the company. But noted leadership development specialists assert that companies are over managed and under led, contending that organizations improve and accomplish their missions when managers are leaders.

Without leaders, there are no followers and the organization doesn't have the mobilized workforce it needs to accomplish its mission.

Leadership Development

It's the *person* that makes a leader, not a title. People have some inherent qualities that contribute to their effectiveness as leaders. But contemporary writers such as Warren Bennis and Stephen Covey make a strong case for the fact that personal attributes and ways of thinking, feeling, and behaving can be developed.

People develop as leaders through observation and introspection (knowing themselves), learning how to behave (influence, motivate, direct, and build trust), and practicing what they learn, especially about interpersonal relationships, team dynamics, and social influence.

Once developed, leadership becomes a way of life. Leaders are life-long learners and observers of the world around them. Passion motivates them to take their social influence outside the organization for the benefit of an industry, the consumer, or the community at large.

People who are personally involved in the community guide their organizations to act in similar fashion by supporting or investing in the community in which they do business. Image and reputation of the company are often measured by the organization's volunteer and/or financial support of community activities and social service projects. This is particularly important if the public perceives an industry as a whole to be self-serving.

■ CONCLUSION

Leaders have a powerful influence over a group or organization and its individual members. The responsible or irresponsible use of that power is a direct reflection of the character of the person who holds the position. People expect their leaders to meet the highest standards of integrity and trustworthiness and to use power fairly and justly. Those who do so are deemed worthy leaders. They succeed in their command when they take charge with decisive direction, draw people into collective efforts, delegate appropriately, and are willing to be accountable for their actions. As leaders inspire a following, they become role models. From this, new leaders emerge.

■ DISCUSSION EXERCISES

What have you learned about yourself as a potential leader? What do you think your greatest challenges will be?

Discuss past experiences in which you felt that your trust in another person was violated—in which you questioned another person's integrity.

How do you assess your personal attributes? Your ability to influence, motivate, and direct other people? Your ability to build a team? To delegate responsibility? To be decisive? To be accountable for your actions? To acknowledge mistakes? Use a scale of one to five (five being highest) to rate yourself.

Do you see yourself as a manager or a leader? How do you relate leadership with the job that you have (or will be doing)?

CHAPTER THREE

MANAGEMENT SKILLS

Think about people you've worked for. What do you admire most about the way they handled the job? What do you admire the least?

What are your strengths as a manager?

If leaders lead people and managers manage work, then "What am I supposed to do?" The answer is straightforward—a manager's job is to get things done through other people.

Managers need followers to do that.

> Try this—Tell a group of people how to walk a serpentine or meandering path. They need to know where to begin and which way to face, how far to go before the path changes direction, whether the path then goes right or left, and on it goes until you've described the entire route.
>
> Can you tell people where to go?

Companies can accomplish their goals when their managers influence, motivate, and direct people—that is, with leadership.

> As for the serpentine—Maybe you just stand up and say, "Follow me!"

Companies are also more successful when managers are transformational rather than protectors of "the way we always do things" and facilitate the company's human resources, provide direction, and then give people the opportunity to unleash their talents.

> Back to the serpentine—Is the path as important as the destination? Did someone in the group have a better idea about how to get from the beginning to the end?

Leadership development is about the personal development that makes people leaders. Couple this with management development and people have the skills to guide human behavior in the workplace.

■ MANAGEMENT STYLES

Management styles are essentially the various ways managers provide direction and use authority and the ways workers are expected to respond. The styles are strikingly different, depending on how managers view their roles and what they think about workers. Workers are to be seen and not heard at one extreme and are seen as valued forces in molding outcomes at the other.

The different philosophies of management also reveal how lines of thinking have changed over the years. Clearly, one management style provides the leadership we expect of today's managers. But the contrasts in styles provide useful lessons about how best to do that.

Dictatorial Style

This is the "I say, you do," Theory X style of management. Don't ask questions; don't offer suggestions. Toe the line or get out. The dictatorial manager has absolute control and never delegates authority. Decision making is unilateral or one-sided—solely the manager's.

The dictatorial manager issues orders, and people are expected to respond promptly and enthusiastically. They must faithfully obey or they will be punished. Often, the manager also micromanages every task, thinking that people wouldn't know what to do if left to their own devices. In fact, any attempt by a worker to exercise initiative is considered an act of defiance.

Obviously, this style of management is oppressive. Although it may still exist in a few settings, dictatorial management was common before managers learned they could influence others without trying to control them. Today, people are more likely to think "Who needs this?" and find a more compassionate or democratic place to work.

Autocratic Style

Autocratic management is a more humanistic or benevolent approach than the dictator's style. The autocratic manager still dominates the scene, but in a less threatening or intimidating way. The manager gives directions (rather than orders) and assigns tasks that suit a person's skills and abilities, which a dictatorial manager does not do. People feel more secure in their jobs (they haven't been set up to fail) and look to the manager to "Just tell me what to do."

Decision making in the autocratic environment is also unilateral, but with a different attitude. Managers see their decision making more as a division of labor than an issue of control. They have the necessary information and expertise to make quality decisions, and workers should do their jobs without the distraction of things their managers are responsible for doing.

Many people respond to autocratic management because it most closely resembles that which they've known as children, students, or workers in other organizations. The autocratic style is also an instinctive posture for managers whose role models are parents, teachers, or former bosses. However, those models can lead to a more dictatorial or micromanagement style than is necessarily constructive.

Participatory Style

Participatory management is the most democratic, humanistic style. This creates the job-rich environment that contemporary theorists favor. Managers are still in charge, but as facilitators, and view workers as valued talent rather than subordinates. The manager prescribes outcomes and delegates authority, and the workers are responsible for achieving those outcomes.

The manager is still responsible for making decisions and is ultimately accountable for everything the workers do. But this self-directed way to work respects people for their individual skills and abilities and gives them an opportunity to influence the work they do.

Participatory management draws upon the manager's leadership skills and gains cooperation (or a following) by engaging people in teamwork, problem solving, brainstorming, and decision making. They may even work with the manager to develop the outcomes they are expected to achieve. This environment motivates people to work, encourages initiative, and inspires people to be creative and grow.

Participatory management is uncomfortable for managers who think they should be more authoritarian, that they give up too much control while they're still on the hook for performance. Certainly, there's risk if the manager fails to provide clear guidance or merely goes through the motions of engaging worker participation only to ignore their contributions. But that's the fault of the manager and not the principles of participatory management.

Laissez-Faire Style

Laissez-faire management is really a contradiction in terms because it is essentially *non*management. Its predominant characteristic is nonintervention. Managers (by title anyway) provide little, if any, guidance and exercise little of the decision-making authority that is customary in their positions.

A laissez-faire environment is the epitome of a self-directed workplace. Either people will individually direct their own work or an unofficial leader will emerge to direct the group. This degree of initiative is desirable for very specialized, technical, or innovative work groups. But, as a general rule, organizations do not formally adopt a laissez-faire style of management.

More commonly, a laissez-faire environment evolves when managers fail to do their jobs. This can happen when managers fear making the wrong decisions or losing popularity, have too many or conflicting roles (sales managers who also sell), or after they've lost control and see little hope of reestablishing their authority. (The independent contractors got too independent, so there's no hope of corralling them again.) In any case, the result is chaos and a department or organization that can't stay on course or meet its goals.

A laissez-faire environment can also breed indifference. People feel that if the manager doesn't care, then why should anyone else? So they do their own thing, if they work at all, and lose interest in being part of the organization. Eventually, the organization can languish into nonexistence.

■ MANAGERIAL BEHAVIOR

Managers have many duties but they all relate to one thing—motivating people.

> Remember the serpentine? Did you notice people's expressions when you tried telling them what you wanted them to do? Did they cooperate and participate in the exercise? Did some people jump in right away while others faded into the background? Did people wonder why you were doing this exercise? Did people tell you what they thought?
>
> One serpentine poses a multitude of questions that frame the job of a manager and the skills needed to do that job.

The ultimate test of a manager's skills is whether people are following. Many things happen, simply because there's a group of people with all their associated human behaviors. A manager needs certain skills to manage all that behavior. Essential skills are grouped under separate headings, but the skills really work together.

- **Observation**—What's going on in the workplace? What are people doing? What are they "saying" with their behavior? What does all of this tell you about what you (the manager) need to do?
- **Communication**—How does what you say and how you say it convince, motivate, or direct people? Do you listen or, more importantly, actually hear what people say? Do you value other people's opinions?
- **Interpersonal Skills**—How do you handle the diverse personalities in the workplace? How do you help them work together? How do your preconceived notions about individual people help or hinder the workplace environment?

- **Team Building**—How do you help everyone use their individual skills and abilities to the best advantage? How do you build team spirit and cohesion? How do you handle dysfunction?
- **Decision Making**—How do you gather the information needed to make quality decisions? How do you engage others in decision making? How do you implement decisions and gain commitment?
- **Negotiation and Conflict Resolution**—How do you do problem solving? How do you handle dissension within the workforce? How do you handle it between you and a worker? How do you address unacceptable behavior?
- **Time Management**—How do you manage work and successfully meet deadlines? How do handle unexpected developments? How do you manage stress?

If managers do their jobs with people, then all the other systems, processes, and procedures that companies hold dear will fall into place.

Managing People

Some noted behavioral scientists, among them Thomas Maslow, Douglas MacGregor, and Fredrick Herzberg, devoted considerable study to human behavior and motivation in the workplace. (Many writings about their findings are readily available in the marketplace.) The crux of their work is that as organizations gain greater understanding of human behavior, they can better manage their human resources. The outgrowth of this is the humanistic, participatory environment that is prevalent in today's organizations.

The science of human behavior is a study all of its own and is not the typical manager's field of expertise. Untrained people can't figure out "what makes people tick" with any degree of certainty and then try to appeal to inner psyches and elicit the desired behavior. The manager often makes faulty assumptions and then takes unjust or inappropriate action.

Managers need a practical way to manage human behavior. A popular approach, which is well described by Ferdinand Fournies in his book *Coaching for Improved Work Performance*, focuses solely on behavior rather than trying to figure out why people behave the way they do. Very simply, the process involves

- learning to observe behavior,
- learning to describe the behavior that is observed, and then
- doing things to elicit behavior that managers consider desirable.

A very basic lesson about human behavior is this—*behavior is a function of the alternatives one sees at the time*. The concept is very simple. A person sizes up a situation, comes up with alternatives about how to act, and then picks one—the behavior. The entire process could take only a second or two or it could take several minutes, hours, days, or weeks. It could be a conscious and deliberate exercise or an unconscious or reflex action.

Emotions, motivations, and sundry other human elements affect the way people assess situations and develop alternatives. Rarely does someone say "I want to look stupid today, so I'll do something stupid." It's far more likely that people don't take the time or have the wherewithal to properly assess a situation and come up with suitable alternatives. Or they don't have the intellectual, emotional, or psychiatric facility to identify appropriate alternatives on which to act.

A bystander may see an alternative that would have been a more desirable course of action. Even the person making the decision may have second thoughts about the choice after the heat of the moment has passed. Behavior is simply a matter of making choices.

From a manager's point of view, those choices fall into two categories—acceptable and unacceptable. Acceptable behavior is often taken for granted because that's what people are supposed to be doing anyway. So, managers look for the undesirable behavior, thinking that they aren't doing their jobs unless they take people to task for behaving in unacceptable ways. Yet, it's important to manage both the acceptable and unacceptable behavior.

Praising behavior. Certainly, the most desirable workplace is one in which people are doing the things they are supposed to do and not cause problems. The best way to keep people on that track is to reinforce desirable behavior. *Behavior that is reinforced is behavior that is repeated.* Reinforcement can be a kind word, a pat on the back, or some more formal kind of praise such as an award.

A manager who is long on criticism and short on praise falls into the same trap many parents do—assuming that acceptable behavior will endure simply out of a sense of "right." But people need to be told they're "doing right." People who feel starved for attention learn, even as children, that the way to be noticed is to act out. Then more undesirable behavior gets more attention.

It's far better to set up a positive cycle that reaps more desirable behavior. Everyone does something worthwhile. Real estate companies tend to focus on production outcomes (sales and listings). But people contribute to the organization, the industry, and their own professional development in many other ways that deserve recognition.

Two simple rules to keep in mind—One is that praise must be genuine. Spouting words of praise for every move people make (especially if the manager has never been particularly effusive) sounds insincere. More harm than good is done unless genuinely praiseworthy behavior is acknowledged.

The second rule is to *praise the performance*, not the performer. Look at the behavior separately from the person. The manager's job is to evaluate behavior that affects a person's work, not to judge the person and all the accompanying motivational, emotional, and character baggage. Even the person with most unpleasant baggage can do acceptable or desirable things.

Many young adults in today's workplace were lavishly praised as children. This "most praised generation" (whom critics call self-centered or narcissistic) is accustomed to copious self-esteem building strokes and can wither in a compliment-deficient workplace. In many companies, this has spawned cultures of praise in which feedback, kudos, and other displays of appreciation are used to codify worth in the workplace.

Skeptics say that this all sounds like mollycoddling, that work isn't supposed to be pleasurable or that managers aren't supposed to help people feel good. The fact is there's a whole lot of benefit and very little risk when managers recognize the good people do, especially when the organization's interests are at stake.

Modifying behavior. This is the part of behavior management that focuses on undesirable or unacceptable behavior. Certainly, managers would like it to stop, but managers can't actually change the behavior. Only the offender can do that.

The manager's objective is to motivate a change in behavior. But people do emotional or instinctive things that won't cause someone else to change. Harping, criticizing every move people make, or yelling, screaming, and threatening (YST) are more likely to anger or frustrate people and cause them to turn a deaf ear. Certainly, anyone can fly off the handle in the heat of the moment. But that flare does more for letting off steam than it does for changing behavior, at least for any longer than it takes to lash out.

Managers can do constructive things to cause behavior to change.

1. **Decide whether the unacceptable behavior deserves attention.** Pick your battles. No one works well in an environment of constant criticism. The stress alone is counterproductive, and eventually people feel that there's no way to please the manager anyway. Intervene only if the achievements of the organization, the individual, or other workers are in jeopardy or there's significant legal or public relations risk.
2. **Clearly describe to the offender the behavior that is unacceptable and the reasons why.** The offender may not even be aware of the manager's displeasure. The person chose an alternative to act on, but the manager saw a preferable one.
3. **Develop an action plan.** This is a participatory exercise with the manager in which the offender devises a plan for doing things differently or preventing such a transition from occurring again. The manager has to agree with the action plan and the offender's behavioral choices.
4. **Follow up to ensure the behavior changes.** This is the step that holds the offender accountable for implementing the action plan.

The manager's role is to praise the change in behavior and coach continued efforts to do things differently.

Managing Generations

Put Baby Boomers, Gen X, and Gen Y together and you get very different attitudes about work and the workplace, which also explains the differences in the attitudes about praise.

The Boomers (born between 1946 and 1964) entered the workforce when autocratic management was more common than not. Gen X (born between 1965 and 1980) came into the workplace when participative management was prevalent, but bosses were still bosses. And Gen Y (born between 1980 and 2000) first entered the workforce several years ago and bumped up against a culture that is often still workplace centered and steeped in tradition.

The culture in many companies was created by the Boomer force, whose attitude is that work is work, and that's done in the office. In fact, if you're not in the office you must not be working (even salespeople are expected to use that as "home base"). The priority in life is to earn a living and all the other benefits of a compassionate workplace are secondary, even though worthwhile amenities.

Gen Y creates the most striking culture clash with managers who expect to interact with their workers face-to-face and can't let go of their need to exercise authority. Gen Ys interact with devices instead of in person and work wherever they can be digitally connected—"Just let me be independent and trust me to do my job."

Gen X sits in the middle, the bridge between two extremes. The Xers are the first children of the technology age, such as it was at the time, and are also largely responsible for raising the most praised generation. That translates easily into the culture of a compassionate workplace, but Xers are also influenced by autocratic environments in which they have worked.

Generational differences bred impatience with the ways of others. But people have to get past the right-versus-wrong way or the workplace has to work "my way." Organizations need the perspectives of multiple generations to be viable. They can achieve that by moving ahead with the times while also respecting the fact that people are products of eras in which they were raised. Technology plays a large role in generational differences but technology can also be a good platform for developing common ground in the workplace.

The distinction for managers is the mobile worker, who uses technology to stay in touch with their jobs and the manager, versus the autonomous worker, who uses technology to work outside the organization with little managerial contact. The latter requires a high degree of trust that the autonomous worker will do the job. The two styles of work resurrect generational differences in the roles of managers and workers. The decision for a real estate company's managers is whether their independent contractors are mobile or autonomous workers.

Team Building

A leader is a good team builder and a manager needs to be one for the same reason—to develop an enthusiastic, cohesive work unit and mobilize the group's efforts.

If the manager does nothing to corral the group, people will do their own thing. That thing can be a variety of activities that satisfy the individuals but may have very little to do with satisfying the organization. People have very personal and sometimes very different reasons for working.

- Some want to be busy and will be perfectly content eking out whatever living they can make doing busywork.
- Some are building their résumés, and a job is but one of a number of entries that will be made.
- Others use the job as a means to an end, the most common being money.
- Some want to contribute to the lives of others and see the organization or its consumers as a means to this end.

There are many more reasons people work. The point is that people work to satisfy personal needs. The organization, on the other hand, has needs (goals) that have to be satisfied as well.

Team building is grounded in the belief that both the organization and the workers benefit from an environment that respects the worth of individuals and encourages their contribution (the participative work culture). Collaborative efforts stimulate creativity and help the organization derive the greatest benefit from people's various skills and abilities. Even if the motives are different, everyone can work toward similar ends and gain satisfaction along the way.

Collective efforts, or teams, are evident in a number of places in an organization. Peers within the group hierarchy, such as members of senior management, first-line supervisors, or members of the sales staff, often work together among themselves. Cross-hierarchy partnerships form between supervisors and the people being supervised. Representatives from all levels within the organization, regardless of the designated hierarchy, work together on specific projects.

In a real estate company comprised of an army of independent contractors, this is one of the best ways to elicit the cooperation of independent salespeople.

Managing Diversity

Everyone has different personalities, talents, styles, and physical and cultural characteristics. The diversity of all of this is what makes people interesting and adds a useful dimension to the workplace.

Conventional wisdom is that organizations benefit from diverse ideas and opinions. When everyone has very similar viewpoints, they look at problems and solutions the same way and don't challenge prevailing ideas or provoke new ones. Diverse viewpoints test the merits of a line of thinking, or a course of action, and stimulate innovation.

The reality is that diverse minds are often conflicting minds. Some people are receptive to alternate viewpoints or can at least agree to respectfully disagree. Others feel annoyed, even threatened, by viewpoints that differ significantly from their own. It's not uncommon for the group to polarize around similar lines of thinking. However, the bond of like-minded people can strengthen more for the we-versus-they principle of the matter than for constructive problem solving.

The easy way out of the potential for conflict or friction on a board, committee, or other work group is to select people with similar viewpoints, even better if those are the same as the person's who makes the selections.

This strategy appeals to managers who see dissent or conflict as a distraction that interferes with efficient decision making. Management essentially manages the group dynamics with the selection process and perhaps also ensures that the group renders the decision that management wants.

A slightly daring approach is to select a token dissenter as well. This works when the person is respected as a provocative thinker or a spokesperson for a certain line of thinking and is a constructive devil's advocate. The strategy is effective when the group leader gives the dissenting voice an opportunity to be heard and test whether others share that person's opinion. The strategy is even more effective when the leader encourages others to "devil" their ideas as well.

However, the token strategy can backfire if the single dissenting voice gets isolated from or tuned out by the rest of the group. Some people simply relish being contrarians or "pot stirrers." One of those can be more disruptive than constructive. Token-for-token-sake becomes nothing more than a transparent exercise to appease those who do not share the mainstream views. (You had a voice; you were just outnumbered.)

A bold approach is to select people with a wide range of viewpoints and give the conventional wisdom a chance to prove the benefit of diversity. This strategy tests the leadership ability of the chair or group leader but it will work, especially if the process is managed well from the start. The leader is in charge but as a facilitator, not as a director of opinion.

Everyone's opinions matter, including those that run counter to the mainstream or even those of the group leader. Conflict, which often also involves egos, typically turns counterproductive when the most vocal or opinionated people monopolize the conversation. The leader's job is to remain neutral, keep the group focused on the heart of the issue, and give the less opinionated voices a chance to be heard. Often those are the ones that help build consensus. The fewer preconceived notions managers have about "the mainstream," the more the company benefits from its diversity as well.

Managing the Manager

The manager is just as human as everyone else, which means the manager's behavior only adds another dimension to the workplace dynamics. Managing the manager is really about how being human can hinder or help the workplace.

Labeling. It's not uncommon for people to use a kind of shorthand to describe other people. This shorthand becomes a label, which typically identifies a dominant feature or characteristic of a person. Labels simply reflect the perceptions of the people assigning the labels.

Labeling is part of human nature, though that doesn't mean it does people any favors. A label may not be a fair or accurate characterization or even the same one everyone would assign to a person. But once attached, labels stick with people everywhere they go.

People also tend to behave in ways that are consistent with their labels. "Successful" generally enhances self-esteem and causes people to strive and live up to their reputations. "Loser" typically causes people to lose confidence or disengage, to feel that if no one thinks they're capable of anything better, then there's no point in trying. In effect, the poor soul has been labeled into failure.

The managing-the-manager part of this discussion says that managers have to think beyond the label. People expect the manager to respect their individual talents and to treat them fairly and justly. Managing labels often leads to inconsistent oversight or intolerance of behavior in one person versus another or creates an appearance of favoritism.

Prejudice. Today's workplace reflects today's general population. Throughout the past decade, the population in the U.S. has become more ethnically diverse. An increasing number of people are multiracial, blends of race and ethnicity, and more people with disabilities are active, productive workers. The workforce is also aging, a large number of whom will be retiring from full-time employment within the next ten years.

The managing-the-manager part of this discussion comes quickly by saying that the manager is very likely to be supervising people whose individual profiles are different from his or her own. This requires learning appropriate behaviors from both a cultural and a legal perspective to properly manage people of differing age, race, color, ethnicity, or gender.

Diversity in the workplace group can also cause people's underlying stereotypes and prejudices to surface or personalities to clash. While it's unlikely that the assembled collection of personalities will be so simpatico that everyone will be best friends, people certainly deserve an accepting and respectful environment in which to work.

The responsibility for creating that environment falls squarely on the manager. Dissension in the workplace can easily arise if the manager is perceived as being more attentive to or more tolerant of some people because of their heritage, lifestyles, or other characteristics. Not only is this unfair but in many cases, it also is illegal. The manager's job is to manage in ways that are solely related to job performance. As the manager embraces diversity, others in the group have a model to follow as well.

Today's workplace, in general, is far more socially aware than once was the case. Companies acknowledge their diversity with flextime and childcare for working parents and adult caregivers, gay-friendly and femininity-friendly environments, zero tolerance for sexual harassment, and heightened awareness of multiple cultural and religious systems. Some companies become role models in these regards.

Work life and personal life. People are rarely able to put things that are happening in their lives into separate compartments. Personal lives spill over into the workplace and vice versa. When all is going well in one sector of a person's life, that wellness often carries over into others. The not-so-well can be dragged along too.

The workplace is a collection of differing degrees of pleasure, disappointment, stress, anger, sadness, major trauma, and even grief. This is not to say that the manager has to become the group's therapist or psychologist. But managers do need to be empathic to the realities of life that everyone has to deal with.

The managing-the-manager part of this scene says that the manager has to guard against allowing events in his or her own life to complicate the group dynamics. Managers are always on stage, so to speak. Because they wield a lot of power over the lives of others, people are ever watchful of a manager's words and actions that indicate acceptance or rejection, approval or disapproval.

People tend to associate the manager's behavior toward them with something they've done rather than with something in the manager's life. The grumbled, quick "hello" as the manager heads back to his or her office can easily be interpreted as criticism or rejection rather than what it really means, that the manager is having a disastrous morning. A simple explanation can prevent erroneous conclusions, the "don't take it personally" kind of words that keep the air clear.

Stress and time management. A number of studies cite real estate sales as one of the most stressful occupations. It's no wonder that real estate offices are charged with high energy, high emotion, and perhaps short fuses. Certainly, the financial pressures that drive today's companies to work harder to stay afloat cannot be ignored. But companies reach a point of diminishing returns when the health and well-being of the workforce is jeopardized.

There's more to life than work. People must make time for play and time for solitude, the battery-charging time that helps us be better people in all sectors of our lives. Unfortunately, there are those who feel that unless people are working at breakneck speed, they are somehow less devoted to their careers or the company.

The final managing-the-manager commentary says that the manager has to learn to carry an immense load of duties and responsibilities, and do so with calm good humor. The manager has to be able to derive personal satisfaction from the job as well. The manager can become a role model (and protect his or her own well-being in the process) by setting realistic expectations about that which is humanly possible to accomplish, establishing priorities, and adopting good time-management skills.

The end result is minimized stress. Interestingly, stress management is one of the most popular topics in workplace training. By helping people to reprogram attitudes and develop healthy lifestyles, everyone, including the company, benefits.

■ ASSUMING THE POSITION

The fitting, final discussion is to look at how a person steps into a management position. Even those who have already taken this step can learn more about being a manager.

Is a Promotion a Good Thing?

The common strategy in the business world of promoting the best technicians into managerial roles is also prevalent in the real estate industry—good salespeople are often elevated to management positions. Presumably they have demonstrated leadership potential and good people skills that transfer well into the realm of management. However, people are often promoted out of the jobs they do best and then wither in administrative jobs.

A promotion is one of the business world's most powerful forms of reward and recognition. People tend to "buck for promotions" for reasons that vary from increased pay to increased responsibility or prestige. Companies tend to overlook people who are complacent or show little interest in moving up and promote those who do. However, companies aren't always very smart about selecting the right people for the right jobs. People don't always accept promotions for the right reasons either.

By the very nature of real estate licensing laws, broker/owners and sales office managers (in some states) must satisfy advanced licensing requirements after serving their dues as salespeople. They arrive at the doorstep of a management or ownership opportunity presumably with enhanced transaction skills and greater knowledge of the business, essentially being promotable at least from a regulatory point of view.

However, regulatory requirements serve one purpose—to protect the public. They don't intend to prescribe attributes and skill sets that make people effective leaders, managers, or business owners. Perhaps that's why you're reading this book or possibly attending a management course.

Some people aspire to manage an office or own a brokerage company and being a salesperson is just the first step in a carefully developed career plan. Others fall into the role because a new opportunity presents itself. Regardless of aspirations or opportunities, a promotion is not a good thing without an affirmative answer to the next question.

Are You Suited for the Job?

Not all leaders are good at supervising people. Simply because a person demonstrates leadership potential or the ability to command a following doesn't necessarily mean that he or she is suited for a people-oriented position. Some leaders are better suited to more outwardly-focused or entrepreneurial endeavors.

Not everyone with good people skills is good at all the things managers do with people. Some managers are especially good at recruiting or team building while others are good counselors or mentors.

Companies often have unrealistic expectations of managers. This is especially true in real estate companies where the sales office manager is expected to manage people, money, and processes while also recruiting, training, and maintaining the office space. Unless the company has designated personnel with specific skill sets and abilities to do some of those jobs, the manager, by default, becomes "all things to all people." That is a tall order to fill, especially if the order doesn't play to a manager's strengths.

The answer to "Are you suited for the job?" is, "It depends. What are your strengths?" People don't always see themselves as others see them, which creates a mismatch between the jobs they do and the ones they are really good at doing. Marcus Buckingham, author of *StandOut* and *Go Put Your Strengths to Work*, and Tom Rath, author of *StrengthsFinder*, contend that people are more effective and satisfied when they play with their "strong suits." Online resources that accompany their books are very good for identifying those strengths.

Certainly, people can acquire new knowledge and skills but they make the greatest strides when they build on their strengths as opposed to trying to do major "makeovers" over their weaknesses.

For people interested in going the new-business-owner route, a number of additional tools for assessing strengths are available. "Entrepreneur IQ" (available at *TheEntrepreneurNextDoor.com*) and the Strong and MBTI Entrepreneur Report that ties the Myers-Briggs personality test to entrepreneurial aptitude assess personality traits. Not everyone agrees there is a singular personality type, but the clear distinguishing trait is confidence in the ability to build a successful business.

How do your strengths align with the job you will be doing? Managers have multiple roles—interpersonal, technical (product or service), and business management. Depending on your job description and scope of authority in the organization, the degree of talent and aptitude needed to play those roles will vary.

How Do You Make the Transition?

The official position of manager creates a class distinction, even if a subtle one, between the supervisor and the people being supervised. The distinction becomes very apparent when managers supervise people who were once their peers, especially in the same organization. The salespeople, who previously saw the manager as "one of us," may feel that the person is worthy of the position and deserves their allegiance. Or they may feel that their peer has betrayed them by becoming "one of them," the management corps.

Gaining the cooperation of subordinates (and acceptance by the management corps as well) depends to a large degree on the way a manager approaches the position. Being boss is not a popularity contest, but the boss doesn't have to be an adversary either. Managers can't be apologetic about being in the position or the decisions they make. But being consumed by an exalted sense of self-importance or an inflated ego only widens the gap between boss and subordinate. Managers gain cooperation by demonstrating genuine respect for the position and the people being supervised.

The salesperson-to-sales-manager transition is additionally burdened by the shift from "doer" to supervisor and watching others do what the manager used to do (or did better). Sometimes, it seems easier and quicker to just take over rather than telling someone else what to do and then wait on the sidelines until that happens. Here is the "you have to let go" lesson about delegating and respecting the abilities of others. They have their job, and you have yours.

New managers and business owners can also be in for a rude awakening when they discover the complexities of running a company and the multitude of issues that affect goal attainment and profitability. As workers in the trenches, they rarely saw (nor was it their job to be concerned with) the real world of the dollars and cents.

Now, everything managers and owners do, including managing people, is related to money, especially with today's cost of doing business. Small businesses are most likely to fail in their first three years because of lack of planning, undercapitalization, unrealistic expectations of a company's productivity in its early years, and the owner's lack of experience in running a business. Established companies face similar financial challenges from time to time as well. Without sound business management skills, the harsh reality is the new manager or owner will be quickly transitioned out of a job.

A successful transition into management or ownership also requires realistic expectations about the personal implications of the move, especially financial ones. Being the owner is not necessarily more lucrative than sharing sales commissions with a broker. A sales manager's compensation may not equate to the income earned as a salesperson either. A sales manager is typically a first-line supervisor (though may be a middle management position) and although at least a small salary or base pay is customary, the substantive income is tied to the production of the manager's salespeople. That may or may not be especially lucrative, depending on the salespeople.

So You Want to Be a Sales Manager?

We'll begin with the assumption that you answered "yes" to the earlier questions. We'll also assume that you have the professional credentials to do a credible job, including the continuing education required to maintain whatever real estate license you have. The *Digest of Real Estate License Laws—United States and Canada* published by the Association of Real Estate License Law Officials (ARELLO) is available for further information. Certainly, professional real estate designations bolster credibility as well.

Credibility is jeopardized if the salespeople know more about real estate transactions than the manager does. While this is not an incurable condition, it says that the manager needs to stay on top of the latest industry and legal developments in order to be a useful resource for the salespeople. Salespeople may, indeed, have more knowledge and better transaction skills than the manager (that's their daily job). But a manager can preserve credibility by demonstrating respect for that superior talent, and can also learn from it.

Finally, we hope that you take this book to heart and learn about managing a business. Even sections that don't apply to your specific job are important for understanding where you fit into the big picture of the company. Numerous opportunities are available to develop business management skills, from collegiate degrees to non-credited seminars and workshops. Some are specific to real estate and others are generic, but a real estate company is like any other for-profit enterprise—they are all businesses, operating on the same fundamental principles of management.

Now we deal with one last question about the job of a sales manager. The earlier comment returns about managing people, processes, and systems while also recruiting, training, and so on. This is the tall order that sets up the manager to fail unless there is a specific (and realistic) job description along with clearly defined performance expectations.

Expectations typically include production goals and perhaps also recruiting quotas. But expectations could also include performance reviews, training activities, or a number of one-on-one meetings with salespeople. The manager's performance could also be measured by expense targets, quality service feedback, or the number of listings that don't sell or sales transactions that fall through.

The dizzying array of things that a manager may be expected to do suggests that only those with superhero strengths need apply. Then, add a major bone of contention in real estate offices—the manager is expected to sell too. Certainly, not all companies' expectations are as extensive as those described. But in smaller companies or in difficult economic times, the sales manager's responsibilities can be extensive.

How do you do the job? This question raises the contentious issue about managers who also sell.

The purists say that the only way to be effective is to devote 100 percent of the time to management. Others argue, especially when the sales staff is small, that it *is* possible, even a financial necessity, to both manage and sell (or provide other professional services). The time devoted to each activity can vary considerably and in some cases, management runs a distant second to sales activities. In some companies, managers who do not routinely sell are encouraged to do so once in a while, just to stay in touch with the marketplace.

Being a full-time manager has its advantages. The job responsibilities are very clear—supervise the activities of the salespeople, coach their performance, and help them reach their goals. The manager can devote full attention to these responsibilities without the distraction of sales activities. Furthermore, the manager is not competing with the salespeople for business.

Blending management and real estate activities is more challenging. Managers can find themselves in an untenable time management tug-of-war, trying to both manage and sell. They are often criticized for neglecting the salespeople or for grabbing leads to fuel their personal business. The manager must learn to play both roles well, preserve harmony in the office, and preserve his or her sanity and personal life in the process.

- **Prioritize responsibilities.** The manager's sales and management priorities are typically defined by the organization—whether one job is primary and the other is a secondary assignment or each has equal priority. Unless the priorities have been clearly stated at the outset, the manager and the broker or supervisor will have conflicting expectations and performance outcomes will be disappointing.
- **Determine the amount of time and effort that must be devoted to each role.** While it might seem like a statement of the obvious, that time and effort should be aligned with priorities, there's more to the time-management challenge than first appears. Administrative, supervisory, and problem-solving tasks can be very time consuming, even if those responsibilities are supposed to be secondary to the sales job. All these new responsibilities are often overwhelming, which tempts new managers to concentrate on the more familiar sales activities. But it's important to take charge of the management job at the outset to be effective for the long haul. The job will become easier with experience.
- **Prepare contingency plans.** The manager will likely be confronted with issues demanding attention on both the management and sales fronts simultaneously. Salespeople count on the manager being available to help when brushfires flare in their transactions, but that can't happen if the manager is busy with his or her own sales. For the benefit of all concerned, the manager needs a backup plan so that someone is available to help either the salespeople's or the manager's transactions move forward.
- **Protect harmony in the office.** Perhaps the most challenging issue to manage is the competition between selling managers and their salespeople. One way to minimize this is by the manager restricting sales activities to previous customers and personal referrals rather than taking leads from the office. In some companies, managers

avoid sales entirely and engage in other income producing activities such as leasing.

- **Maximize the use of technology.** This is a statement of the obvious in today's world of wireless and cellular technology, but the benefits of mobile devices cannot be overstated. The good news is the manager can handle multiple activities at one time from one location. The bad news is the manager is on duty 24/7, unless there are specific guidelines about by whom and under what circumstances the manager may be contacted after certain hours. Everyone needs a personal life, including the manager.

The reasons people want to be a sales manager vary from the desire to climb the organization's ladder to the opportunity to help others develop their careers. Our premise is that if you step into the job with your eyes wide open and the right "bag of tools," you will take a good first step into the ranks of management. Talking to other sales managers helps prepare for that step too.

CONCLUSION

With a keen understanding of the human dynamics in the workplace and sharp interpersonal and business management skills, a manager can successfully direct the company's human resources. The style of management—dictatorial, autocratic, participatory, or laissez-faire, or a variation on any of those themes—sets the tone for the environment in which people work. That environment is also a melting pot of individuals and behaviors, including the manager's, that need to be guided in constructive ways so that the workplace supports desirable outcomes for the organization.

DISCUSSION EXERCISES

Discuss the management style that most closely approximates your instinctive style. What is most constructive about your approach? What is most destructive? How would you revise your style based on what you've learned?

What tendencies do you have that work for or against you as a manager?

What have you learned about approaching the behavior of your salespeople? Consider typical scenarios or problems in your office and ways you would handle them.

What have you learned about your strengths and the job that you are suited for?

What do you expect to be your greatest assets and challenges in making the transition into a management position? If you're already in management, what would you do the same or differently if you had to make the transition again?

CHAPTER FOUR

COMMUNICATIONS AND DECISION MAKING

What's the best way for people to communicate with you? Talk to you? Send you an e-mail? Find you on Facebook?

How do you get other people to pay attention to what you have to say? Or what you want them to do?

How do you find out what you need to know? How do you tell others what they need to know? Seemingly straightforward questions, but the answers are more complicated than simply ask and tell.

> Subject: Meeting Notice
>
> It has come to my attention that we need to have a meeting to discuss listing production. The suggestion has been made that a workshop would be a good idea so on Tuesday, March 26, 2013 I ask all of the sales staff to be in the conference room at 10:00 a.m. Be prepared to discuss why listings don't sell has increased.
>
> I look forward to seeing you then.
>
> M.J. Doe, Sales Manager

If you send this memo—

Will you know if anyone is coming on March 26th?

Will the sales staff know exactly what will happen or what's in it for them?

Did someone make a decision that they need to know about?

Will people be inspired to log the date in their calendar (which is also a Jewish holiday that year)?

Or did people delete or toss the memo before even reading it?

What does this memo say about the writer, especially if it gets forwarded or passed around in the company?

The answers are all about communicating effectively.

■ ORAL COMMUNICATION

We learn, often as salespeople, about the sender-receiver-atmosphere-message cycle in oral communication. We learn to effectively express ourselves and convey our intended message, and to watch, listen, and ask questions of others so that we get their messages straight.

People communicate with tone of voice, facial expressions, and body language or mannerisms that often reveal more about their thoughts and feelings than words do. And even words don't tell all. Often the most important message is hidden behind the words. So we restate or question what we heard to clarify the message (commonly known as active listening skills).

We have the benefit of all the visual and auditory messages that people exchange when we communicate face-to-face. We can also pick the time and place for especially critical conversations or discussions to minimize distractions that can distort communication.

We lose the visual benefits and can't control the setting (or distractions) with telephone conversations and audio conferencing, but voice alone still gives us a useful interactive exchange. That is, unless we're dropping messages in voice mailboxes. These systems satisfy the sender's need to ask or tell but don't guarantee what the receiver hears or does with the message.

Technology is efficient and serves useful purposes, but it has also significantly altered the way we communicate.

■ BUSINESS WRITING

Digital media is responsible for the most dramatic change in the way we communicate. Personal contact is diminishing, and we communicate more with the written than spoken word. This also means that we are doing more work in writing than we do face-to-face.

We don't have to become professional writers or journalists, but we do have to learn to communicate with the written word as effectively as we do in person.

Good business writing also cures the "I told you…I asked you…I sent you…" problems of lost, overlooked, and discarded words. Digital technology has reduced the amount of paper but hasn't reduced (and perhaps has increased) the volume of words that cycle through the workplace, often in redundant electronic and paper formats. People adopt self-protective strategies to manage the assault—the wastebasket and the delete button.

Salespeople know AIDA—attention, interest, desire, and action. Business writing has to accomplish the same thing.

> How about M.J.'s memo—Did it lose your attention at the very beginning, with the subject line?

We can learn about good writing when we think about what we don't like in what we read.

Back to M.J.'s memo—Was it clear and concise? Well organized? Well written? Did it provide enough or too little information? State a clear purpose? Appeal to your needs? Inspire you to attend?

When writing for business consider that

- Writing is writing, regardless of the delivery system—digital or paper, e-mail or text, a document attachment, or a report that lives online in the digital "clouds."
- Once we send our words, we can't take them back, shred them, or control where they go. Every written word can live forever and become a liability for the company and fodder for everyone to use as they please.
- Grammar, punctuation, and spelling *do* matter. People may not recognize the "good," but many more people than we realize notice the mistakes.
- Good writers *rewrite*. Even the shortest text messages need a second look before they're sent. We don't have to make a project out of writing, but we do have to project the right message.
- Writing has to capture the eye or make a visual impression in order to capture the mind. This is the writing equivalent of "we eat with our eyes" that uses short paragraphs, white space, and formats (i.e. bullet lists, bold-face and italics) to sell readers on the writer's words.
- Writing says a lot about the writer's professional abilities. Sloppy or disorganized writing (and grammatical errors) tarnishes reputations, jeopardizes promotions, and can create more problems than the words are intended to solve.

So, how do we write well? We have to resist the tendency to dash-and-send and start with a plan. This doesn't have to take a lot of time, just a little thought. A good book about business writing and a style manual will help sharpen writing skills, too.

Goal and Audience

First, we need a clearly defined goal. The goal focuses on "What do I want to accomplish?" To get attendance at a meeting or seminar? To share important information? To request information? To solve a problem?

Business writing serves several general purposes—to inform, persuade, motivate or inspire, document, or build relationships. Writing often serves multiple purposes but still needs a primary goal so that the words don't wander and leave the reader to wonder "Why should I bother reading?"

We also have to know who the audience is. This tells the writer how to appeal to the intended receivers. What do they know and what do they need to know? What are their positive and negative hot buttons? What's the writer's relationship with the audience? What are the demographics (age, language proficiency, education level, professional status, etc.)? The more the writer figures out about the receivers, the more effective the communication will be.

Managers often complicate communications with copious requests for status reports, feedback, and assorted other words that satisfy the managers but are just clutter to the people who receive them. The words make a stronger statement if they are written with a clearly defined goal and appeal to the audience.

Once the goal and audience are defined, everything else can fall into place.

Content and Organization

This is the what-to-say and how-to-present-it step that assembles words that suit the goal and the audience. Unfortunately, many people start writing content without thinking about the organization, and miss the goal and the audience too.

List the content and then pare out items that aren't essential to the goal or won't resonate with the audience. Make sure important facts are included as well. This avoids the report request that goes out without a deadline or the seminar notice that includes the date but omits the times.

Then organize the content. People often begin memos, announcements, and even business letters with general information, which is usually rather uninspired, and then work through the specifics. This descending-outline form of thinking commonly loses readers before they get to the meat of the message.

Organize for a strong beginning and a strong ending. Think "above the fold" or top placement so the first words people see on their computers or mobile devices or in the first paragraph of a document accomplishes AIDA. Once people are hooked, they'll read through the middle (as long as it's clear and logically presented) and reach the conclusion. A strong conclusion makes a lasting impression and reinforces the beginning.

This organization plan also works for lengthy reports. An executive summary, which is a synopsis of the most important findings or facts, gives the report a strong beginning. People get the important need-to-know, which is supported by the rest of the report as well as a cover sheet that helps them locate the report in the future. A strong ending frames specific conclusions from the report.

Write and Rewrite

Just as we do in oral communication, we use language to convey our written message. But we also have to use words that give writing the personality that's missing without personal contact. It's your writing, make it sound like you.

Long gone is the stilted, convoluted, and long-winded writing style that was common in business years ago. Even in academia (and textbooks), writing has a warmer or more personal tone, sounding more like the way people talk today. In fact, one of the tests of good writing is whether you can read it well out loud.

Adopt a writing style that suits you, the specific audience you're writing to, and the nature of the writing—personal text or e-mail, casual memo or announcement, or formal report or business letter.

- Write direct sentences with strong nouns (not the nebulous "it") and verbs. Vary sentence length for interest and make sure pronouns are aligned with nouns (people, they) and phrases relate to one another. (M.J. didn't ask people on March 26; M.J. meant to ask people to attend on that date.)

- Make the "rules" work for the type or nature of the message. Although certain basic rules of grammar, spelling, and punctuation apply, not all rules are cast in stone. Commas are pauses that can make a statement clear or more powerful, or can distract from the flow of the message. Colons are more formal while the em dash (—) is less so and also creates visual interest.
- Use grammar and spell check in software programs but remember they aren't infallible. Auto-correct has contributed to many embarrassing messages, and programs don't always catch the "hear" and "here" kinds of mistakes either.
- Use language the audience can relate to, especially for people who aren't likely familiar with industry terminology or lingo. Think generations, too. An informal tone (such as the "hey" greeting) appeals to some but offends other people. And beware the shorthand of text messaging. It belongs only in a text and only if you're sure the receiver understands the code ("lol" could be a very inappropriate "laugh").
- Make the writing style fit your relationship with the receivers. A letter to solve a customer relations problem will be more formal than a casual e-mail, as will an e-mail to superiors than one to peers.
- Choose words carefully, especially when delivering potentially unpopular or inflammatory information. The tendency is to sugarcoat or bury the point to avoid unpleasantness, but that often stirs more controversy than a clearer, more precise message would. Strive for a positive reaction, or at least one that is minimally negative.
- Remember that written words live forever. Avoid flip, comical, critical, and discriminatory remarks even in the most casual text messages.

The rewrite goes quickly. Think less-is-more and get rid of the word clutter. Regardless of how much you like some sentences, let go of ones that make the same statement but just in a different way. Pare out excess adjectives and adverbs. "Devastating" is already bad and doesn't need "very." A "short" timeframe is short and doesn't need "very" as well.

Read the words out loud, fix the places where you stumble, and make sure you accomplished your goal. A second pair of eyes can see things the writer misses and while all writing doesn't need a proofreader, the extra eyes should definitely see important memos, letters, and formal reports.

> How would you rewrite M.J.'s memo?
>
> Subject: Meeting Notice
>
> It has come to my attention that we need to have a meeting to discuss listing production. The suggestion has been made that a workshop would be a good idea so on Tuesday, March 26, 2013 I ask all of the sales staff to be in the conference room at 10:00 a.m. Be prepared to discuss why listings don't sell has increased.
>
> I look forward to seeing you then.
>
> M.J. Doe, Sales Manager

Headlines and Delivery

Think "subject line that sells" and a delivery method that reaches the intended audience. All the great writing won't matter if people don't open the e-mail or don't receive the message in the first place.

Good headlines are easily identified by headlines that get overlooked. "Meeting notice," "announcement," "for your information," and assorted other short but generic words are only marginally informative and certainly don't compel the reader to think, feel, or do anything.

Think about what you can say in a few powerful words that captures the goal of the writing. Generally, the headline needs to say what and why that's a good thing for the receiver. Also think about where the headline will appear. The subject line of an e-mail has to capture the mind in the first few words in case the entire line doesn't display on the reader's device.

Think outside your own box when picking digital media. Regardless of what's customary or easy for the sender, the media has to be customary or easy for the receiver. That means all receivers, who may have a variety of different preferences. You can't make everyone make text their preference just by sending only texts. Often a variety of media is desirable anyway, especially for calling attention to other messages.

■ PICK YOUR FORUM

The principles behind good business writing can pay immense dividends when applied to every oral and written word that flows through today's workplace.

All information that is important to the organization flows through its managers. Or it should. They are vital information links with superiors, subordinates, and the external community, which puts managers in the informational "seat of power." They can use that power responsibly, share what they know and do so timely and accurately. Or they can be filters or gatekeepers.

Certainly, confidentiality and legal liability must be considered. But the manager is not serving anyone well by telling people only what they want to hear or telling them only what the manager wants them to hear for a self-serving purpose. Little problems can eventually become big ones and more difficult to solve.

Pick your forum is about picking the right venue or media for the occasion. Don't waste people's time with a meeting when a memo would do. And don't drop bombs in a meeting or an e-mail or text that should be explained individually and in person. The objective is to communicate efficiently but also to do it effectively.

Say It Face-to-Face

Personal matters need to be handled one on one, in person. The most obvious are goal-setting exercises and performance reviews, but performance problems, disciplinary issues, and management decisions that affect only certain people should be handled personally as well. The primary virtue of face-to-face meetings is the conversation that is exchanged in a confidential and distraction-free setting.

One-on-one meetings are time consuming for the manager, especially with a large staff, but the benefits of personal attention and the quality and quantity of the information exchange far outweighs the time involved. People should not be subjected to the manager's displeasure or blindsided by life-changing news in front of other people. Managers should not hide behind an e-mail or text message to tell people unfavorable news, which can easily circulate uncontrollably or inappropriately throughout the company (or beyond).

Face-to-face meetings circumvent the "look at the text I just got from the manager" stories that really deserved a personal conversation. These meetings can also test-drive a decision and gain buy-in before it's publicly announced as well.

Put It in Writing

We have numerous outlets for accomplishing the more work-is-done-in-writing style of business today. The only practical way to deliver a lot of information and provide "hard copy" of news or announcements, updates, and lengthy reports is in written media. But we also have interactive options that do more than simply deliver one-sided words. The objective is to make the media we chose work to its best advantage.

E-mail. If the choice is e-mail or the postal service's "snail mail," e-mail wins. But an e-mail is only as effective as the way it's presented.

First of all, people don't scroll. The initial words have to catch their attention (the strong beginning "above the fold") so people are compelled to move on down the screen. But they won't stay tuned to text-heavy pages or long paragraphs. Bullet or number lists can keep them hooked but if the subject matter is long or complicated, a better strategy is to pare it down into several e-mails (or make it a document attachment).

Think, too, about the visual format for the benefit of aging eyes and people with vision challenges and for differences in devices. Avoid fancy fonts and colors that are difficult to discern or could display differently in various devices. Use minimum 12-point type with no more than 60 characters per line and don't shout with ALL CAPS. Remember, too, that not all e-mail programs support HTML, so fancy formatting and graphics can get lost and the e-mail will look very strange.

The best test of a subject line is whether people see the e-mail. Some programs can be set to indicate the receiver got the e-mail, or you can send a follow-up e-mail, which also reinforces the first one.

E-mails are often classified or graded for importance. The most overused appeal to the receiver is "high importance." One way to look at this is that we should send only important messages. On the other hand, not every message is time sensitive or urgent enough to demand immediate attention. Use calls for action judiciously so they don't lose their intended effect.

Blogs. Blogs and social media (Facebook, MySpace, and LinkedIn) are rapidly taking over e-mail in the digital race for our attention. They appeal to our hyper-spontaneous need to tell and ask and have been a major force in shifting us from personal to digital contact.

Blog sites created for internal business purposes are appealing for the same reason that people use them in their personal lives—the manager and the workforce can interact in real time. Even the announcement of a meeting or seminar can fuel a conversation that can further promote benefits, answer questions, and help people prepare to discuss the subject at hand.

Blogs are good not only for posting time-sensitive news and information but are also very effective for engaging participation in formal problem solving, brainstorming, and decision-making processes. The workforce has a venue to share opinions, provide feedback (perhaps vent as well), and offer suggestions (an electronic suggestion box).

The rules of good business writing apply to blogging as well. Blog posts tend to be highly conversational, but even the give-and-take in one or two sentences can memorialize unfortunate commentary. Posts should not be written on the fly or in the heat of the moment and should never be sent without being reread.

Managers tend to be wary of blogs, perhaps because of their reputation for unbridled content. But uninhibited commentary can provide the manager with a good opportunity to quickly defuse dissension or foster constructive thinking.

Because blogs have become so popular, they have taken over the interactive platform for internal communication. Some companies also have their own Wikis, which are essentially interactive encyclopedias or repositories of information for use by a company's workforce. Blogs and Wikis are even more useful with an RSS (Really Simple Syndication), which essentially inventories and catalogues the content, so that people have a search engine or Web feed for the information.

Texts and tweets. The epitome of speed and efficiency is the text and tweet. Texts are super efficient for making plans, sending reminder announcements, and exchanging ideas quickly. People often prefer a text message to a voice phone call. Short messaging systems, such as Twitter, accomplish the same thing, all within a limited number of characters.

Beware the speed and convenience, however. Instant messages tend to be instant reactions that can have disastrous consequences. Don't "speak" until the words are carefully framed and written well. Character limitations also limit the clarity of a message, which leaves readers to fill in the words behind the message perhaps incorrectly. Grammar and punctuation count, too, and it's just as easy to capitalize words even within character limits.

Microsoft® Word®, Adobe® PDF, and Microsoft® PowerPoint®.[1] A final word is that software programs provide a variety of options for capturing written words, each of which is desirable for different applications.

Most of us are accustomed to preparing text in Microsoft® Word®. This provides the most convenient options for drafting and editing, and merges well with Microsoft® Excel® spreadsheet software. A Word document can also be edited using track changes, which is very useful for proofing or creating a document with group participation.

Adobe® PDF (Portable Document File) is the most desirable format for circulating a document. Word documents can easily be converted to PDFs, which preserves the content and the format as the author intended. Although PDFs can be edited, the process is more cumbersome and works only if the editing feature is enabled by the creator of the PDF document.

PowerPoint presentation software offers the most dynamic graphic options but the program is intended to support, and not be a substitute for, a word processing program. PowerPoint software is essentially a visual publishing program that is used to create compelling presentations. The best way to use PowerPoint software is to start with material that is drafted in Word and then create the visual presentation. PowerPoint format is not a good option for distributing files because they can't be opened by all readers.

---

1 All trademarks are the property of their respective owners.

Also think about secure cloud services such as Dropbox™ and YouSendit® for lengthy documents instead of attaching them to e-mails.

Hold a Meeting

The business meeting may seem like a dying event today, given the popularity of digital media. But meetings serve a purpose that can't be achieved otherwise. The most obvious is the ability to share information with a number of people at the same time and engage in controlled group discussion.

Business meetings compete with e-mails, text messages, and a mountain of paperwork for the attention of an increasingly mobile workforce for whom the physical office (let alone group events) is increasingly less relevant. A meeting has to rise above all that competition so that people don't feel it's another time-wasting exercise. The major culprits are meetings devoted to information that should have been delivered by a memo or a report. Make a meeting work with good planning and time management.

- **Hook people into the meeting.** Think benefits. A meeting has to have a clearly defined purpose that gives people a reason to attend. They need to see "What's in it for me?" to give up their time. If a meeting can't deliver those benefits, then there's no reason to have one, even if it is a weekly or monthly ritual.
- **Make the meeting relevant.** Gather the right people—those for whom the subject at hand is applicable—and give them ample opportunity to participate. A major reason for holding a meeting is for people to share their views, express opinions, and ask questions. They don't come to hear a lecture.
- **Publish an agenda.** Tell people what's going to happen ahead of time. This not only shows that there's actually a plan for the meeting but also helps people get into the proper mindset. Often meeting materials are distributed for people to review ahead of time as well. This advanced planning also forces the person conducting the meeting to prepare ahead of time, which makes for more efficient use of meeting time for all involved.
- **Take charge.** Start on time, get to the subject matter quickly, and proceed through an orderly agenda. Anticipate objections and prepare to politely, but firmly, handle problems. Even a free-flowing

exchange of ideas (or a meeting purposely structured with a minimal agenda) needs firm guidance to keep the discussion on track.

- **Avoid the pitfalls.** Establish a firm cell-phone-off rule that applies to everyone, including the presenter. Don't waste people's time by starting late, repeating opening remarks for the benefit of latecomers, or preaching about attendance or punctuality. The people who need to hear the sermon aren't there anyway. Beware the disgruntled, the attention-seekers, or the ringleaders of resistance. They have an agenda, too, and will attempt to seize the moment to advance their cause, especially if they feel others in the group are of like mind. The one downside to publishing an agenda ahead of time is people have a chance to pre-form opinions, so choose your words wisely.
- **When it's over, it's over.** Punctual endings are as important as timely beginnings. Respect people's time. If the agenda is too ambitious for the time allotted, draw the meeting to a close and pick up at a later date (perhaps at a mutually agreeable time selected by the group before it disbands). If people start to depart before the meeting is formally adjourned, figure out where the meeting went astray.

The manager's reputation for holding a well-planned, well-managed meeting with a constructive agenda encourages people to give their undivided attention. They may even look forward to the next meeting.

Speaking in Public

Several comments about public speaking are suitable at this point because there are a lot of similarities between good business meetings and successful public speaking engagements.

Regardless of where the manager is on stage, be it a weekly sales meeting, a training program, or a local REALTOR® or Rotary luncheon, the platform is easier for some people to step onto than for others. Some can even feel the butterflies in the pit of the stomach at the mere suggestion of speaking in front of a group. Nevertheless, the platform comes with the job, and there are ways people can learn to be effective on that platform. There are also fine organizations, like Toastmasters International, to help sharpen public speaking skills.

The key to effective public speaking is good preparation, certainly more than can be accomplished in a panicked hour before the scheduled event.

Just as a meeting needs a clear purpose and good organization so, too, does the public speaker's message. It also needs to be rehearsed in some respect so that the speaker can deliver the message and handle the group dynamics with confidence.

Pick the right topic. Even when the speaker has been given some general suggestions, the choice of the specific topic has to appeal to the audience's interests, level of experience, and motivation for attending. That choice isn't always easy, especially when speaking to a large, diverse group, so the message has to strike a chord with at least the majority in the audience. A word of caution is that what the speaker (the presumed expert) thinks the people need to hear and what the audience thinks they need to know can be two distinctly different things. Think benefits, again.

While everyone who addresses a group wants to feel accepted, that doesn't mean that thought-provoking or possibly controversial messages have to be avoided. The point of the presentation is to make a difference in the lives of the people who come to listen. Sometimes, challenging their thinking or comfort level is a good thing.

The message, whether it's a 20-minute speech or a three-hour business or training session, generally flows by

1. telling people what you're going to say,
2. telling them your tale, and then,
3. telling them what you told them.

The first step is the introduction, the "hook" that captures people's attention and provides the objective of and rationale for the program. This also helps to focus everyone's minds (including the speaker's) on the agenda and minimizes the tendency to consume time with idle chatter and announcements. The second step is the substantive content, which is about 80 percent of the time allotted. The last step is a conclusion or summary, the "close" that, depending on the nature of the program, may be a brief statement or a more detailed wrap-up of the major points that were discussed.

A carefully developed message deserves a thoughtful delivery plan. Simple things, like where the speaker will stand, how the room will be arranged, and what media will be used (overhead projectors, PowerPoint presentations, and sound systems) can make or break a program and should be prescreened ahead of time. The importance of using technology cannot be overstated. That said, there's nothing so unnerving as to show up with an entirely media-dependent presentation that won't work, so a "plan b" for this eventuality isn't a bad idea, either.

The actual delivery of the presentation, regardless of the occasion, requires some preparation to successfully manage all the dynamics of the event.

- **Plan for the setting.** Anticipate the arrangement of the venue, including where the speaker will stand and how best to communicate with the group. Some settings are less formal and more conducive to interaction between the speaker and the group than is typically the case with large assemblies for a keynote address or a formal luncheon speech. Nonetheless, good public speakers learn to communicate over and around podiums and other barriers or shortcomings of a particular venue.
- **Rehearse.** Though it may sound foolish, even 15 minutes in the limelight deserves a run-through to deliver a powerful, interesting message that fits the allotted time. That run-through may be a full rehearsal in front of a mirror with attention to inflection and eye contact or some quiet time devoted to mentally "talking through" the presentation.
- **Plan for questions and comments from the audience.** Some speakers are able to control the presentation while dealing with questions and comments along the way; others prefer to handle audience participation at the end. The important point is to give the audience an opportunity to interact with the speaker and resolve any questions before they leave. Audience participation also minimizes the feeling that people are getting a lecture.
- **Be prepared to go with the flow.** Only the speaker knows whether the presentation is going according to plan. Thoughts get scrabbled, speakers lose their place, and even make mistakes, but no misstep is so egregious that the speaker can't acknowledge it with good humor and then get back on track. With experience, speakers learn to think

on their feet, take cues from the audience, "go off script," and deliver stellar programs.

- **Choose humor wisely.** Humor must fit the speaker's style, personality, and, certainly, the nature of the subject matter. Some people are good at telling jokes, while others are better at telling light-hearted tales or using humorous examples to make a point. The caveat is that audiences can easily be distracted by or misinterpret humor, and there's no humor in offending people.

DECISION MAKING

We gauge leaders by their decisiveness and managers by their ability to make decisions. All that we learn about communication plays a significant role in giving managers the information they need to frame proper guidance and telling people what they need to know.

Information is the force behind all decisions. The quality of those decisions is directly related to the quantity, accuracy, and timeliness of the information on which those decisions are based.

Decisions fall into four general categories.

1. **Entrepreneurial or institutional decisions.** These involve significant strategic directions, policies, or fundamental systems within the organization.
2. **Corrective decisions.** These resolve problems, dilemmas, or crises that require solutions to keep the organization on track or to maintain order in its systems and processes.
3. **Resource decisions.** These involve the allocation of personnel or money.
4. **Mediation decisions.** These are essentially negotiated solutions, primarily involving personnel issues and customer service.

Decision-making processes vary. One process is very deliberate and methodical, analyzing situations and evaluating a wide range of options before deciding on a course of action. Another is equally analytical but goes through this process more quickly. Some focus on the long-range implications when making short-range decisions while others focus on the immediacy and are less concerned about long-term ramifications.

Different modes of decision making are appropriate in different situations. Therein lies another aspect of decisions—deciding when a quick versus more deliberate process is appropriate or even when not to interfere.

People sometimes get frustrated with managers, a case of violated expectations, in a sense. People expect direction but get none, or the direction is too slow in coming. Or people expect a more studied course of action but get what appears to be a quick fix instead. People who are inclined to be quick decision makers are put off when others chose a more deliberate approach and vice versa. When managers make a conscious decision to do nothing, others may feel that they have abdicated their responsibility.

Classic Decision Making

Classic decision making is a deliberate, methodical process. It is somewhat like a scientific model, involving seven very rational or logical steps.

1. **Define the situation**—clearly describe the problem or circumstance and the cause or causes.
2. **Develop alternatives**—list all the possible courses of action to solve the problem or address the situation.
3. **Evaluate alternatives**—consider the pluses and minuses, feasibility, short- and/or long-term ramifications, and the perceived acceptance of each option.
4. **Select the appropriate alternative**—decide on the most desirable course of action, which then becomes the decision.
5. **Implement the decision**—inform the appropriate people about the decision and institute any necessary changes in policies, procedures, or systems that are affected by the decision.
6. **Follow through**—monitor the implementation of the decision to ensure that the new directive has been institutionalized.
7. **Evaluate the outcome**—decide whether the decision produced the desired results. Did it do what it was supposed to do? Address the

situation or correct the problem? If the wrong alternative was chosen or the implementation was faulty, take corrective action.

Used in its purest form, classic decision making is a formal process that is undertaken by an individual manager, a team of managers, or a cross section of people within the organization. This methodical approach is especially valuable when the defined situation significantly affects major policies and procedures. Deliberations through each of the steps are intended to produce the most carefully framed decision, with all possible implications being considered, so that the decision has the greatest chance of addressing the situation and being implemented successfully.

The classic model is also the mode of decision making that is inherently customary for some managers, even to the extent that they can mentally run through the same series of steps and come up with a viable decision in a relatively short time frame. Some variation on the theme of the model may be constructed to accommodate the nature of the situation, available response time, and the importance of short-term versus long-term implications of the alternatives.

Variables in Decision Making

Regardless of whether the classic model is used or the manager makes a spur-of-the-moment decision, the quality of the decision is tied to several variables—information, expertise, human behavior, and consensus versus majority.

The classic model presumes that the information people are working with is complete, accurate, and timely, but the same rules apply to any decision-making process. Emotional or biased observations, cooked books, or months-old financial reports skew the definition of the situation at the outset as well as the analysis of alternative solutions. If the gatekeepers are hindering the flow of information or diverse viewpoints and data sources aren't considered, the quality of the decision will suffer.

Another variable is the business or technical expertise of the decision makers. The classic model presumes they have sufficient skill and professional insight to properly define the situation and generate and evaluate alternatives. Their solutions may not be perfect, but the quality of the decisions is directly related to the knowledge, skill, and business sophistication of the people who make them. While one person may be totally capable, often a group provides a breadth of perspective and expertise that is desirable.

There is also the human variable involved in decision making. Personal agenda, bias, or a quest to protect one's turf or authority can color the view of the situation, the alternatives, and even the final decision. Regardless of the process, there is some amount of gut instinct or intuition that may factor into the equation, sometimes for good reasons and with good outcomes.

Personality traits also play a role in the way we make decisions. People who tend to see the world as black-or-white are often less likely to consider other people's opinions, are less anxious about making the wrong choices, and are more likely to make quick decisions. People who see the variations of grey in the world are more likely to be receptive to multiple points of view and very thoughtful about making the right choice. They are often hesitant or reluctant decision makers, perhaps to even rethink or regret a decision once it is made.

When a group of people is engaged in the process, the human dynamics can be even more interesting. Mix the quick with the ambivalent decision-making personalities and the impatient ones tire of the pondering their counterparts are inclined to do. Sometimes coalitions form in favor of a certain alternative for a variety of reasons that have little to do with the business merits of a course of action and more to do with organizational or personal dynamics.

Classic decision making presumes the final conclusion is a consensus of the group, which means everyone agrees the decision is the most suitable one even if some people are less than 100 percent enthusiastic about it. If the group can't reach consensus, the decision winds up being the alternative that got the majority vote, which means there is opposition that can cause dissension or even hinder the implementation of the decision.

Implementing Decisions

Implementation is the action step that not only communicates a decision but also mobilizes resources, processes, and procedures to support the decision. Decision making is little more than an academic exercise if only the people who were involved know what was decided and the organization fails to align its operations to support the decision.

People in many organizations can tell "I didn't know that" tales about changes in policy or procedures, all as a result of management's failure to communicate. The people who need to know didn't get the message, or the message itself wasn't clear enough or didn't make an impression.

A decision that makes sense to the people who made it must be communicated so that it makes sense to all the people who are affected by it. A new process that enhances operations in one department may seem cumbersome or ill-advised in others. But people are more willing to implement decisions they understand. Managers don't have to justify or defend a decision, but they can certainly advance the cause for implementation when they explain the rationale or logic behind the thinking, especially from a companywide perspective.

Often the unknown variable is the degree of acceptance a decision will receive. The decision may be welcomed if management corrects a long-standing problem or does something the workers think is especially helpful. Or the decision may change policies or procedures that people were content with or didn't think needed to be changed in the first place.

Everyone in management must present a unified front in support of the decision. Not all decisions will be popular, but if senior management has decided that certain procedures are to be adopted in the sales offices, then that's what the sales managers are responsible for implementing. If people sense dissension, they are less likely to cooperate or may even sabotage a decision.

When major changes in the organization are contemplated, management must guard the confidentiality of a decision until it can be properly announced and explained. Otherwise, the company grapevine can start an undertow of rumors and half-truths that can undermine the decision even before people hear the official announcement. Typically, organizations launch major initiatives with great fanfare, including advance teasers or internal public relations hype to create positive excitement, while minimizing negative anxiety.

The final step is to make sure the decision has been institutionalized and is producing the desired results. Decisions are not cast in stone. Some institute changes or start initiatives that take time to produce results or can't be reversed quickly, so any follow-up decision, even one that resets a timetable, is a good thing.

■ CONCLUSION

The flow of information in an organization serves many purposes for managers, the people they supervise, and the people the managers report to. Funneling the volume of information in ways that reach the intended audiences in a timely, accurate, and compelling manner is the challenge of good communications. Organizations depend on the fluid exchange of information to function efficiently so that managers can make quality decisions and their directives can be implemented.

■ DISCUSSION EXERCISES

What do you see as the strengths and weaknesses of the ways management in your organization communicates? How well informed do you feel about what is going on in your company? How does that aid or hamper your ability to do your job?

Critique some of your business writing. How can you improve your writing based on what you've learned? What does a rewrite look like?

What works and doesn't work for the audiences with whom you communicate? Text, e-mail, blogs, a combination?

How worthwhile are the meetings that are typically conducted in your company? If you have been responsible for meetings, what has been successful and what has been problematic about your meetings?

Think about a business decision that you or senior management has recently made. How do you assess the decision-making process and the way the decision was implemented?

IN CONCLUSION OF UNIT I

Armed with an understanding of the interpersonal, informational, and decision-making roles of a manager, the manager can assume a leadership position, make the decisions that are essential in the job, and command a following of the people on whom the organization depends for its very existence. This is a tall order, but with well-developed skills, the manager can successfully assume the position and the responsibilities that it confers, and find fulfillment and enjoyment in the journey.

■ THE SCENARIO

Having read this unit, what is your analysis of the following scenario?

The broker was sitting alone in her office, having retreated to its solitude after a disturbing meeting that afternoon with the "Chairman's Circle." This is a group of salespeople who are chosen by their offices' sales staffs to be their representatives at periodic meetings with the broker. The Circle acts like the "eyes and ears" within the organization, sharing insight and providing feedback, to help the broker stay in touch with what's going on in her multimillion-dollar, multi-departmental company.

The original topic of conversation that was supposed to be the subject for that afternoon's meeting is not nearly as important as the issue that eventually surfaced.

It all began when someone mentioned the company's relocation program. The comment was a passing reference to a procedure that this salesperson's manager had explained at a recent office meeting. But that comment opened the floodgates and turned the Circle's meeting into a full-blown discussion about relocation referrals. The more conversation she heard, the more the broker realized that the program she thought was carefully laid out to be fair, equitable, and efficient wasn't working that way at all.

She learned that several of the office managers, for whatever reason, had neglected to discuss the company's relocation procedures with their sales staffs. Moreover, it appeared that some of the managers had totally disregarded the company program and implemented their own procedures for distributing relocation referrals, and in at least one case, the salesperson suspected that the manager was keeping the best referrals for himself.

The crowning blow was the revelation that the company's relocation director, who outwardly said all the right words at the senior management team meetings, seemed to be playing favorites with certain offices, and in some cases with selected salespeople, without regard to published procedures. These were procedures that the relocation director had designed, that the senior management team had approved, and that the sales office managers had been fully briefed on.

During the disquieting hour the broker spent in her office after the meeting, she became increasingly disheartened. Recognizing that the distribution of relocation referrals is one of the most thorny issues to manage in any brokerage company, it's conceivable that the spirited discussion simply vented some typically competitive viewpoints. But the more she thought about it, the more convinced she was that what she'd heard said much more about the sales office managers and the relocation director who worked for the company, or at least the way they were perceived. All of which reflected on the broker as well.

■ THE ANALYSIS

After the discussions in this first unit, the situations that the broker faced should be fairly clear. Her Chairman's Circle is characteristic of the participatory culture that is prevalent in today's organizations, and certainly it did what she'd hoped it would do—be a way for her to gather information. Wisely, she decided to let the conversation flow rather than reining it back to her preplanned agenda. The time seemed to be right just to let people talk, and the more they did, the more they revealed.

One breakdown centered on the way decisions about the referral policy had been implemented. Clearly, there was not a unified voice or support within the managerial ranks because the policy had not been discussed, and in some cases had been circumvented entirely, by some of the office managers.

The unknown variables are whether some of the managers just had more pressing matters to discuss with their sales staffs, whether the policy was basically flawed, or whether some of the managers had overstepped the bounds of their authority by instituting their own procedures. In one case, the selling manager's priority appeared to be his or her personal business over that of the sales staff. All of this needs further investigation by the broker.

The breakdown at the senior management level is particularly disturbing because the person in a position of authority is exercising that authority in irresponsible ways. The unknowns in this situation, which the broker needs to explore, are whether the broker misjudged the person she put in that position, or whether there are other dynamics surrounding the policies or the people who interface with the relocation department that are causing the system to unravel.

In the final analysis, trust has been violated—faith that people in the organization had in the trustworthiness of their leaders and the trust the broker had placed in the office managers and the relocation director to do the jobs she expected of them. While none of this is absolutely fatal, as long as the broker takes some steps to get everything back on track, it's disheartening to make these discoveries, especially because it takes more time to re-engender trust than it does to lose it. If you were the broker, what would you do now?

UNIT II
PLANNING THE ORGANIZATION

Organizations engage in a mass of activities which are grouped under functions. The first of those is planning. This is the step that sets all of the wheels in motion and guides virtually everything an organization does and all the decisions that are made.

Planning, however, is the function that is often given the least attention. Typically, people focus more on "doing" than planning what to do. Management expert Peter Drucker observed that most people spend more time working at doing things right rather than working at doing the right things. Planning charts the course for doing the right things.

Certainly, any new business needs to be armed with a plan. But that's not the end of planning. Organizations need to revisit the process periodically to ensure that they continue doing the right things and set new courses as needed. Organizations sometimes also develop auxiliary plans so they have ready courses of action in case the business environment changes dramatically.

Planning involves more than simply writing down some goals. In fact, developing goals or objectives, and the supporting activities is one of the last steps in the process. The process begins with several steps that gather specific information and proceeds as follows:

- Analyze the external business environment
- Analyze the external marketplace and the internal company environment
- Develop the plan and supporting activities
- Implement the plan by assigning responsibilities and allocating resources

Planning begins with what is known as a *situational* or *environmental analysis*. This is the informational part of the process that assesses the prevailing external and internal climate, identifies opportunities and barriers that confront the organization, and does some forecasting for the future. As in most things management does, the informational part of the process is most critical. Without this, there's no assurance that the organization will be doing the right things or that the things it plans to do are feasible. The situational analysis provides the information for making the right decisions.

Many resources are available from which to gather information about local and general trends and conditions, including census data and general business and real estate–specific research that can be accessed on the Internet. An excellent resource about industry trends is the *Swanepoel Trends Report* by Stefan Swanepoel.

The chapters in this unit lead you through the planning process. The broker/owner (and senior management in a large organization) is typically involved in all aspects of planning to develop the strategic or general plan for the company. Department managers or managers of sales offices are usually involved in certain aspects of planning, especially those that relate to their specific areas of responsibility. A familiarity with the entire process, however, is necessary to understand how a plan fits together.

CHAPTER FIVE

ANALYZING THE BUSINESS ENVIRONMENT

What factors currently have the most effect on the general business climate in your area? And on real estate companies?

What role will these factors, or others, play in the future?

The most compelling lessons about the economic meltdown that began in 2007 tell us that

- a company's plan is only as good as the analysis of the business environment and the assumptions we make about the future.
- assumptions must anticipate change, including change that will negatively affect the company.
- contingency planning is as important as the master plan because the business environment will change.
- intervention must be swift for the company to remain a viable economic organization.

These words could sound too negative during a thriving economy but that's the very time a company has to be wary of the alternative. Business is supposed to be exciting and rewarding, not a gloom-and-doom proposition, but a company can't reap the rewards if it can't triumph over the inevitable forces of change.

This is the first chapter of two that lead up to an actual plan. And why does it take two chapters to get to that point? Why can't we just write a plan and get on with the business of doing business?

The answer is very simple—business plans fail when they aren't supported with cold, hard facts. A plan is only as good as the research that supports it. Quantified evidence demonstrates opportunities and reveals pitfalls, which establishes credibility for the plan.

Even the best managed companies can't be viable economic organizations if their leaders miss the game-changers in the business environment and don't strategically place their organizations to take advantage of opportunities. That strategic placement involves forecasts. The unknown variable, of course, is that the future can't be measured in quantified terms, which means forecasts have to be based on well-studied lessons, both past and present.

■ ECONOMIC FACTORS

History proves the overwhelming positive and negative effects of economic factors on the business environment. Companies want evidence that the good times will continue and warning about the approaching bad times, but the economy doesn't always cooperate by providing that evidence, especially when domestic politics and global forces are also at play.

However, economists and business analysts follow a number of key economic indicators, which business planners need to follow as well, to form assumptions. The most learned economists and analysts don't always agree on what the indicators mean for what lies ahead, but often a combination of indicators provides a fairly reliable picture of the economy.

Gross Domestic Product

The gross domestic product (GDP) is the broadest indicator of the strength of the economy, showing the economic output and growth. Healthy industrialized economies have an average annual increase in the range of

3 percent. A higher percentage indicates that the economy is overheating. In the United States, a sharp decline has historically resulted in stagnant growth. The GDP that the government releases each quarter indicates how the economy is faring as the year progresses.

Inflationary Cycles

A healthy economy should generate a low, stable rate of inflation. During the 1990s, the United States enjoyed slow, steady economic growth, with inflation hovering around 3 percent per year and even less toward the end of the decade. That trend, along with optimism in the stock market, continued until 2001 when inflation began to accelerate, the stock market started to lose ground and unemployment began to climb. Inflation then slowed, capital spending started to rise, and the stock market regained lost ground and more to set record highs in 2007. Then, we headed into the Great Recession.

As trite as it sounds, what goes up eventually comes down, and vice versa. For an indicator of where we are in inflationary cycles, look at the spread between short-term interest rates set by the Federal Reserve and the interest rates on long-term bonds.

- If the spread is large or getting larger—the government is trying to fuel the economy by loosening its monetary policy. This encourages people to spend and grow the economy.
- If the spread is small or shrinking—the government is attempting to cool the economy by tightening the money supply. This discourages people from spending to guard against another inflationary spiral.

In recent years, the Federal Reserve (the Fed) has managed inflation with gentle, though sufficient, adjustments in interest rates to keep inflation in check. Those efforts during the 1990s prevented inflation from it riding the extreme peaks and valleys of previous decades. The Federal Reserve continued its vigilant management of inflation and lowered interest rates when economic stimulus was needed after the tech-stock bubble burst in 2000–2001.

The Fed's low interest rates fostered considerable economic growth, but this action also had unintended consequences. Interest rates were at their lowest point in a generation and created an extraordinary credit boom. But that prompted unexpected extraordinary risk-taking, which sent billions of dollars in subprime mortgage loans into foreclosure. The fallout rocked financial sectors (and put some lenders into bankruptcy), tightened credit, canceled corporate takeover plans, and in the summer of 2007, set up a tidal wave of volatility in the stock market.

Stimulating economic growth and keeping inflation in check is clearly a balancing act. Even during the stock market's turbulence in the summer of 2007, the economy appeared to be relatively strong and inflation was under control. But by the fall of that year, credit markets had seized and the threat of recession loomed. The Fed cut short-term interest rates by 50 basis points sooner than it wanted to in an attempt to shore up a rapidly weakening economy, an action that renewed concerns over rising inflation.

We did get the Great Recession. But one of the few cautiously optimistic signs throughout was that inflation was relatively well contained, despite repeated reductions in short-term interest rates. The Fed held rates at their lowest levels in decades in an attempt to stimulate borrowing, but it took many months for the effect to start the economy back on a growth path.

Consumers don't usually see the rate of inflation the same way the government does, though. The government gauges inflation with the consumer pricing index, while consumers gauge it with their checkbooks. The hard sell to consumers is a consumer pricing index that indicates inflation is under control, while the real world of rising costs of gas, groceries, and utilities is straining their budgets. The disconnect between indexes and checkbooks comes from the fact that measures of core inflation do not include food, fuel, and energy, the very prices that have risen dramatically in recent years.

Certainly, business planning is easier during periods of stable inflation, when economic indicators are relatively predictable and the economy is in a steady growth mode. But this is also when it's easy to get lulled into a false sense of security. Overly aggressive optimism can leave a company vulnerable when the economy begins to slow unless the company is vigilant and makes timely adjustments, especially in volatile times.

Consumer Confidence

The line between economic growth and the prospect of recession is often quite thin. The decision rests in the hands of consumers, whose spending represents two-thirds of our nation's income.

The consumers' willingness to spend is tied to their sense of financial security and general attitude about the state of the economy. Turmoil works on their psyche, with emotions often being the powerful but unpredictable driving force behind spending, especially when big-ticket purchases are involved.

Retailers that deal in food, clothing, and low-cost consumer goods can gauge consumer confidence by watching trends in monthly sales. But dealers in less-frequently purchased items (vehicles, home appliances, and houses) are more dependent on longer-term sales trends, interest rates, and repair-versus-replace and retrofit-old-versus-buy-new behaviors to judge future business. These trends are closely monitored by a number of analysts, with some of the most complete research being available from the National Association of REALTORS®.

Consumers are sturdiest when they have job security, wages that are sufficient to support their cost of living, and minimal debt. These factors can be evaluated with unemployment and job-growth rates (which the government publishes each month) and the Federal Reserve's data about ratio of debt obligations to after-tax income. Consumers also signal confidence when they make discretionary expenditures on such items as high-end consumer goods, second homes, and vacation properties.

Consumer confidence is most challenging for over 60 percent of low- and moderate-income households, who spend at least 50 percent or more of their income on housing alone, and for people living on fixed incomes (including the elderly) for whom the costs of housing and daily living often increase more rapidly than their income. Low interest rates, which are good for the housing market, don't signal good times for people who rely primarily on investment income for their living expenses either.

The Housing Market

The housing market is one indicator economists agree is a relatively sound gauge of the strength of the economy. Real estate-related enterprises certainly have a vested interest in the housing market, but when the market deflated in the middle of this decade, we saw proof that as housing goes, so goes a lot of other markets. Consequently, real estate enterprises are not the only businesses that have a huge stake in the housing market regaining momentum after it loses its footing.

A number of years ago we'd have written about consumers sitting on a precarious perch when the Federal Deposit Insurance Corporation reported that home-price appreciation outpaced income growth in 38 out of 50 states during March 2004 to March 2005. As prices increased 6.7 percentage points faster than income, median-income buyers simply could not afford median-priced properties with traditional loans. Interest-only, low- and no-down payment, and adjustable-rate loans, which accounted for a little over half of the home mortgage lending in 2005, made those appreciated prices affordable and even fueled appreciation. In the meantime, headlines started to warn of a housing bubble about to burst.

As with any first mention of negative news for the housing market, pundits (the real estate industry's included) countered that the market was, in fact, quite healthy. The really significant story in the third quarter of 2005 that slipped under the radar was the growing anxiety of stock market experts who saw worrisome signs for the banking sector and predicted the possibility of credit problems down the road.

It's easy to see wisdom in archived headlines, but the warnings were there if more people had paid attention. Indeed, the housing bubble did lose its air and a number of mortgages went into foreclosure. In the big scheme of things, the loans in jeopardy represented only a small percentage of those that were outstanding. But that was the tip of a much bigger story about mortgage fraud and credit woes for the entire marketplace, which left many to wonder how fast the housing industry would right itself in a new era of tighter credit policies.

The race and pause of the housing market is a dose of cyclical realism. Certainly, some areas of the country (even city to city) are more dramatically affected by market cycles than others. Sales volume (often distinguished between existing and new houses), new-housing starts, and housing prices are all factors in these cycles. When word spreads that prices have dropped 10 percent in an area where they had gained 100 percent or more, the missing part of the message is that the blush came off appreciation.

The Great Recession took more than the blush off appreciation and left thousands of homeowners upside down, with outstanding mortgage balances exceeding the market value of their properties. The deeper the recession, the more economic forces that are needed to restore consumer confidence and fuel the housing market as well.

Unemployment and job-growth rates have been as closely watched as the number of home sales, not just as separate indicators but for their collective effect. When companies are back in the hiring mode, the real estate market regains strength as well. But those also have localized impacts, with not all regions of the country or individual cities having similar experiences.

A community's economic growth and development efforts have a bearing as well. Watching the job-growth rate for several months as businesses expand, downsize, or move into or out of an area will help forecast potential real estate business.

■ POLITICAL FACTORS

Depending on prevailing political ideologies, sympathies, and priorities, the effect public policymakers have on the business environment can vary. Republicans and Democrats see the role of government differently, especially its role in stimulating business and job growth. The parties (and individual politicians) also have differing views about budget matters, tax cuts, entitlement programs, and a host of other issues that directly or indirectly, but nevertheless ultimately, affect consumers and the corporate community.

Swinging with changes in the political landscape is not easy, and most business planners avoid devising plans that align with the political ideology currently in power. Nothing's as fickle as politics, and power can shift unexpectedly due to a variety of circumstances that are not readily predictable. There is a role, however, for political vigilance in the planning process. The agendas of federal, state, and local policymakers can certainly affect corporate operations, community development, and the housing industry, all of which have a direct bearing on a real estate company.

Corporate Development

All of a company's best efforts to grow revenue can be quickly neutralized by government regulations and tax policies. Businesses (as opposed to people) often bear the brunt of the government's quest for revenue, making corporate and business privilege taxes in one form or another a significant cost of doing business. Companies are additionally burdened with costs to comply with regulations, including the administration of employee benefit and retirement plans.

Some locales are more business-friendly than others. Some states' incorporation and accompanying tax laws make attractive seats for corporations. Companies can also be affected by the role of business development in the overall economic development plan of a state or local political subdivision. In areas where incentives are offered to attract businesses and stimulate accompanying job growth, a company may be inspired to take advantage of these opportunities. A more favorable business climate is also an incentive for established businesses to remain in these areas.

Without venturing into the appropriateness of a particular ideology, the fact remains that the treatment of businesses is subject to political forces. Unless business planners are conscious of strategies being contemplated in the political agenda at all levels of government, companies can be in for a rude and, possibly, costly awakening.

Economic Growth and Development

Community economic growth and development policies can affect a real estate company in a variety of ways, in addition to the possible incentives for business development.

The fundamental challenge in economic growth and development efforts is to balance benefits with costs, both in terms of money and the amount of regulatory intervention that may be needed. Preserving the quality of life for a community's residents, revitalizing aging neighborhoods or enhancing the utility of the land, and strengthening a community's economic base serve desirable and often very necessary purposes.

The price, however, is that growth stresses existing infrastructures (sewer, water, and transportation systems) and community resources (schools, libraries, and public safety services). Those stresses also stir up residents to fight growth, or any change in their neighborhoods for that matter, simply out of a desire to preserve the community as they've known it.

Even when residents want their deteriorating or blighted neighborhoods to be revitalized and the social problems that often accompany them to be eliminated, people frequently grow impatient with the amount of time and money required to upright these neighborhoods.

The resolution of the cost-versus-benefit equation comes in different forms, again depending on political views of the government's role. On one hand, government should be highly engaged, with significant regulatory intervention and financial commitment to brick and mortar, entitlement programs, and economic stimulus packages. On the other hand, the private sector should drive economic growth and development, the thought being that opportunities abound for the private sector's benefit. The government should participate only to the extent that it helps free enterprise to function.

The real estate industry has always been a staunch supporter of private property rights. Not only can overly aggressive restrictions impede the fundamental rights of ownership but aggressive land-use plans, zoning ordinances, and building codes can discourage development and exacerbate the very problems they intend to solve. The participation by a company's leaders in economic development provides valuable perspective.

All of this means that sound economic growth and development policies ultimately benefit real estate and create numerous opportunities in the marketplace. Regardless of whether the priorities are job growth, enhanced educational opportunities, improved transportation, or land-use enhancement, the outcome is a community that is more attractive to more people, all of whom represent potential real estate business.

Environmental Issues

As policymakers seek ways to protect public health and safety and the environment, both the property owner and the real estate industry have been saddled with volumes of regulations. In essence, environmental issues have become real estate issues.

While serving environmental interests, which in many cases also have health-related components, is a noble and necessary cause, the solutions often tangle with private property rights and the checkbooks of sellers, purchasers, and developers of real estate. Enforcement of the solutions often brings an additional price in the legal liability for all parties involved, including real estate practitioners.

Although many environmental issues are universally important (including health and safety issues in the workplace), issues that have the most noticeable effect on a real estate company can vary by geographic area. Forestry, water, or wildlife concerns are especially significant in some areas. In others, the age of buildings and the construction materials and methods that have been used over time make issues like lead-based paint, asbestos, and toxic molds particularly significant.

The ever-expanding list of federal, state, and local regulations; health-related studies; and civil cases that have been adjudicated expands the future impacts on the real estate business. They affect the amount and nature of potential business, the costs of complying with regulations, and perhaps most importantly, can significantly affect the company's liability exposure and insurance needs.

Regulating the Industry

While many public policies regulate the real estate industry in some fashion, public law and rule give the industry a host of laws and regulations that are specific to its business. The number is considerable when you consider state licensing laws; federal and state antitrust laws; consumer laws; the Real Estate Settlement Procedures Act (RESPA); the Foreign Investment in Real Property Act (FIRPTA); federal, state, and local fair housing laws; the Americans with Disabilities Act; data security laws; anti-solicitation laws; and the Truth-in-Lending Act.

The challenge is to monitor all the developments as laws are amended and new ones are passed. And little is forgiven for ignorance. Several trends have had a particular hand in shaping the way real estate companies do business, driven in part by a heightened emphasis on consumer rights, in a word, *disclosure*—disclosure of agency relationships, disclosure of property conditions, disclosure of environmental substances, disclosure of financing terms, and disclosure of the way that various service providers participate with one another in real estate transactions.

Additional responsibilities mean additional paperwork—and additional liability for the broker, especially if the salespeople are careless about complying with these requirements.

While the industry's laws may not necessarily have a major impact on the volume of business a company can forecast, they certainly affect the way a company does business. Laws that foster universal licensure of salespeople will also have a bearing on the business. Because of the intricacy of the volume of laws, smart business planners engage the company's legal counsel in the planning process as well.

■ SOCIOLOGICAL FACTORS

The social or demographic environment is the people factor that affects virtually every aspect of a company's business, from its workforce to its clientele. Companies that manufacture consumer goods and deliver consumer services (that's where real estate fits in) devote considerable resources to studying population demographics.

The demographic study is the part of the analysis of the business environment that provides the most quantifiable support for the assumptions behind a business plan. While the number of people is useful information, the demographics or profiles of those people (age, education level, cultural origin, and so on) are particularly helpful for tailoring products and services, delivery systems, and advertising programs that suit the available pool of potential consumers. Figure 5.1 provides an interesting profile of the population.

The U.S. Census Bureau dissects data by region, state, and city, and also estimates demographic trends, including shifts in population. For real estate companies, data that are especially helpful for planning include

- age and sex compositions,
- cultural composition (Asian, Hispanic, etc.),
- homeownership and rental distributions,
- household and family composition (number of people, ages, generations),
- housing characteristics, and
- population distributions.

FIGURE 5.1
Age of General Population and Various Types of Citizenry

	25–34 Years Old		35–44 Years Old		45–64 Years Old		65+ Years Old		
	No.†	% of Total	No.†	% of Total	No.†	% of Total	No.†	% of Total	Total
General Population*									
1995	42	16	42	16	15.5	20	33.5	13	263
2000	38	14	45	16	60.0	22	35.0	13	276
2005	37	13	43	15	70.0	24	37.0	13	288
2010	38	13	40	13	79.0	26	40.0	13	300
White (Not Hispanic)									
1995	29.50	11.0	31.50	12.0	41.0	15.5	28.75	11.0	
2000	25.75	9.3	32.75	11.9	46.5	16.8	29.50	10.7	
2005	24.00	8.3	30.00	10.4	53.5	18.6	30.25	10.1	
2010	24.50	8.2	26.25	8.8	58.5	19.5	32.25	10.8	
African American									
1995	5.50	2.0	5.00	2.0	5.25	2.0	2.75	1.1	
2000	5.25	1.9	5.50	2.0	6.25	2.2	3.00	1.0	
2005	5.25	1.8	5.50	1.9	7.75	2.7	3.00	1.0	
2010	5.50	1.8	5.25	1.7	9.00	3.0	3.50	1.2	
Hispanics									
1995	5.00	2.0	4.0	1.5	3.75	1.5	1.5	0.5	
2000	5.25	1.9	5.0	1.8	4.75	1.7	2.0	0.7	
2005	5.25	1.8	5.5	1.9	6.25	2.2	2.5	0.9	
2010	5.75	1.9	5.5	1.8	7.75	2.6	3.0	1.0	

*These numbers do not consider people who are younger than 25 years old. Because people under 25 years of age are not included, the numbers do not add up to 100 percent. They are U.S. Census Bureau data estimates, which predate the 2010 Census.
†Numbers are in millions of people.

Baby Boomers and Their Offspring

The Boomers and their offspring are not only a force in the workplace (see Chapter 3) but a force in the marketplace. The Boomers have been a driving force for many years, simply because of their sheer numbers. This population has affected virtually every system it touched in its advance through life, from the public schools to the business community and the housing industry. They have been a force to reckon with during their maximum wage-earning years and continue to be as they demand goods and services that suit their maturing lifestyles.

Gen X, as the offspring of the Boomers are known, is the first true technology generation. The Gen Xers have never known life without microwave ovens, cable television, or portable phones (let alone cell phones). They have achieved financial independence, raised their own families, and parented their own baby boom of Gen Ys, or the "echo generation."

Gen Y is now entering the workforce, which also means they are becoming a consuming force in the marketplace. This is the device generation for whom smart phones, tablets, and the Internet are staples in life, a factor that plays a huge role in the products and services companies develop and where those goods are placed and advertised. They are very environmentally conscious and feel a great sense of entitlement.

Certainly, all of these developments affect demand for housing—not just in the number of units but also in style, size, and amenities. While Boomers are downsizing, their children are upsizing. Generally, Gen X prefers a home that reflects today's more active and casual lifestyles, and is better technologically appointed and more environmentally-friendly than the homes of their parents.

The eldest Gen Ys are in the housing market now, too, looking for homes that are a lot like the ones they grew up in. This is the social-media generation that collaborates extensively with friends (who also play a role in Gen Y's home buying decisions) and builds real estate relationships with information, which imposes a high level of expectation in the quantity and quality of the information a company's Web site and its salespeople deliver.

Gen Ys rely extensively on virtual tours (which means they actually visit fewer properties than older generations do) and are accustomed to getting what they want at the price they want to pay, just as they do by trolling the Internet for other purchases they make.

In recent years, companies shifted their focus from the Boomers to the 25-to-35-year-old age group (some even to the 18-to-24-year-olds) to capture a market base for the future. But this focus also takes products or services that appeal to the older consumer out of the marketplace and increases the generation gap in advertising that leaves many with an "I didn't get that" point of the message.

Maturing Adults

Many companies are now refocusing on the Boomers, the old force in the marketplace that's still sizable and has attractive financial capacity. They outnumbered the 18–24-year-old population in the 2010 U.S. Census, with the over-65 crowd numbering 40,268,000 million (5,493,000 of whom were over 85) as compared to 30,672,000 million 18–24-year-olds.

It's no wonder that many industries, real estate included, have made the senior population a priority target market. However, this is a diverse group rather than one stereotypical senior population. The pre-65-, 65-to-75-, and over-75-year-old age groups each have different needs and lifestyles.

The 75-and-older category has been retired for some time (in many cases because of corporations encouraging early exits as they streamlined operations) and have found engaging ways to enjoy active retirement. The next younger group is working longer, sometimes more because of financial necessity than by choice, but is merging work with a more recreational, relaxed lifestyle.

Where does the maturing population want to live? Surveys indicate that at least four out of ten Boomers intend to move during their retirement years, with nearly one third expecting to downsize their housing. But the most prevalent answer is that people want to live at home as they age, wherever that home is. Aging-in-place is a growing trend, with people striving to live independently along with the support of in-home services, if necessary.

In some households, this means multigenerational living as older, less physically or financially independent seniors move in with their adult children, with those adults becoming the senior adults' caregivers. There are also households where young seniors are their young grandchildren's caregivers. These trends create unique housing requirements, often to accommodate multiple generations in separate quarters under one roof.

Population Shifts

The population in the United States is more mobile than in other advanced industrial economies. According to the Census Bureau, the average American moves 12 times in a lifetime.

Population shifts are driven primarily by employment opportunities, but today's younger generations are also more inclined to explore new venues for their climatic, recreational, or cultural appeal than previous generations were. Even though the nation's population continues to grow, some parts of the country have experienced population decline. These shifts create opportunities for real estate companies in areas with population increases, but challenge other communities and their real estate companies to find ways to remain vital.

Culturally Diverse Population

As the population grows, so does its cultural diversity and the number of foreign-born homeowners. The increasing diversity of our population is due to an influx of temporary residents working for international corporations as well as to immigration. The National Association of Home Builders and the National Association of REALTORS® trend estimates are helpful in gauging demand and preparing to serve culturally diverse consumers.

The general public appears to receive more accurate and comprehensive information about home ownership and the home-buying process than even English-dominant language minorities do. Given the size of the minority population, opportunities abound for real estate companies that are prepared to serve a culturally diverse clientele. But this means that only those companies that understand the uniqueness of cultures and have a staff that is familiar with multinational customs and language can benefit.

Anyone who has traveled abroad has experienced first-hand the wonder, and the isolation, of different customs and unfamiliar languages. It's striking to note that people in many countries are fluent in multiple languages, with English often being the second or third language studied by young people during their formal education. It's also not uncommon to find public signage, restaurant menus, and the like in English as well as the local language.

Turning the tables, one quickly sees that this land of opportunity is also one that has been somewhat lax in its development of multilingual and multicultural understanding. While language is the most obvious hurdle for immigrants, even among English speakers, differences in customs, taboos, and business etiquette pose daily challenges.

A resource for preparing a real estate company's sales staff to serve this population is the cultural diversity training and certificate program that has been jointly developed by the National Association of REALTORS® and the Department of Housing and Urban Development (HUD). The National

Association of Hispanic Real Estate Professionals, formed by Latino licensees, is also developing curriculum to help all licensees serve the lucrative Hispanic market.

■ CONCLUSION

Hopefully, the obvious conclusion is the importance of strategically positioning a company in the local business environment. Although there's some uncertainty associated with that environment, with the watchful eye of management, a company can be less vulnerable. How well a company does is a function of how well management analyzes factors in the local environment that have a bearing on its operations and how pragmatic, and perhaps bold, management is when predicting the future.

■ DISCUSSION EXERCISES

Discuss the most dramatic economic, political, and social changes in your area and the ways real estate companies have coped with them. Have any real estate businesses in your area failed or dramatically changed their operations recently? What do you think were the causes?

What conditions in the business environment in your area impact other businesses more than they impact real estate companies? Impact real estate companies more than other businesses?

What segments of the population (by age, culture, etc.) will have the greatest impact on the future workforce for your company? Your clientele?

6

CHAPTER SIX

ANALYZING THE MARKET

Who are the consumers of your company's services?

What do they really need a real estate company to do for them?

How well is your company positioned to serve today's consumers now? And in the future?

A company can't succeed simply because its owner(s) believe there's a place for the company in the marketplace. There's always competition, whether from another company in a similar business or from a company providing a product or service the consumer considers a suitable or preferable alternative.

Continuing with the cold-hard-fact part of planning, the next step is a market analysis. A market analysis converts what "we believe" into hard evidence about—Who are the consumers of real estate services? Where are they located? What services do they need? Where do they go to get those services?

Lest someone say, "I already know the answers," the flaw in that line of thinking is that a marketplace changes. Not just in the number and profile of consumers but also in the where and how they satisfy their needs (in other words, consumer behavior). This is the part of the equation that has changed most. People investigate the Internet first and make choices based on what they learn online. This is also where a company's competition figures into the equation. Do people pick brand (the name and reputation of the company) or pick the company because of its Web site or social networking page?

A critical piece of the market analysis is an assessment of the company, that is, the internal environment. This reveals how well the company does in the marketplace by comparing what is learned about the consumers with what is learned about the company. This tells the company what it should continue to do, do differently, or cease doing entirely.

The cease-entirely decisions are the ones companies often struggle with most. Like a favorite old shoe, companies get comfortable with the old, familiar activities that were once the foundation of their success. But because companies don't have unlimited human or financial resources, they can rarely afford to keep adding to their agenda without eventually retiring some of their "old shoes." A market analysis can help make those hard decisions.

But the market analysis (or any data-centered activity) is only as valid as the objectivity of people doing the analysis. People tend to form assumptions and then seek data to support those assumptions rather than use data to form assumptions and guide decision making.

ANALYZING BUSINESS OPPORTUNITIES

Analyzing opportunities is really a process of looking at all the available options in the marketplace. While a company can't take advantage of every business opportunity, it's important to first consider all possible avenues. This is what stimulates creative thinking and helps an organization move forward rather than being restricted by old business patterns. Later in the process, options can be eliminated.

Geographic Markets

There are a variety of ways to look at the marketplace. One is geographically. Today's geographic market bears little resemblance to the local, neighborhood real estate market we once knew.

The mobility of today's population means that the once-loyal customer bases that brokerage companies could count on are moving to other communities. Even where population numbers remain the same, the shifting population means that customers don't stay in one place long enough to develop the depth of allegiance to local vendors that is typical when consumers stay in one community for a lifetime. The result is that most brokerage companies can no longer survive solely on business generated in a highly localized geographic market.

Consumers don't see the market in narrow geographic terms either. The Internet has opened the doors to a borderless marketplace, satisfying the mobile consumer's wanderlust and thirst for information about any part of the country or the world. The virtual reality of this evolution is the ability to "tour" properties located most anywhere. That virtual "walkthrough" also means that consumers have already seen a lot of properties before deciding which geographic area to pursue.

The middle ground is a regional approach. That region can be several communities or several counties, depending on the density of the population and the diversity of the properties. Although some real estate companies have tentacles (branches or affiliated corporations) that reach into many states, they, too, are regional specialists. A regional marketplace enables companies to develop their brand and foster customer loyalty, or serve past customers with a wider range of geographic options.

As the geographic view of the marketplace expands, so does the MLS. Today's MLSs have not only expanded their inventories, but they also have expanded their services.

- Local MLSs have merged to form large, regional systems to expand the geographic area for which listing inventory can be accessed.
- Real estate companies have banded together to form integrated databases, essentially structuring their own MLSs.
- MLSs have linked their listing inventories with Internet sites to provide consumers with electronic access to their members' listings.

Because today's MLSs are highly computerized, they can assemble and distribute a much broader range of timely, useful information. Ultimately, the goal is to provide the resources companies need to meet the demands of today's consumers.

Referral networks. Referral networks have been used for a number of years to serve broader geographic markets. A broker can refer buyers and sellers to a broker in another marketplace or to another real estate company whose service or expertise is more suitable for those consumers. Some networks are independent; others are connected with national franchises and corporations. Companies also establish their own internal systems to funnel referrals between offices or departments.

Referral networks are advantageous because the added service a company can provide to a consumer also means added revenue for the company. Consumers benefit, as well, because referrals take the guesswork out of selecting suitable licensees to help them.

Referral networks also provide a number of additional services for their members, ranging from opportunities to network with other broker members and training programs for their salespeople to regional or national advertising programs. Some brokers feel this is an especially important feature because the network can provide market identity that the company could not otherwise attain for itself.

If state licensing laws permit, a broker may also be able to promote the company's listings in other states. A broker in another state could expand the exposure of a unique listing by targeting potential purchasers or investors in your area. Or you could advertise a property located in another state that belongs to a buyer with whom you are currently working. By expediting the sale of your buyer's property, you can expedite the buyer's purchase with you.

While intercity referral networks are attractive, they are only as valuable as the cost-versus-benefit equation allows. Decisions should be guided by the answers to—How many referrals can be expected? Is there high turnover or a large transferee market in the area? Does the company need the affiliation to compete with other firms in the area? Will a national advertising campaign produce significant results for the company? What is the cost of affiliation compared with the costs of other networks?

In the final analysis, can affiliation with a commercial referral network do things a company and its sales staff can't do more effectively themselves? Is it a valuable addition to the informal networking with potential consumers and other real estate practitioners that the company customarily does?

Relocation networks. These may be part of, or in addition to, intercity referral networks. Though their ultimate purpose is to help people establish residence in another geographic area as they move within their companies or to other employers, relocation networks can be structured in a number of ways.

One way is through corporate relocation management companies, otherwise known as *third-party equity contractors*. These companies enter into agreements with large corporations to handle employee transfers. The relocation companies generally team up with reliable local real estate companies in each community in which their clients have an office or plant.

The downside of these arrangements is that the relocation company may expect the real estate company to provide services above and beyond those it normally provides.

- For listings, services could include yard care, plumbing (winterizing), supervising painting and other cosmetic repairs, and providing weekly or monthly status reports of merchandising efforts.
- For buyers, corporations may expect buyer representation (buyer agency) and perhaps other assistance to help a family relocate to a new community.

In order to accommodate these demands and retain relocation company business, the real estate company may decide that it's necessary to appoint a relocation director who is trained specifically to supervise these transactions and orchestrate the myriad of details associated with the services the corporate relocation company expects. The relocation director should assign referrals to the company's salespeople and not also be an active salesperson.

Another way for a real estate company to assist local employers is by developing its own contact network and structuring services similar to those of the corporate relocation companies. Some employers provide their own in-house relocation assistance to current and newly hired employees. Other employers do not provide any organized relocation assistance. Both of these cases are opportunities for a company to design programs tailored to meet the needs of employers and their transferees.

Any of these relocation arrangements offers the potential to generate additional income. They also can be costly, in some cases as much as 40 percent of revenue earned. Again, affiliation is worthwhile only if the additional benefits justify the cost. Additional staff time must be allocated to these services. Furthermore, and perhaps most significant, third-party equity contractors charge brokerage companies numerous fees for handling referral transactions.

Another question to answer is how the corporate relocation company practice of charging "after the fact" fees affects the brokerage company. These fees are assessed for servicing a buyer or seller who is the employee of a relocation corporation's client, even though no formal referral was established or disclosed at the time the salesperson began working with the individual.

Service Markets

Another way to look at the marketplace is by services. While there are a number of ways to segment services, for the purpose of this discussion the focus is services related to various kinds of property.

Companies must make strategic decisions about whether to be generalists or specialists, or whether to offer a broad or a narrow range of services. In small or rural markets, a company is more likely to be a generalist, doing such things as selling and leasing residential and commercial properties, brokering industrial or recreational land, and appraising and managing real estate. Typically, this strategy is driven by the fact that there is not sufficient demand for any one, or a select few, services for a company to be profitable otherwise.

Being a generalist is demanding and requires considerable knowledge about many aspects of real estate. Unless the broker has that expertise, or can hire it, and can adequately supervise all of these activities, trying to be all things to all people can be very unrealistic and even disastrous.

Specialization is as common in the real estate industry as it is elsewhere in the business world. This strategy is appealing when there is sufficient demand for a specialized service and the company has considerable expertise in that specialty. The company should not venture into a specialty just because there's a demand to fill, however. There's too much liability for the company unless it has the appropriate, skilled talent.

Even a residential sales specialty requires that the company decide which transaction services to provide. Services might be limited to marketing properties and following the transactions through to settlement. Or the company may serve only buyers or also provide mortgage brokerage and title or escrow services.

Niche marketing. The ultimate in specialization is niche marketing—targeting very specific or narrow segments of the market with specialized, focused services. Niche marketing appeals to consumers by satisfying a need for unique or distinctive expertise and offers some exciting opportunities for the company to be innovative and distinguish itself from the competition.

By looking at the local demographics of the population, the profile of land uses in the area, and the competition's target markets, business planners can identify niche opportunities. Look at census data and other industry and consumer research, as well as any distinctive skill or expertise that members of the sales staff have that would appeal to a specific niche market.

A market niche could be a specific kind of property, such as luxury homes, condominiums, resort, vacation or waterfront properties, ranches, farms, prestige properties, or new construction. Or the niche could be a specific consumer population, perhaps one that is underserved or one with whom you have unique commonality or particular sympathy.

The most obvious consumer niches are populations such as senior citizens or international buyers. Or the niche may be singles, people with disabilities, or first-time buyers. The caveat is that when certain populations are targeted while others are ignored, the company can inadvertently violate the fair housing laws. Niche marketing must be done carefully to avoid discriminating against people in the protected classes.

There can be drawbacks to niche marketing. "Putting all of your eggs in one basket" if that market is too specialized or there's a sudden downturn in the targeted market may not provide enough business to sustain a profitable operation. A company can minimize its vulnerability by selecting several niches.

Niche marketing can be a viable strategy only as long as the company has the expertise to gain the confidence of the niche's patronage. Don't pick it just because there are business opportunities. A property niche requires considerable knowledge about its ownership, use, transfer, and any special laws that affect it. A population niche requires knowledge about its uniqueness and perhaps specialized services that population requires.

Beyond residential brokerage. The real estate industry is much more than houses, though the residential business seems to get more attention, perhaps because of the housing market's high profile on the economic barometer. This does not suggest, however, that other types of property are not a critical part of the economy. From a business management point of view, however, the fundamental principles of running a company are universal, regardless of the type of property the company handles.

A real estate company may specialize in investment properties, commercial sales or leasing, industrial properties, commercial farming, real estate development, auctions, or property exchanges. Depending on the state's licensing laws, the company may also consider brokering businesses. Any of these specialties requires a wide range of expertise (and perhaps additional licenses) relating to the use and operation of a property, including government regulations and tax laws.

For example, serving real estate investors requires a broad base of knowledge about tax laws as well as real estate to help people make wise decisions about acquiring, managing, and disposing of their investments. That also means understanding the current laws governing exchanges. Or a company may specialize in real estate counseling. This endeavor requires sophisticated analysis of the investor's circumstances and real estate holdings and then providing educated, objective advice.

Agency Services

Another way to segment the service market is by the nature of the assistance consumers want real estate companies to provide. Do they want to be served as customers, or as clients? Furthermore, do they really understand the differences so they can make educated choices?

In the history of the real estate industry, few topics have prompted as much discussion as agency relationships. The industry has been buffeted about as state regulators, consumer advocacy groups, and the industry itself began challenging one of its most fundamental practices, that being the common law of agency.

When the client or principal was the seller and the customer was the buyer, the licensee's fiduciary obligations to the seller were very clear. Although some people would argue that licensees treated buyers more like clients than customers anyway, that still left buyers without formal representation. So, buyer agency emerged. This, too, should be straightforward. Just turn the tables so the buyer is the client and the seller is the customer.

The discussion could end very simply at this point by saying "study the consumers in your marketplace and decide whether they want to be customers or clients." This falls into the "what services do they want" part of the market analysis. Then align company operations with the marketplace, consistent with the basic principle of a consumer-driven business. This would tell the company whether exclusive agency, serving either buyer-clients *or* seller-clients, is suitable.

The agency story gets much more complicated, though, because of the desire of brokerage companies to preserve client relationships with sellers while also adding buyers to their client lists. This would not be so problematic from a legal perspective if a company's client-seller and client-buyer are engaged in distinctly separate transactions and impervious firewalls could be built within the company's systems so that confidences and proprietary information of each client could be scrupulously protected.

Although the marketplace hasn't necessarily indicated that the consumer wants client services to sell a property and also client services to buy another one through the same company, that's what some brokerage companies have assumed. Or perhaps the companies are driven by profit motives. In any event, this strategy does appeal to the one-stop-shop preference of many consumers. However, it's not nearly as easy for a company to provide as might be assumed.

The next part of the agency story is that license law officials in a number of states entered the fray with a regulatory solution—designated agency. This was a landmark development because real estate license laws have historically been rooted in the common law of agency, which steadfastly prohibits dual agency (though some states' real estate laws have permitted it with informed consent).

Designated agency is a construct that attempts to shield the principal broker from dual agency conflicts by permitting the appointment of specific licensees within the company to act as a client's exclusive agent.

Designated agency has received a mixed reception. Proponents welcome it as practical solution for resolving their dual agency dilemmas. Though they have found that, even with the regulators' attempts to protect client interests with internal company procedures, implementing the solution has meant navigating a maze of intricate situations in the real world of real estate transactions that don't fall into neatly prescribed procedures.

Critics see designated agency as an implausible notion that only creates more dilemmas, not the least of which is that designated agency is an attempt to circumvent or rewrite common law to suit a selected purpose, one that creates conflicting principles in law and will eventually prompt litigation. It's also been said that designated agency is still dual agency dressed up in different clothes and doesn't properly serve the interests of clients on either side of the transaction because designated agency sets aside selected principles of the fiduciary relationship.

As the dual and designated agency maze became even more confusing, some states' laws provided a way out—no agency. Known by various names, the most common being transactional brokerage, this platform presumes to preclude any implications of agency by treating both buyers and sellers as customers in the same transaction, thus eliminating the conflicts that arise from multiple fiduciary relationships. Commonly, the licensee (who is not an "agent" per se) has certain statutorily prescribed duties to these customers, but state law does not consider the duties to rise to the level of a fiduciary. A party who desires representation may still request it and enter into a contract accordingly.

Regardless of where your state's law sits in the transformation of agency practices, one universal practice emerged—*agency disclosure*. While the legal details vary, the common purpose is to ensure that consumers are able to make reasonably informed decisions about the relationships they form with licensees.

Certainly, the laws that prevail in the state where the company does business are those with which the company must comply. It's possible that the law will undergo more transformations as agency practices are refined. In the meantime, the broker/owner must determine the company's agency policies, and the company must develop services and systems to support those policies. In the context of a market analysis, the policy should suit the demands of the consumer.

- If state law permits nonagency, the broker may decide to serve all consumers (sellers and buyers) as customers, rather than as clients. This is a significant departure from customary practices in many states, so consumers may not fully understand the implications of nonagency (nonfiduciary) services.
- If state law permits both agency and nonagency relationships, the broker must decide for whom client versus customer services will be provided. Because consumers typically have preconceived notions about what licensees do, the broker cannot assume they understand the distinction. This is another persuasive argument in favor of agency disclosure laws.
- In states where the laws permit the full range of agency relationships, the broker has more complicated decisions to make: Does the firm represent buyers/tenants or sellers/landlords, or both in the same transaction? Is subagency permitted by state law? If so, how will this affect the company's policies?
- If state law permits designated agency, the broker has to decide, first, whether to use it, and if "yes," then how it will be implemented, particularly the internal procedures that are essential for protecting the interests of all concerned.

Despite the fact that major transformations in agency law are more than a decade old, relatively straightforward definitions haven't been easily converted into actual practice. Whatever decisions a broker makes about the company's agency policies have to be supported by procedures (and training programs) that address the unique circumstances the salespeople encounter each day.

Serving sellers. What do sellers want? The standard answer is that they want their properties sold at the best possible price in the shortest period of time, with minimum hassle and expense, and maximum market exposure. The rest of the answer is not so predictable, and therein lies a major pitfall for a real estate company. One size, so to speak, does not necessarily fit all sellers.

An analysis of the marketplace will tell you whether sellers want a standard listing package, complete with agency representation, MLS and Internet exposure, company advertising, and the customary oversight of the transaction through to closing. Or whether sellers want a tailored plan, one in which the seller undertakes some activities (perhaps with the aid of the Internet) and the real estate company provides selected other services. Certainly, the fees that a seller is willing to pay in either case must be commensurate with the services that are received.

While not all real estate companies agree with the tailored plan of services, an increasing number of companies each year are adopting the a-la-carte approach to servicing consumers. In some markets, real estate companies have joined forces with sellers to help them by doing such things as posting their properties in the MLS, helping them with their advertising, or agreeing to bring prospective buyers to the properties. *Agree* is the operative word, because these arrangements must be put in contract form, spelling out the terms of service the company will provide.

This brings us back to the discussion of representation again. Not all contracts between brokers and sellers are necessarily agency agreements. Where state law permits, the broker may provide a tailored plan of services that does not include representation, if that is the seller's desire.

Otherwise, there are several kinds of contracts that are customarily used to provide representation. The brokerage company needs to decide whether to use open listings or one of the two types of exclusive listings. As a member of an MLS, though, that decision may have already have been made because it's not uncommon for MLS rules to require the use of certain types of listings. Those rules, however, are being scrutinized under antitrust laws where they restrict broker practices and, consequently, choices for the consumer.

Open listings are rarely satisfactory for either the owner or the broker. They create considerable controversy over procuring cause and, in the case of multiple brokers showing the property, who is entitled to a commission. Open listings may also mean that the owner misses out on some of the marketing or other services that would typically be provided under an exclusive arrangement. However, this objection can be mitigated to some extent by promoting these listings to buyer or tenant representatives.

The customs in the marketplace and preferences of sellers should guide decisions about the type of listing agreements used. Company policy may be to enter into only exclusive-right-to-sell agreements or to provide alternatives in selected, unique situations. Even exclusive agency agreements do not eliminate controversy, but they may be tolerable in certain cases.

Serving buyers. What do buyers want? The standard answer has been that they want maximum service to help them select a suitable property and guide them seamlessly through all aspects of a purchase. Most want an advocate, someone to look out for their interests and provide advice and counsel in their decision making.

In today's marketplace, that answer is still valid, but there are some significant twists. One is the point at which buyers want to engage the services of a brokerage company. Buyers now come to the salesperson armed with far more information about price, property, and process than they once did, all gathered from the Internet. As disarming as this might be for some salespeople, many more say that they can spend better quality and less quantity time with better informed buyers.

The part of the market analysis that studies buyer behavior must include a look at the way buyers use the Internet, the sites they visit (including the company's), and the services buyers really want from a brokerage company. This then leads to a study of fees, especially fee-for-service pricing. Today's consumers look much more critically at the cost of brokerage services, especially full-service commissions, and are forcing companies to offer a-la-carte plans or tailored services for buyers.

The other twist is the issue of representation, which until recently had to be provided by the buyer's attorney. Now, an overwhelming majority of brokerage companies provide that representation. Some companies have chosen to limit their business to buyer representation (known as *exclusive buyer's agents* or *EBAs*), and in fact, the professional council of buyer's agents continues to gain membership each year.

Bear in mind that buyers are not the clients and have no representation until an agency relationship is established. This happens by virtue of all the lessons one learns about agency and how relationships are established, both purposefully and inadvertently. *Disclosure itself doesn't create agency.*

Buyer representation agreements come in various written forms, similar to the options available in listing agreements, with similar advantages and disadvantages. Decisions to use an open agreement or one of two forms of exclusive contracts, again, rests with the broker and becomes the policy for the company and its salespeople. The preference in the marketplace must also be considered.

Defining *Your* Market

This is the part of the market analysis that captures the hardest data about the pool of people and properties that will mean business for the company. The numbers or quantitative evidence can help the company make final decisions about market segments and services. While exploring the marketplace, several opportunities will draw your attention. To test assumptions about whether they will be good for the company, ask

- How many potential users of the services are there?
- How many of those users can your company reasonably expect to capture (as compared to the other brokerage firms in the area)?
- How many properties of specific types are there in your area?
- How many of those properties are likely to sell during the next two to three years?
- How many of those sales can your company reasonably expect to capture?

Demographic data (Chapter 5) are particularly helpful in the quest for answers. Demographics reveal age, education level, income and employment, household composition, and whether people rent or own homes. These data are much more useful for assessing business potential than simply head-count, as in population density. The data also can be used to see how a broader or narrower geographic market would affect business potential.

Although companies can engage their own study to identify potential markets for products or services, this is a costly venture. Information that is readily available in the public domain, such as census data, can usually serve the purpose. Local municipalities and school districts, utility companies, public and private social service agencies, and collegiate institutions are good resources as well. Often, these groups also do forecasting that may be useful for the company's purposes.

Study land uses. Zoning maps, community development groups, and collegiate institutions provide a wealth of information for analyzing the number of properties in various land-use classifications. Compare this data with the needs of various segments of the population.

The trends that develop over time are especially helpful for identifying marketplace potential. Track the changes in the demographics and how the land-use and development trends accommodate those changes, which in some areas reveal a return to the commuting and consumer conveniences of urban living. Demand for environmental-friendly and "green" building is also increasing. If one segment is growing more rapidly than the supply of suitable property, for example, there will be greater demand than there is supply. The reverse is also true.

Finally, look at sales data. The register of deeds (or the office where real property transfers are recorded) and MLS statistics not only reveal the number of various types of properties that have transferred but also sales prices. By adding the sales prices of the properties and dividing that total by the number of transactions, the average price of a transaction can be determined.

Separate that data by brokerage company. Compare the number, average price, and types of properties that each company (including yours) handled. Look at several years' data, considering the economic conditions that

FIGURE 6.1
Analyzing Potential in the Market

$$\frac{\text{Total prices of properties sold in an area}}{\text{Total number of sales}} = \text{Average sale price in an area}$$

Average sale price × Number of sales transactions for one brokerage company = Gross sales volume

$$\frac{\text{Number of sales transactions for one brokerage company}}{\text{Total number of sales in the market}} = \text{Percentage of the market}$$

Using these simple calculations, you can analyze the sales data by the types of properties being sold and the percentage of the market you or your competitors command by type of property or total volume. You can then begin forecasting goals for your company.

prevailed at the time, to help forecast average prices and numbers of transactions. Those forecasts may have to be fairly conservative to account for the time needed for a local market to recover from a slump or recession and the depressed prices that could be associated with that scenario. (See Figure 6.1.)

The purpose of working through this process is to help identify target markets with sufficient business potential. Because the population profile changes over time, it's important to revisit this process periodically to be sure that the organization is still in tune with the marketplace.

■ ANALYZING THE COMPETITION

Firms jockey for position in the marketplace, striving to do business a little better than, or a little differently from, their competitors. Competition forces companies to press the limits of their creativity and provides consumers with the price and product or service benefits of a free enterprise system.

Competition is also a cleansing process, the survival of the fittest. The survivors have learned from their competitors' mistakes and how to take advantage of the opportunities their competitors create for them.

The way competitors compete is by scrutinizing what each other is doing. So an important piece of a company's market analysis is a look at the competition. (Consider, too, that the competition is looking at you as well.)

Consumers also watch the competition, though the way they see competing companies and the competitors see one another is different. Consumers often see little distinction between the services each real estate company offers. The *absence* of a service is often more noticeable than the services that *are* offered. On the other hand, the industry sees more differences than similarities. Perhaps that is because the industry tends to attach more importance to certain aspects of a company or its services than the consumer does.

The challenge is to differentiate between your company and the competition in ways that are meaningful to the consumer.

Market Share

It's conceivable that the market opportunities your company identifies are ones that your competitors are looking at, too. This suggests that an important part of a market analysis is a study of not just the opportunities but capacity in those opportunities.

This is why it's called market "share." A company can't be successful by specializing in condominiums if there are only a few developments in the area and one broker is already very competent and successful in that specialty. This is not to suggest that a company must avoid markets that are already being served. But it's much easier to succeed, at least initially, by targeting a market in which there are ample opportunities.

It's also conceivable that a company has identified a unique opportunity because it matches with a unique talent the company has that the competition does not. In this case, the company will be the one-and-only who is serving a particular target market. That may be the good news (no competition) but it may also be a sign that the strategy could be less lucrative or more risky than it appears. Studied risk, however, does not discourage entrepreneurial business people.

Analyzing market share is not an occasional event but an ongoing activity for most brokerage companies. Tracking the company's market share compared to its competitors provides key pieces of information for gauging company performance throughout the year.

Competitive Edge

Many of the decisions a company makes about how to serve its target markets are influenced by what the competition does. Should it join a franchise or a referral or relocation network? Where should sales offices be located? Should the company buy billboard advertising or a paid infomercial on television?

Should the company do any of these things because the competition does? Or because it doesn't? When looking at the competition, pay closest attention to firms that are similar in size to your company and serve similar target markets. Trying to go head-to-head with a large company's financial resources is not very feasible for a small company.

Attend any professional conference or convention, open any trade publication, or even check your e-mail and you'll find an incredible array of marketing and advertising tools, communications devices, and sundry other tips, tools, and programs promoted to enhance your business (all at a cost, of course).

Here's another cost-versus-benefit analysis. While it's tempting to buy into every attraction, the cost can far outweigh the benefit if the consumer sees little value or the company's competitive position is not enhanced appreciably. Decide which ones are absolutely necessary to stay in the running and defer those that would be merely nice enhancements until you have discretionary dollars.

Affiliations. Begin by looking at your competitors' affiliations. Are the majority connected with franchises, national corporations, or networks? How many are independent? Is MLS membership necessary? A company doesn't have to do what everyone else does, but it should not eliminate options that are needed to be competitive. Most of these organizations have production statistics and cost comparisons from other, similar markets to use in an analysis. Also, talk to brokers who have relinquished their affiliations with organizations you are considering. Their experiences can be very telling.

Location. Study the locations of other offices. There's more method than madness in the selection of office sites. Cheap office space may be available off the beaten path. But your competitors will benefit from your being in business more than you will if they are more accessible to or within the travel patterns of the clientele you intend to attract. Is the area saturated with offices, particularly in relation to the number of potential customers in a targeted market? How relevant is an office in your marketplace? With the amount of business done out-of-office increasing, a prime customer-service location may not be important.

Marketing strategies. Study the advertising and marketing strategies of other firms. Advertising and promotional strategies are designed to promote the company as well as to showcase it above the competition. Visit their Web sites. How do you rate their appearance, ease of navigation, content, and most importantly, the interactive features that would cause site visitors to do business with those companies? Do any companies have downloadable apps? What other digital venues does the competition use? Facebook, Twitter, blogs?

Just because someone else does something doesn't necessarily mean that's the right tool for you. It's too costly to "buy" the market, so you have to make wise choices. But absence is often more costly, especially in the digital marketplace. The services of public relations or advertising professionals are invaluable when assessing marketing strategies.

Consumer services. In addition to the types of agency and nonagency services being offered, look at the competition's services, such as home warranty or guaranteed buyback programs; decorating or furnishing allowances; cross-purchasing or affinity programs; or closing cost credits, to name a few. Here again, the point is not to mimic the competition, but to assess the competitive merits of various services.

Be innovative. A new tip, tool, or process that you've learned about that the competition has not yet embraced may be something to consider. New ideas are refreshing, but they are also untested. What attracts a consumer in one part of the country could fizzle in another, so it's important to think about local consumer behavior. If a very unconventional approach is being considered, think about why no one else is doing it. It may have been tried before, but with disastrous results. Or it may have been an idea ahead of its time, which means the time could be right, now.

Recruiting advantages. Typically, a competitive analysis focuses on the external marketplace. But a company also needs to think about how its marketplace strategies affect the ability to attract and retain salespeople. Salespeople are the ones most directly affected by what a company does to rise or fall against the competition. They also know what services their personal followers expect.

While this is not to say that a company should be dictated to by the sales staff, it does say that the salespeople have considerable insight and as much (if not more) at stake in the decisions companies make to enhance, add, or eliminate a service. When the competition offers a tool or process that is especially effective and your company does not, that ultimately affects recruiting and turnover.

■ ANALYZING YOUR ORGANIZATION

This is the internal environmental analysis that an organization must do. It's captured during the discussion of the market analysis because the company is an integral part of that marketplace. Often the most valuable lessons a company learns about itself are the result of looking at the consumers and competitive forces in the marketplace. Gathering some consumers in a focus group (perhaps past customers) is a good way to find out what they think.

Before a company can convert the information learned in a market analysis into a meaningful and achievable action plan, it needs to take an objective and critical look at all of its current structures, systems, and processes. The result may be a reaffirmation that the company is doing the right things or a sober awakening that the company is not properly aligned to do the things the market now indicates are right.

Ask the following questions.

- How do the company's current services align with those the market analysis indicates are suitable? With the services offered by the competition? Which services generate profits, and which ones do not? What services should be added, eliminated, or altered?

- How effective and efficient is the organization's current structure? How well does each office, division, and department function internally and within the entire organization? What systems and procedures need to be enhanced or eliminated to make the organization function more efficiently? What changes are needed as a result of the market analysis?
- What is the financial position of the organization? Does its income meet its needs? Meet projections? Or is the company running at a deficit? Is the available cash sufficient to fund operations? Or does the organization have to rely on outside sources of funding? Is the budgeting process adequate to manage the company's financial affairs? What does the organization need to do to enhance its financial position or fund initiatives that are critical to its success?
- Are the right people doing the right jobs? Are there positions that should be added or eliminated? Are there personnel changes (management, staff, or sales personnel) that should be made to better align talent with responsibilities? What personnel changes would be needed as a result of the market analysis?
- What is the physical condition of the offices? Of the equipment and technology? Are there improvements that will increase the efficiency of the company's operation or enhance its image?
- How well do the salespeople perform? What is the per-person production? What are their strengths and weaknesses? What should the company be doing to enhance their performance?
- Has the company gained or lost salespeople? Why? Are the company's recruiting efforts working? How many salespeople should the company have on staff?
- Has the company met its previously stated objectives? Its production forecasts? What is the company's market share, and is it on target with projections? Has the company gained or lost ground? Why?

These are some of the most critical questions that need answers before deciding what to commit to a plan. Notice that this analysis is another informational exercise, often requiring quantified numbers. The answers to these questions are useful throughout the year as management monitors company performance as well. Involve the salespeople, too. They have the front-line perspective that isn't necessarily revealed by statistics.

■ CONCLUSION

The market analysis, along with the analysis of the business climate, arms the company with the information it needs to decide how the organization should respond to seize opportunities and prepare for the challenges that lie ahead. The information will guide decisions about target markets and services and the ways the company will position itself in the competitive environment. Virtually every decision, from the development of the business plan and financial projections to the development of marketing and advertising programs, will be affected by the information gathered during this process.

■ DISCUSSION EXERCISES

Discuss the methodology you would use to analyze the marketplace. What do you already know, and what do you need to find out, about the consumers and the property in your area? What sources of information would you use?

Discuss the methodology you would use to analyze your competition. What do you know, and what do you need to find out, about the firms and their services that affect your company?

What innovative services or business strategies not currently prevalent in your area do you think would work?

Discuss the methodology you would use to analyze your company. What internal procedures already exist to gather the information you need? What systems should your company implement to give you the quality, reliable data you need?

CHAPTER SEVEN

7

DEVELOPING A PLAN

In what way, if any, will the mission of your organization change in the coming years?

What should the company's priorities or principal efforts be? How should those to be accomplished?

Business planners can form some notions about what the company should be doing while analyzing the business climate and the marketplace. But notions are vague and don't provide enough guidance. It's like embarking on a trip without a specific destination in mind. Even when you have a destination, you need a map to get you there. A plan identifies a specific destination for the company and the methodology for reaching that destination.

If your company has paid little attention to planning or has a formal-looking document (a plan) the management team hasn't seen for a while, that's not particularly unusual. Companies short-circuit the planning process for a variety of reasons, most of them related to time, money, and talent. Those who do allocate (or acquire) the necessary resources often lack the systems or procedures needed to make the plan a living document, an integral part of the company's operations.

Yes, planning does take time and money. But the amount of company time and money devoted to planning is relatively small in comparison with the benefit of ensuring that the company uses its resources for the right things. This pays enormous dividends, especially if the company avoids financial calamity. Even companies hanging on by a thin thread will spend money for a sound business plan to get back on track.

With respect to talent, sound business planning does require some skill. That's not to say that the company can't do it in-house. The company may have the personnel who can lead the process and develop good plans, similar to the framework discussed in this unit.

If that talent doesn't exist, though, the company has to be willing to seek the help of outside counsel—a business-savvy associate, a professional planning consultant, or a resource from a local college, university, or association of business professionals. Often, the fresh perspective of an outsider is very beneficial. The amount of time company personnel can devote to special projects and the organization's financial situation will affect the division of labor between in-house and outside personnel.

■ PLANNING RATIONALE

Several general concepts about planning are important to keep in mind. They affect the way plans are developed as well as the way plans are used.

- The *purpose of a plan* is to direct the organization's financial and human resources to those selected activities that will yield the greatest return on investment. Conversely, plans prevent the organization from devoting resources to activities (regardless of tradition) that produce meager results. A plan tells the organization how to work smart.
- A properly constructed plan tells the organization *what* it wants to accomplish and provides a general framework for *how* the organization intends to do this. Plans turn aspirations into concrete expectations. Plans contain specific, measurable goals and a methodology, including timeframes, to tell the organization how to accomplish them.

Specificity provides benchmarks so the organization can determine whether it's accomplishing what it set out to do.

- A plan helps the organization be *resilient*. Organizations must be responsive, but they also must resist the temptation to abandon course at the sight of each intimidating change. With thoughtful forecasting, the company will have a plan that empowers it to function in the contemporary environment. By anticipating changes and restructuring activities, if necessary, the organization can keep pace with contemporary times and stay on course during turbulent ones.
- The *foundation* of a plan is an analysis of the past, present, and likely future. A plan is only as good as the information gathering and filtering processes in the situational analysis and the assumptions about future cause and effect. Planners must avoid underestimating the competition and overstating the company's abilities, including revenue capacity.
- Planning activities must be *integrated* throughout the organization. This means that planning must occur at all levels of the organization. After upper management defines the long-range plan, lower levels of management plan activities around the goals for which they are responsible. A business plan has little value unless all units of the organization are working in concert with one another.
- Planning requires *commitment* from everyone in the organization. This means people must "buy into" the plan. Otherwise, they will stride off on their own path, which defeats the purpose of having a plan in the first place. People are more likely to be committed when they see that the plan evolved from a deliberate, logical decision-making process. Engaging people from various levels in the organization not only provides multiple perspectives but also gives people a sense of ownership, which enhances commitment.
- A plan must be *implemented*. Unfortunately, the planning documents in some organizations are stowed in a drawer as soon as they are printed, never to see the light of day again. Some organizations use the documents for awhile and then stray off on some other path, as if the documents never existed. But an organization cannot afford to squander resources on projects that are not utilized.

- Planning is the most fundamental management activity. From this flows virtually every business decision that is made. A plan is also useful for building credibility with people outside the organization. Lenders, suppliers, and potential business affiliates want to see that the company has a thoughtfully prepared business plan, which they then use in their decision-making processes.
- A business plan is only a management *tool.* It should not take the fun out of being in business or stifle enthusiasm or creativity. In fact, a properly designed and implemented plan should have an inspiring, positive effect on the organization. Be flexible!
- If a plan doesn't materialize as expected during the first year, don't give up. (This is where leadership's entrepreneurial spirit is an asset.) Because a plan is reviewed periodically, the company can make adjustments if necessary and set more realistic or achievable goals. It's difficult to anticipate, especially for a new business venture, how long it will take to reach certain plateaus.

YOUR BUSINESS PLAN

The information gathered from the situational analysis is now used to actually develop plans. Pertinent information that must be considered revolves around that which has been learned about the

- business environment,
- marketplace (consumers and competitors),
- company's services and compatibility with demand,
- organization of the company's sales and marketing activities (strengths and weaknesses),
- company's human resources,
- organization of the company's operating structure and technology systems, and
- company's financial position.

There are various levels of planning, some more comprehensive and long term than others. The beginning point is a long-range blueprint (a master plan, in a sense) for the organization. A typical long-range plan spans three to five years. In recent years, organizations have found that a three-year timeframe is more feasible because of the dynamic environment. Formally, this is known as a long-range, general, or strategic plan.

The point is best made by saying that *good long-range planning enables the company to be a meaningful specific rather than a wandering generality*. Some organizations don't plan farther out than one or two years. But that's typically not a long enough period to implement a plan and gauge performance, especially of new endeavors. It takes time to solidify the company's position with a new target market or to reap the benefits of a franchise affiliation.

Furthermore, without a long-range plan, the temptation is far too great to shift course each year when instant results do not materialize. Valuable human and financial resources can be expended in one direction, only to be diverted in another direction and then another. Although organizations must be responsive to change, these must be deliberate and thoughtful responses.

Would you rather push a rope or pull a rope to get it from one place to another? It takes little effort to push one end of the rope. But when you do, where does it go; how many turns does it take? Isn't it more productive to take hold of one end and pull the rope? In doing so, you can control where it goes. But you have to know in which direction to head. And the longer the rope, the longer it takes for the tail to line up behind the leader.

Organizations are like the longer rope. Many facets of an organization have to be aligned in position behind the leader (the plan). The larger or more complex the organization, the more cumbersome the process. If the plan calls for some dramatic changes, there's the very element of change that an organization's culture and its people may not readily adjust to. All of this simply strengthens the argument in favor of a longer-term plan.

Planning terminology can vary. Professional strategic planners have individual preferences and sometimes put their own spin on terminology. The important thing to remember is what each part of the plan should tell you. Figure 7.1 shows how the pieces fit together.

FIGURE 7.1
Outline of the Components of a Plan

Mission Statement

- General Objective
  - Goal
    - Strategy
      - Tactics
    - Strategy
      - Tactics
- General Objective
  - Goal
    - Strategy
      - Tactics
    - Strategy
      - Tactics

Mission

The development of the long-range plan begins with the answers to several important questions.

- What is the company's purpose for being in business?
- What specifically does the business do?
- Where should the company be in the future that is different from where it is today?

The answers define the mission, the organization's fundamental purpose for existing. This is the foundation on which the business enterprise is built. Defining a mission is a thought-provoking exercise that critically assesses the organization to validate its basic reason for being and, most important, forms a vision of its reason for existing in the future.

These thoughts are then crystallized in one or several concise sentences that become the **mission statement**. These words very simply say what the organization is about. Everything it does must support the mission. If something doesn't support the mission, then the organization shouldn't be doing it. Profitability is not the purpose, but rather validation that the organization is doing the right things in pursuit of a clearly defined mission.

The mission statement is a critical first step in developing a plan (or prescribing the right things) because everything else that follows must support the mission.

General Objectives

Next, expand on the mission statement by identifying **general objectives**. Perhaps the best way to characterize these is by the terminology that's currently in vogue—initiatives or competencies. They crystallize what the organization needs to focus on to accomplish its mission in the contemporary environment. Essentially, *general objectives*, *initiatives*, or *competencies* (whatever you choose to call them) become the organization's priorities during the timeframe of the plan (three or five years).

The number of general objectives is typically a function of the size and complexity of the organization and the capacity of its human and financial resources. For a fairly small organization, two general objectives are likely most feasible. Larger organizations typically don't choose more than four. Although, even a very large, complex organization may choose only one or two competencies so that all efforts are mobilized in a highly focused direction.

To demonstrate what general objectives or initiatives look like, consider this.

■ **CASE IN POINT** The situational analysis reveals that one of the most critical issues is the role of technology in everything the company does. The analysis also reveals that the company, which had been a leader in the first-time homebuyer market, has been losing market share. Yet, that population has been growing and with the low interest rates and proliferation of incentives for first-time homebuyers, this target market has great potential.

Converting this to objectives, one might be "to fully integrate the use of the latest technology throughout the organization." Another objective might be "to make homeownership a reality for first-time buyers throughout the metropolitan area."

Notice that these particular initiatives or competencies affect the entire organization. Even the one that focuses on a target market suggests that the company's public relations messages, marketing and advertising themes, mortgage department activities, and perhaps other parts of the company in addition to the individual sales offices, will have a role to play. Although these illustrations have companywide impact, the organization can establish objectives that are less broad, in which case a particular department or group of sales offices becomes a priority.

The mission statement and general objectives tell what the company *aspires* to do. But they don't tell the organization how to accomplish that.

Think about planning the same way you would describe a sports game. First, you identify the game and the general theme of the game (the mission statement and general objectives). Now, you have to tell people what the object of the game is; these are the company's goals. Then, describe the series of plays that will get the team to the goal; these are the strategies the company will use to reach its goals. Finally, lay out the sequence of steps that will be needed to execute plays; these are the tactics that implement the plan.

Goals

The next step is to spell out the goals of the "game." Each general objective is supported by a number of specific **goals**. These are the end results the organization wants to achieve. They break down the aspirational or futuristic nature of the general objectives into manageable accomplishments and show how the organization intends to achieve its objectives.

Goals must be translated into specific words that tell precisely how to focus the organization's resources. They have four characteristics.

1. Specific or identifiable
2. Measurable (quantitative)
3. Attainable
4. Framed in time (beginning and completion dates)

Words like increase, maximize, decrease, or minimize, with nothing more specific or measurable, don't provide the detail needed to determine whether the organization is on target. Specific goals would say "increase by 100 transactions," "increase by 25 percent," or "$500,000 in gross commissions." You may hesitate to make such precise statements because they represent a commitment that is easily scrutinized, and failure is obvious. But specifics are needed to give the organization readily identifiable *outcomes* for measuring the results of its efforts.

Timeframes also add specificity. If you want to increase your activity in a particular service by 100 transactions, do you mean in one year, two years, or six months? A timeframe serves as a benchmark for determining achievements. A lack of timeframes can leave the organization floundering just as badly as if it didn't have any goals. An accomplishment that is significant enough to be a goal has to be achieved in a timely fashion.

Goals must challenge the organization to move forward, but they also must be attainable. The object is to make the best use of a company's resources, not to frustrate the effort with unrealistic expectations.

Goals must be properly aligned with the capacity of the organization's financial and human resources. Or a part of the plan must be devoted to enhancing resources or systems to accomplish a goal. The best way to set realistic goals is with the information gained from the situational analysis. The business environment, the marketplace, and the company's past performance all affect future accomplishments.

Before setting a goal related to revenue or number of transactions, evaluate past production figures. Then, decide the amount of gross revenue you want to generate. Convert this figure to a number of transactions by determining the previous average commission and dividing the new gross figure by that amount. Now, decide on the distribution of listings and sales; compare these figures with previous activity. This then tells you whether the gross income or transaction projections are realistic.

Using other historical data, you can set goals relating to such achievements as the percentage of the market share you want to capture, the volume of business generated by various types of properties, or the volume of business generated from rentals and sales or other services.

With verifiable, measurable goals the organization has data with which to assess the organization's accomplishments during the plan's three- or five-year life. If the goals were unrealistic or unanticipated changes in the marketplace occurred, the company may have to revise the quantitative measures and the time frames in subsequent years. But don't change the numbers in the plan just to make your organization look better. The harsh reality may be that the organization is really straying off course. Face the facts and do something about it.

Strategies

After setting goals, the next step is their supporting **strategies**. These prescribe the methodology for accomplishing each goal. Long-range planning is otherwise known as *strategic planning* because it provides not just goals but also the strategic methodology for accomplishing them. In light of the game analogy, people need to know what steps to take to "score." Strategies provide those directions.

Strategies get to the heart of the hard decisions needed to convert goals into game-winning accomplishments. Look at what the organization currently does and decide what it needs to continue doing or do differently or new things it needs to do. Also consider the obstacles or roadblocks the organization could encounter and how will it overcome them. All of this reveals what the company needs to do to align systems, processes, procedures, and, most important, the human and financial resources in concert with the goals.

The strategy part of a plan is also where the phase-out of an activity that is no longer suitable is addressed. If certain customary activities no longer contribute to the achievement of an objective, they should be discontinued.

Figure 7.2 shows how goals and strategies support a general objective. If you have decided that one of the company's niche markets is vacation properties and second homes, for example, a portion of your business plan could be developed following this format.

Not all goals may be production-related. An earlier example about a general objective relating to technology could be supported with a goal about upgrading the company's computer system and strategies to make that happen. Another goal about an interactive Web site with strategies to build or enhance it could be suitable. An accompanying strategy may also be to reduce the amount of newspaper advertising.

FIGURE 7.2
Goals and Strategies

General Objective—To provide real estate services relating to vacation properties and second homes.

- **Goal**—To obtain 48 listings of properties suitable as vacation properties or second homes within the next 24 months. (Now you need to define strategies to get these listings.)
  - **Strategy**—Assemble the professional knowledge necessary to identify suitable properties, including buyer's preferences, lifestyles, and desirable amenities.
  - **Strategy**—Train the sales associates to identify and list suitable properties.
  - **Strategy**—Develop a network with developers of these properties.
- **Goal**—To close 36 sales transactions within the next 24 months. (Now you need to define strategies to acquire the sales.)
  - **Strategy**—Train the sales associates to work with potential buyers.
  - **Strategy**—Develop marketing and advertising programs to promote these properties to the target population.
  - **Strategy**—Develop an outreach program to target potential buyers in other geographic areas.
- **Goal**—To increase vacation- and second-home market share to 40 percent of the company's total sales production within three years.
  - **Strategy**—Establish a business unit within the organization to provide a wide variety of services to people who own or desire vacation properties or second homes.

Similarly, a goal to establish a new business unit, such as a relocation department, or to open a branch office by a certain target date could be supported with strategies to make the necessary preparations and plan the allocation of resources to that end. A goal to trim back a certain operation could be supported with strategies to assimilate those activities and personnel elsewhere in the organization.

Contingency Plans

Because planning involves forecasting, the more futuristic the forecast, the fewer variables there are that can be predicted with great certainty. While most situations in the business environment, the marketplace, or within the company don't occur without some warning, circumstances can arise that could send a company scurrying to adjust.

A company can be prepared to make necessary adjustments by developing **contingency plans**. Not all master plans have this component. Companies develop contingency plans when there are significant indicators that a change in circumstances is a distinct possibility but not yet certain or close enough on the horizon to be incorporated in the plan.

Contingency plans are simply alternative goals and strategies that will be implemented in the event they are needed. It's impossible to move forward when the company is busy circling the wagons in a time of crisis. Contingency planning is a proactive measure that prevents the organization from being thrown for a loop and protects against knee-jerk reactions in the heat of the moment that could divert resources in careless or uncontrolled ways. It takes a little extra time to wander down the "what if" path of a major exodus in the job market, for instance, but it's an ace in the hole (which the competition may not have) that could pay enormous dividends.

Putting All the Pieces Together

A business plan is unique for each organization. Plans are not "packaged programs" that someone else has developed. Nor can you borrow another organization's and make it yours. If your organization is inflicted with the "just give me the words" ailment, it won't have a plan that supports your company's mission and general objectives and the goals, strategies, and timeframes or measurements that are suitable for *your* organization in *your* marketplace.

A major benefit of planning is the *process itself* or the discussions that ensue as various viewpoints, creative ideas, and possible solutions are shared. In other words, a plan is not a document that the broker prepares while sitting alone in the backroom, even in a small organization. Planning is a participatory exercise that fosters teamwork and engages people who have a stake in the outcomes in ways that enhance the plan's implementation. No doubt, all of this looks familiar in the context of the first unit's discussions.

The players in the process certainly include senior management and perhaps also a cross section of representatives from other levels in the organization, including sales staff. In a small brokerage company, the broker, and perhaps a sales manager or selected salespeople, are involved. The leader of the project could be a designated member of senior management or an outside consultant.

While the design of the actual planning meetings can vary, they generally involve tasks first being assigned to gather the research in the situational analysis. This pre-meeting preparation jumpstarts the program and forms the basis of initial discussions as people react to the discoveries and reach consensus on the major impacts on the organization.

These conclusions eventually become the basis of the general objectives. Because objectives go hand-in-hand with the mission, the planning group must visit the mission statement (or develop it if the company doesn't have a clearly defined one) to decide whether it's still viable. Then goals and strategies can be developed.

This can be a very efficient exercise, with the bulk of the work being accomplished perhaps in a two-day retreat. Once the situational discussion concludes and mission and general objectives are codified, the goal and strategy parts come together rather quickly, building on the ideas that were offered in the earlier discussion. Conducting planning meetings requires strong leadership so that discussions flow freely but stay on point and eventually achieve consensus. That may also mean helping people with divergent views, self-protecting instincts, and other bones they want to pick—make some concessions.

When all is said, someone commits the plan to writing and circulates a draft to all the participants to be sure it says what everyone agreed to. Once everyone concurs, then it's ready to go. The actual planning document generally has several components.

- Table of Contents
- Executive Summary—the condensed version of the plan
- Summary of the Situational Analysis—the key factors that show the rationale behind the plan (which is just as useful for future reference as the actual plan)
- Mission Statement
- General Objectives (or Initiatives or Competencies)
- Goals and Strategies—the key outcomes of the plan, supported by their respective strategies

The final item that is written when the planning document is assembled is the executive summary. This is a several-page report that presents the essence of the plan and provides a user-friendly reference for the document. The summary is also the part of the document that outsiders—lenders and investors—typically look at first, so it must present a persuasive argument for the merits of the plan.

The summary includes a brief history of the company; its current activities, particularly its distinguishing features and services, and position in the marketplace; and important factors about its financial position. The summary has to be supported by hard evidence (research, statistics) of the key risks and opportunities on which the plan is based, along with general objectives (or competencies) and significant goals that indicate what the company intends to do about them.

IMPLEMENTING A PLAN

Notice that after all is said, it's not done. The written document is only the beginning. The plan needs to be converted into action. This is the part of the process that brings the plan to life by defining activities and, most important, charging people with the responsibility for accomplishing them. The plan forms the basis for an annual business plan.

Tactical Planning

Using the game analogy again, tactics tell the team how to execute the plays of the game. *Tactical* or *activity* planning directs the workflow under the strategies.

In the strategies illustrated in Figure 7.2, there is still more the company needs to know about what to do. In the training strategy, what is the plan for developing and implementing the training? In the strategy relating to marketing and advertising, what specific marketing and promotional activities are needed? If a new business unit is to be created, what must be done to assemble the necessary money and personnel and define the work for the department?

When do any of these things have to be accomplished? Are the necessary resources and talent readily available in-house, or are there activities that need to be outsourced?

Tactical planning answers these questions. In doing so, it breaks down the plan into manageable pieces of work. Otherwise, the scope of the task can look overwhelming. (No wonder organizations just shove the document into a bottom drawer.)

This phase of planning also identifies responsibilities. Normally, the work units that are affected by the strategies are responsible for the tactical or activity planning. They're most familiar with the work and, because they are accountable for accomplishment, they need to be engaged in the process.

A sales office that is charged with achieving a production quota is the work unit that should decide how to reach it. Even though this is typically a participatory process, the manager is ultimately responsible for the outcomes, which includes seeing that resources are not diverted to counterproductive activities.

The Business Plan

A business plan is the company's work plan for the year. It comes together very easily because it's simply an extrapolation of the goals and strategies that were benchmarked for completion that year, perhaps with some refinements, and makes them priorities. A business plan can also include new strategies that may be needed to address emerging situations that can threaten the attainment of goals in the master plan.

The mention of refinements means that projections of numbers, dollars, and timeframes when the plan was first developed may need to be revised. Because there are more "knowns" than conjectures since the first planning discussions, the next 12-month period can be forecast with greater certainty. Projections may be revised downward because of developments in the business climate, the marketplace, or the company so as not to frustrate the organization. But it's also permissible to revise projections upward. If the company is ahead in the game, keep it winning.

The business plan typically becomes the working document that managers at all levels in the organization use to monitor progress throughout the year. Many of the quantitative measures can easily be segmented by quarters so that management has readily identifiable benchmarks. It's a lot easier to manage by quarters than it is to figure out how to make up for lost time in the last few months of the year.

Along the way, management can also identify activities that should be restructured or new strategies that could be recommended for the next year.

Back to the Long-Range Plan

By reviewing the long-range plan when the business plan is prepared each year, management can gauge the company's progress and the validity of the long-range plan. In so doing, management can determine whether the company is still on the right course or needs to revise the plan to respond to changes within the organization, the marketplace, or the business climate.

The long-range plan can be easily updated with each year's review, essentially recasting the plan for three years by adding a new third year each year. This does not mean that the company keeps changing courses or moving the goalposts farther away. It means that the essence of the plan can be used to build the next one, essentially providing continuity as the company moves forward.

Look at the assumptions from the situational analysis and evaluate which ones are still valid and those that need to be revised. (This is where the most recent company performance data are helpful.) From that, the rest of the components of the plan can be evaluated and tweaked as necessary. As goals or strategies are accomplished, they can be replaced with new ones as appropriate. This way a company can be flexible, continue to grow, and respond to change without getting jerked off course on a whim. Even the most comprehensive planning processes typically build on the previous plan.

■ CONCLUSION

With some thoughtful design and practice, planning will become as routine as any other business activity. A sound long-range plan becomes the foundation for the company's operations. Other phases of planning simply bring the plan to life by defining activities needed to implement the plan and giving the company it's "marching orders" for the coming year. An annual review of the long-range plan forms the basis for the next plan. This way management is constantly providing the vision for the organization that will help it prosper in the future.

■ DISCUSSION EXERCISES

Identify one general objective and then develop appropriate supporting goals.

Prepare several strategies that could be implemented around these goals. Are the strategies identifiable, measurable, attainable, and framed in time?

Using one of your strategies, define appropriate tactics or activities.

Now, are there any significant contingencies that should be planned for? If so, what would those plans be?

IN CONCLUSION OF UNIT II

Armed with a business plan, a manager is prepared to move on to the other management functions. This can be done with some assurance that the right course has been charted, particularly because of the amount of research that went into the development of the plan. The company has its marching orders, and it is now up to management to guide all the other systems, procedures, and resources accordingly.

■ THE SCENARIO

Having read this unit, what is your analysis of the following scenario?

One bright Thursday morning, the managers of the company's 15 sales offices gathered for their monthly meeting with senior management. (That's the broker of record and the three regional managers who oversee the sales offices located within their geographic areas.) The hottest item on the pre-published agenda was "revenue projections for the coming year."

For the past week, the sales office managers had been scrambling through their files trying to figure out what "number" they will put on the table when it's their turn to tell the assembled group how much money each of their offices will bring into the company next year.

While senior management is sitting in eager anticipation of what the office managers are going to say on Thursday morning, the office managers are struggling to figure out how to cope with their assignment. They could briefly review year-to-date production and pick a number so that they have something to say at the meeting. They could analyze the past several years' income and expense statements and come up with a conservative number, then look like heroes when their offices exceed projections later on. Or they could be really gutsy, predict record-setting accomplishments, and impress everyone on Thursday morning with their go-getting, winning attitude. Then they can deal with the consequences next year when they fall short.

By the conclusion of Thursday's meeting, each manager's projection has been recorded on a flip chart. The managers had not offered, nor were they asked for, a rationale for their projections, so it's conceivable that they could have used any one of the above-noted methods to come up with their numbers. Nevertheless, after the sums on the flip chart were totaled, senior management took the managers to task by saying that the grand total did not live up to senior management's expectations.

The meeting ended with both the office managers and senior management feeling totally frustrated over what should have been done to project next year's revenue.

■ THE ANALYSIS

The discussions in this second unit should shed some light on the debacle in the Thursday morning management meeting.

The purpose of the monthly meeting, being to solicit input from the sales office managers with respect to the next year's revenue projections, is a worthy participatory exercise. The best people to state the case are those who are most familiar with the work of their respective offices. It's also better for the people who will ultimately be responsible for accomplishing a goal be involved in its development. The fact that people left the meeting feeling frustrated, though, says everyone should have known what the expectations were.

If senior management had developed a business plan for the coming year, the office managers should have been told what it was, rather than being told after the fact that they were off-base. If senior management didn't have any plan, but rather expected the meeting exercise to at least produce a revenue goal for next year (a questionable notion, at best), then no one should have been disappointed. If senior management expected to gather information to use in developing a plan for the coming year, then the input should have been respectfully accepted, even if it wasn't what management wanted to hear.

The fact that the office managers were thrashing around in a variety of modes as they prepared for the meeting says they were ill equipped for the task. They lacked the necessary information and a uniform and skillful methodology to produce valid numbers. It also appears that revenue-projecting exercises don't get their due respect. It could be because they are uncomfortable or because sales managers don't feel their voices will be heard anyway, so there's no point in wasting a lot of time and effort. Maybe the real source of their frustration is that senior management is out of touch with the realities of life in the sales offices and the industry.

While there are several ways to engage senior and office managers in planning exercises and produce useful outcomes, the hardest thing for either level of management to cope with is not being on the same page of the program. Office managers want to have input, but they also need some direction. In other words, when the organization does not have a master plan, the individual units within the organization don't know what they need to be doing.

THE SUMMARY

Throughout this unit we have developed the various stages involved in the planning process. Depending on whether you are the broker/owner, a senior manager in a large organization, a sales manager, or a department manager, your involvement in these phases will probably be different. As a guide for understanding your function in the process, the following summary is provided.

- Analyzing the Business Climate
  - The broker/owner along with senior management conducts the analysis and may use outside resources.
  - Other managers could be invited by the broker/owner to participate. Beyond that, they need to understand how the analysis impacts the planning process.

- Analyzing the Market
  - The responsibilities are similar to those described above.
  - Other levels of management, such as a sales manager, can provide valuable insight about the marketplace, the competition, and the current state of the company.
- Developing the Plan
  - The Long Range or Master Plan

    The broker/owner and senior management are primarily responsible for developing the long-range plan and any contingency plans. Though other levels of management may be invited to participate in the development of the long-range plan, the owners and senior management are primarily responsible for implementing the plan.
  - The Business Plan

    The broker/owner and senior management are primarily responsible for developing the business plan.

    All levels of management are responsible for monitoring their areas of responsibility to accomplish the business plan.
  - Tactical Planning

    All levels of management, and possibly others in the organization, are involved in planning the activities that are needed to accomplish certain strategies prescribed in the long-range plan.

UNIT III
ORGANIZING THE ORGANIZATION

There once was a day when "Here's the desk; here's the phone; good luck, you're on your own" said just about all there was to say about where a real estate salesperson would be working. Indeed, it was an office, with a desk or two and some phones, and maybe a Girl-Friday-type who ran the broker's office while he and a few salespeople hit the road, armed with sheer determination and gut instinct, to drum up business.

That real estate deal could just as well have been written on the back of a used envelope or a diner napkin. Not many laws to worry about that could send anyone to a court of litigation. High-tech was a car with air-conditioning. Multi-list was a pile of listing sheets in a binder that had to be sorted through to replace the outdated with the new. Training was what the salesperson learned at the arm of the broker. Company information systems were the pages in the bookkeeper's ledger.

No, this isn't novel fiction. And from a business management point of view, there's not a lot about a company that had to be planned or organized, either. Unquestionably, all of this bears little resemblance to the industry today. It does make a point about the reasons for walking a meticulous path through today's business management study.

The plan that was formed in the previous unit now needs organization—the who, what, where, and how decisions that make the company do what the plan says are the right things to do. Like planning, organizing is an ongoing activity. With each year's business plan and each major overhaul of the long-term plan, the same decisions have to be visited so that, as plans change, so do the organization's structure and systems. Otherwise, the company's progress is as hamstrung as it would be without any plan at all.

The organizing function essentially groups activities and resources so that a company can operate effectively and efficiently and be an economically viable enterprise. To do this, the company needs

- structure for its ownership, business alliances, and human resources;
- physical facilities, properly provisioned with communications and information systems;
- financial structure to properly manage the company's financial resources;
- policies and procedures to prescribe how business is conducted; and
- marketing and advertising with which to generate business.

The blueprint for the company's structure is the company's plan. In bringing the plan to life, the organization also takes on its own personality. While there may be some general boundaries to guide decisions and, certainly, some hard lines drawn by law, the organizational structure, facilities, policies and procedures, and marketing and advertising strategies are individual to each company. The chapters in this unit are devoted to organizing the company so that it is prepared to accomplish its mission.

If you're the broker/owner or a senior manager in a large organization, you will be responsible for the major legal and financial decisions. This will also include company policy. If you are a sales office or department manager, you most likely will have some authority to make financial decisions and to develop operating systems within your office or department.

CHAPTER EIGHT

STRUCTURING THE ORGANIZATION

How are the real estate companies in your area structured? Their ownership, affiliations, staffing, departmental systems, and the scope of authority of their sales managers?

What has changed in recent years? Why?

The structure of an organization is essentially the framework for a company's operations. The legal form of ownership, professional affiliations, organizational chart (the way activities are grouped), and chain of command (the hierarchy) all provide structure so that the organization can function.

The operating structure will vary, depending on the kind and scope of work the company does (back to its plan) and the company's stage in its life cycle.

■ LIFE CYCLES

Every company goes through stages in life and, just like people do, have different needs and different modes of operation from birth to old age. Also like people, longevity is not assured without some intervention to remain healthy and relevant.

The start-up company is in the *birth* stage, typically characterized by a fairly modest scope of work (and most likely, a tight budget) and an efficient, though streamlined, operating structure so it can get on its feet. Whether it does get on its feet in the first place depends on how well its founders identify the need in the marketplace for their new venture and provision the enterprise with a solid business plan and sufficient capital. New businesses don't survive just on bright ideas.

Once the company survives the most vulnerable first one to three years, it can become more ambitious. In organizational life cycling this is the *growth* stage. As its name implies, the company expands the work that it started doing and/or stretches into new markets or endeavors. This is typically the most energetic time in an organization's life. Depending on the nature of the work it does, how well it's tapped into the marketplace, and the aggressiveness of its leadership, this stage can be short-lived or can endure for five, ten, or more years.

Organizations also have a *midlife*, though not necessarily a crisis. If there's to be one, the crisis is more likely to arise during a company's most aggressive years (the growth stage), when making the right decisions at the right time can be most challenging. Midlife is less aggressive and growth is more gradual, eventually to reach neutral growth or the stability stage of life. The midlife organization is typically grounded with a very solid market position, which it can also take advantage of with the addition of a new venture. But that can also be a vulnerable position if the winds of the marketplace shift and the organization doesn't shift its strategies as well.

Then there's the *maturity* stage, which is characterized by long-term stability. This is the point at which long-established companies can reap the benefits of their endurance in the marketplace. This is also when maintaining the level of profitability they are accustomed to, let alone growing profit, can be more challenging. Companies can age out of relevance, especially if they're afflicted with "that's the way we've always done it, and it works" notion while the competition and the marketplace move on in new directions.

A mature company has to remain energetic so that it maintains its stature in the marketplace. Companies often do this with mergers or acquisitions or an innovative strategy, or by restructuring their internal operations to work smarter and more cost efficiently.

Midlife and maturity should suggest that the company has the experience to be smart about doing business in whatever the prevailing environment. If a company uses that to its advantage, it can endure. The point is to make the most of the "middle age" and "elder statesman" years. Otherwise, the company will discover the last step in maturity—*decline*. Although companies in decline can reengineer and reenergize their operations, the loss of momentum and position in the marketplace makes the task far more imposing than if they had preempted the decline in earlier years.

The framework or operating structure of a company (and a company's plan) must change as the organization cycles through the various stages of life. Ownership may be reconfigured, adding new owners or severing relationships with current ones. Business affiliations may change as new alliances are adopted or existing ones are discontinued. Operations may expand to include new business sectors or scale back to reduce the number of services. In essence, operating strategies must empower the organization to function.

■ LEGAL OWNERSHIP

One of the most fundamental decisions is the who and the how with respect to the company's ownership.

The broker may be the sole owner of the business or join forces with other owners. The salespeople may have an ownership position in the company, an increasingly more common practice. The lone worker or one who employs only one or two salespeople may feel comfortable being a sole proprietor. However, other forms of ownership may be preferable.

Because these decisions have complex legal and tax implications, the advice of professional counsel is strongly advised. State licensing laws may specify certain ownership positions for the responsible broker and officers of a corporation, which must also be considered.

Sole Proprietorship

In a sole proprietorship, the broker is the sole owner. The broker hangs out a shingle, personally reaps all of the rewards of being in business, and bears all personal liability for its losses. The sole proprietor has exclusive command over the business, without the entanglements of other owners, so the success or failure of the enterprise is attributable to one person.

Presumably, the owner embarks on this venture because the person has certain technical (as in real estate) and business expertise to make this a worthwhile endeavor. While it may be appealing to own a business and "run it the way I want to," the sole owner doesn't have the benefit of other stakeholders to provide advice or counsel. A sole proprietor isn't insulated from personal liability either, which means the owner has essentially put all of his or her assets and creditworthiness on the line for the business.

The sole proprietor is solely responsible for the longevity of the enterprise and the livelihood of anyone who works for the owner. If that person becomes incapacitated or dies, the business is vulnerable unless the owner has provided legal directives or prepared a plan of succession to cover these eventualities. (State real estate license law may also stipulate certain procedures.)

Often proprietors see their businesses as valued legacies for family members. However, without the technical expertise or commitment to perpetuate the enterprise, the business may not endure. Various studies indicate that fewer than 35 percent of family businesses survive under the second generation. Even more sobering is that by the third generation, only 12 percent of those enterprises in this country are still in business. (See a discussion about succession in Chapter 18.)

Corporations

A corporation is a sole legal entity created under state laws of incorporation. Although it's an association of one or more persons (as stockholders), a corporation is treated as a single individual that has legal capacity to contract and otherwise conduct its affairs as prescribed by the articles of incorporation.

A corporation may be closely held, meaning that the shares of stock are owned by relatively few people, all or most of whom are directly involved in the corporation's business. Or the corporation may be publicly owned, meaning that the corporate shares are publicly traded in accordance with securities and exchange laws.

Corporate structures are appealing for several reasons.

- **Limited liability.** Liability incurred by the corporation becomes an obligation of the corporation, not of the individual owners. Unless a shareholder has signed a personal guarantee for the corporation's obligations, actions for damages, judgments, or bankruptcies will not affect the person's assets. Only the amount of the stockholder's investment in the corporation is at risk.
- **Perpetual existence.** Because a corporation is a legal entity that exists indefinitely (until and unless it is properly dissolved), it technically never dies. Any officer who dies, retires, or resigns can be replaced.
- **Centralized management.** The stockholders elect a board of directors that, in turn, elects a slate of officers. The officers are responsible for the general affairs of the corporation. At least one of the officers, the licensed broker, is directly responsible for the real estate brokerage activities under state license law.
- **Transferability.** The corporate stock may be transferred freely from one stockholder to another.
- **Lack of income limitations.** A corporation may have an unlimited number of stockholders and is permitted to earn an unlimited amount of income.

One of the major disadvantages of a corporation is that profits are taxed twice—once at the corporate level (before dividends are distributed) and again as dividends are distributed to the stockholders. Salaries paid to the officers are not considered profits, so they are taxable only to the individuals who receive them. Losses may not be passed on to the stockholders, but may be applied to the corporation's future earnings. Any capital gains realized by the corporation are passed on to the stockholders as ordinary income.

Brokers who incorporate have customarily retained their ownership positions as closely held or private corporations. Some brokers have taken their corporations public and circulated offerings of their stock on the major stock exchanges. Motives vary for doing this, including the ability to infuse cash into the corporation and to give staff, particularly managers and salespeople, an ownership stake in the company.

Any corporate strategy should be evaluated with the help of an accountant and a corporate or tax attorney, particularly because corporate and tax laws are constantly changing.

S Corporation

The S corporation (S corp) offers the same first four advantages of a corporation and overcomes one of the major disadvantages, the double taxation. Income, losses, and capital gains are passed directly to the stockholders. They, rather than the corporation, pay taxes (or deduct losses) on their personal tax returns.

There are restrictions on S corps. The number of shareholders (as prescribed by state S corp law) is limited and not more than 25 percent of the S corp's income may be generated from passive investments, such as stock dividends, rental of investment properties, and interest from money deposits. If the S corp is engaged primarily in real estate brokerage activities, these restrictions may not be burdensome. But without professional advice, it is easy to make mistakes and jeopardize the S corporation status.

Recently, individual real estate licensees, particularly sales teams, have formed S corps (or other legal relationships as permitted by state license law). Presumably this is done to provide a personal liability shield but in the case of sales teams, the S corp also provides legal structure for the team and the management of its affairs. However, salespeople should not pursue a formal relationship without proper legal and tax advice.

Most real estate licensing laws did not originally contemplate the scenario of a person (or persons) who is an underlying licensee of the employing broker also forming a corporate entity. The relationship between the broker and the licensee (or individual licensees) is clear. But unless the entity is licensed or state law addresses these arrangements in some other way, questions can arise over the entity's relationship with the broker, including whether the entity (as opposed to the individuals) is practicing real estate without a license or can be compensated by the broker.

General Partnership

A partnership is an organization formed under a state's Uniform Partnership Act in which two or more co-owners engage in business for a profit. All of the owners are general partners and share full personal liability for the debts or other obligations of the partnership. The partnership itself does not pay taxes, although it does file an information return that reports the income distributed to each partner. The partners are responsible for paying their own individual taxes. Losses or capital gains also are passed along to the partners.

A partnership can hold a real estate broker's license, provided each partner who is engaged in the real estate business is also a licensed broker. Unlike a corporation, a general partnership is not a sole legal entity and doesn't have a life of its own. The death, withdrawal, bankruptcy, or legal disability of any of the general partners will dissolve the partnership. It's advisable to seek counsel before forming a general partnership, including assistance in writing a partnership agreement.

Limited Partnership

A limited partnership is a venture in which one person (or a group of people), known as the general partner(s), organizes and operates a partnership. Other members of the partnership, the limited partners, are merely investors. These individuals don't personally participate in the operation of the partnership or its business. They share in the profits from the efforts of the general partner and are liable for losses only to the extent of their investment. General partners, however, have unlimited liability and their actions are closely regulated by state and federal agencies, including the manner in which limited-partner investors are solicited.

Limited Liability Companies

Personal liability and corporate income taxes are the two most persuasive issues that affect the choice of ownership structure. Many states have laws that enable businesses to operate as limited liability companies (LLCs). The investors in LLCs are members, rather than partners or shareholders, who have membership interests (rather than stock) in the company.

LLCs may be an appealing alternative to S corporations and limited partnerships. Some of the restrictions that are imposed on an S corporation can be avoided. An LLC partially limits the liability that otherwise exists in a limited partnership, provided the appropriate steps are taken to accomplish this. Regulations and fees for establishing LLCs vary considerably from state to state, so professional guidance is essential.

■ MODE OF OPERATION

Once the most desirable form of legal ownership is determined, the next issue to consider is the mode of operation. That is, whether the company is going to be independent or affiliated in some fashion with other organizations. Generally, the competitive advantage or disadvantage and the benefits and drawbacks for the company influence this decision.

Independent

An independent business appeals both to owners, who want maximum freedom to guide their affairs, and to consumers, who want to do business directly with people who own and operate their own companies. In this mode of operation, the business enterprise is totally self-reliant. This go-it-alone strategy means that the company's success is due to its efforts alone. This also means that the company confronts its struggles alone as well. There are no supportive benefits such as those available when companies are affiliated with one another.

Franchise

A franchise is essentially a "packaged program" for a business, presumably a proven formula for running a business that provides a tested product or service that has appeal in the marketplace. The owner of the franchise authorizes franchisees to engage in this patented or copyrighted business, with the expectation that the franchisees will make money for themselves and for the owner of the franchise.

Franchisees are independent business owners who, at the same time, are affiliated with other companies who are part of the franchise's network. The most common reason real estate companies choose affiliation is to gain more power in the marketplace than an independent company could otherwise achieve for itself. Companies choose franchises based on the principal focus of the franchise.

- **Marketing and advertising.** While all franchises provide brand name or identity, that brand identity is the primary focus of many franchises. The appeal is their professional marketing and advertising programs, typically including television, radio, or print media campaigns; Web site links; and brochures, newsletters, signs, and other marketing tools. National franchises also have the purchasing power to assemble coupon and merchant-discount programs, and other cross-marketing strategies.

- **Target market services.** These franchises' primary focus is specific consumer services, such as counseling owners who want to sell their properties themselves or services associated with buyer agency. The primary advantage of consumer-service-oriented franchises is the technical expertise they offer to the franchisees. These franchises appeal to companies whose business focus is similar to the franchise's focus.
- **Business operations.** These are the franchises that provide operating structures, such as the 100 percent commission companies and the pyramid ownership plans. The appeal of these franchises is they offer greater financial benefits to the salespeople than are customary in other kinds of organizations.

Ultimately, brand-name recognition is the primary benefit of a franchise. This can be a blessing or a curse for a company, though. Consumers often remember the name of the franchise rather than the name of the individual firm. So a company needs to promote its individual identity while also linking itself with the franchise. Some franchises grant exclusivity or limit the number of franchisees in geographic areas while others do not, so the company may not achieve the power in the marketplace that it expected.

A franchise's power in the marketplace is also a function of the success or failure of the individual franchisees. Franchises often provide business development expertise to protect the reputation of the brand and franchise revenue. Frequently, there are also training programs and seminars for the salespeople and leadership and management programs for the brokers.

Franchise affiliation provides a logical connection for referrals with other franchisees around the country. However, this association can also be a drawback. If consumers have had unsatisfactory experiences with one franchisee, they may resist referrals to others (even though these may have been just isolated events). It's best to become acquainted with other franchisees to decide whether this is a desirable group with whom to affiliate. It's advantageous, though not a necessity, to share similar philosophies of doing business as well.

One of the downsides of affiliation is the franchised service or product itself. Not all franchises are successful everywhere. The brand may not have the power in a particular marketplace that it commands elsewhere, or it may have had a storied past after franchisees in an area started up and failed or disassociated from the franchise.

The popularity of brands shifts, which also creates a shift in franchise affiliation. Keller Williams® Realty and Sotheby's International Realty were not even in the franchising business in the late 1980s but have commanded a prominent position with established brands like RE/MAX®, Coldwell Banker®, and Century 21®. Others, like Help-U-Sell® and Red Carpet®, went through very difficult times but may well be reestablishing their position. Some of the most recent entries, like Weichert® Realty, Assist-2-Sell®, and ZipRealty™, are also making inroads in the marketplace and competing for franchisees.

The benefits of franchise affiliation come with a price, in some cases a very substantial one. The entrepreneur who dreamed up the franchise and took it out for a test drive shares it with a profit motive, not out of a sense of generosity.

Franchise costs typically include entry and exit fees, monthly royalties (predetermined or production-based amounts, and sometimes both), and transaction-specific charges for referrals or other franchise services. Often there are also mandatory expenditures or vendor-purchasing agreements that must be honored, all of which have to be analyzed in conjunction with the benefits that could be anticipated from franchise affiliation.

The cost-benefit analysis can be a daunting task, but the importance of due diligence cannot be overstated. The Federal Trade Commission requires franchisors to provide a great deal of information about the franchise in a standardized format, known as the uniform franchise offering circular (UFOC). (Some states have similar requirements as well.) The UFOC intends to help prospective franchisees make informed decisions before signing an agreement.

As lengthy as the disclosure is (sometimes hundreds of pages), a critical piece of information is not required—the historical data about franchisees' earnings. This is a persuasive argument for talking to people who are affiliated with the franchise before making a final decision.

The company's legal counsel should also scrutinize the contract because franchise agreements often give franchisors considerable latitude to change operating procedures while also restricting the franchisees' ability to pursue legal action against the franchisor.

Once convinced that the benefits warrant the expense, the company must decide how to foot the bill. Generally, the company pays the initial fee but ongoing costs of affiliation may be borne solely by the company or shared with the salespeople. Salespeople will resent the financial obligation, however, unless they feel the franchise affiliation benefits their production.

National Corporations

A number of national corporations have been attracted to the real estate business in recent years. Often, the goal is to strengthen their operations by engaging in diverse but compatible enterprises. The ability to link the products and services of these enterprises in cross-marketing programs is an additional enticement.

National corporations typically purchase existing local real estate firms, selecting those that meet certain criteria for size or market share. The terms of the agreement with the corporation will determine the structure of the company under the corporate umbrella, the broker/owner role and responsibilities in the organization, and the degree of financial independence (or dependence) the company will have.

Once the business is sold to a national corporation, the broker/owner essentially becomes a manager. While this means relinquishing some prestige and decision-making authority, the attractive trade-off may be the power of the corporate name along with advertising and promotional programs and strategies to enhance the company's internal operations. Depending on the financial arrangements, the company may also realize an infusion of cash with which to enhance its brokerage activities.

Local Affiliations

Although the trend in many areas is to affiliate with nationally-known brands or corporations, some brokers prefer to maintain their local identity. They also want the competitive advantage and cost efficiency of collective power.

This can be done by forming local associations or franchises and pooling financial resources for such expenses as training, marketing, and advertising programs and secretarial and accounting services. Brokers can also pool their expertise, as professional sales teams, to offer complementary services such as land development, commercial leasing, and property management. Because each of these ventures is individually structured, there is no standard financial arrangement.

Collectively, brokers can increase their power in the market by capitalizing on the market share of each firm and creating local name recognition for new affiliates. But companies need to consider the image and success of the associated firms. The rising-star company may be providing greater benefits to the weaker firms than it will reap in return. On the other hand, jointly capturing a larger share of the market benefits everyone.

An informal way brokers can achieve cost efficiencies is to share office space, housing their independent operations under one roof and sharing rent, common facilities (such as conference rooms), and secretarial and accounting staff. Because several brokers are working out of the same physical location, consumers may not see the businesses as distinctly separate enterprises. It's important to be sure that the arrangements meet any office requirements prescribed by state license law.

There are several downsides to shared-office arrangements, unless eventualities are properly addressed ahead of time. One is the liability for one broker's unpaid bills that could become the responsibility of the other brokers. Controversy can also arise over entitlement to customers. In addition, litigation between a consumer and one of the brokers could unexpectedly draw another broker into the proceedings, simply by virtue of the affiliation.

Affiliated Business Arrangements

An affiliated business arrangement (AfBA) is a network of interrelated companies, owned by one holding corporation, that offer services tied to a real estate transaction. The most obvious are mortgage lending, title insurance, and settlement services.

For years real estate brokers have sought ways to enhance the services they offer consumers. Today this strategy is even more important to satisfy the consumers' quest for seamless transactions. AfBAs provide the interrelated services consumers desire and provide the operational structure real estate companies covet to coordinate and control a transaction. The linkage of services through AfBAs also links sources of revenue.

While AfBAs are appealing, significant capital is needed to set up separate companies, and no one should venture into these arrangements without considerable legal oversight, in light of antitrust concerns and the Real Estate Settlement Procedures Act.

Multiple Listing Services

The discussion of affiliations would be incomplete without once again mentioning multiple listing services (MLSs). Regardless of whether the company is independent, a franchisee, or part of a national corporation, MLS membership may be an important facet of its operation. Depending on the strategies in the company's business plan, MLS membership may be important not only for serving consumers but also for the company's competitive position in the marketplace.

■ MERGERS AND ACQUISITIONS

The distinction between a merger and an acquisition is more academic than real. In practice, companies combine in very individual ways under legal arrangements that suit their specific purposes. The allure of an alliance is also individual, though the intended gain is efficiency and/or effectiveness for the organizations. These alliances may also be tied to a company's growth objectives. (See discussion in Chapter 17.) Your company may be searching for an alliance or yours may be the company being courted by another. In either case, the goal is to combine forces in ways that are a win-win for both organizations as they become one.

For the company being pursued, joining forces with another may provide additional financial resources with which to aggressively pursue selected company objectives or achieve greater power in the marketplace. Depending on the role the broker/owner would have, this may be an opportunity to relinquish some management responsibilities and concentrate on activities in which she or he has particular expertise or interest. This may also be the most suitable way to phase into retirement.

For the company doing the pursuing, joining forces with another may be the most suitable way to expand operations, or gain managerial or staff talent or other assets to strengthen the organization or its position in the marketplace. If a company's business plan calls for adding new products or services or expanding geographic territory, purchasing an existing company that offers these features is one way to accomplish those goals.

Although a company could expand by opening a new office or starting a new division, acquiring another business could accomplish the same purpose more efficiently. An existing business has an established presence in the marketplace, experienced personnel, a physical office site complete with furnishings and equipment, and possibly a franchise affiliation. All of these assets take time and money to establish. The business also has a proven cash flow, which is an advantage if financing is needed to acquire the company.

Even though an acquisition eliminates some of the unpredictable variables associated with starting a new enterprise or opening a branch office, this strategy is not without risk. Often the motive for acquiring a real estate business is to capture its sales talent. However, the market position of the acquired business can quickly deteriorate if that talent is lost, making this a very costly recruiting exercise. In fact, upheaval is often seen as a prime opportunity for others to court the company's personnel.

In the corporate world, some people have gained celebrated reputations as merger and acquisition specialists because of their keen ability to evaluate business enterprises, find good fits, and orchestrate successful transitions. This is not to say that a company in quest of an alliance can't go it alone, but it does make the point that these projects require considerable skill to forge a happy and profitable match.

Evaluating a Business

Any merger or acquisition requires that the company principals be astute consumers. The win may be for the company being acquired if its owners are unloading problems and frustrations. But the venture is not a win for the company that now shoulders the burden of worn-out equipment, a staff of malcontents, a franchise affiliation that is more costly than beneficial, an office location that is no longer viable, or more debt or other liability than was anticipated. Consider the answers to several questions.

- Why is the business for sale? Are the current owners just ready to retire, or are they bailing out because they can't make a go of the business any longer?
- What are the business's primary assets (or appeal)? What are its liabilities?
- How much is the business really worth? Is the profit overstated or understated? Has the owner deferred expenditures that should have been made? (The profit will look better than it really should.) Or is the business incurring expenses that should be trimmed? (The profit won't look as good as it could.)
- What's the reputation of the business in the marketplace? In the case of a merger in which both companies will retain some identity, will the association portray a positive message?
- How well is the company managed? Is it a well-run organization that just needs the power in the marketplace that can be achieved with affiliation? Or is it a lingering organization that can be made better with more astute oversight?

Evaluating or appraising a business is a difficult task. Like any appraisal, the validity of the evaluation is a function of the quantity and quality of the information that is available. Not all business owners freely open all records for perusal or accurately state the true state of affairs. Also, like any appraisal, there is some amount of subjectivity involved, even in quantified measures. After all is said in the appraisal, the value and the price of a business may differ, depending on the motivations of the parties.

Frequently, real estate brokers have the expertise to evaluate a business. However, because they are directly involved in the venture and not totally objective, the advice of an accountant who can expertly assess the company's financial statements is a wise addition to the decision-making process.

Return on investment (ROI) is the most widely accepted valuation approach—expressed as present value returned on investment, internal rate of return, or financial rate of return. In any case, these theoretical approaches to value require a large amount of financial data to produce the numbers with which to analyze an investment. While working through the analysis, also consider that the business being analyzed may not continue to be the same business, so any of its assets could be worth either more or less after the merger or acquisition.

Look closely at all aspects of the organization, especially those that made the company attractive in the first place. Determine the value of that which is being purchased—the name, current listings, pending sales, all or some of the company's services (property management or mortgage business), office equipment (or leases), employees or salespeople, contracts (such as advertising, franchise, or multiple listing service), or office location. Sometimes, all a purchaser wants is the sales unit, leaving the seller with the rest of the business assets and liabilities.

Goodwill. The length of time the company has been in business and the way it's integrated into the new organization will affect the value of the company's name and goodwill. The quality of listings and volume of sales transactions may improve or decrease. Because the salespeople have a significant bearing on these aspects of the business, a mass exodus can seriously jeopardize the value of goodwill or the quality of the listings and sales.

Organizational culture. Because business cultures and management philosophies differ, the effect of new leadership on the overall operation of the current firm must be considered, including the

- planning philosophy,
- organizational structure and business systems,
- staffing or personnel assignments and supervisory responsibilities,
- training and professional development programs,
- allocation of financial resources and financial management systems, and
- management styles.

Certainly, the more compatible the organizations are, the more attractive the acquisition or merger will be. That's not to suggest that dissimilar organizations can't blend successfully, but any transition takes time while people learn to function under new business philosophies, management styles, and operating systems. The greater the differences, the longer the transition period and the time before the venture can reach its financial potential. Highly divergent cultures and business philosophies are often not good candidates for these ventures.

The success or failure of a merger or acquisition rests in the hands of the people who work for the organization. When cultural and philosophical differences are great, considerable retraining may be needed. It's also likely that people will resist the merger, take matters into their own hands, and find other places of employment. All of this has cost implications as well.

Transition

The structure of the merger or acquisition will dictate a number of things. It may be that little will change, other than the name of the acquired company. Or the change may be more dramatic, with closure of the acquired company's offices and the assignment of personnel to other offices. Or the newly blended organization may be a fully integrated merger of leadership, systems, and personnel, all doing business as a new entity under a company name that is a blend of the previous companies' or a name that reflects a fresh start for both companies.

Regardless of the specific arrangements of the venture, the companies need a transition plan. The outward things people see (like company name and signature) are a minor part of the story. The companies need to ensure that business runs smoothly so that the venture proves to be financially rewarding in as efficient a timeframe as possible. A transition plan needs to address several things.

- **Containment.** Even before the legal documents are signed, rumors start circulating. One could hope they are harbingers of excitement and positive outcomes, but invariably rumors thrive on the negative, which can threaten relationships with staff (particularly salespeople), customers, clients, and others in the business community.

  Companies need a plan to contain the news and retain staff and business relationships until they are ready to make their formal announcement. In other words, they need to maintain control and assure everyone that all is well.

- **Organization.** After the closing and formal announcement of the venture is not the time to decide how the companies are going to do business. A smooth transition requires a well-thought-out plan for leadership and assignment of responsibilities, operating policies and procedures, business systems, and the allocation of personnel.

  The object of the exercise is to design an efficient operating structure during the transition period. This is an interim plan that enables the organization to get up and running while it phases in various changes that will become permanent.

- **Launch.** Two audiences are affected by the merger or acquisition—the internal community (the workforce) and the external community. The company needs a good marketing plan to convey the message of its new identity to these two audiences. This requires considerable advanced planning so that the organization is armed with signage and promotional materials and is prepared to capture the minds and hearts of its audiences when it makes the public announcement.

  The initial kickoff is a fast-paced, high-energy time, typically beginning with an exciting event for company staff that is then followed with announcements to current customers and clients (they should not hear the news third-hand) and, finally, the community at large.

Once the company is prepared for the fanfare and has a road map to get business underway, the hard work begins. During the first two weeks after the fanfare, the company needs to get staff on board with the company's services and business policies and procedures. Much of the success of the new venture depends on the way leadership, especially of the acquiring company, conducts itself. People are often skeptical or feel insecure, and they certainly resent being steamrolled. The more respectful and patient leadership is and the stronger the partnership between management and staff, the smoother the transition will be.

A well-known fact of mergers and acquisitions is that duplicate systems, redundant personnel, and divergent business philosophies mean that some people could lose their jobs. The new company's production policies may mean that marginal salespeople will be terminated; duplicate administrative departments mean that excess personnel must be assimilated elsewhere in the organization (sometimes by demotion) or let go. People may leave rather than wait for management to decide their fate. Unless management has a plan for retention and succession, the organization may lose the very people it wanted to keep.

■ INTERNAL STRUCTURE

An internal operating structure is essentially the organization of work. In a single-person organization, the structure is very simple—one person is the organization and is responsible for all facets of its operations. As the scope of work grows, the structure of the organization becomes more complex. Work has to be properly organized so the company can work efficiently but, most importantly, provides a structure that motivates and inspires the people who do the work. The process of structuring work involves six steps.

1. Identify all the work required by the company's business plan
2. Group interrelated tasks associated with that work
3. Assign those collected tasks to work groups (Groups generally have certain primary functions that relate to administrative, operating, and product or service activities.)
4. Convert that work into job positions (Analyze the relationship and scope of work that can reasonably be accomplished by an individual, considering the time and effort involved.)
5. Determine the roles and responsibilities associated with each position. This becomes a job description for the position.
6. Identify the skill sets or talent needed to perform each job and discharge the responsibilities of the position

Essentially, this process arranges work in a rationale or logical scheme—it tells the company what needs to be done and who is needed to do it. A real estate company's work may be grouped by property type (residential, commercial, etc.) or by services (brokerage, property management, appraising, etc.). There may also be groups that provide administrative support and manage the information systems. As the organization grows larger or more decentralized, its efficiency becomes more dependent on these work groups.

A start-up company obviously goes through this process from scratch. But organizations revisit the process periodically to ensure that work is arranged efficiently and the human resources are properly aligned. Are there better ways to group work? Are there job positions that should be added, eliminated, or reconfigured? Are the skills and talents of current personnel properly aligned with their jobs? Or are some workers better suited to other jobs? This process also forms the basis for recruiting, hiring, and training.

One-Person Organization

If you are a one-person business, you are the broker, salesperson, and manager. A one-person organization is a singularly self-directed enterprise in which the owner *is* the business. Although the organization structure is simplistic (especially without other people to supervise), that doesn't mean the work is simplistic.

The chief one-and-only person has all the responsibilities of running the business, from managing its financial affairs and marketing and advertising activities to actually delivering the enterprise's core services. This requires the owner to have multiple business skills and the time to devote to multiple tasks (or to outsource certain functions).

Being the singular independent businessperson can be exhilarating, but the work that can be accomplished is limited by how much one person can do. Obviously, the enterprise depends solely on the revenue that one person can generate. With all of the responsibilities the owner has, the biggest challenge is finding enough time to generate new business and grow revenue.

One- to Ten-Agent Organization

A one- to ten-agent organization is a small, centralized operation. (See Figure 8.1.) The broker/owner role now includes supervisory responsibilities. This means that skill sets are required to supervise the organization's human resources in addition to those required for the other business management responsibilities.

Obviously, with more hands on board, the capacity of the organization expands. More work can be accomplished and the company can sustain more consistent operations and generate a steadier stream of revenue than when the company is totally dependent on one person's efforts.

FIGURE 8.1
One- to Ten-Agent Organization

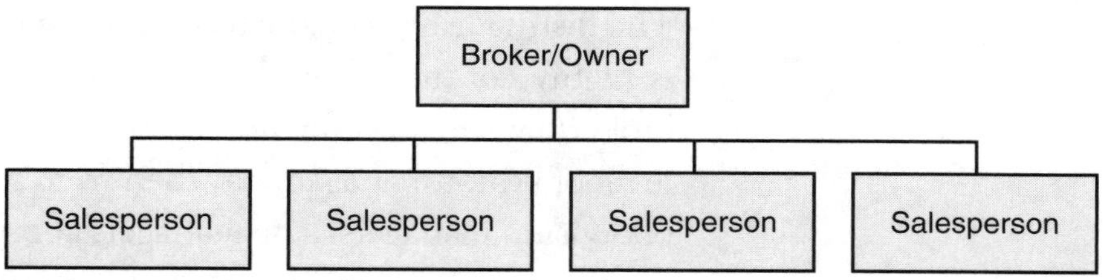

Growth means that the cost of doing business increases and the organization becomes more complex. Increased cost of facilities, information systems, and other support services that today's salespeople expect can be disproportionately expensive per person until the organization grows closer to the eight- to ten-agent size, unless a very small number of salespeople are highly productive. Nonselling and other clerical staff will likely be needed to support administration functions as well.

All of this means that there are more human variables to manage. As soon as one salesperson is hired, the broker becomes a sales manager. Typically, one-tenth of the broker's time is devoted to this activity. With each additional salesperson, another tenth of the broker's time is added to sales management activities. As the sales staff grows, the broker has less time to devote to sales activities and may eventually become a full-time sales manager (unless one is hired).

Monolithic Organization

A monolithic organization is a highly centralized operation, functioning as a single (mono) unit, with work being structured to flow from one singular source of authority at the top of the organization. The one-person and one- to ten-agent organizations are monolithic in the sense that one person at the top of the organization (the broker/owner) is the chief in charge of the entire scope of the organization's work.

As human and financial resources permit, the scope of work expands, with the result being that work is grouped in more focused ways. Hence, there may be a number of work groups (departments or divisions) that are responsible for accomplishing various goals in the business plan. Some are directly responsible for delivering the company's core services, and others are responsible for administrative functions that support the salespeople and the internal operation of the company. (See Figure 8.2.)

The distinguishing characteristic of a monolithic organization is that work is highly controlled by the top of the organization. This is normally the broker/owner or president. Authority flows from this position to the next level of senior management, then from senior management to department or division managers. The managers at each level are responsible for directing their work groups, but they do so only within the limits authorized by the immediate superior. Decision making is highly controlled by one or only a few individuals in upper management, leaving subordinate positions with little authority.

The skill sets or talent required for each position reflects the scope of work that is assigned to those positions. Because the work becomes more focused the lower the position on the organization chart, skill sets become more task oriented. A training director in a monolithic organization, for example, has little influence over other aspects of the company's administration, so this position is likely to require only very specific training skills. Broader business management skill sets would be required of the top three positions in Figure 8.2.

Although nothing about the formal organization chart changes, the physical efficiency of work and the control over human factors can differ, depending on whether all work groups are housed under one roof or at

FIGURE 8.2
Monolithic Organization

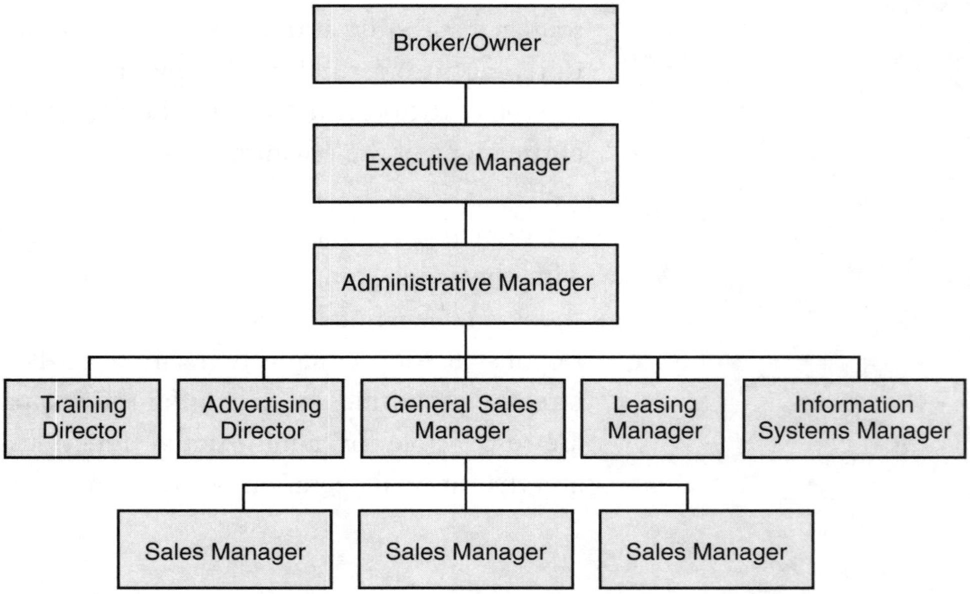

scattered sites. The most important consideration, though, is that physical space must comfortably house the scope of work and provide flexibility, so that as the organization grows, people are not working in overcrowded, morale-defeating conditions.

Housing all of the company's operations in one location can be efficient, reducing the facility cost per person and function, and enhancing the coordination of activities among departments. It's easier for senior management to supervise all activities though, taken to the extreme, highly controlling managers use centralization to keep everyone under the one-roof microscope. Multiple facilities can also be efficient, though, with sales offices being strategically placed for their purposes and administrative functions housed elsewhere.

Decentralized Organization

A decentralized organization consists of a number of work groups or departments, but, unlike a monolithic organization, there are fewer layers of management at the top of the organization. As demonstrated in Figure 8.3, authority is delegated from the top of the organization to the next management level. The managers or directors of those work groups have the authority to direct their groups' activities, operating essentially as individual business units.

Decentralized operations are more horizontal than monolithic ones (which are clearly more vertical) and are often viewed as more functionally efficient. With fewer levels of management to bog down the process, organizations can be more responsive or resilient. Managers or directors can freely direct the work for which they are responsible, essentially making the calls rather than waiting for direction from intermediaries.

FIGURE 8.3
Decentralized Organization

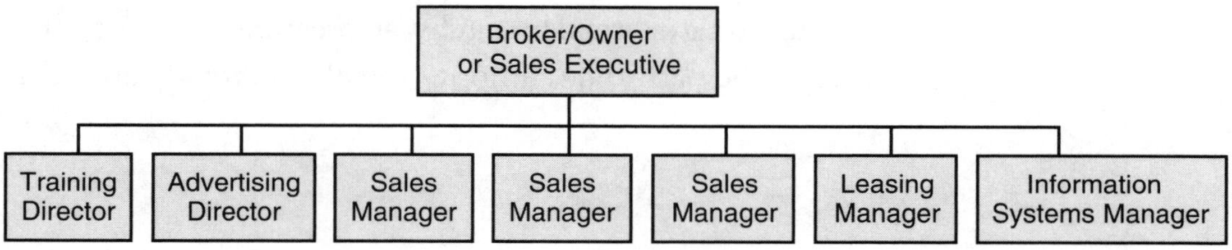

Frequently, the work groups are structured as individual **profit centers**. This means that each unit functions on its own financial platform and is expected to produce enough income to cover its costs of operation plus make a profit for the company. Work units that are responsible for a company's core services (like sales divisions or offices) are often set up as profit centers.

Typically, administrative functions are centralized. Setting up accounting and information management, marketing, and training departments for the entire organization, rather than duplicating these activities in each work unit, is more cost-efficient and standardizes certain activities that are necessary for the organization to run smoothly. That standardization, however, does not mean that administrative departments ignore the needs of other business units. Processes and procedures must be tailored to support the various requirements of these units.

The challenge in a decentralized organization is to achieve the proper balance between autonomy and control. While each work group functions independently, all units must function as a unified organization, operating under the same business philosophy and company policies and procedures. Decentralized organizations maintain order by fostering teamwork among the managers or directors of the various business units and by selecting individuals who can exercise prudent use of authority.

■ CHAIN OF COMMAND

The organization of work involves an orderly organization of responsibilities so that people know exactly the scope of work for which they are accountable. People also need to know exactly who their superiors are so they know from whom to take direction. Otherwise, work evolves in a chaotic manner, lines of authority become vague, and people wind up asserting themselves in places they don't belong.

By establishing a formal hierarchy, an organization charts the chain of command or the path that authority travels to provide an orderly process for making decisions, issuing instructions, and commanding or directing work. In real estate organizations there are typically two types of authority.

1. **Staff authority**, which is given to the people who are responsible for support services, the work groups providing administrative support. These groups contribute *indirectly* to the achievement of the company's objectives. They provide services such as accounting, marketing and advertising, training, purchasing (materials for the operation of the business), and maintenance.
2. **Line authority**, which is given to the people who are responsible for contributing *directly* to the achievement of the company's objectives. These include work groups such as the sales offices or the property management, leasing, or new construction departments.

The organization's chart shows very clearly how each position functions within the context of all other positions in the organization. Positions that are connected by direct lines of authority must directly interface with one another. Positions outside those direct lines often have some degree of interdependence, though no authority to direct one another's activities. A sales office manager, for example, often interfaces with accounting and marketing departments, but has no authority to direct process or policy in those departments.

Job Descriptions

The way to put the meat on the bones of an organization chart and expressly state how positions function is with job descriptions. A **job description** converts the scope of authority conferred on a position by describing the responsibilities of that position. The description also shows how the person in the position interfaces with superiors, subordinates, and others in the organization when there is no direct line of responsibility.

A job description tells people where they fit into the big picture of the company—to whom they are to report, the positions that report to them, and exactly what their responsibilities are versus the responsibilities of others. Poor job descriptions recite chores or tasks associated with a job. A properly written job description explains (describes) the activities for which a person is *accountable*. This tells people what the critical elements of their jobs are within the organization and provides a basis for assessing performance.

Don't assume people know what a job entails. In the case of salespeople, it's tempting to say that they already know what to do—get sales and listings. But that's not a suitable job description. Are they responsible for meeting production goals or complying with the law or company policies? Furthermore, it's not appropriate to chastise a person for failing to properly discharge responsibilities if he or she hasn't been explicitly told what they are.

Job descriptions provide a tool with which to identify skill sets required for the positions. Basically, "what does a person need to be able to do to handle the responsibilities for which he or she is accountable?" Typically, the larger the scope of responsibility, the more diverse the skill sets are. Job descriptions are also used to periodically evaluate the assignment of responsibilities within the organization and identify more efficient assignments if necessary.

Informal Organization

Regardless of the way positions appear on a chart, most organizations have an informal structure. This is because work overlaps and doesn't always fit neatly into a chart. Often, this means that systems or processes are needed to facilitate the flow of work outside the formal chart so that the organization can function as an efficient enterprise.

■ **CASE IN POINT** According to the formal organization, the manager of a sales office is responsible for managing that office's advertising budget, and the salespeople in that office operate under the manager's directives with respect to listing advertising. That's straightforward.

Then along comes a listing that is assigned to one of those salespeople by the manager of the relocation department who is responsible for all aspects of a listing that comes through the relocation network, including the advertising. Now there are two separate authorities for managing listing advertising and two separate bosses the salesperson has to follow, depending on the source of the listing.

This is a prime example of the way work doesn't always fit neatly into a chart. Obviously, the goal is to get the listings advertised. But authority must be clearly delineated so that the office manager maintains control over the aspects of advertising for which that position is responsible, while also facilitating the work for which the relocation director is responsible. Most importantly, the salespeople need to know which boss's directives to follow in which situations.

The major challenge in managing the informal structure of an organization is maintaining order. The formal structure typically provides direct lines of reporting, with one boss and one person's directives to follow. The order of the organization in this case is very clear. Order can begin to unravel when lines of authority become blurred or people have multiple bosses. Conflicts arise over accountability (easy to pass the buck), and multiple (and perhaps conflicting) directives are confusing at best and often result in undesirable actions.

Processes or systems are needed to clearly provide for cases in which people are permitted to work outside the formal structure and the authority bosses have in those situations. Otherwise, people will create their own informal structure. Sometimes they do this anyway, regardless of the company's formal or sanctioned informal structure.

- People shop for decisions, seeking the answers they want to hear, regardless of whether the person they seek out is the boss or has the authority to make the decision. In these cases, all people want is someone to concur with a course of action they wanted to take.
- Some people want to exercise more authority than they've been granted, so they manage work or decide matters that are beyond their scope of authority. While people sometimes take on more responsibility than they've been authorized for laudable reasons, the disruptive influences are those who do so with some self-serving purpose or agenda.
- When people don't agree with a company policy or procedure, they may give directions or make decisions that are beyond their scope of authority primarily for the purpose of countermanding or derailing company procedures.
- When management fails to provide decisive leadership, people leapfrog over the immediate supervisor and go to the next higher-up for a decision or decide matters for themselves. These are cases in which management has failed to do its job or hasn't responded promptly enough for people to do their jobs.
- When company processes or procedures are inefficient or impractical, people will ignore them or find their own, better ways of doing things. A supervisor's approval or authorization from another depart-

ment's supervisor that seems unnecessary or unduly restricts the flow of work will be circumvented.

Management is responsible for preserving order and chain of command, which includes fulfilling the responsibilities for which the managers are accountable and refraining from interjecting themselves into other managers' areas of responsibility. People work outside the formal organization structure for a variety of reasons, any of which should be management's wake-up call that work is not properly organized, that the wrong people are in positions of authority, or that the people in positions of authority are not fulfilling their responsibilities.

■ **CASE IN POINT** As the broker of a small company, you hire a sales manager who, among other things, is responsible for assigning referrals. A salesperson approaches you directly with a plea for a referral, feeling that you'll be receptive because the two of you have previously had a close working relationship.

If you intervene, you undermine the authority of the sales manager. This can also be interpreted by the salesperson as your public acknowledgment that the manager has not properly done his or her job. Ultimately, the chain of command unravels because you've authorized the salesperson to ignore it. To preserve order,

- you could ask the salesperson to raise the issue with the manager (and if the salesperson doesn't, it could be that the salesperson was seeking preferential treatment from you), or
- you could approach the manager along with the salesperson and inquire about the status of referral assignments.

Either approach demonstrates to both the sales manager and the salesperson that you respect the manager's authority. Your intervention also demonstrates that you are responsive by addressing an issue that, if ignored, could mushroom into a major problem. A disgruntled salesperson could turn other salespeople against the company's referral system. (Repeated queries about referrals, however, could indicate a more serious problem that should be addressed with the manager.)

■ CONCLUSION

Giving structure to an organization gives it the orderly form it needs to execute the business plan. The broker (and other owners, if there are any) must decide the most suitable form of legal ownership and appropriate business affiliations. These involve decisions about the degree of independence or interdependence the company and its principals will have with other organizations.

As the scope of work grows or becomes more complex, the company can get disorganized, or even become dysfunctional. Organizations need an internal structure that groups work in a logical, efficient manner and a chain of command that clearly defines the path of decision-making authority. Job descriptions tell people the breadth and limits of what they are expected to do. Just as the business plan provides a blueprint around which the company is organized, the structure of the organization provides a road map for assembling the tools for the business and allocating its resources.

■ DISCUSSION EXERCISES

Chart your current organization. What is its formal structure? What activities is each work unit responsible for accomplishing? What personnel are assigned to each work group and who is the supervisor?

What is the informal structure of your current organization? How does this differ from the formal organization? What problems, if any, arise from people working within the informal rather than the formal structure of the company?

Select a position in your company and prepare a job description for that position.

Using your organization (or one you're familiar with), analyze its life-cycle stage. When do you think it will enter the next stage, and what do you think it should be doing in the meantime?

CHAPTER NINE

STRUCTURING BUSINESS SYSTEMS

What will the business office of tomorrow look like? Where will it be?

What do companies have to do differently to support the way people work today?

Just as people need housing, a company needs a physical plant or facility in which to do business. While that facility may be as humble or state-of-the-art as resources allow, it needs to be sufficiently efficient so that people can do their jobs—at the very least, the basic "house."

That basic facility, today, is not the desk/phone office of yesteryear. For all companies in today's business world, technology plays a major role in the way people do their jobs, companies manage their information, and the public interfaces with the organizations. This has altered virtually everything companies used to think about the where and what of their offices.

One thing that has not changed is the need to project an image of the company. This is the "dress-up" space the public (and a potential recruit) sees that showcases what the company thinks of itself and instills confidence that this is a good place to do business. Impressive corporate headquarters, the monuments of stability or affluence, can accomplish this. For real estate companies, the people they need to impress (the consumers) have less reason to visit the tower of power and are much more likely to meet the company in the sales office, if they visit at all.

While the seat of the company and the sales office may be one and the same, the two have distinctly separate functions. In business management parlance, there's something known as backroom operations. This is the behind-the-scenes administrative function that the public doesn't and has no need to see. With today's technology, that function revolves around a computer system, which can be connected, operated, and managed virtually anywhere.

All of this says that facilities have to be tailored to suit the work. In doing so, the company creates environments that are conducive to efficient operations and makes the best use of its financial resources. As a company's plans change, the facilities change as well. Although a new office site or updated décor, furnishings, or equipment might look tempting, only those that support the organization's plan and priorities are appropriate to consider.

Many resources are available to help evaluate physical needs, design facilities, and automate a business so that the company gets the best value for its dollar.

■ YOUR OFFICE

Real estate licensing laws are still rooted, in one fashion or another, in the permanence of a physical office complete with fixed signage, telephones, and the like. That requirement was instituted years ago after fly-by-night operators fled the scene with a buyer's money as quickly as they arrived and then couldn't be found. A fixed office that was approved by the regulators intended to anchor the broker with a professional presence in a permanent space.

Any salespeople the broker employed would also have to work out of that approved location as well. Today, the broker's and the salespeople's official place of business is still the address of the office approved by the state's regulators. That office, however, is no longer the salesperson's primary base of operations. In fact, technology and innovation have changed the entire face of business offices.

The purpose of an office has flip-flopped. Instead of being the place people go to work, the office today is a place that supports wherever they work. This evolution is not unique to the real estate industry. Nearly every business enterprise has workforce populations who have disengaged from the company office.

Real estate companies view sales offices differently. Many have streamlined their offices, focusing on the areas that their customers and clients use and consolidating work areas. Others see the offices as central hubs of activity and are generous in their design and allotment of space to both the public and work-space areas.

Then there are the brokers who favor virtual offices. A *virtual office* combines off-site communications with a high-profile professional address, which reduces the cost of traditional offices while also maintaining a professional presence. A broker can establish an office that includes reception courtesies, business meeting space, and other on-site business amenities at a fraction of the cost of purchased or leased space. The broker can also be supported by remote services (receptionist, answering service, voicemail, and virtual assistant).

In effect, the majority of real estate salespeople today have virtual offices. They work off-site but use the company's office as their official mailing address and business meeting and service center, with on-site personnel being their receptionists, answering services, and support assistants.

If the quest is for sales office space that is essentially marketing space for the company, the starting point is the market analysis.

- Where are the company's target markets located?
- What are their consuming patterns?
- Does the office need to be within the traffic patterns (vehicular or pedestrian) they are likely to travel?

- How likely are they to be "walk-in" business for the company?
- How important to the salespeople is the proximity of the office to those consumers?

As companies expand their geographic view of their businesses, the neighborhood sales office becomes less important than the company's ability to interface with consumers electronically. With fewer reasons for consumers to actually set foot in the company's buildings, a longer distance to travel on occasion may not be a major deterrent.

Add to consideration the part of the market analysis that looked at the competition and market shares.

- Where do the company's most significant competitors have offices?
- How much potential business is there in those locations?
- Does the company have to be located in the same locations to preserve or increase market share in its target markets?
- How much name recognition does the company have in the target market area?

There's a common fear that if a company does not have a presence where the competition is located, the company will lose. But if there's not enough business to support everyone, it may be better to chart new territory. On the other hand, if there's a concentration of other brokerage firms in an area, that could indicate they've identified an area with great potential.

If the purpose of the office quest is to open a branch office, the value of the company's name recognition in the new area should be considered. This is not to say that a company shouldn't blaze a trail into markets where it's not well known, but the company does need to factor a marketing and advertising program into the cost of the new facility. Salespeople should not be expected to bear the entire cost of self-promotion when the company relocates them to a new office.

Office space for primarily administrative purposes should support the operation of the company's various business units. There's no need to pay the price for a prime location when the work has low public profile. The important consideration is the efficiency with which work units and their managers will interface with one another. The supervisor of the marketing department, for example, is better off being located in the same place as the staff that person supervises.

Site

Armed with that analysis, the actual site selection can begin to take shape. Notice that all of this amounts to the company going through a buyer qualification process before starting its "house hunting." (Practice what the industry preaches.)

Visibility of a sales office (and its signage) is important if the company expects a lot of consumer traffic. The office doesn't have to be on a main road, but must at least be in a place where consumers can find it before they get lost to the competition. While a free-standing building may provide the most visible office and signage (and ownership opportunity, if that's a consideration), higher density sites (shopping centers, malls, office complexes) are not necessarily inferior, depending on the actual space that is available and sign placement that is permitted.

The person who goes office shopping doesn't always see the same things a consumer would see, particularly if the shopper is familiar with the area. The barrier in the middle of a four-lane highway without easy access from the opposite side of the road may not raise a red flag to the person who is accustomed to dealing with it. An out-of-the-way location can be a constant source of aggravation for the person who has to give directions to people who are unfamiliar with the area.

How important is parking? Even a commercial brokerage company located in a central business district can frustrate customers when parking can't be easily located. Suburban sites, especially in malls and office complexes, can be equally frustrating. Before signing a lease or purchasing a building, visit the site at various times of day and on different days of the week to get a good sense of capacity.

Consider, too, the parking for staff, especially as needs peak and wane dramatically according to work patterns and schedules of office events. Otherwise, the office manager can become a parking lot attendant trying to keep spaces intended for customers free from salespeople who just stop by.

Size

The change in purpose of today's office has greatly reduced the amount of square footage needed. While the work an office supports can be accommodated in a variety of physical configurations (which also affects the amount of floor space that is needed), the first consideration is the nature of the work it has to support—people, equipment, and public image.

Today's real estate sales office is primarily an informational and support center. This means accommodating management and support staff (which may also include a salesperson's assistant) and office and telecommunications equipment. Because this office is typically the only place where the consumer actually meets the company (the image space), an attractive reception area and comfortable conference rooms are a priority.

With more people working at home, and the fact that they can easily carry the contents of their desks in increasingly smaller electronic containers, there's less and less they need in the brokerage office. Of course, a lot of this depends on how technologically advanced the company's operations are. If contract files reside in the company's database, for example, they can be accessed through a secure Internet connection or by intranet.

Cost efficiency is the key. With minimal reason to provide desk space for the sales staff, a few workstations for those occasions when salespeople do need to be in the office are all that is necessary. The challenge is to match space available with anticipated need. Otherwise, a lot of floor space sits idle on occasion and people are clogging hallways at other times. The best guides are the company's workplace policies and the work patterns of its salespeople.

One strategy for managing workstations, which is used in a number of business enterprises, is known as *hotelling*. As its name implies, it's a reservation system (though without the fee). With a phone call, e-mail, or Web site calendar, the salesperson can reserve a workstation for the desired time or in another office site that has availability. Because of the unpredictable nature of the real estate business, this system has to be quickly responsive.

If the company views the office as the principal working headquarters for the sales staff, significantly more space is required. A rule of thumb is approximately 100 square feet of floor space per salesperson, depending on how the space is configured. Partitioning single offices will require more space than an open or bull pen arrangement.

Calculate desk cost to see how many salespeople are needed to cover this overhead and make a profit. A very expensive site can be a self-defeating proposition for the manager if the anticipated number of salespeople is an impracticably large number of people for one person to supervise. A larger support staff would be needed as well.

Use the checklist in Figure 9.1 to identify which areas are essential for the company and those that are desirable or optional. Don't overlook the importance of public areas, such as reception areas, conference rooms, restroom facilities, and refreshment centers. The back office space (staff, equipment, and supplies) should not be the leftovers, but a pleasant environment that promotes maximum efficiency.

When selecting office space, it's also wise to consider how training programs, sales meetings, and other group events will be accommodated. The worst place to conduct these is at desks or workstations. Electronic capability is also needed so that audio and video conferencing and satellite delivery can be used. Renting outside facilities on an as-needed basis may be more cost-efficient than setting aside space that will be used infrequently.

Unless the company has someone on staff who is skilled in designing office space, the services of a professional space planner are invaluable for helping to select the most cost-efficient space, identify areas that can be used for multiple purposes, and plan flexibility for future expansion or contraction.

Legal issues. Several legal issues must be considered before signing on the dotted line of a lease or purchase agreement. One of these is the state licensing law. In most jurisdictions, even if the specific office requirements are minimal, the facility must be inspected before the office can be opened for business. Local zoning ordinances must also be checked to be sure the intended use is in compliance and that signage and parking requirements are satisfied. Any necessary occupancy permits and/or occupational licenses must also be obtained.

The facility must also comply with the Americans with Disabilities Act (ADA). Because a real estate company provides services to the public, the

FIGURE 9.1
Space Area Checklist

	Essential	Desirable	Optional
Reception Area			
Customer			
Receptionist			
Display Area			
Desk Space			
Management			
Salespeople			
Personal Assistants			
Secretarial			
Accounting/Bookkeeping			
Advertising/Promotions			
Research/Data Collection			
Others			
Work/Equipment Area(s)			
Computer(s)			
Fax Machine(s)			
Copy/Duplicating			
Telecommunications			
Conference Area(s)			
Filing			
Storage			
Office Supplies			
Signs, Promotional Materials, etc.			
Records			
Coat Closets			
Rest Room(s)			
Coffee Bar/Kitchen			
Training/Audiovisual			
Library			
Children's Play Area			

office (whether it's owned or leased) must be accessible to people with disabilities. Or the company must be prepared to provide accommodations that will enable a person with a disability to access the company's services. The company also has obligations as an employer under ADA.

Consider ADA *before* selecting the office space rather than after moving in. Some sites may be readily accessible while others may require considerable, costly retrofit. An architect or someone versed in the law can review the facility and recommend the most suitable ways to comply with ADA. Architectural or structural barriers pose the greatest challenge. ADA provides acceptable alternatives in the event that altering the structure to overcome barriers is an undue hardship.

Entry barriers (which can be overcome with a ramp or call button at a suitable height for a person using a wheelchair) are not the only considerations. If the public is customarily given access to rest rooms, refreshments, and other comforts in the office, these must also be accessible by people with disabilities.

Design and Décor

Now comes the task of designing and decorating the office. Figures 9.2 and 9.3 provide some preliminary ideas for a floor plan. Figure 9.4 provides a checklist of things to consider at the remodeling, decorating, and furnishing stages. Some companies use similar floor plans and décor, including the company's signature color scheme, in all of their offices to reinforce their image and provide added efficiency for people who sometimes work in several office locations.

Public areas. The reception area introduces the company and makes its first impression by what the public sees, hears, smells, and feels. A calm inviting atmosphere, free of distractions from the hubbub in the "back room" and harsh paging systems, creates a professional welcome. (Provide the receptionist, staff, or floor person a suitably inviting workspace as well.) Think about how visitors will spend their time in the waiting area and provide comfortable seating that is stocked with informative or promotional material and perhaps an interactive video display.

Conference rooms are as important showcases for the company as the reception area and should be similarly comfortable and distraction-free. The public should not have to walk through staff work areas to get to conference rooms, nor should salespeople have to entertain customers at workstations or desks. Equip conference rooms with telephones, computers, WiFi, and video facilities. These are not optional expenditures if the rooms serve multiple purposes for meetings, closings, and additional workstation space.

FIGURE 9.2
Sample Office Arrangement

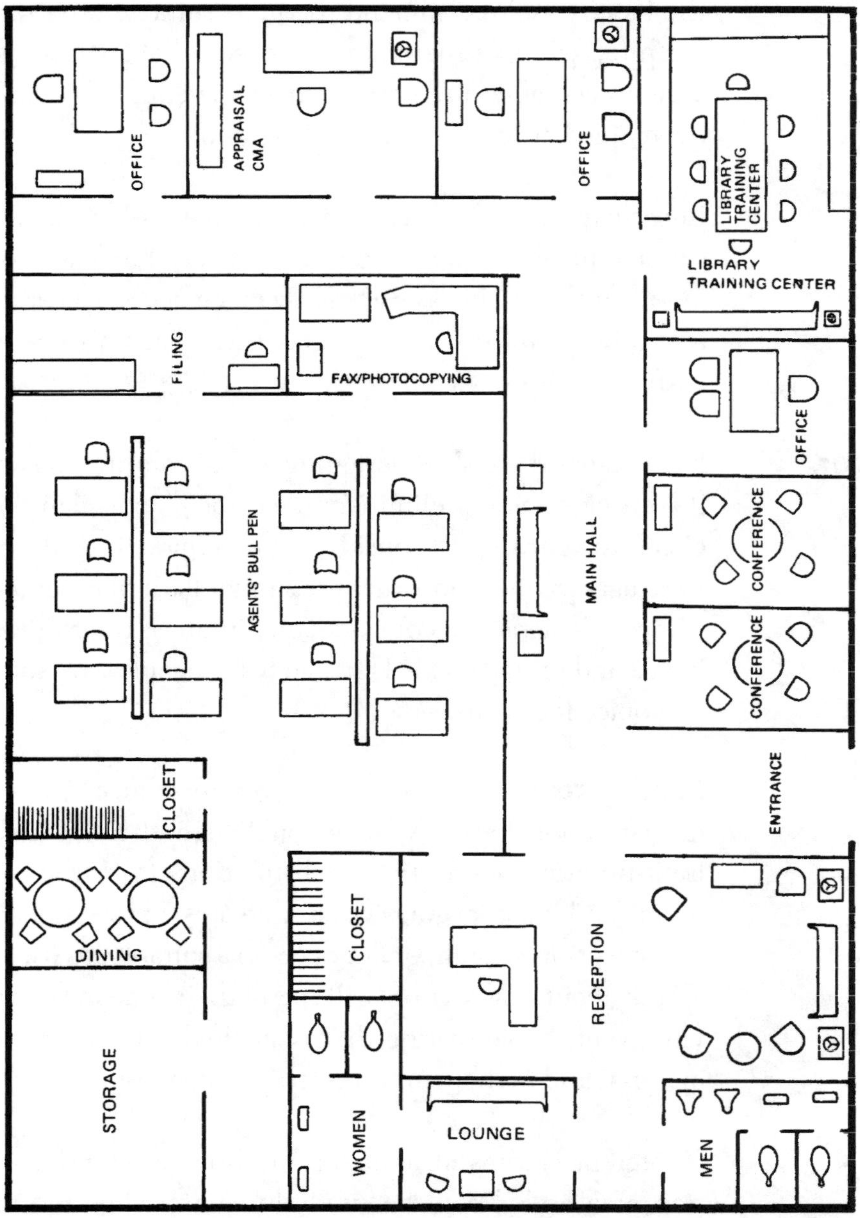

FIGURE 9.3
Additional Office Layout

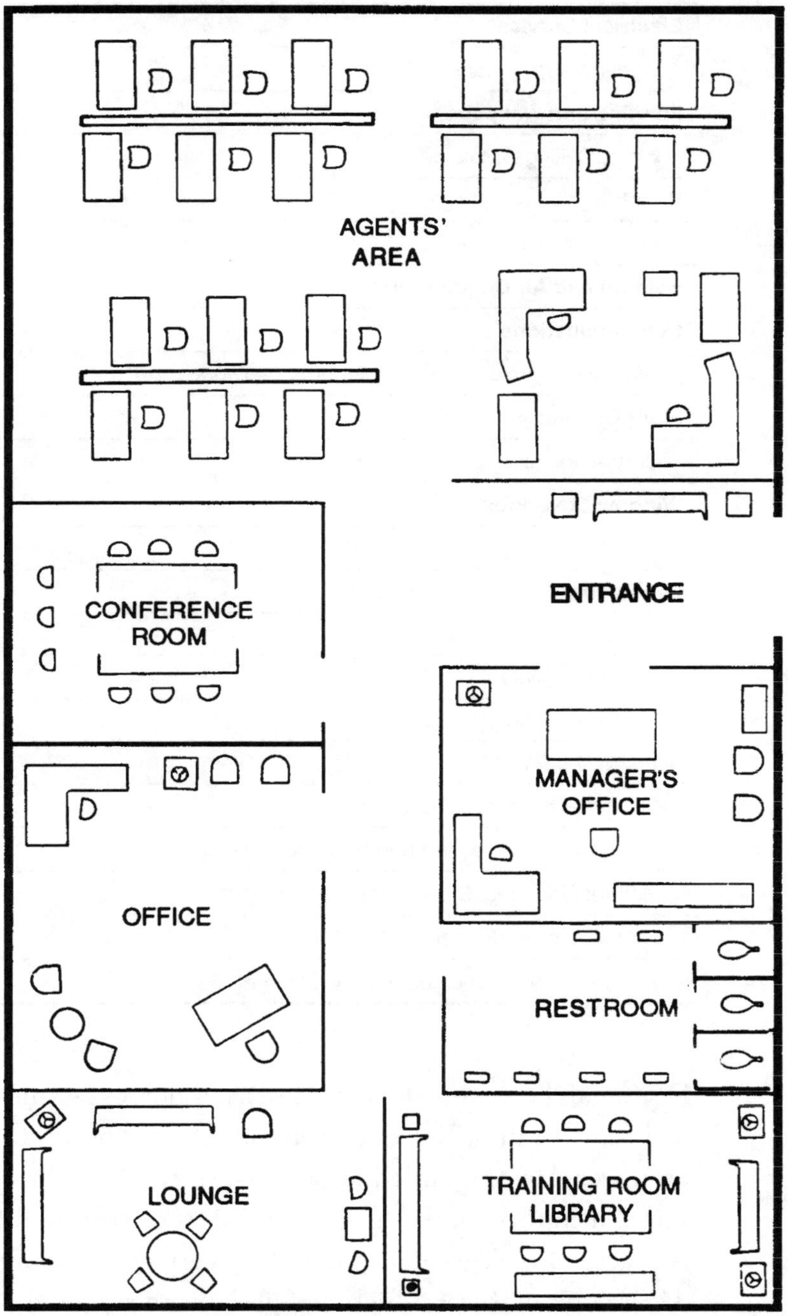

FIGURE 9.4
Remodeling, Decorating, and Furnishing Checklist

Carpentry
Partitions, Paneling, Shelving, Doors
Electrical Service
Lighting and Switches, Outlets for Equipment
Painting and Wallpaper
Walls, Ceilings, Moldings
Plumbing
Rest Rooms, Kitchen
Heating and Air Conditioning
Communications
Telephones, Fax Machines, Modems, Networks
Floor Coverings
Carpeting, Tile
Window Coverings
Blinds, Drapes
Furnishings
Desks and Chairs
Vinyl Floor Mats
Credenzas and Filing Cabinets
Computer Stands
Conference Room Chairs and Tables
Reception Area Seating and Receptionist Unit
Pictures, Plaques, Clocks, and Bulletin Boards
Lamps and Wastebaskets
Workroom Table/Counter, Supply Cabinet

Décor can be as upscale or modest as resources permit. There are two things to keep in mind, however. One is safety. The pretty ceramic-tiled floors on a wet day, the curled floor mats, or the frayed carpeting can be a lawsuit waiting to happen if someone slips or trips and falls. The other issue is practicality. Very cheap could be very expensive in the long run if the décor can't withstand high use, abuse, and repeated cleaning and then has to be replaced. Also, think about how child-friendly and ADA-friendly the environment is.

Work areas. Regardless of how much floor space is devoted to work areas, the space should be separate from the public areas and support an efficient flow of work and the interaction of people and systems.

Think about how work activities are grouped. The sales-support staff and the salespeople should be readily accessible to one another, and the administrative-support staff should be readily accessible to the broker or manager. Equipment and supplies should be conveniently located for the people who use them. Areas like the broker's and/or manager's office, kitchen, and restrooms serve both public and private purposes and should be readily accessible without having to trail through the backroom work area.

Mapping the space for the sales staff involves more than simply allocating square feet on the floor for desks. A trend in office design, including in the corporate world, is the *open office*. This resembles the corral or bull pen arrangement that has been used for a number of years in the real estate industry.

The appeal is that people can more freely interact with one another without barriers of individual office walls, which inspires creative thinking and joint problem solving. Because not all workers are in the office at the same time, this environment is especially helpful for fostering teamwork and camaraderie when they are present. The open arrangement also means that less floor space per person is needed and space can easily be reconfigured as needs change.

This communal environment has its critics, however. For the most part, they object to the disruption and distraction that can interfere with concentration and privacy (particularly on the telephone) and affect client confidentiality. This environment also reveals to management the less flattering aspects of human behavior that fail to respect others' business leads and personal belongings, all of which add to the things a manager has to manage.

In companies where separate offices have been viewed as a status symbol, the communal, classless environment may be difficult to adjust to and may seem like a demotion. A lesson can be learned from a president and CEO of a major Fortune 500 company who was so committed to the benefits of the open environment that he insisted that he and his senior advisers work in open offices (just like the rest of the company's workforce). Granted, the workstations are mahogany-framed glass, but the space is not otherwise any larger or more prestigious than that of anyone else in the company. Private or confidential work is done in small conference rooms.

Equipment and furnishings. Floor planning requires some thought about the configuration of the hardware and furnishings that will eventually be put into place. While today's technology is less dependent on the hardwire connections than previously were required, an office customarily uses more permanent and, in some cases, much more complex systems than residential users do. In fact, today's sophisticated systems are appealingly accommodated in buildings that are blackwired (institutionally outfitted with the connectivity to support electronic communications) or provide wireless service.

Regardless of the connectivity and accompanying power sources that are required, the placement of those utilities and the furniture and equipment must be compatible with one another. Otherwise, the wire jungle becomes a tripping hazard or the power source is across the room from where the photocopy machine should be. Although utilities can be moved, it's cheaper to think about their placement before hardwiring an installation, rather than discovering later on that it's misplaced.

An office can be furnished in variety of imaginative ways to create an appealing décor. Furniture comes in a variety of qualities at a variety of prices. Often, better quality, used furniture is less costly than new, inferior furniture. And while small desks are less expensive, they are unsatisfactory if most of the work surface is occupied by equipment.

■ COMMUNICATIONS AND INFORMATION SYSTEMS

All the bricks and sticks aside, the real "mortar" for a company is technology. Technology is cited in numerous surveys of real estate industry leaders as one of the most significant forces that has shaped (or reshaped) the industry and will continue to be a driving force in the future. Technology is also cited as one of the most significant costs of doing business.

The heart of that technology is the computer system. This is the centerpiece for virtually all of a company's information and communication efforts. Integration is the key because both hardware, or equipment, and software must be compatible for the system to provide the seamless processes users require. So dependent are today's companies on their computers that they are nearly out of business when their systems go down. A company can also be in for untold distress if records are lost and the time comes to defend a lawsuit or answer to a regulatory agency.

Although a single-person start-up company could be provisioned with the best PC deal found in an advertising circular, that purchasing strategy is not recommended. Powering up a business, as well as upgrading an existing system, is considerably different than buying for even the most techno-savvy personal user. The computer (or its central processor or server) is a massive datacenter that must efficiently perform many diverse functions. The system can easily frustrate or hamper operations if it doesn't have enough power, capacity, or integrated compatibility to capture, manage, warehouse, and deliver vast amounts of data.

The first step in provisioning or upgrading technology is to get professional advice. Business systems analysts, telecommunications specialists, and computer consultants are all possible resources for analyzing a company's needs, recommending (and even designing) integrated hardware and software solutions, and getting the new system up and running.

The point is to invest wisely in the technology that best serves the company's needs, avoiding features that will never be used while also anticipating future requirements. ("Future" is just a matter of a year or two for electronic technology.) Bargain-priced and outdated systems will be technological nightmares, especially if they are odd or incompatible with other technology currently or commonly in use.

The System

A company's computer system can be as state-of-the-art or as basic as financial resources and operator expertise permit. The system is an assemblage of a number of hardware and software components to serve multiple computing purposes for multiple users in a variety of locations all at the same time.

What does the system need to be able to do this? The details vary with the size and complexity of a company's business, the number of internal and mobile users, and the way the company interfaces with the public. Specific software selections are best guided by a professional, but the essential features are the same.

- **Data management.** This is the creation, collection, conversion, and retrieval of information (data). Word processing, spreadsheet, and financial and accounting functions are the most common. Operating systems, often augmented by separate software programs, convert scanned documents into electronic formats, reformat data, index content, and merge data for various uses. An important part of that function is the Web-interface that brings downloaded data (documents, e-mails, and other information captured from the Internet) into the database.
- **Networking.** This connects users to data and offices, to the central database (server), and manages traffic with the database within the company, otherwise known as an *intranet.* Thanks to wireless technology, not all users are physically connected by hardwire any longer, but all networks require software that supports communications between the database and the users. The more users there are at any one time, the more powerful that communication needs to be so that data transmits quickly. Under the heading of networking fall telecommunication, videoconferencing, and interactive blog and wiki capability.
- **Server.** This is the "brain" of the system that serves information to connected computers. The server runs programs, stores data (files), and provides Internet connections. This may sound very straightforward, but it really understates the immense power required to support all of the demands on a server, especially with networking. When the server is down, users can't access the central database or the "brains" of the operation. The server may be supported by a Web host that manages the Internet traffic to the company's Web site, as well as manages those of many other companies.
- **Security.** This is the function that protects the database from unauthorized access and infection. Data encryption, firewalls, and intrusion detection are all software functions that are essential for

protecting the database. The risks increase exponentially with each user, mobile unit, and wireless and removable device that connects to the company's system. (See more about this in Chapter 18.)

- **Storage.** This is the warehouse function that must also provide user-friendly retrieval. Companies commonly underestimate the capacity of the infrastructure needed to handle all the running applications plus house a vast mass of information. That data can quickly consume the server's or processor's storage space, even with compression software, and although removable storage is an option, it can be very inconvenient. Tapping into a hosted or on-demand (online) server or "cloud" services can provide convenient and sizable storage.

A company's computer system is not just a "filing cabinet" that can easily be accessed; it must be interactive as well. Today's systems can be even more interactive with *virtual computing*, sometimes called *cloud computing*, that gives users remote access to data and documents through a Web browser. Services such as Google Docs, Dropbox, and YouSendIt provide storage as well as remote access for synchronizing and sharing files with computers or devices on which the respective software is installed. This also gives salespeople a link to the forms, promotional materials, and other data needed to do their jobs.

Software

One of the best ways to select hardware is to first consider the software that will be (or is being) used. The capacity, speed, and memory that are required for a hard drive or central processor are affected by demands of the various software applications that will be running. Although software can be custom designed, this is rarely cost-efficient, especially for a small organization. With the wide selection of commercially available software, that's not really necessary. It's also better not to take the chance that customized software could be friendly only to the designer or incompatible with other software the company uses.

Considerable money can be spent on what appear to be intriguing software programs that don't deliver as promised, are difficult to use, or don't get used at all once they're installed. Mistakes can be avoided by talking to other users of software being considered, getting professional advice (also helpful to evaluate compatibility with other software the company uses), and evaluating the technical support provided by the software manufacturer. How readily accessible and affordable is it?

In addition to an operating system, essential software for a real estate company includes:

- **Financial management.** The most obvious is the accounting function, which can be handled with spreadsheet, money management, or more sophisticated accounting software. Pairing that data with specific financial management or multifunction software can provide the analyses that help managers monitor and critique the company's operations.
- **Sales management.** This is the real estate-specific software that can monitor transaction activity, pending closings, and listings about to expire; track business by region, office, or salesperson; forecast cash flow for the coming months; and monitor the performance of salespeople at any given time. Real estate trends in the area can be monitored as well. (Some programs offer as many as 38 assessments of a company's operations.) All of this information is, then, readily available for a market analysis, too.
- **Word processing.** Word processing serves the obvious purpose of doing what typewriters once did but with the advantage of committing correspondence, reports, routinely used forms, promotional materials, and the like to the electronic database. Then they can be retrieved for reference, reuse, editing, or distribution. A word processing program is also an essential companion to a wide variety of other text-oriented software, like real estate contract programs, and is the program into which text documents downloaded from the Internet are saved.
- **Internet.** The basics include connectivity by whatever software the Internet service provider (ISP) requires and navigation, which can be achieved with a browser such as Internet Explorer that is commonly included in operating systems. Because Web sites are so vital to communication and marketing today, an essential part of a company's basic Internet capability is a Web site. A variety of software programs are available, though the services of a Web site professional may provide the most desirable site design and management, which

must also include site-visitor tracking, links with other sites, and frequent updates of site content.

- **Virus protection and firewalls.** Firewalls are barriers constructed by software programs around selected files or systems to protect against intrusion. Internet security (some of which resides in operating systems) and antivirus software are intended to protect the system from viruses and assorted other intrusions that can corrupt files or take over a system. With the prevalence of nefarious activity, multiple programs are desirable, the expectation being that at least one will be able to intercept an intrusion.
- **Utilities.** These are the system management programs that keep other software programs and certain aspects of the hardware working efficiently. Although some utility functions are part of the operating system, a separate utility program (such as Norton Utilities) has more features that can enhance the functioning of the operating system.

Software that is nice to have (considered essential in some companies) includes desktop publishing programs and real estate-related programs. Desktop publishing requires a slightly more skilled user than word processing programs but has powerful design, layout, and graphic capability, which is extremely desirable for in-house preparation of professional presentations, brochures, and newsletters. The company may provide sales-related software for salespeople and personal assistants, but because salespeople commonly have their own and an array of resources available to them online, companies are more inclined to use software to support the in-house management of transactions.

With any software the company installs comes the risk of *copyright infringement*. The purchaser of a copyrighted program (the company) is the only authorized user. While the program can reside in the company's system for in-house use, company personnel must be clearly prohibited from downloading those programs onto their personal computers. Pirating programs seems to be an offense that few take seriously, but that doesn't excuse the action, and an aggressive enforcer can create untold misery for all involved. Suitably direct company policies can minimize potential problems.

Hardware

The physical hardware decisions fall into place fairly easily after the software investigation. That's also when the users will be identified (by jobs the software supports) and where they are located. Decisions must also be made about the amount of hardware that will be available to the sales staff and the workstation connections that will be provided for personally owned hardware.

The professional systems adviser can help assemble the appropriate hardware system (central processing unit, monitors, keyboards, connections, and peripherals, such as printers and scanners) and design the layout. With wireless routers and remote desktops and laptops with wireless cards, the workstation layout can be much more flexible.

Connectivity also becomes a hardware issue. The number of company locations, the number of people at each location, and the capacity of the various Internet service providers (ISPs) will affect hardware and wiring requirements.

The choice of an Internet service is primarily a function of the cost (which is often different for businesses than for residential users) and efficiency of use. Different technologies have different system requirements, which also affect the speed of transmission. Another consideration is the frequency of downtime (inability to access the Internet) and navigating efficiency. Also, some ISPs do a better job than others at managing spam (unsolicited e-mails) and intrusions.

One final decision is what, if any, role an outsourced server will play in the system. The computing power of a server is fixed and can't grow or supply occasional bursts of power as needs arise. Upgrading to larger servers can be quite costly and impractical. One solution is to lease server space, which is especially suitable for a large company. An alternative is to use on-demand virtual servers, which are typically more appealing to small and midsized companies. Hosted hardware or grids supply supercomputing power to users on a pay-as-you-go basis, much like utility companies deliver electricity.

System Maintenance

Once a computer system is installed or upgraded, it has to be maintained. Software updates must be captured (if not automatically downloaded), full-system antivirus scans must be run (even when operations are scheduled to run automatically, hands-on attention is also required), and certain software utility functions must be run periodically to keep the central processor or server humming at peak efficiency.

Built-up clutter, fragmented files, registry issues, and other inefficiencies won't necessarily paralyze the system, but they can certainly slow down performance and consume valuable drive space. Although a utility program can continually run in the background and certain maintenance functions can be scheduled to perform automatically, some sweep, defrag, and other clean-up functions have to be manually initiated. (Think about who in the company is going to do this maintenance.)

Technical Support

Certainly, large companies can ill-afford to do business without an information technology (IT) department. Midsized and even small companies, though, are just as vulnerable to hardware failures, software breakdowns, and network snarls. More problems arise as more users are connected, especially at the hands of people who just happen to hit the wrong key. Today, many computer system problems originate from Internet intrusions, which can be quite challenging to overcome.

Even with technical support available from software and hardware companies, someone in-house must be savvy enough to communicate the problem and keystroke through solutions. If that someone has other jobs to do, valuable productive time is lost to the company's computer troubles, even if the problem is solved with minimal panic and frustration. But as good as technical support is at many technology companies, solutions often require a number of calls and can, in the process, create new problems. Bottom line—budget and pay for technical support. Every company needs a computer tech to call who will promptly respond.

Preserving the Database

As advantageous as it is to store all the company's data and documents on a computer, that database is vulnerable if there's a hardware or software failure. An essential part of managing the system is a routine plan for backing up or preserving data. In basic computer lingo, there's a difference between "back up" and "copy," which affects the way in which data can be used for future applications. Any preservation plan should be guided by a professional, who is most likely to be the person to troubleshoot a major meltdown anyway.

Data can be preserved on a variety of media, depending on the nature and amount of data involved. For specific files or relatively small amounts of data, USB flash drives or CDs should be adequate. Large systems are typically backed up on synchronized tapes or ghosted to secondary hard drives.

The risk is that a virus or other threat can be preserved (which defeats one of the purposes of the exercise), so any backup plan must include a vigilant antivirus plan. The important point is to institutionalize routine backup procedures (without simply printing more paper to file).

The next issue is what to do with the backup medium. The most secure protection against fire, natural disaster, and theft is to store the medium off-site. Secondary hard drives are the most efficient way to get a full system of data restored, but they reside in the central computer, which makes them vulnerable to on-site events. (Removable tape may be a desirable secondary backup.) Small media like pen drives and CDs can easily get misplaced (or pilfered), so the company needs trusted personnel to be in charge of securing backup media in a safe location.

Other Modes of Communicating

As important as an e-mail and Web site address are today, a business still needs a telephone (which is also a requirement of many real estate licensing laws). But that, too, has gone high-tech with automated answering and voice messaging systems. The stand-alone fax machine has also gone high-tech, now with virtual faxes that cycle through the company's computer system.

Voice messaging. The appeal of today's automated telephone systems is they require less human intervention. Calls are automatically answered and relayed directly to the recipient's mailbox, with no need for messages and phone numbers to be transcribed (or mistranscribed). The system can act as a central messaging center, which is an attractive feature for multi-office companies (especially where toll costs could deter callers), and also provides the opportunity to deliver promotional or informative outgoing messages.

The appeal of these systems for the workforce is that messages often eliminate the phone-tag cycle and allow the recipient to hear the exact message left by the caller. Voice mailboxes are secure (protecting confidential information) and are available 24 hours a day with remote access. Mailboxes can also be used for people to leave themselves messages, like to-do lists or reminders.

The public, on the other hand, is not so fond of these systems after encountering too many overly long phone trees and improperly designed menu options. Some systems do, indeed, try the patience of even the most patient callers, especially when no option suits the caller's purpose or permits a caller to speak to a human being. To overcome negative public relations, some companies have abandoned the automated answering feature (or shortened it) so that callers can actually speak with someone, who can then direct the call to the appropriate person or mailbox.

Another downside is that people in the workplace have learned how to dodge the system. Nothing is more frustrating for a manager than to watch someone ignore a ringing phone and let the call transfer to voice mail. That's also immensely aggravating (and potentially problematic) for the caller who has urgent business. People often are far too tempted to screen calls, and many are not particularly diligent about emptying their mailboxes or returning calls.

Facsimile machines and electronic fax. A facsimile machine has been as common as a telephone in business offices. If the alternative is postal mail, fax is certainly faster, easier, and cheaper, and when a printed document with a personal signature (like a contract) is essential, fax is a suitable medium.

The major downside is that fax machines operate in fixed locations, which may not necessarily be near the person who needs to receive the communiqué. This can be overcome by software and Internet services that send and receive faxed documents in electronic formats, transmitted by e-mail attachment or online server, or delivered to a stand-alone fax machine. Documents can also be stored just as any other electronic file would be.

Electronic faxes are paperless, which makes them easier to manage, and can be sent and received from any location where there's an Internet connection. If a paper document is needed, the faxed document can be printed on a stand-alone fax machine or computer printer. Internet fax services (which do involve a fee) provide the additional advantages of increased privacy and security as well as backup against lost documents.

A fax machine still costs money, though the purchase price is much more reasonable than it once was, and multifunction machines (combining telephone, fax modem, computer printer, and scanner) are an even better value. Good-quality paper is another expense, but the majority of the operating cost is the telephone line, especially for lengthy documents. Economies can be achieved with a basic, no-frills phone line. Computers with fax capability and efficient Internet connections can shorten transmission time.

Communicating with People Who Are Hearing Impaired

Today's technology opens many avenues for people who are deaf or hearing impaired. Text Telephones (TTs), formerly known as TDDs, are typewriter-like units that display conversation in text on a screen. A TT "talks" with another text telephone or a computer so that people can communicate with one another, regardless of auditory capacity.

This is an important tool for a real estate company. Under ADA, the company is required to provide accommodations so that people can access and partake of the company's services. Installing a TT in one or more of the company's offices or using other services the local phone company offers to serve people who are hearing impaired are alternatives that should be explored. The company must also be prepared to accommodate people throughout a transaction, typically with oral or sign language interpreters. Local organizations that service this population can provide valuable assistance.

Communicating with People Who Are Visually Impaired

Technology also provides numerous opportunities for people who are blind or have limited vision. Large- or raised-print publications can easily be produced on computers and photocopier machines. Real estate documents and other print material can be converted to audiocassettes or attached to e-mail documents for users who have audio-supported computer software. A local organization that services this population can provide additional advice. The bottom line is that a real estate company is required under ADA to provide accommodations for people with visual impairments.

As a practical matter, any person who's discovered that aging eyes don't cope with small-print documents anymore will appreciate a large-print version. A little extra time at the computer or copy machine to enlarge a document is just good business.

Multilingual Communications

A final, good-business comment, which could also have fair housing implications, is about communicating with people whose first language is not English. As the population becomes increasingly diverse, multilingual services become increasingly important. While Spanish language documents are more prevalent in this country than once was the case, more can be done to enhance multilingual communications. Multilingual members of the company staff, translators at a local college or university, and multilingual materials on the Internet are all resources to help a company serve diverse clientele.

■ FACILITIES MANAGEMENT

Keep it clean, keep it safe, keep it well maintained, and keep its costs under control—a very short, perhaps overly simplistic, way of saying what managing facilities is about. Without venturing into the full lesson on facilities management (which can be a professional specialty of its own), the point is to give a heads-up to the manager on site about some things that deserve a watchful eye.

Depending on company philosophy, the clean-safe-maintenance-cost exercises may have different priorities. But cost-containment should not mean that the work environment is uncomfortable, unpleasant, or unsafe. The Office of Health and Safety Administration (OSHA) has a number of things to say about the workplace environment, including the requirement for companies to display the OSHA poster in the workplace. Furthermore, just good common sense is good business, regardless of legal implications.

Security in the Office

A fact of life today is that no place is 100 percent secure from a determined intruder. But steps must be taken to protect the facilities, staff, and customers and clients. The company may not see an office as a warehouse of salable equipment or a convenient route through which a person can easily escape with that equipment. If a collection of keys to the company's listings (including the addresses!) is readily accessible to the staff, those keys also are readily accessible to anyone else. A professional security firm should be called on to conduct a security audit of the facilities.

Beginning with the exterior of the building, the exterior, the parking lot, and all entrances should be well-lighted. Shrubbery should be trimmed to eliminate hiding places. Windows should be double-paned and double-locked. Exterior doors should be metal or thick wood and have double-side-keyed deadbolt locks. Change the locks or alarm codes periodically to protect against lost keys and unauthorized entry. Don't overlook the roof to be sure that there are no hiding places or possible sites for entry.

Protect the listings. Code the addresses on keys and lock them in a secure location. Keep track of lockboxes so that you know the properties on which they are installed. Fortunately, today's lockboxes are less vulnerable to vandalism or unauthorized entry and typically have tracking systems with which to monitor entries. Nevertheless, keys, keypads, and combinations do fall into the hands of unauthorized people on occasion.

Establish security procedures to keep the staff out of harm's way. Use sign-out sheets and call-in systems so that the whereabouts of staff outside the office are known and a threatening encounter can be detected. Establish a code or warning system so that a person can summon help and alert others to a danger. Identify a secure location in the office where personnel can go, and plan an escape route so they can get out in case of a problem.

Salespeople can additionally protect themselves by guarding the amount of personal information they distribute on their Web and social media sites and in their promotional materials. An increasing number of companies are requiring personal identification from customers and clients before salespeople go into the field with them. (NAR has a program on personal safety that is very useful.)

Safety in the Office

Provide a safe environment for staff and the public. Their safety is not just a matter of legal liability but a practical consideration as well. Take steps to prevent accidents and prepare to respond to a fire or medical emergency.

- Program telephones with emergency numbers and be sure everyone knows how to use them.
- Install smoke detectors in all the appropriate places and be sure they are functioning properly. If the building has a sprinkler system, be sure it works properly as well.
- Purchase a first-aid kit and fire extinguishers, particularly for the workroom. Instruct everyone how to use these items so that people don't create more problems than they solve.
- Familiarize people with safety procedures. More injuries and loss of life occur when people ignore the alarms that were intended to protect them. Conduct fire and disaster drills, including for weather-related emergencies.

- Secure handrails and clear walks and stairways of obstacles.
- Make certain the electrical service is adequate to accommodate the computers and other office equipment and appliances.
- Familiarize yourself with the labor laws in your state to be sure you comply with any safety requirements.

CONCLUSION

With well-selected facilities that are suitably provisioned with the equipment and other systems a company needs to function efficiently, the organization has the physical tools for its trade. While all of this can be a significant part of a company's initial investment and continuing operating budget, the dollar is well spent when it enhances the company's image and the environment in which its people work. Because of the way people work today, the company's communications and information management systems are just as important (if not more so) as its physical plant.

DISCUSSION EXERCISES

Critique a real estate office with which you are familiar, considering its general location, its site, and its design or layout.

What communications and information systems do you consider to be essential for your business to run efficiently and effectively? Which are desirable and optional?

Outline the steps you would take to open a branch office.

What does your company do, or what provisions are in place, to aid customers and clients who have visual or hearing impairments, or are non-English speakers?

10

CHAPTER TEN

STRUCTURING THE FINANCES

How much money do you need to start a business? To keep it running?

What do you need to do to keep the company on a healthy financial track?

The two resources that companies depend on most are human and financial. Unless the company properly allocates its financial resources, none of the company's systems, processes, or people can accomplish what the company's plan says to do. In other words, the plan and the money have to be aligned.

The financial management people see themselves as the holders of the purse strings or the controllers of what a company does. Others think the financial management folks ought to be paving the way "green," facilitating (rather than controlling) the company's operations. But there's only so much money to go around. Alignment means putting the available money in the right places so the company can do the right things.

Business plans and financial plans go hand in hand. If a company intends to open a new office, upgrade its computer system, increase its promotion, or implement a more competitive sales commission plan, the company needs a financial plan to make these things happen, while also keeping existing systems and services operating. Financing and budgets are part of that financial planning.

■ THE FINANCIALS

The place to begin a discussion of finances is with an elementary guide to financial statements, commonly known as *the financials*. These statements provide a picture of an organization's fiscal condition, captured in a variety of ways, depending on the kind of statement.

Certainly, the principal owners and senior management must be able to interpret the statements, but even the lowest manager on the totem pole needs to be able to decipher reports. The company's financials also give business planners, lenders, investors, and potential buyers (as part of their due diligence) essential decision-making information.

The platform on which financials are prepared is known as *double entry* bookkeeping. This is a system of capturing *debits* and *credits*, each offsetting the other, to result in an equal balance. Considerable expertise (the accountant's) is required to properly categorize and interpret data in accordance with legal and generally acceptable accounting practices. Novice business owners and managers especially (though often the most experienced, too) can benefit from a professional's explanation of what these reports reveal about the organization's financial condition.

Balance Sheet

A balance sheet reports the organization's assets, liabilities, and owner equity and provides a snapshot of the organization's general financial position or condition as of the date it is prepared.

- Assets consist of what the company owns that exist as cash or can be converted to cash in less than one year. Depending on the nature of the organization's business and current holdings, entries are categorized as either current or fixed assets.
- Liabilities are obligations incurred during the normal course of doing business, including those to creditors. Tax obligations, employee

benefit and mandatory pension programs, and restricted funds are also entered as liabilities.

- Owner equity is the net worth of the business, the difference between assets and liabilities. This also includes net income and the equity financing provided by investors (as opposed to financing provided by creditors).

The entries on a balance sheet must balance. That is, total assets and total liabilities plus owner equity should be identical figures. An accountant can interpret the significance of the entries, though perhaps the most useful observations are gained by comparing balance sheets over several years' time, particularly the ratio of owner equity to liabilities. This is the number that owners or stockholders of the organization have the greatest personal stake in.

Income Statement

An income statement, sometimes known as an *income and expense* or *profit and loss* statement, is a picture of an organization's financial performance during a particular period of time. Twelve-month reports generally coincide with the company's operating calendar, stated as January 1 to December 31 or some other fiscal operating year. The income statement tells how the company got to the balance sheet.

The income side of the report reflects all of the revenue generated by the company in the ordinary course of doing business. The expense side reflects expenses incurred in generating that income. Each expense entry is charged against the income account that incurred the expense. A review of individual income and expense accounts reveals those that are most productive or incur the greatest expense. The total income over total expense is net income, commonly called (pretax) *profit*. If expense exceeds income, the bottom line shows a negative number.

Several accounting methods can be used to report income and expense. The *cash* method reports entries in the period they were paid. For instance, a sale in February that is collected in April is entered as *April* revenue. The *accrual* method reports entries in the period they occurred. That February sale would be entered as *February* revenue.

The accountant can best advise which method is most suitable for the company. Regardless of the method used, however, the same principle must be applied to both income and expense entries. Shifting accounting methods requires very studious decisions, rather than simply using whatever method makes the picture look better.

There are also various accounting methods to treat inventory, which real estate companies are unlikely to have. An accountant can explain those procedures, though, if they apply.

Income. Depending on the company's primary and ancillary services and accompanying fee structures, income to a real estate company is most likely derived from

- **Brokerage fees**—the commissions that are generated by the salespeople and those received from cooperating brokers and fees generated from a-la-carte menus of services. Any commissions generated by the broker/owner and other managerial personnel may be included as well (though to get a true picture of sales staff productivity, these amounts are not part of that analysis).
- **Additional service fees**—activities such as appraising or property management or fees for referrals generated by referring customers and clients to other brokerage companies or to other business units providing services like insurance, title or escrow, and mortgage lending.
- **Transaction fees**—administrative service fees collected from each transaction that are intended to offset a variety of internal operating costs associated with delivering real estate brokerage services. (However, see the discussion later in the chapter about RESPA's view of these fees.)

Expense. Operating expenses fall into two categories.

1. **Fixed expenses**—rent, dues and fees, salaries, taxes and license fees, insurance, and depreciation (funding for depreciation on equipment, buildings, and automobiles the company owns)
2. **Variable expenses**—advertising and promotion, utilities, equipment and supplies, and cost of sales

Cost of sales includes commissions paid to the salespeople and brokers cooperating in the transactions, overrides paid to the sales manager, and fees attributed to individual transactions, such as MLS, franchise, and referral or relocation fees. Cost of sales is variable expense because expenditures fluctuate with production volume; commission splits and the number of cooperating broker transactions; and referral, relocation, and franchise fees.

Cash Flow Statement

A cash flow statement reports the cash position of the organization. It focuses on the company's cash-generating operations, showing the cash balance plus cash generated (receipts) and how cash is used (disbursements).

Receipts and disbursements differ from revenue and expenses shown on other financials because the cash flow statement does not include accounts receivable and accounts payable—that is, they are still pending collection and payment.

Cash is the liquid asset that fuels a company's operations as opposed to assets shown on the balance sheet that would have to be traded or liquidated for cash. The greater the cash, the more agile a company can be. Many companies in today's business world operate on very lean cash positions (and are successful), so they must manage cash flow carefully.

Many business analysts consider the cash flow statement to be a company's most important financial statement because it shows how well the company's cash-producing activities perform and provides the most accurate picture of how well positioned the company is to withstand adversity or seize opportunities. Sizable cash balances provide the wherewithal for companies to grow without incurring debt. Cash also makes companies attractive takeover targets—that cash often being the lure more than other aspects of the company.

A cash flow statement also shows how the organization uses cash in its day-to-day operations. By analyzing cash receipts and cash disbursements over a period of time, management can assess how much liquid capital is required to meet monthly obligations, especially as cash flows at different rates each month. The cyclical nature of the real estate business and the time lag between signatures on the contracts and settlement makes that flow particularly erratic.

This analysis is then used to develop a *cash management plan*. The objective of that plan is to provision the company with the right amount of cash at the right time and make the best use of cash until it is needed to meet the company's obligations.

One part of that plan puts cash to work with collection policies that bring cash in quickly so it can earn interest and payment policies that maximize earnings before cash must be disbursed. Cash is generally allocated between interest-earning, liquid-asset accounts (i.e., money market accounts), and certificates of deposit with maturities that coincide with dates that cash must be disbursed. (Banking institutions often provide attractive cash management arrangements for businesses.) Large excesses of cash (especially if cash is being accumulated for a capital expenditure or growth initiative) are normally managed separately from the bill-paying money.

The other part of that plan provides a strategy for coping with significant cash deficits. This part of the plan may not be necessary, but if it is, methodical planning in advance is far more desirable than scrabbling for cash in a crisis mode. Cash requirements can be satisfied by liquidating assets or going outside the organization to borrow money or find investors. Each of these alternatives can take time to arrange, cost money, and have lingering consequences that have to be weighed (including possible legal ramifications).

■ FINANCIAL RESOURCES

Financing is an integral part of a company's financial structure rather than an isolated or short-term event, even for companies that are flush with cash. For a start-up company, financing *is* the financial structure, but any company relies to some degree on aid from outside resources, especially to grow. Those outside resources fall into one of two general categories.

1. **Debt financing**—loans
2. **Equity financing**—ownership interests

Planning and managing the use of outside resources is a critical part of financial management. Each of these resources has advantages and disadvantages as well as cost and timing issues. In this management effort, timing is everything. Too much money too soon unduly increases costs either in interest payments or premature, diluted ownership positions. Too little money too late unduly stresses operations and can result in missed business opportunities or less prudent decisions in the chase for money. That last-minute money may be readily available, but also at a greater cost.

Financial Projections

The key to the wise use of outside resources is wise forecasting. A diligent analysis of past and present operations (back to the company's financials), particularly money-flow patterns, provides a basis for projecting future need. Financial projections must also accommodate any new strategic initiatives that are outlined in the business plan.

Start-up companies have the added challenge that they have no history on which to base projections. New business owners can easily fall into the trap of underestimating the competition and the cost of doing business (though veteran business owners can be similarly afflicted). In addition to the obvious capital needed to put a business in place, companies need money to bridge what can be a wide gap between the first day of business and the time they break even—and the even longer time before they make solid profits.

Depending on how the company is structured and the affiliations and services needed to compete in the marketplace, the capital requirements of a real estate business will vary. Basic necessities, however, typically include:

- Legal fees (establish the business)
- Accounting fees (advice and to set up books)
- Telecommunications and computerization (equipment and installation)
- Initial fees for affiliations (MLS, franchise, etc.) and professional associations
- Business licenses and taxes
- Office space (buy or rent, remodeling)
- Office equipment (facsimile machines, duplicating equipment, desks, chairs, file cabinets, etc.)

- Office supplies
- Personnel (payroll and Social Security, workers' comp, unemployment, income tax withholding)
- Graphics (logo, signs, stationery)
- Promotion and advertising (initial entry into the marketplace)
- Signage (office and yard signs)

Depending on how the total cost of these items compares with the amount of money on hand plus that which can be gathered from other sources, additional expenditures could be considered. Or the company needs more cost-efficient ways to provide the basic necessities. Consider whether leasing versus purchasing items such as office space, telephone systems, or duplicating equipment is more feasible.

Start-up companies are most vulnerable when they lack the capital needed to operate until they break even. *Be conservative when estimating income and generous when estimating expenses*. Overestimate expenses by 10 percent to cover the miscellaneous and the unexpected. Although the math can overstate the capital required, it's better to apply for a larger loan (if a loan is required) than to try persuading a lender to advance more money after just a few months. A three-to-five-year span to the break-even point is a typical projection. In the meantime, companies have to withstand operating losses and may also have to make additional capital expenditures to be competitive.

Cash flow must also be factored into start-up capital requirements. A considerable amount of bill-paying cash goes out before an appreciable amount of cash flows in to minimize the drain on capital reserves. The first year is the most treacherous, though a company should expect to be totally capital-dependent for at least the first six months. That capital may very well be funded by the proprietor's personal credit cards, which adds to the personal risk of starting a business. It's a risk many people are willing to take, though, because nearly half of small start-ups are funded with personal credit.

Procuring Financing

The first step in procuring financing is to engage an attorney and an accountant and make them an integral part of the decision-making process. They are also good resources for networking with potential lenders or investors and making the necessary introductions. The Small Business Administration (*www.sba.gov*) is a valuable resource for estimating start-up costs, as well as for obtaining loans. The local branch of the Service Core of Retired Executives (SCORE) may also have expertise that can help work through some of these decisions as well.

The decision-making process consists of evaluating financial projections and determining the appropriateness of debt or equity financing. One or the other is typically more desirable, depending on the purpose for which financing is needed, the amount, the urgency and duration of the need, tax consequences, the relationship the company's owners desire to have with others, and the creditworthiness of the company. All of these considerations have legal as well as financial implications.

Equity financing gives investors the opportunity to be part of an enterprise they feel has attractive growth or earnings potential instead of sitting on the sidelines simply as note-holders. Generally, equity financing is desirable for capital expansion or improvements rather than for covering temporary cash-flow requirements. Because equity financing involves restructuring ownership, and possibly business operations (if the investors are going to have an active role in the organization), these are more complicated and time-consuming ventures to arrange and aren't suitable for quick cash.

Debt financing is preferable when the company's principals don't want to relinquish any ownership position, and it provides tax-deductible interest payments (a feature the accountant may advise is preferable). Depending on the size and quality of the company's assets and its credit standing, debt financing is generally more versatile, serving both long-term and short-term needs, and may also provide an open line of credit if the company is a worthy risk. Especially when dealing with a lender with whom the company has an established relationship, financing can often be arranged relatively quickly if time is a consideration.

Financing Portfolio

Regardless of the chosen resource, the company has to "package a worthy pitch," that is, a financing portfolio. This is especially true for the start-up company, which has to convince a lender or an investor that a business venture that doesn't yet exist, has no assets (collateral) and no proven track record, is a worthy risk. Early-stage companies face similar challenges because they are still trying to prove themselves as viable enterprises. That said, however, it's usually easier for these companies to arrange debt rather than equity financing.

Unless debt financing can be arranged privately (family, friends, or business associates, with debt perhaps being convertible to stock at some point), the logical place to go is an institutional lender. Banks and the Small Business Administration are good sources, as are government incentive programs for emerging companies and, if applicable, programs for minority-owned businesses.

The first barrier is the office door of the bank officer, who is typically subjected to numerous business schemes and entrepreneurial ideas that are proposed as can't-fail ventures. That barrier is more difficult to penetrate if the proposing business owner has no established professional reputation or personal banking relationship with the institution. The known entity is more likely to get noticed and if that connection does not exist, the introduction by other business owners (or the company's attorney or accountant) is often the key to opening that door.

A company that has a previously established relationship with the lender and is seeking a relatively small sum of money may be asked to simply complete a loan application that the lender can then process through a computer scoring system to evaluate the request.

Otherwise, a fairly comprehensive financing portfolio will be required so the request can be scrutinized in detail and considered by a lending committee or potential investors. The portfolio should be easy to read, get to the point, and stand out on the pile of all the other applications on the lender's desk. It begins with an introduction of the company and the request in a three-paragraph summary of the merits of the proposal. The balance of the portfolio substantiates the request by

- educating the potential lender or investor about the business's industry and the marketplace;
- demonstrating the industry and business management expertise of the company's principals and that they are character worthy (personal résumés and a list of references are typically part of this);

- describing the company's business and its operations, including a business plan, the financial statements, and budgets; and
- demonstrating a sound plan for using and repaying the money that is requested.

That substantiation must be captured in quantifiable terms, the hard facts that support assumptions behind the business plan. Puffery and generalities won't get serious consideration. Lenders and investors want evidence that there's a problem to solve in the marketplace and a candid assessment of the company's skills and abilities and the company's competition. Surprisingly, competition can also demonstrate that others think endeavor is worthwhile. Financial appeals need to demonstrate how the company will address the real world challenges of being in business.

Ultimately, lenders and investors want to be able to assess their exposure or risk in the venture. They are rarely willing to bankroll a venture in which their risk is greater than the company's (or its principals') risk. This means that the company (or its principals, if they must personally guarantee the loan) must be willing to place a significant amount of capital or collateral on the line. For the principals, this means risking personal assets, which can have significantly more financial implications than simply funding their business.

Once the company gets the money, the relationship it maintains with the lender is as important as the one that got it the money. In a sense, the lender becomes a partner. Good communication with that stakeholder affects future borrowing power but also becomes a valuable safety net in the event all does not go as the company planned.

Business owners are far too inclined to prematurely boast the good news about the company and drag their feet with the bad, but it's far better to tell the tales in reverse. Lenders respect a heads-up warning (that may eventually prove to be a nonevent) and a realistic assessment of the value of a company's accomplishments.

■ GENERAL OPERATING BUDGET

A general operating budget is an essential part of a company's financial structure. A budget serves the same purpose as a business plan—it provides a road map. In this case, it's a map of how the company intends to allocate its financial resources in the context of projected income and expenses (normally for a one-year timeframe) to support the company's business plan. *Projected* is the operative word. These are forecasts or targets that are intended to keep the organization on track.

Budgets are more or less useful, depending on how realistic the projections are. They need to be based on quantifiable evidence and sound analysis of internal and external factors that affect income and cost of operations. Overly ambitious revenue or overly conservative expense estimates may make the profit forecast look good, but they don't provide the key indicators needed to critically assess the financial health of the organization and make good decisions.

A balanced budget (one in which expenses don't exceed revenue) intends to help a company live within its means. If a sizable expenditure is required to accomplish a goal, the company has to find offsetting revenue to make this happen. The alternative is to construct a deficit budget, which says that the company expects to spend more than it makes.

A deficit can be tolerated on occasion if an excessive expenditure has high probability of significantly enhancing revenue in coming years. But a company can't tolerate many years of deficit spending before reserves have been depleted or debt far exceeds the value of the business.

A general operating budget resembles an income statement to the extent that the line items are similar. (See Figure 10.1.) This helps the company measure actual income and expense entries against those that are budgeted. Companies commonly also prepare a variety of more specific budgets to guide such things as departmental, office, or functional activities.

Gross Income

The data gathered during the situational analysis can serve as the basis for developing realistic revenue projections. These targets may also have been benchmarked in the company's business plan. For budgeting purposes, the exercise is simply one of mathematically converting services to revenue.

FIGURE 10.1
Income and Operating Expense Budget

GROSS INCOME		
Commissions on in-house sales	$__________	
Commission received from cooperating transactions	$__________	
Referral fees	$__________	
Other fees for service	$__________	
Total Gross Income		$__________
GENERAL OPERATING EXPENSES		
Commissions paid to salespeople	$__________	
Commissions paid to cooperating brokers	$__________	
Overrides paid to managers	$__________	
Relocation and referral fees	$__________	
MLS fees	$__________	
Franchise fees	$__________	
Other	$__________	
Total Cost of Sales		$__________
Marketing and advertising consultant	$__________	
Classified advertising	$__________	
Institutional advertising	$__________	
Direct mail	$__________	
Brochures	$__________	
Television/radio	$__________	
Signs	$__________	
Telephone directories	$__________	
Other	$__________	
Total Marketing and Advertising		$__________
Rent	$__________	
Utilities	$__________	
Janitorial services	$__________	
Trash/recycling removal	$__________	
Other	$__________	
Total Occupancy		$__________

FIGURE 10.1
Income and Operating Expense Budget (Cont.)

Equipment maintenance/supplies	$__________	
Office supplies	$__________	
Postage and overnight delivery	$__________	
Packaging and shipping	$__________	
Bulk mail permits	$__________	
Printing	$__________	
Lockboxes	$__________	
Kitchen/beverage	$__________	
Other	$__________	
Total Equipment and Supplies		$__________
Professional dues	$__________	
Membership fees	$__________	
Subscriptions	$__________	
Total Dues and Publications		$__________
Accounting services	$__________	
Legal services	$__________	
Computer consultant	$__________	
Communications services	$__________	
Telephone	$__________	
Paging services	$__________	
Computer information networks	$__________	
Insurance	$__________	
Comprehensive business policy	$__________	
Workers' compensation	$__________	
Errors and omissions	$__________	
Credit bureau	$__________	
Total Services and Fees		$__________
Managerial salaries	$__________	
Secretarial and clerical salaries	$__________	
Other	$__________	
Fringe benefits	$__________	
Total Salaries		$__________

FIGURE 10.1
Income and Operating Expense Budget (Cont.)

Real estate licenses	$__________	
Business licenses	$__________	
Taxes	$__________	
Income taxes	$__________	
Social Security	$__________	
Unemployment	$__________	
Other	$__________	
Total Taxes and Licenses		$__________
Awards	$__________	
Incentive programs and contests	$__________	
Education	$__________	
Conferences and conventions	$__________	
Travel and entertainment	$__________	
Auto expenses	$__________	
Petty cash	$__________	
Other	$__________	
Total Miscellaneous		$__________
Interest on loans	$__________	
Bank account charges	$__________	
Total Bank Charges		$__________
Total Operating Expenses		$__________
NET INCOME		
Total Gross Income	$__________	
Less Total Operating Expenses	$__________	
NET INCOME		$__________

Transaction revenue can be determined by first multiplying the average sale price of a property by the number of transactions expected. The result is gross sales volume. Then, calculate the amount of income that can be expected from the gross sales.

Price-setting decisions. Before making this final calculation, however, the company must decide how to charge for its services. Companies that manufacture goods have more hard costs (raw material, manufacturing, packaging, distribution, labor) on which to base pricing decisions than service businesses do. The challenge for service businesses is to translate cost and value into price. Service providers and consumers often have disparate views of value, especially when consumers expect to receive more services for the price than the provider intends to deliver.

While any pricing decision affects the income statement, a motive to maximize revenue over time or maximize the number of unit sales to reduce unit cost will not have the desired effect if the price upsets other variables. In other words, you can't just put a bigger price tag on services and expect the bottom line to turn out better.

Pricing decisions involve determining what the market will bear and at what point a price increase will reduce volume or revenue. This essentially pushes the envelope on price, pushing price to its maximum level before it has a negative effect. Other variables include competitive factors, the type of consumer (some being exceedingly price-and-value- or bargain-conscious and others being boutique or concierge clientele), the power of company brand name or image, and the perceived value of its services' benefits. Unless all of these are considered, any price could have a self-defeating effect.

The practice of charging transaction or administrative fees offers several lessons about pricing. The companies that blazed the trail proved that the market (at least, in some parts of the country) would bear the price. This is also an example of segmented price—the basic price of the service remains the same while a separate price is added. All were argued by the companies as necessary charges to cover expenses, especially with shrinking profit margins. Other companies followed suit and then the market was further tested when companies started increasing the fees.

There's nothing wrong with segmented pricing per se, as long as the total price is represented as a blended commission (the negotiated amount of commission plus a flat fee) and is fully disclosed.

But there *is* a problem under the Real Estate Settlement Procedures Act (RESPA) with separate, add-on fees for services that are provided as part of the transaction anyway. Regardless of what the add-on fees are called (sometimes known as "ABC" fees for administrative brokerage commission), they do not provide a demonstrable benefit to the consumer or an additional real estate settlement service as required by RESPA. (*Busby v. JRHBW Realty, Inc. d/b/a Realty South* in the U.S. District Court for the Northern District of Alabama.) An even safer way to defray the cost of overhead is to charge a higher rate of commission.

Another commission versus fee-for-service decision involves a-la-carte menus of services. Companies that offer these options face another pricing decision—what fees are suitable for each service or should attractive prices be offered for "packages" of services. (*Real Estate, a la Carte*, by Julie Garton-Good, provides some helpful insight.) The companies that blaze the trail have the additional challenge of forecasting income without a track record or historical data as a guide.

There are also the alternatives of charging either hourly or contingency fees, similar to the way other professionals charge for their services. An hourly charge could be capped at some amount for a month's service. A contingency fee could be collected when an agency agreement is signed, and a performance clause could provide for the return of the initial fee if the company is unable to perform the stated service within a certain time period. The company could also include reimbursement for expenses in either of these cases.

Price must be based on sound business rationale, not based on the logic that that's what everyone else charges. Pricing decisions must take into account legal restrictions. A company cannot afford to ignore the antitrust laws or state licensing laws, such as those that prohibit advance fees or reimbursement for expenses. (See Chapter 17 for an additional discussion about pricing strategies and maximizing income.)

Operating Expenses

The gross income forecast is next offset with a forecast of operating expenses. Fixed expenses (rent, salaries, insurance, and the like) are easier to forecast because these are already known. Variable expenses are more difficult and also require the most management to control. The caveat in forecasting variable expenses is that too often managers pad their expenses so they look like heroes when they come in under budget. Obviously, this does as much harm to the budget process as being overly conservative.

Because each company's business plan is different, operating expenses will reflect expenditures needed to implement the plan. Although the way these expenses are categorized may differ, depending on the accountant's design of the company's statements or the computer software program used, typical expenses that must be budgeted fall into several general categories.

Cost of sales, or transaction expense. This category of expenses includes direct transaction or service costs (commissions, referral and franchise fees, and the like) and expenditures made to assist a transaction to settlement, such as minor repairs or the purchase of an appliance. For the typical real estate company, this category of expense is one of its largest.

Once was the day when real estate companies used calculations of company dollar to determine the amount of money available for operational expenses. *Company dollar* is the amount of gross revenue that remains after cost of sales has been deducted. Today, companies more commonly use the format of an income statement and enter these costs as operating expenses because, in fact, that's what they are.

Marketing and advertising expense. These include costs to develop marketing and advertising strategies and design the materials. Costs also include the placement or distribution of classified, institutional, listing, and recruiting advertising and signs (for sale, sold, and open house); media and/or online advertising; and directory listings. Web site design and maintenance may either be categorized as marketing or communications expense.

Occupancy. These are the "housing costs," which include rent, utilities, janitorial services, and trash/recycling removal. Depending on the terms of the lease, some of these expenses may be included in the rent. If the company owns its office building, mortgage payments, even though not considered a pure expense, must be budgeted.

Equipment and supplies. These include the rental or maintenance of, as well as the purchase of supplies for, equipment such as computers, duplicating equipment, fax machines, and audiovisual aids. This category also includes postage (including overnight delivery) and packaging, shipping, bulk-mail permits, printing, office supplies, lockboxes, and kitchen and restroom supplies.

Dues and publications. These include the broker's and the company's dues in professional and industry organizations, and MLS and franchise fees; subscriptions for directories, newspapers, and magazines; and other dues for organizations such as the credit bureau and chamber of commerce.

Service fees. These expenses include accounting and bookkeeping services, various insurance policies (see discussion about insurance in Chapter 18), legal services, credit reports, computer consultant, and communications services, including basic, local and long-distance telephone service, fax and computer lines, and Internet services.

Salaries. These are salaries for the broker (unless the broker doesn't take one), managers, secretarial and clerical personnel, and other employees, including the training director, relocation director, and marketing director. Also included are employee-related costs, such as medical and dental insurance and other fringe benefits.

Taxes and licenses. This includes real estate licenses for the broker and the company, business licenses, and taxes, including payroll taxes (income taxes, Social Security, and unemployment taxes).

Miscellaneous expenses. Although these can be categorized in a variety of ways on an expense statement, the items include awards, incentives and contests, education, conferences and conventions, travel and entertainment, auto expenses, and petty cash.

Bank charges. This includes payments on debt and service charges on bank accounts and credit card services.

Repairs and replacements. These include the repair and replacement of equipment the company owns, which are expenses that must be budgeted for even though, in strict accounting terms, they are asset expenditures that are depreciated.

Reserve for contingencies. Companies need to plan for contingencies. The most fiscally sound way to do this is to allocate a certain amount of anticipated revenue to the company's reserve account. In effect, this is a savings plan that causes the company to set aside reserves for unexpected expenses or for capturing opportunities that present themselves. It's tempting to eliminate this line, particularly because it reduces anticipated net income (which means the company doesn't look as profitable), but prudent financial management suggests this is an important safety net.

Net Income

After projecting the income and deducting the anticipated expenses, the difference is the anticipated net income (projected profit) for the year. This can be a sobering moment if there's no profit or, worse, a deficit. The process of developing a budget is as important as the final product because it forces management to consider and reconsider its projections on both the gross income and expense side of the ledger and find the most cost-effective ways to allocate the company's resources (personnel).

The outcome of budget discussions may be a change in company policy. It might be that the salespeople will have to share advertising expenses, or franchise or MLS fees. They may also have to pay for the use of the copier, office supplies, promotional brochures, postage, or fax. Any of these options could improve budget projections and the way the company manages its financial resources, but they could have a negative effect on the company's human resources.

Unless the company has a 100 percent commission structure and assesses a desk charge, the company could find that its ability to attract and retain sales talent is jeopardized. Salespeople resent being "nickel-and-dimed," especially if carried to extremes with charges for each envelope, cup of coffee, or form the secretary prepares. Although it's common in most areas for salespeople to share in some operating expenses, the salespeople will go elsewhere to work if a company's compensation and expense structure is seriously out of line with the competition.

Profit Centers

Certain aspects of the general operating budget can be budgeted in greater detail. Similar to the way planning is done (the business plan for the entire organization being then broken down into more detailed plans at lower levels in the organization), each work unit (department or sales office) develops its own detailed budget.

When companies designate these work units as **profit centers**, this means that each unit is charged with the responsibility for generating the income it needs to cover its costs of operations and make a profit for the company as a whole. The budget process in this case generally begins with the work unit being charged with producing a certain amount of profit. The work unit then embarks on a budget process to figure out how much income and expense to project to reach that profit goal.

Variable Expense Budgets

A general operating budget cites categories of expenses that are allocated for specific purposes. To guide the use of these funds, variable expense budgets are needed to identify individual expenditures within those categories. These more specific budgets are particularly helpful for monitoring expenditures throughout the year.

For example, an amount designated for marketing and advertising is broken down into various marketing and advertising activities. It's not uncommon in large companies to delegate this budgeting responsibility to the marketing director, who then becomes responsible for deciding the best way to use the funds. Once the budget is formed, the manager also becomes responsible for keeping these expenses in line with the budget.

Monthly Operating Budgets

Monthly operating budgets are simply monthly benchmarks, typically one-twelfth of the year's projections for each budgeted line item. Most computer software programs can trigger these computations.

These numbers are useful for comparing the *actual* income and expense figures with the *budget* numbers to monitor performance throughout the year. The actuals may be ahead on certain lines and behind on others, particularly because of monthly variations, but next month the numbers may shift. The most important things to look at are the bottom line and income and expenses that appear to be significantly lagging or exceeding projections.

It's best not to change the budget during the year. While that might make management feel better, that doesn't change the status of the organization. Any expenses that seem to be getting out of control after three months should be evaluated (some may be seasonal), and damage-control measures should be planned. That's not to say that the measures have to be implemented, but at least there's a battle plan if expenses significantly exceed income.

PRUDENT PROCEDURES

A company's financial statements are presumed to portray an accurate picture of a company's financial condition, but that picture is only as truthful as the financial database from which those statements are generated. That database includes general ledgers, income and expense ledgers, accounts payable and accounts receivable ledgers, payroll and commission records, and trust and escrow account ledgers. Generally acceptable accounting principles establish the standards or proper methodology for setting up the various ledgers, collecting, posting, maintaining, and verifying data and conducting audits.

Today's bookkeeping and accounting functions are typically supported with computer software, but manpower is still required to compile and input the financial data and maintain the records. Software can eliminate some errors, but the ledgers are still only as accurate as people make them. Even the most meticulous bookkeepers make mistakes on occasion, though systems of checks-and-balances in accounting practices can identify those errors so corrections can be made.

The most egregious errors are caused by gross negligence and nefarious schemes. Senior management or the sole owner is ultimately accountable for the truthfulness and accuracy of the company's financial records, which means being accountable for every person and step involved in the recordkeeping process.

The obvious standard for performance is zero tolerance for mishandling the company's money and financial records, which includes senior management as well. The scandals of "cooked books" and loan fraud are most often orchestrated at the senior level of the organization. But misappropriation of funds can be orchestrated at any level of an organization.

Trust or Escrow Accounts

The principal broker in a real estate company has the added responsibility of handling other people's money. Their funds must be scrupulously protected and accounted for, not just because that's good business but because that's the law—the real estate licensing law.

Specific procedures vary from state to state, but the commonality is the broker must maintain separate trust or escrow accounts and ensure that entrusted funds are not commingled with the company's general operating funds.

Although trust or escrow accounts should be set up and managed in accord with generally accepted accounting principles, real estate licensing laws typically spell out certain procedures for handling deposits and withdrawals along with information relating to a transaction that must be posted with each deposit. Some states' laws are quite specific about the manner in which bank statements for escrow accounts are reconciled. Evidence of the company's compliance with all of a state's trust or escrow account regulations must be available for inspection if requested by a regulatory agency. (See Figure 10.2 for a sample trust/escrow ledger.)

FIGURE 10.2
Trust/Escrow Ledger

TRUST/ESCROW LEDGER

Street Address	Town	County	State	Zip Code	❑ Sale ❑ Rental

Seller/Landlord	Purchaser/Tenant
Name ______	Name ______
Address______	Address______
City ______ State ______ Zip______	City ______ State ______ Zip______
Telephone (Home) ______ (Work) ______	Telephone (Home) ______ (Work) ______

Miscellaneous Comments

Date	Received from/on Behalf of or Paid to	Amount Received	Received By	Check No.	Amount Paid	Balance

The internal processes a company establishes to handle escrow money, security deposits, rent checks, and other transaction-related funds are critical to the company's compliance with licensing laws. Funds must be accounted for from the time they are received (normally by the salesperson) to the time they are deposited and then disbursed. The longer the chain of events and the more people who handle a check before it is finally deposited, the greater the likelihood a check will stray or miss a deposit deadline. The same is true for the chain of events for withdrawal and disbursement.

A desirable solution is a transmittal form that accompanies the funds, which includes a sign-off and date each step of the way. Only certain people should be authorized to participate in that chain of events (which may also be prescribed by licensing law).

Security

Protect the money and the money data. This simple statement says much about the systems and procedures a company needs to ensure that the company's assets and its records are secure. Not only does this speak volumes about the need to protect financial data files with encryption, firewalls, and passwords, but it also raises a host of other security issues.

One of the best first lines of defense is to limit the number of people who have access to financial data and money. Senior management should be the only authorized personnel, in addition to bookkeeping and accounting staff. Certainly, the object is to protect sensitive information, but highly-centralized control also prevents tampering with the data by unauthorized persons. Because software systems track entry and use of the data, errant behavior (even by authorized persons) can be readily detected and those responsible can be held accountable.

Money is normally secured with internal systems of checks and balances. Selective access to checkbooks, inventories of company assets (including equipment and serial numbers), and records management procedures are essential safeguards against misappropriation, internal theft, or embezzlement. A recent report by the Association of Certified Fraud Examiners found that embezzlement is on the rise and is a particular problem for small companies, accounting for about 46 percent of all workplace fraud.

Best practices that protect against workplace fraud or embezzlement (which auditors commonly look for when they conduct their reviews) include:

- Separating the accounts receivable function from the accounts payable function so that unauthorized money can't be hidden with offsetting entries.
- Authorizing only certain individuals to approve disbursements and establishing a document trail to hold them accountable. Electronic disbursements are most vulnerable without sufficient safeguards.
- Requiring that two people handle payroll—one to write the checks and one to distribute them. This may sound inefficient, but the easiest way for someone to skim money is by writing and pocketing a check. An option is to outsource the payroll function. No one handling payroll should be authorized to approve pay rates.
- Requiring that checks in excess of a certain amount be approved by the owner of the company or a designated senior manager. Companies can also require dual signatures on checks. The logistics can be a problem, but this can be overcome with sufficient lead time so that checks can be disbursed timely. Under no circumstances should dual-signature checks sit in a checkbook pre-signed by one of the parties.
- Reconciling all bank statements monthly so that any discrepancies can be tracked down quickly. Most theft occurs over a period of time, so the sooner errant funds are detected the less the company loses.

Finally, zero tolerance for mishandling funds must be supported with specific termination policies for people who do.

■ CONCLUSION

Structuring a company's finances is a function of aligning its resources in the most cost-efficient ways to accomplish the company's business plan. Essentially, this means putting the right amount of money in the right place at the right time. This is a multifunction project that involves diligent study of the company's financials, forecasting need, and building in the proper safeguards to ensure that the financial resources are used wisely.

Budgets are one of the most useful tools for keeping a tight rein on the organization's finances. All of this is an information function that rises or falls on the vigilance of management, as it monitors the financial health of the organization and takes the necessary steps to maximize resources and minimize expense.

■ DISCUSSION EXERCISES

Obtain a copy of a company's financials or an annual stockholder report and discuss what you learn from that information.

What issues relating to the marketplace and your organization would affect the development of a general operating budget for your company or a budget for your office or department?

Discuss the financial management procedures that are required by your state's license law, particularly those that address the management of an escrow or trust account.

What effect have cost-containment or cost-sharing arrangements had on your sales staff (recruitment or retention)? On buyers? On sellers?

11

CHAPTER ELEVEN

BUSINESS POLICIES AND PROCEDURES

Do business organizations, in general, suffer from a lack of ethics, or a lack of trust? Is your company trustworthy?

Is real estate a profession or a business?

Returning to the game analogy that's been used before, people need to know the rules of the game so they know how to execute the plays. In a business organization, people need to know the what and the why of the company policies and the how, when, and who of the procedures.

A company's "rulebook" is really a book of behavior that is grounded in the company's philosophy of doing business. That philosophy is established by the company's owner(s) or senior managers, which means that the company's rules of fair play and ethics reflect the values of its leaders (see Chapter 2). Admirable leaders foster admirable institutions. The opposite is also true.

Recall that we are willing to align with people we trust. The same is true about the institutions they lead. The company's rules have to demonstrate that this is a company people can trust—a company that is concerned about the welfare of others and delivers on its promises to the people who work for it and to the public with whom it does business. The most trusted companies deal from a position of strength.

However, all the right words about benevolence, commitments, and even ethical behaviors won't cure the lack of trust people have in dysfunctional organizations. We create function with policies and procedures to ensure that the company can deliver on the words.

Policies and procedures evolve as much from practice as from written rule. But regardless of how they originate, policies and procedures need to be committed to in writing. This prevents misunderstandings, provides consistency (which is extremely important when certain matters of law are involved), and minimizes the amount of time managers devote to directing processes, solving problems, and resolving controversy. People can essentially govern themselves in most situations. The company's written rules are generally provided in several publications.

- A policy and procedures manual—the general operations manual that spells out the rules and processes that govern all of the company's operations
- A personnel procedures manual—the human resource "bible" for managers that directs internal procedures governing employment and employee relations (this manual is meant for managers, not for employees)
- An employee handbook—the general circulation document for everyone who works for the company that tells people the day-to-day rules of conduct

Similar to the rulebook in a game, the company's rules must also provide sanctions for the offenders. In other words, the rules must have teeth so that people take them seriously and know there are consequences for digressions.

Several rules about making rules:

- Policies and procedures must help the organization work efficiently, not bog it down with cumbersome processes. Although the principal owner(s) and senior managers are primarily responsible for developing the rules, the managers who are most familiar with operations that are affected by certain policies or procedures need to be part of the development process as well. They know when rules are (and aren't) necessary and how best to design them.

- Policies and procedures manuals, personnel procedure manuals, and employee handbooks are all individualized documents. While there are many resources (including on the Internet) to help develop these manuals, the actual substance must support the culture and organizational systems and processes of the individual company. These aren't documents that one pirates and then just changes the company name on the pages.
- People need to know what the rules are. The company has to protect against the "I didn't know that" claims by delivering copies of handbooks and manuals to each person and obtaining written acknowledgment of their receipt. This is one time that paper is preferable over digital formats. However, the documents can live in the company's database for reference.
- All policies and procedures must withstand legal scrutiny. As necessary as the rules are for creating order, they can create considerable disorder if they violate the law or cause litigation. The company attorney must be involved in developing policies and procedures.
- Rules, once adopted, must be followed. Herein lies another legal pitfall. In the event of litigation, both the rules and the actual conduct are scrutinized. Despite all the written words, the organization is defenseless if the behavior is not consistent with those words. As a practical matter, there's little point in developing policies and procedures and then ignoring them.
- Policies and procedures must be revised periodically to support changes in the law, the industry, and the organization; and to eliminate outdated or conflicting rules. Loose-leaf binders are most satisfactory so that only individual pages (including dates of revisions) can be replaced. Electronic documents are easily revised, but revisions can be overlooked unless people are properly informed of the changes.
- Finally, the project of developing rules for the organization's game is not as overwhelming as it may sound. Certain policies and proce-

dures are already in practice and just need to be committed to writing. The things that management spends most of its time directing or resolving are prime candidates to be addressed in the organization's manuals as well.

■ BUSINESS ETHICS

A code of conduct is one of the most fundamental sets of "rules." The code sets forth the company's value system and the right or morally correct way for it to do business—in other words, the company's ethics.

Ethics involves morality and a set of beliefs that guides actions and defines behavior as good or bad, right or wrong, or morally approved or disapproved. Various groups and cultures as well as individuals develop their own definitions, and consequently, their own beliefs about what is right, wrong, good, bad, and so forth. Business organizations form sets of beliefs or creeds as well.

Although there is no one universal value system, that doesn't mean that different sets of values govern our personal lives and another one governs business. Peter Drucker, in his book *Management: Tasks, Responsibilities, Practices*, argues that there is no such thing as separate ethics for business. One ethical standard must govern all areas of our lives. *There is not a different standard of right for making money.*

The fundamental ethical principle of professional conduct is "Above all, do no harm."

The Heart of Ethics

Those words are short and simple, but the practice often adds the "as long as..." qualifier, generally one that relates to making money or maximizing profit. Companies make statements about ideals and social responsibility, which are good for marketing or image-building, but are constantly challenged to fulfill those commitments when money or power is involved.

Why is achieving one standard, as Peter Drucker espouses, so difficult? Why is it that Wall Street is rocked by scandals, students cheat on college exams, or government officials are forced to resign in disgrace?

Some people will say, "Don't these people know any better?" Others might say, "I'd do the same thing they did," "I'll not likely get caught," or "They must have had a good reason." Not everyone sees behavior the same way, so it's no wonder companies struggle to get everyone on the same page.

The cause goes back to the lessons we learn about the root of people's value systems (past experiences, family upbringing, cultural influences, traditions, etc.) and the principles that guide morality and, therefore, guide behavior.

Because everyone doesn't come out of the "same mold," the challenge is to bring people with divergent value systems together. Society does this with rules. These rules fall into two general categories—*laws*, which are the rules established by government (including consequences for violators), and *ethics*, which are driven by morality, values, and principles of individuals in the group as well as the group as a whole. Behavior can then be described as legal or illegal, ethical or unethical. Because some laws may appear to be unethical, ethics may impose a higher standard for conduct.

Management in an organization establishes value systems, which can range from moral, social, and aesthetic values to economic, legal, and political values. The company's value system forms the culture of the organization and becomes the way a company does business. Michael O'Connor and Ken Blanchard, authors of *Managing by Values*, contend that values are extraordinarily powerful forces in shaping an organization and dictating business practices.

A real estate company must live within the framework of an ever-expanding body of law that intends to protect consumers. While those laws tell licensees what is expected of them in a legal context, a company also needs to articulate the value system and principles that govern its business practices so the workers understand what the company expects of them.

That system forms the basis for the company's code of ethics. Committing a code to writing accomplishes the telling part, but equally important is enforcement so that people actually practice what the company preaches.

Code of Ethics

The mention of a code of ethics in the real estate industry brings to mind the codes that are established by the industry's professional organizations, such as the National Association of REALTORS®. While these codes serve a useful purpose for the industry (though some would argue that they are not as effective as they ought to be), industry codes do not supplant the need for an individual company to establish its own code of ethics as well.

A code of ethics reflects the company's business philosophy and the value principles on which that philosophy is based. If the philosophy is similar to that of NAR, the basis is the Golden Rule—"Do unto others as you would have others do unto you." Behavior is guided by the answer to "How would I want someone to act toward me?"

A company's code of ethics says that these are the principles we live by. Generally, these statements cover the company's relationships with its consumers and others in the business community (including competitors) as well as internal relationships between boss and subordinate and among peers. Some statements are aspirational and others address specific practices along with standards by which they are measured to guide conduct during the ordinary course of doing business. In a real estate company, these usually relate to the way the company delivers its services.

If the company subscribes to an industry code of ethics, then the company's code should support, rather than conflict with, the practices the industry code prescribes. Of course, the company can always impose higher standards of conduct for its organization as well.

Institutionalizing Ethics

Institutionalizing ethics means integrating ethics throughout the organization.

1. Clearly state the ethical conduct that is expected.
2. Establish systems within the organization to ensure that the behavior is consistent with the words.
3. Provide penalties for people who deviate from the code of ethics.

In other words, once the company adopts a code of ethics, the organization must be committed to *following it*. This requires the active participation of everyone in the organization. People must focus not only on the results but also on the process to achieve those results.

Ethical practices occur when the process is not compromised or bypassed to achieve a result. If a company's attitude is, "I don't care how you do it, just get it done," this says that the result is more important than how the result was achieved. The ethical code becomes meaningless if senior management tolerates or ignores behavior that is contrary to the values it has established.

Although businesses need to survive financially, they need to decide what price they are willing to pay for pursuing a dollar. A commitment to ethical conduct is one of a company's most valuable assets. Doing what's right is not always the easiest course of action, nor does it always produce immediate financial rewards. But *there is simply no right way to do the wrong thing.*

A company can institutionalize its code of ethics in several ways.

- **Put the code of ethics in writing.** Ethical standards are meaningless when they are simply elusive intangibles. Written statements memorialize the code, leave no room for ambiguity, and provide evidence for enforcement. That is, as long as the words are specific. It's not sufficient to say "integrity is expected of every salesperson." Instead, describe the behavior that exemplifies integrity. A code of ethics that is too vague is merely window dressing rather than a meaningful script.
- **Communicate the code of ethics.** Everyone in the organization needs to be told what the code of conduct is. This can be done through training and orientation programs, pamphlets, letters, and, most important, by management's example. The company should also communicate with the public. This can be accomplished in brochures, contracts, and advertising. The actual behavior of the company's people, however, makes the most powerful public statement.
- **Demonstrate that the code of ethics is important.** All levels of management must lead by example to gain commitment from others in the organization. There is no such thing as two sets of acceptable behavior, one for management and another for those being managed. Management must be consistent, meaning it's not OK to ignore the

code in certain situations, regardless of the financial gain that would result.

The institutionalization of ethics is measured not only by actual behavior but also by how employees, customers, and clients *perceive* the ethics of the company. Because the managers are responsible for creating an ethical environment in the company, they can take a lot of the credit or share the blame for this perception.

- **Enforce the code of ethics.** The most powerful way to institutionalize ethics is to address violations. Unethical behavior persists when organizations fail to aggressively pursue enforcement. Often enforcement requires the removal of barriers that discourage people from stepping forward and informing upper management about unethical conduct. Otherwise, the organization is functioning with a code of silence rather than a code of ethics.

  Provide directives about to whom suspected unethical behavior is to be reported, how disputes will be investigated and resolved, and a series of penalties that will be assessed for violations. Then do it!

- **Reinforce the code of ethics.** Constant exposure is essential for reinforcement. The code should be a centerpiece in workshops and seminars, either by devoting sessions exclusively to the topic or by incorporating the subject in other discussions. The failure of many sales training sessions is they ignore ethical behavior in the pursuit of successful selling behavior. Training should prepare people for the ethical dilemmas they might encounter and develop possible solutions for these dilemmas.

Ethics can be either managed or mismanaged. Management can be serious about upholding the company's code of ethics (and any industry codes the company pledges to follow) and can foster the level of professionalism codes intend to achieve, or management can look the other way and simply ignore the issue. Companies in which managers choose the latter option could suffer undesirable consequences. Because some unethical conduct is also illegal, the company's legal liability is significantly increased and the penalties can be costly.

PROFESSIONALISM

The term *profession* is used by people (and industries) who see their endeavors—and want others to see them—as worthy of the stature commonly associated with undertakings that require highly specialized knowledge and skill and intense academic training in the classic sense of learned professions. Some people may say that's an inappropriate or self-impressed view of an endeavor, and others would say that it's possible for endeavors to rise to that stature.

The term *professional* is used (including in this text) in the context of conduct that is distinguished by exemplary knowledge, skill, and ability in a field of endeavor and the commendable character of the person so engaged (truthfulness, honesty, integrity, and the like). For the purposes of this discussion, "professional" is distinguished from the "ethical," which is rooted in morality and value systems, while professional encompasses a broader set of traits and behaviors.

Without venturing into the debate about whether a person can be professional and not also ethical (or vice versa), the fact is that both are elusive concepts without prescribed standards and descriptive behaviors.

A common theme of authors who write about professionalism is the character traits that distinguish a person as a professional, which are the very traits we ascribe to our leaders (see Chapter 2), and the exemplary way people conduct themselves and strive to excel. James R. Ball does his own exemplary job of describing behaviors in his book, *Professionalism Is for Everyone*.

Even very ordinary jobs can be done with professional class by people who don't settle for mediocrity, who continually strive to enhance their competence, not just in knowledge but in performance, take pride in their work, serve others, and rise above the crowd. Whether real estate rises to the level of a profession in the classic sense as the industry prefers to be recognized is a worthwhile debate. But anyone in any job can do it professionally.

Professional Standards

We ascribe certain core competencies to professions, which in service businesses are often characterized as minimum service standards. A provider who doesn't perform at least the minimum is presumed in some fashion to be less professional than one who does. Competitors assert that they are more professional because they deliver higher levels of services than their industry counterparts do.

Herein lies the discord between "full service" real estate companies and companies with alternative business models, ranging from counseling sellers about selling their own homes to virtual brokerage based solely on the Internet. They clash over which business model is more professional but in so doing raise huge antitrust concerns that the full-service traditionalists are attempting to control the marketplace or restrict the business models that give the consumer choices in services and prices.

The industry's licensing bodies have attempted to define minimum service standards for their licensees. Although the regulators have the authority to prescribe certain standards of conduct to protect the public (consumers), they learned that attempting to define certain services overstepped the boundaries of antitrust laws and interfered with free enterprise. (Some regulations survived legal challenge and others have been rescinded.)

Professionalism expects people to strive for excellence in whatever their endeavors but never intended to suggest that one business model or set of services is necessarily more professional than another.

Companies strive for professionalism by prescribing standards of excellence for themselves and all who work for them. This often begins with a pledge or commitment to their customers and clients that becomes part of the company's philosophy of doing business. That pledge is given meaning by describing professional behaviors and standards the company sets for its services (quality services standards are discussed in Chapter 17). The commitment may also include certain knowledge, skill, and ability enhancements the workforce strives to achieve.

■ POLICIES AND PROCEDURES

The various manuals that a company prepares are the handbooks that tell people "the way we work" in the organization. Certainly, the code of ethics makes statements about how to work, either in a separate piece or as part of other manuals. But all of these handbooks or manuals delve into the organization's work processes, describing the way the company's services are delivered and the way people and documents flow. Policies and procedures are especially valuable for

- providing ready answers for many of the dilemmas people face during the course of daily operations.
- setting rules by which everyone shall play.
- helping to resolve conflicts before they arise.
- providing a risk-management tool for both the company and its staff.

Careful wording in written policies is extremely important. Litigation and employment disputes can arise out of accusations that policies created contracts (though that's certainly not the intention) or constituted promises the company failed to fulfill. Obviously, this is a good argument in favor of making sure that the company attorney reviews the company's words. Written policies should contain statements that management can make changes at its discretion at any time and has the right to interpret and administer policies as changing circumstances warrant.

Just as with ethics, company policy and procedures must be institutionalized. Everyone in the organization should have a copy of the general operations manual and the employee handbook, and should be encouraged to refer to them. These are an essential part of orientation for new staff as well. Management must also stand behind the policies and procedures, enforce them consistently, and administer sanctions as warranted. Once a manager ignores some of the rules or permits some people to circumvent them, the order that the rules intended to create no longer exists.

Because a company's manuals are declarations that can have legal implications, not only the procedures but also the stated words must be framed within the law. The most significant laws are those that affect real estate practices, antitrust, employment and the workplace, and civil rights. A real estate company that employs independent contractors must also differentiate between workplace procedures for them versus employees.

Because the manuals reflect a company's philosophy and operations, the substance is individual. However, there are certain subjects or processes that are typically addressed, some of which apply to everyone who works in the organization and others that apply to selected personnel or departments. The format of the manuals and the arrangement of content are individual as well, with some being more detailed or appropriate for employee handbooks. A human resource consultant and the company's attorney are invaluable advisers in these projects.

General Business Policies

As a foundation for all that follows in a general operations manual or employee handbook, the place to begin is by describing the company—its mission statement, a brief history of the organization, and a description of its target markets by geographic area and types of properties or services. This is also where the company's general philosophy of doing business is explained. All of these pronouncements affect *everyone* who works for the company and also tell the public who the company is.

The company's general operating structure needs to be explained, including the organization chart and relationships with superiors and senior management. Generally these issues are addressed with policy statements that reflect the culture, workplace environment, and management style of the organization. This often also includes an *open door policy*, which speaks about the accessibility of management (including the principal owner or broker) by everyone who works for the company. The purpose of these statements is to explain the organization's hierarchy and the way people interact with one another.

In a real estate company, the policy discussion must also address some very critical issues that relate to its services. Aside from the need to provide policy and supporting procedures (remember the how, when, and who), the company cannot afford to leave potential legal landmines unattended. The company has the right to expect that all workers, including independent contractors, conduct themselves in a legal and ethical manner.

Agency. The broker must clearly define the company's policy regarding law of agency relationships. The policy must state whether the firm represents buyers/tenants, sellers/landlords or both as disclosed dual agents or as designated agents, and state a position about subagency.

Procedures must explain how fiduciary obligations are to be fulfilled, including agency disclosure, and how those obligations are preserved (especially confidentiality and loyalty) if the company practices disclosed dual agency or designated agency. If state law permits nonagency (or nonrepresentation), the company needs policies and accompanying procedures relating to those services. (Sample office agency policies are available from the National Association of REALTORS®.)

Antitrust. Because real estate practices are constantly scrutinized for antitrust violations, a company's policies must address the prohibited acts of price fixing, group boycotting, territorial assignments, and tying agreements. Policies should explain the business rationale for the company's fees and its various fee structures. Equally important are procedures that tell all personnel what they need to do and say in their representations of the company's fees to protect the company from antitrust violations.

Equal opportunity. The company should express its philosophical commitment to equal opportunity in housing and employment. Then establish specific policies and procedures to ensure that everyone in the organization serves all customers and clients properly under federal, state, and local fair housing, civil rights, and disability laws. Personnel policies and procedures must comply with all applicable employment and disability laws.

The company could also participate in affirmative action programs. An example is the Fair Housing Partnership Agreement that the National Association of REALTORS® and the Department of Housing and Urban Development have jointly signed. This is a voluntary program in which participants can further equal opportunity in housing by engaging in certain advertising practices and outreach programs in the community.

Real estate license law and rules and regulations. A policy should state that all of the activities in the organization must comply with the state's licensing laws. Any procedure that is defined throughout the operations manual should support this policy. Because the company must not permit unlicensed employees to engage in activities for which licensure is required, procedures should address what unlicensed people can and cannot do.

This is also a good place to discuss the company's policy with respect to personal assistants—whether they are licensed or unlicensed or employees of the company or a salesperson—and the specific activities they are permitted to perform.

General workplace policies and procedures. A number of rules for the workplace and accompanying procedures tell people about the day-to-day life in the organization. These apply to everyone, regardless of their position in the company or their IRS employment status (independent contractor or employee). Typically, these issues are included in an employee handbook, but the placement is not as important as the topics that are covered. Human resource supports are available on the Internet but commonly suggested topics include:

- Equal employment opportunity (including cultural diversity)
- Nonharassment, including sexual harassment (between staff members, management and staff and employees/independent contractors, and customers and clients—see NAR's sample policy)
- Drug and alcohol use/abuse (what, where, and procedures if violations of policy occur)
- Smoking and nonsmoking (in the workplace and with customers and clients)
- Violence in the workplace, and personal safety and security issues (including procedures to protect personnel and precautions for salespeople in the field, as well as the company's policy about acceptable self-defense measures; i.e., Mace™, firearms, etc.)
- Standards of conduct (including issues such as theft, conflict of interest, and violations of laws, ethics, and policies)
- Job enrichment and professional growth (workplace philosophy and opportunities, including education and training)
- Confidentiality (company matters as well as client confidences and personal information to protect against identity theft)
- Public relations (image of the organization)
- Actions on behalf of the organization (who, what, and procedures)

- Nonsolicitation (prevent disruption in the workplace)
- Use of company property and equipment
- Computer, Internet, and social media usage (Some companies draft separate policy manuals for computer usage, Internet use, and social media.) Issues to address include
  - — hardware systems (physical security of equipment);
  - — mobile devices and removal media (use of personal tablets, laptops, smart phones, and removable devices like USB flash drives to interface with the company's computer system; the loss or theft of personal devices or media containing company or related data);
  - — user accounts, passwords, and protected files;
  - — copyrighted software (permissible use and legal issues);
  - — handling attachments and forwarding messages (e-mail);
  - — computer viruses (defenses of company system, including scanning attachments and user CDs and disks);
  - — use of secure sites when transmitting personal data, credit information, and the like to protect against identity theft;
  - — prohibited activities (frivolous and personal use of internal network and Internet, including harassing and offensive content);
  - — protection of intellectual property and Internet downloads (typically prohibited);
  - — use of the company's social media sites (who monitors, posts, and takes down material and compliance with laws, including state license law);
  - — company monitoring of computer and Internet usage (including user waiver of right of privacy); and
  - — directions for handling system failures.
- Emergencies (workplace as well as personal)
- Termination (independent contractors and employees, and grievance procedures for them)

- About the work day
  - Office hours (including procedures for after-hours in the workplace)
  - Holidays (including accommodations for cultural and religious preferences)
  - Personal phone calls (including emergency procedures and reimbursement of charges)
  - Dress policy (general professional appearance)

Employee Policies

In addition to the items above, a number of issues are addressed in policies that relate specifically to employees.

- Categories of employment and related fringe benefits
- Employment of minors
- Employment of relatives
- Meal and break times
- Pay procedures
- Travel/expense accounts (if any)
- Overtime
- Absenteeism and tardiness
- Layoffs
- Disciplinary actions
- Resignation and discharge
- Vacation and leave
  - Personal days
  - Vacation time
  - Sick time
  - Jury duty
  - Bereavement leave

— Military leave

— Family and medical leave (check requirements under the federal Family and Medical Leave Act and any related state laws)

A number of state and federal laws protect employees in the workplace, the IRS distinction between employees and independent contractors not necessarily being relevant in these laws. The best advice is legal advice to be sure that all employment policies and procedures and conditions in the workplace comply with these laws.

Procedures for Independent Contractors/Salespeople

Although salespeople often enter into independent contractor agreements with the company, that work status should be reaffirmed with careful wording in the company's policy and procedures (another argument in favor of engaging legal counsel). The policies and procedures should address a number of issues.

- Sales teams (the way they are accommodated in the company, including notification to management about how the team has structured its relationship)
- Relationships between the company and qualified legal entities as permitted by state license law (whether the company recognizes such legal associations as corporations or partnerships formed by the licensee(s) and associated administrative procedures, including whether the company will pay the legal association or the individual licensees)
- Part-time agents, full-time agents, and mobile officing (including definitions, hiring policies, and the way people work)
- Referrals (procedures for distributing in-house leads and referrals between salespeople and referrals to other companies)
- Cooperation among salespeople in-house (including sharing customers and clients)
- Standards for servicing customers and clients (listings, sales, and other applicable services)
- Open house procedures (including sales procedures and safety precautions)

- Transactions
  - Listing and buyer agency agreements (types, situations in which each is used, policy on written versus oral agreements)
  - Forms and contracts (policy for written and oral contracts, written disclosures, contingency forms, transmittal to company files and to contract signatories, and record keeping)
  - Escrow money (tracking procedures, deposits and withdrawals, cooperating broker procedures, disputes)
  - Litigation and legal expenses
  - Settlement or escrow procedures
- Commission programs
- Insurance (coinsurance on autos, errors and omissions)
- Dues and fees (professional association, MLS, franchise)
- Education and designations
- Advertising and marketing procedures (who pays and for what, which media are used, frequency, content and approval of copy even when salesperson is paying the bill, solicitation)
- Web sites, blogs, social media, and Internet advertising (requirements of license law, copyright and trademark infringement, defamation, sexual harassment, discrimination, wire fraud)
- Telephone, fax, and e-mail solicitations (including do-not-call-list rules, spam, and other solicitation laws)
- Telephone procedures (personal and business calls, phone log, who gets the lead on an inquiry, expectations for returning messages)
- Dissemination of information (about the company and its listings, including the nature of information to be discussed on the phone and who is permitted to disseminate what information)
- Lockboxes and signs (inventory control procedures, who pays)
- Postage, printing, and direct mail (who pays, limits, review of copy)

- Attendance (*recommendations* for floor time, sales meetings, training sessions)
- Parking at the office
- Salespeople selling and purchasing real estate for themselves
- Handling disputes (between salespeople, with customers and clients, with licensees in other firms)
- Termination (disposition of listings, leads, pending closings)

■ CONCLUSION

Many systems and processes need to come together so that an organization can function. The company's policies and procedures are one more of those systems. The purpose is essentially to tell people how the company does business and provide orderly processes so that the company can function efficiently. Not only are manuals of policies and procedures good reference materials to help people self-direct their work but they also provide a framework within which management can manage the daily affairs of the organization.

■ DISCUSSION EXERCISES

Does your company have a code of ethics? If so, are there conflicts between what the company preaches and the way it practices?

Illustrate a typical ethical dilemma that you encountered in daily practice. How was it resolved? Could it have been resolved differently? How?

Discuss typical problems that arise in your company and how these could be resolved by a well-written company policy and procedures manual.

Are there issues other than those outlined in this chapter that you have found particularly helpful to include in a policy and procedures manual? If so, how have they been addressed?

CHAPTER TWELVE

12

MARKETING AND ADVERTISING

What media attract the attention of today's consumers?

How are companies using technology to reach today's consumers?
What can you think of doing that others aren't doing?

Marketing is about packaging and placement—packaging a product that appeals to the consumer and placing the product where the consumer will see it and act. Product can be a box of cereal or jug of laundry detergent, dressed up in a package that says "buy me." Placement is the shelf space and advertising venue(s) that captures the consumers' attention and inspires them to buy.

The same principles apply to anything a company supplies in the marketplace. A real estate company's product is its service and information (including listings), which the company has to package to appeal to the consumer and place or promote in ways that produce buyers.

The way for a company to grow its business is to increase its base of consumers. Anyone who is likely to want the type of service the company (or its competitors) offers is the audience for the company's marketing efforts.

Just as a company needs a business plan, the company needs a plan to generate business from that audience.

A marketing plan provides the messaging that puts a face on the company and its services, and gets that face in the right places to capture the minds of consumers. Some people characterize marketing as a head game—who ever gets into the head of the consumer wins. There are many tools of the advertising trade that convey attention-getting messages, make an impression, and cause people to act. Capturing that head takes some finesse and creativity, which benefits from the imagination and skill of professional marketing and advertising specialists.

■ MARKET IDENTITY

First the company needs to make a statement about itself. That's its market identity, otherwise known as its *brand*. Brand is established with the company's name, its logo, and its slogan. All of this becomes the company's *signature*.

A signature makes a powerful, concise statement about who the company is and what it does everywhere the signature appears—the sign on the office, yard signs, business cards, letterhead, brochures, and Web pages—and makes an even more powerful statement when affiliated companies are recognized under the same banner (such as with franchises).

Once established, the brand becomes a company's most valuable asset in the marketplace. Companies vigorously protect their brands against infringement, often with legal actions over names, slogans, or graphics that can confuse or mislead the public. The company that attempts to infringe only further proves the value of well-established brands.

What's in a Name?

The name has to tell the consumer what's unique about the company's value or service. Even with franchise affiliation, the company needs its own identity. Small businesses rarely give enough thought to the choice of a name and then get lost in the crowd or convey the wrong message about what they do. Even if real estate is obvious, the company has to distinguish itself from other real estate companies.

One way to do that is with the name of the broker. A person's name is unique to that organization and may well convey value if the broker has a respected or established reputation in the community. That name can be a powerful draw, but can also give people the impression that they'll be working directly with the broker, particularly if the company is small.

Another way is to choose a fictitious business name (FBN). It may relate to a specialty, a geographic area, or some other distinctive feature of the company. Some people consider the alphabetical position of the name in telephone and business directories as well.

FBNs have to be compelling and original. It takes a little research to find one that is not currently in use, which can be done by "Googling" various ideas and searching the registry of the department of state government that approves FBNs. Generally, names that imply the existence of a nonexistent partnership or corporation, and ones that contain words like Bank, Insurance, Escrow, Trust, Federal, National, State, United States, Reserve, or Deposit Insurance will not be approved.

The company also needs to select an Internet domain name. The name should be closely related to the company name and easy for users to recall. It often takes some trial and error to find one that is available and also pairs well with the company name. The availability of a domain name may affect the final choice of an FBN. Test-drive names with friends to gauge reaction before making the final decisions.

The procedures for approving and certifying a fictitious name vary from state to state, as do the license law requirements for real estate company names. An FBN is usually advertised in a local general circulation newspaper for a period of time before a certificate is issued. The company may also have to record a certificate in the city or county where it will do business. A corporation is not usually required to file a certificate because the corporation, as a legal entity, is entitled to use its own name.

What's in a Signature?

A signature is the shorthand or the sound bite that creates brand recognition. A signature makes a short but powerful statement with words, colors, and graphics that stick in people's minds. Think about company signatures that stick in your mind. Some are readily recognized by their color schemes (like real estate franchises). Others have catchy slogans or logos, like the apple or golden arches that are recognized worldwide.

Think "signature that sizzles." Sizzle is the attention-grabbing, impression-making characteristic of a signature. Even the most conservative institution (like a bank) needs a sizzling signature. This is the art of creative design that professionals know best, that crafts a signature that matches the company with the profile of the consumers the company wants to attract.

The design must also look smart in a variety of formats. One that looks good on a billboard may not look so fine when it's scaled down for a classified ad or a business card. Striking colors or screened backgrounds work for color print and Web pages, but may lose the punch in a black-and-white presentation. While it may not be possible to cover all these bases, a professional can craft a design that suits the media that are most likely to be used.

Professionals can also help gauge consumer reaction and determine when it's time to redesign the signature. As a company ages through its life cycles, it may need a new face that appeals to the contemporary consumer—the new color scheme, slogan, or graphic that says the company is in step with the times. A new signature may be so bold as to bear no resemblance to the old but something recognizable from the old signature is typically included to preserve identity with established patrons.

When companies undergo significant change, they often need to change the signature. After the merger of two firms, the new company needs to make its own statement. Depending on the merger's strategic direction, the signature may combine a recognizable feature from the previous two companies or may cast an entirely new image. (For dishonorable reasons, a new name and signature may be used to shield the true identity of a company as it continues to prey with its nefarious schemes.)

What's the Plan?

Once the company has a signature and can be readily identified from its listing ads to the sponsorship jerseys for the girls' softball team, the next step is to develop a plan for selling its brand.

Companies promote their brand and make themselves visible in a multitude of ways, ranging from paid advertising to e-newsletters and blogs. Companies also need a theme for their messaging and a coordinated strategy for making public appearances in a number of venues and driving consumers to each of those venues.

A marketing plan (similar to a business plan) provides that strategy by answering "What does the company want to say, who is the intended audience, and how can it be reached?" Just as with business writing (see Chapter 4), the answers focus the message and the delivery method to appeal to the targeted audiences.

Where does advertising fit in? Think "purpose, population, and price." A company can't afford to market itself in every advertising medium or to waste money on distracting messages. Some promotional tools and media are most beneficial for institutional purposes (promoting the company) while others are better for promoting specific services or properties. Some reach broad audiences and others target more focused ones.

The goal of purpose-price-and-population is to pick the venue that serves the purpose and reaches the desired population for the best price. Obviously, the most cost-efficient price is the one that reaches the largest number of people in that population. A short but intense, integrated campaign rather than less frequent appearances in a longer, drawn-out one, provides greater benefit for the same amount of money.

■ THE DIGITAL MEDIA BUSINESS

Marketing programs once combined newspaper advertising and classified listings with glossy print brochures, newsletters, and bulk-advertising mailers. Display advertising meant billboards along the side of the road, and mass media was broadcast TV and radio.

Today's display advertising is an online banner or digital video, and the Web is as mass as it gets. Even traditional print media have gone digital as well, with content and advertising in both print and digital formats. Everything companies do in today's marketing programs drives consumers to the digital addresses where the companies can be found.

But marketing is not just about the digital delivery of information and company messages. It's also about using digital media to build two-way relationships with consumers. Consumers are flocking to blogs, social networking sites, and virtual worlds, all possible because of the Internet, and that's where companies' marketing plans have to go, too.

The objective is not just to talk to the consumer but to get the consumer involved in the marketing process. The Web 2.0 world offers vast opportunities to do that but marketers have to think about ways to stimulate the conversation and create reasons for the consumer to participate.

Web Sites

A company's online presence is today's most powerful marketing tool. Web sites are, in a sense, today's mass media and electronic billboards for the company's signature and message, which includes consumer information and "classified" advertising. But the sites are effective only when they rise above all the other Internet sites and deliver what the visitors are looking for.

Today's Internet-savvy visitors surf in search of the most informative, easily navigated, and interactive sites. Simply getting people to a site is a major task. Once there, however, visitors have very little (if any) brand loyalty so first impressions must be outstanding for them to commit the site to their "favorites" lists. Professional site developers know best how to make that first impression and deliver what today's surfers are looking for, a task that is far too important to lose valuable time to mistakes and the inevitable trial and error of do-it-yourselfers.

Web sites are compelling because of two things—design and content. The programmer and designer (often one and the same) are focused on the technology that drives the site and the graphics that make it look sharp. But those efforts have to support the marketing mind, which are the goals of the site, the audience, and the messaging and features that draw people's attention. Sites are fairly static once they are built, but the content is fluid, meaning that it will constantly change. The site essentially provides a template for those words.

The power of words. A Web site is written for viewers or users, not readers. People scan, looking for information they want, which may not necessarily be what you write, unless you know your audience. Headlines have to hook the eye of the scanners, as does the content.

Web writing is the epitome of less-is-more, with short words, short sentences, and short paragraphs (no more than three sentences). Even well-written copy in a promotional brochure typically won't work. Web copy has to be about half the length of print copy (remember the scanning eye), which also means there's no room for the promotional hype and hyperbole that is common in advertising copy (that's not what a site visitor wants anyway). Marketing messages have a theme and useful sound bites, but those have to be tailored for use on a Web site.

Also think globally. Although the general caveat about using industry terminology and lingo applies, Web writers have to be additionally aware of the fact that not all site viewers are native English speakers—even those who may not be familiar with (and can be offended by) expressions and slang in our colloquial vocabularies. A translation widget for other languages may be a good idea, too. This is another case of know your audience.

The power of Web words has added meaning because words drive search engines, and search engines drive visitors to landing pages, which aren't necessarily the company's home page.

Web pages have to finesse the search engines with keywords or phrases that people "Google" or "Bing." Cracking that code takes some trial and error, but a good starting point is to experiment with your own searches and see what results you get. The object is to identify the words that will drive search engines to call up your site. You also need to run that test again from time to time because people's search preferences change.

Search engines are also as "human" as the visitors, in that they rank sites by how much useful information the sites contain and they don't look far down a page to determine which ones get top billing. Although you can pay for site placement, you can start with strong words in the headlines and placing meaty content at the beginning of a page. Site maps (which can be generated by online services) also help appeal to the search engines.

Web sites are more than the company's home page, and in fact, many users rarely see that one. A site is essentially its own engine that drives viewers from page to page and even to outside resources. Sites are most useful when information is grouped in blocks by page, with hyperlinks to other pages.

Although each page is self-contained, some information will be repeated for the benefit of visitors who don't view the pages in any particular order.

An interactive community. Surfers today look for sites where they can communicate with the vendor, ask questions, provide feedback, or offer opinions. From a business development perspective, a site that gives visitors the opportunity to request assistance, complete a survey or form, or take some other action provides a centralized lead-gathering process for the company.

But this means that the company must respond quickly and efficiently, even if by automated acknowledgment, until someone supplies a more substantive reply. And the most socially interactive surfers expect that to happen today, not tomorrow. Someone has to be responsible for responding or handling inquiries and tracking the site's performance.

Enhanced site placement. A company can go the extra mile to get its site noticed by paying for a sponsored site, which is essentially a form of paid advertising. Some people think the return is well worth the expense while others don't, because Internet surfers often avoid sponsored sites.

An alternative is to subscribe to a pay-per-click service, which takes charge of placing the site in return for a fee that is tied to the number of viewers that click on the site. Another approach is to arrange links with other sites. Some sites are more compatible for linking, and some offer better exposure than others (perhaps for a fee).

Accessibility. Just as places of public accommodations must be accessible to people with disabilities (which includes real estate offices), Web sites, too, must be accessible. Many of the compelling visual features that site designers favor are problematic for people who are blind or have low vision.

The technology people commonly use, such as screen readers that translate text to speech and translate text to Braille, can't interpret photos, charts, colored-coded displays, or graphics. Some site features are also troublesome for people who adjust colors or fonts on their monitors or use text enlargement or high contrast settings to accommodate their visual challenges. The

ADA.gov Web site provides guidance for accessible sites, including several suggestions.

- Add text to images. In fact, you can also add HTML codes for screen readers and tags that include words that are more descriptive of an image than the ones seen on the site.
- Post documents in text-based formats. PDFs are the most desirable formats for posting forms, brochures, and other documents. Because PDFs aren't accessible to screen readers, printed matter should be available as text documents as well.
- Include audio descriptions and captions for video and other multimedia.

A Web site is only as good as it is useful and informative for every visitor.

Site management. Web sites are not a launch-it-and-forget-it proposition. Once you establish a following with compelling design and content, you have to hold on to it. Generally, Web sites are redesigned every three years to maintain their contemporary look, but they can always be improved in the meantime with an additional landing page, a more user-friendly click-through, or a new interactive feature.

Invaluable messaging opportunities are missed unless the content is routinely updated. Because people expect to find the hottest topics and most contemporary information, the public relations cost is huge if months-old "news" is still posted or sold properties are still advertised for sale. A linked site may not still be desirable either, as the site owner changes its content.

A sobering note about site management is that not everything that happens on the Internet is moral, ethical, or legal. Some people use their technology know-how to wreak havoc for no particular reason other than because they can. Others have more nefarious reasons and devise schemes to capture business or damage a competitor's business. Web sites can be infected, altered, or spoofed (linked to another site), perhaps to one that is especially embarrassing. No company can afford to let these events go unnoticed.

Ownership. Domain names and site content are assets, known as **intellectual property**, which owners frequently protect by copyright or trademark.

This is a two-way street—the company must protect the ownership of its property and must respect the copyrights and trademarks of other owners (and not use their property without permission). Listings are proprietary information and should be posted only according to the MLS rules.

Another ownership issue involves the leads generated by a site. Site visitors provide contact information for the purpose of doing business with that vendor, not for the information to be traded or sold. If the company (or its salespeople) intends to share or sell that information, that intention must be readily disclosed along with the option to opt out.

Blogs and Social Media

Blogs and social media sites are the most interactive tools in today's marketing programs. Businesses are rapidly learning that they are as conspicuously absent from the public eye if they don't have a blog site or Facebook page as they once were without a Web site.

These sites are inexpensive outlets for the company's message, with the added advantage that the company can control the story and interact with the public in real time. The company can say exactly what it wants to say directly to the public, rather than being subjected to the whims of newspaper editors, or radio and TV station reporters who filter or put their own spin on a story.

Just as with a Web site, the goal is to establish a following. The same content rules apply for blog and social media sites—commentary has to be current, compelling, and informative. The company sells itself by being a go-to resource with commentary about issues that interest consumers or hot topics in the public domain (not company commercials).

Blogs and social media sites are most effective when they inspire consumers to join in the conversation with the company and with other consumers. Consumers can sell the company themselves with their flattering comments or experiences. Their commentary is also useful for developing products or services and for identifying customer service problems. Even negative comments provide instant opportunities to acknowledge concerns and minimize the public relations fallout.

Keep several rules in mind about posting.

- **Respect copyrights.** Don't post words that were originally written by someone else without permission and beware the temptation to copy-and-paste from another blogger or Web site. The more creative or original your words, the less likely you are to raise questions about copyright infringement.
- **Respect people's opinions.** No good purpose is served by being argumentative or by chiming in on negative conversations about a competitor. Conversations often are freewheeling, but let consumers have their say-so among themselves and weigh in only if you can make a constructive contribution.
- **Reread before posting.** Instant messaging can mean instant regret over cavalier or flip comments. Beware obscenities and discriminatory comments. Although the site owner will most likely be protected against such comments contributed by third parties, the site owner is liable for his or her own commentary.

Mini-blogs or short messaging services, such as Twitter, are the quintessential instant-engagement venues. The same rules for blogging apply to mini-blogs but these messages are shorter, often capture attention faster, and are great for messaging about the company's other media sites. A Twitter following is an essential part of today's marketing plan, not only for branding and delivering information but also for drawing immediate attention to customer service problems.

Like Web sites, managing blog and social media sites takes work. Someone has to be in charge of posting and monitoring the conversation. That same person is likely to also monitor other sites and join in those conversations. This job is indispensible in today's digital media marketing business.

The Apps World

The most contemporary plea in the digital marketplace is "download our app." The world of apps has grown beyond the novelty of games and entertainment to become a powerful (and fun) way to capture a following and drive information. Once an app is downloaded (most often from the Web site), the company assumes a position in the consumers' portable devices. Although apps take techno-savvy and money to develop (a growing resource in digital marketing), they provide a very contemporary marketing tool for a company's message, especially for listings and special events.

Online Advertising

Companies often see their own Web sites as their online advertising. Certainly, those sites provide an excellent outlet for promoting listings and the company. But as more consumers turn to digital venues, companies have to look for additional non-print venues to showcase their brand.

The online advertising business has matured, surpassing newspaper revenue for the first time in 2010, to become at least a $26 billion business. Nearly one-fourth of the recent growth is attributed to banner and video ads. Even traditional print media have gone digital with Web advertising outlets, often giving advertisers messaging opportunities in a variety of formats for package prices.

Online advertising is the most contemporary and affordable way to reach mass markets. Picking online venues is like picking any other mass media—it's a function of purpose, population, and price.

Web site managers can track visitor behavior—the pages that visitors view, the amount of time they stay connected to a page, whether they interact with or download a page, and the performance of links to other pages or sites. Major media sites (like Facebook and Google Search) also mine data about the consumer interests of their visitors so that advertising can be matched to specific target audiences.

Ad placement is all about going where your audience is for the price you can afford to pay. A banner ad on the site of a business that a homebuyer or property owner is likely to visit may be an option. Or the company can advertise on premium media sites for prices that range from several dollars to $15 for a thousand views, depending on the targeting options and where the ad appears on the site.

■ TRADITION MEETS THE 21ST CENTURY

Conventional tools of the marketing and advertising trade still have their place in the digital world. Some are most suitable for institutional advertising (to promote the company) and others are suited for promoting listings or launching a new service. But they all have a digital component today, either by their means of delivery or by driving consumers to the company's digital addresses.

Broadcast and Print Media

Broadcast and print media have been the best tools for reaching a large number of people at one time, even in specific target audiences. Today's technology has changed the behavior of those audiences, which has changed both the way consumers use broadcast and print media and the way those media outlets serve their audiences.

Broadcast and print media have traditionally been major sources of public information and, while they still play a huge role in people's lives, the media reach their audiences through the Internet and WiFi, laptops and iPads, Kindles and Nooks, smart phones and apps. And audiences can tune into programming at any time that suits them.

Just as the media have found their way into the lives of their mobile viewers, listeners, and readers, a company's marketing program can do so as well with paid advertising, public service announcements, press releases, interviews, or listing-presentation programs.

Media outlets compile audience and reader profiles along with exposure and circulation data that are useful for matching media with the company's target markets and identifying the number of consumers that can be reached. If the primary audience is not a cross section of the population, the marketing program must also include media that reach the general population to avoid violating fair housing laws.

Cost of advertising is a good indicator of the size and consumer value of the audience. Display and classified advertising in a general-circulation, subscription newspaper is more expensive than in a free neighborhood circular. Broadcast airtime during the midnight-to-5-AM hours can be half the cost (or less) of prime-time hours. But either case may not deliver enough of a suitable audience to justify the expense, even at the cheaper rates. Some stations offer packaged time slots that include preferred time as well as off-hours, which may be a good deal. Radio is generally less expensive than broadcast TV, at any time of day.

Cable TV is an attractive alternative, especially since the programming gap between cable and network stations has closed. National cable stations offer more attractively priced commercial time for local advertisers than broadcast stations and can deliver worthwhile audience exposure. Local or community stations are even less expensive, but they have fewer and more localized viewers. Cable bulletin boards are also options, especially for promoting individual listings.

Media specialists can help identify suitable placement alternatives and tailor messaging to suit the venue. A consultant can also help with a sponsored listing magazine show or interactive TV or radio program. These are ambitious projects because of the programming and production effort involved and while they are popular in some markets, the information is just as likely to be broadcasted through a company's Web site today.

Press Releases

The company's message is most credible when third parties, especially the media, think the story is worthwhile. Press releases bring those stories to the media's attention, with the expectation that the media will pick up the story and run with it. Think of press releases from a public relations point of view.

Company events are opportunities to create a story for the media—the launch of new products or services, honors or awards, historic milestones or landmark celebrations, community service projects or human-interest tales. The story has to strike a chord with the public because it's awe inspiring, heartwarming, or unique (and is not a commercial for the company).

Current events are also story opportunities. Media, especially in large metropolitan markets, work for circulation or ratings and are interested in stories that play to the contemporary headlines. The company can contribute research, statistics, or a professional perspective to those headlines.

Even with a media-worthy story, the press release has to capture an editor's attention. This is another exercise in business writing that begins with a goal, which is generally to gain publicity for or increase the visibility of the company, and catches the editor's eye with a crisp headline that crystallizes the message (remember that writing is visual). The most important information is presented at the outset, particularly because that's only as far as the editor may read, and continues by answering who, what, where, how, and when. The body of the release is written in third-person newspaper style—with short words, sentences and paragraphs.

Present the story in a factual manner, without editorializing, and avoid jargon, clichés, and empty adjectives and phrases. Press releases are written as finished copy so they can be read on air, so test that by reading it out loud. And be sure to catch spelling errors and typos because the editors will definitely notice them. Regardless of how carefully the copy is written, however, an editor may still rewrite or use only portions of the release.

Finally, prepare the release so that it can be e-mailed (most media accept only an electronic format). Be sure to include the release date, the date and place of the event or story, contact information including a phone number, and the company's digital addresses. Attach photos or graphics for interest and e-mail in advance of the release date. Don't give the media an excuse to eliminate your story because it didn't rise to the top of the pile of hundreds they receive with enough advance notice.

Letters to the Editor

A faithful observer of current events may get sufficiently stirred by the public discourse on radio or television or in the local newspaper or halls of government to comment on matters that involve real estate. A letter to the editor can offer the professional perspective to the public discourse. Today, that letter may be an e-mail to the editor or posted on an editor's or reporter's blog site.

There are some caveats, however. Commentary can be passionate but unsubstantiated or emotional ramblings or exceedingly controversial positions will not advance the cause and could alienate the company's clientele in the process. Viewpoints must be logically presented and concise to be worthy of print on the editorial page. Also, consider how the tone of a message can change if the letter is edited (if that's the editor's policy).

Media Resource

A marketing plan targets the consumer but the media also hear those marketing messages. Reporters and real estate editors are always looking for good spokespersons and authoritative resources to provide the ready sound bites that add credibility or professional perspective to their stories.

You can build relationships with the media and become their valued resource if you understand how they work. Reporters work on tight deadlines so they need immediate access to their resources. They also have limited space or airtime to work with, and often preconceived notions or slant for the story they (or their editors) want to tell.

Media personnel turn to their resources for guidance or background information or for a quotable comment. People are quotable because of their stature, their expertise, or their provocative or insightful comments. But their commentary is used as it suits the reporter's space and purpose, which means that what you say and what you get in print or on air may not be what you expected. But it's the reporter's story, not yours.

You can be very helpful and sound well versed if you follow several basic steps. Reporters normally contact their resources by telephone, often with the mention of a specific topic of interest. The most constructive way to handle the inquiry is by offering to return the call in several minutes. Use the interim time to compile statistics or other pertinent information and frame the points you want to make in carefully worded remarks.

This not only makes you sound particularly knowledgeable but also minimizes the likelihood of being misquoted or having off-the-cuff or embarrassing remarks memorialized in print or on the airwaves. However, the remark can be skewed, depending on where the comment is placed within the rest of the story, or can be further edited, which can distort the message. Bottom line is the expert can be misquoted, but that's simply a fact of life in the limelight.

Comments can be clearly stated as "off the record," which the reporter must respect. If the media are looking for an official position, be sure that only the person who is authorized to speak on behalf of the company provides those comments.

Once a relationship is established, the media are more likely to be receptive to a heads-up announcement for a story or other comments the expert resource chooses to make, including those in press releases.

Newsletters

Newsletters serve many purposes, but the most useful from the consumers' point of view is one that educates. This is an ideal way to satisfy their quest for information with articles about emerging trends, changes in the law, recent court cases, and real estate-related government regulations, while showcasing the company at the same time.

Although newsletter content is likely to appear on a company's Web site, the marketing plan may include a separate newsletter that can be distributed (electronically or in print) to customers and clients, local newspapers or magazines, or professional publications.

Regardless of the forum, the content still must be current, factually accurate and, most important, not create public relations or legal problems. Any interpretation of laws or legal cases must include a disclaimer (unless credited to a properly licensed attorney), editorial comments must clearly be identified as such (though some editorializing is not worth the risk of controversy), and any reproduction of someone else's writing must be done with the original author's or publisher's permission. Once original content is prepared, copyright it.

Flyers and Brochures

Printed flyers and brochures have been staple marketing tools for years. Simply because they are in print on paper, brochures and flyers give people something tangible to read and hang on to. Traditionally, they have been distributed in person and by mail, but these tools also pair well with today's technology and digital media.

Both tools are visually-appealing messaging opportunities, but they serve different informational purposes. Flyers are the "short sheet," one-page (but no more than two) promotional pieces that are typically single-message focused. They can be written and produced relatively easily, and cheaply, and distributed in a variety of ways, including by e-blasts through a company's e-mail service provider.

Good flyers have a limited number of large-type words and lots of white space so they can be read and absorbed quickly. Flyers catch the eye with strong headlines, get to the point of the message quickly, and use the arrangement of words with bullet lists and short paragraphs and sentences to sell the reader.

Brochures are the glossy image makers, with their artful design, layout, and graphics. The copy can tell the company story, spotlight a particular aspect of the company's services or its premier listings, or promote the company as a good career choice. Professional-looking brochures that are also well written are indispensible in marketing.

Brochures are typically the flattery pieces. (If the company doesn't believe it itself, it's hard to expect the consumer to believe in the company.) But brag-and-boast can be a major turn-off if there's more puff than substance. Although company accomplishments and designations mean something to the industry, they mean little to the general public unless they are translated into solid benefits for the consumer. Be truthful and realistic (don't make promises that can't be kept) and be sure that all content complies with state license law.

Spend wisely both in quality and quantity. Although brochures can be self-developed with desktop publishing programs, the company image is too valuable to scrimp on expense. The project should be out sourced to a professional unless the company has on-staff talent who can prepare striking design and sharp copy.

Brochures have limited shelf life but the per-piece cost drops as the size of the print run increases. A larger print run is generally a wiser expenditure but only as long as the brochures are used before the content is out of date. Once the initial design and layout are done, minor copy or photo changes are relatively inexpensive to make for another print run. Typically brochures are also committed to PDFs so they can be downloaded or circulated electronically.

The even higher-tech versions of a brochure are PowerPoint presentations and digital videos. Technology-supported marketing tools put the glitz and glamour on a story with high-impact visuals and/or captivating audio, which appeals especially to the digital-media oriented consumer. These tools also pair well with Web site and closed-circuit broadcasts, and are portable on the salespeople's pads and laptops as well.

Directories

The paper version of the Yellow Pages-type telephone directory is gradually being replaced by online directories. A sponsored business listing in an online directory or on a map Web site is as useful in a marketing program as it has been in print directories. An online listing has the added feature of interactive maps and GPS on many sites. These listings are also a good way to drive users to the company's digital addresses.

Branding Opportunities

The really creative part of marketing thinks up unique venues for a company's signature. Companies have promoted their brand on billboards, taxicab placards and automobile signs, tabletop placemats, and, of course, open house and yard signs. Companies have imprinted just about every imaginable give-away, from memo pads to mouse pads. They support ball teams with jerseys and community events with booths, and have also flown high in their hot air balloons. It's all about brand and driving viewers to digital addresses. You don't have to spend a lot of money—just make the expenditure memorable.

■ MARKETING PROPERTIES

Unless the company exclusively represents buyers, promoting listings is a significant part of a company's marketing activities and one that the sellers expect the company to perform with utmost skill.

Unfortunately, too many salespeople see the signature on a listing contract as the end of their responsibility to the company rather than the beginning of their responsibility to the property owners. Some of that is the company's fault if it focuses on quotas rather than on service. A property worth listing is worth marketing.

The marketing plan for listings involves as much common sense as advertising skill and knowledge of the laws that govern advertising practices. A rule of thumb is "if this was my property, how would I want to see it showcased?" The answer, of course, is in the best light. A property needs to be really ready for show (if not, some staging may be desirable), a realistic listing price, flattering pictures, and appealingly descriptive words.

While some marketing strategies achieve higher results than others in different market areas, the goal is to get the listing in the public eye. A company's own statistics can be used to determine how that eye is most effectively captured in its market area.

Photography

Digital media is also a visual media. Today's digital photography produces outstanding results and is particularly useful for a variety of electronic formats. Photographs can be attached to e-mails, uploaded to the Internet, and compiled in video. They can also be used for interactive videos and virtual tours on the Internet.

The "a picture is worth a thousand words" notion takes on new meaning for a company's advertising budget. A company (or the salesperson who's paying the bill) can ill afford to spend money on an ad that showcases a property that isn't ready for show, a tree or a brown hillside instead of the house, or a snowcapped roof when the tulips are fading into summertime.

The company can make much more effective advertising expenditures with an investment in good equipment and a talented photographer (if the salespeople can't do it well), along with a policy that only timely photographs will be used. Any photo taken by someone outside the company might be copyrighted, in which case permission is needed before it can be used.

Regardless of where the words appear (classified advertising, a Web site, or a script for a TV promotion), the price the company pays for marketing the property is worthwhile only if the ad copy is effective. While the listing salesperson is most familiar with the property and presumed to be the best person to write the ad, this also presumes the salesperson (or assistant) has the skill to write effective copy.

There are a variety of solutions to the poor-copy problem. Figure 12.1 is a form on which a salesperson can prepare notes to guide the development of an ad, particularly the sections on the right side of the form. With the help of computer software or hints from ad-writing seminars (including classes the company decides are necessary to offer), the salesperson can compile better copy. Or the company can use a copy specialist.

The copy must create a word picture of the property or communicate a message that generates attention, interest, desire, and action (AIDA). Numerous studies indicate that the three most important features in an ad are the neighborhood (location), the size of the property, and the price. As a practical matter, while abbreviations are common, not everyone understands a 4BR, 2B, hse w/EIK, FR, and 2 FPs. Make the ad make sense to the public.

Certainly, good ad copy enhances the chances that the listing will capture the right buyer. But even readers who aren't attracted to the specific prop-

FIGURE 12.1
Ad Copy Form

CLIENT'S NAME:		SP.:	WHAT MAKES THIS HOUSE DIFFERENT FROM ALL OTHER HOUSES ON THE MARKET AT THIS TIME? (USP—UNIQUE SELLING PROPOSITION)	
ADDRESS:		LED NO.:		
TOWN:		AGE:		
LIST PRICE:		LIST DATE:		
STYLE:		EXT.:	WHO DO YOU SEE BUYING THIS HOUSE?:	
ROOMS:	DR:	FAM. RM.:		
BR:		E-I-KIT:		
BATH:	FULL:	HALF:	LIST AN INDIVIDUAL FEATURE AND DESCRIBE THE BENEFIT OF THAT FEATURE TO A BUYER	
FINISHED BASE:				
FPLC:	WHERE:	TYPE:	SPECIAL FEATURE:	BENEFIT:
# GARAGE:		CENT. AIR:		
POOL:		DESCRIBE:		
PROP. SIZE:				
ITEMS INCLUDED:				
WALL TO WALL: ________		SELF CLEAN OVEN: _______		
REFRIG: ________		CENT. VAC.: _______		
WASHER: ________		INTERCOM: _______		
DRYER: ________		OTHER: _______		
SPECIAL INSTRUCTIONS AS TO ADVERTISING COMMITTMENTS:				
			1-Year Homeowner's Warranty Included: __Yes __No	

erty can be sufficiently impressed by the company's professional marketing skill.

Legal issues. Ultimately, the broker is responsible for the representations made in an ad, regardless of whether it is paid for by the company or the company's salesperson. The company has significant legal, as well as public relations, risk if laws are violated or the property is not accurately represented. *Monitoring advertising on Web sites, including the salespeople's own, is an essential risk-management activity.*

Superlative comments or opinions are permissible, misrepresentations of facts are not. If a house is described as "energy efficient," the typical reader expects superior insulation or cost-saving features, not just ordinary construction. Brand names, such as Thermopane®, should be used only when the named product is actually used. A typographical error (3 bedrooms instead of 2) is untruthful, regardless of whether the company's salesperson, the typist, or the publisher of the ad made the mistake.

An ad must truthfully represent the owner's position and protect the broker's fiduciary responsibility to the owner. Only the price authorized by the owner may be advertised (not unauthorized reductions), and confidential information that could compromise the owner's negotiating position cannot be disclosed ("owner anxious" unless authorized by the owner).

The state licensing laws may address issues that are revealed in the answers to

- Does the advertisement of a listing have to include the licensed name of the firm? The phone number? In the case of multiple offices, which phone number?
- What conditions or restrictions are imposed when salespeople include their names and phone numbers? What about personal voice mail and cell phone numbers?
- What are the procedures for advertising on the Internet?
- What are the requirements if the broker or a salesperson advertises property that is personally owned?

While financing terms may be appealing, the representations must comply with the truth-in-lending laws. General expressions, such as "owner will finance" or "liberal terms available," are permissible. But "only $1,000 down" is dangerously misleading and is permitted only if the specific loan terms are included (the amount of the loan, amount of the down payment, amount of the monthly payments, and length of the term).

Is the language nondiscriminatory? The fair housing laws prohibit making, printing, or publishing any statement that indicates any preference, limitation, or discrimination based on race, color, religion, sex, familial status, handicap, or national origin. If you're unsure about the language, consult the Federal Fair Housing Advertising Regulations, which are available on the Internet.

For example, language such as *whites only, Hispanic neighborhood, Christian home, adults only, adults preferred* or *older neighborhood, singles, no children, walking distance to the synagogue, one block from the Italian club,* and *good parish schools* are considered discriminatory. It is permissible to say *mother-in-law quarters, family room, walk to bus stop, bachelor pad, great view,* or *wheelchair ramp*. These are federal guidelines, so be sure to consult local and state legal references as well.

Ad Placement

From the company point of view, advertising serves dual purposes—to promote listings and to promote the company. The property owner, on the other hand, is concerned about only one thing—"my property." Sellers see advertising as their right of entitlement for listing the property, expecting that an ad will directly contribute to the sale of the property.

Although classified advertising in print media is still part of some marketing plans, the Internet is the most in-demand outlet for listings. They may be posted on the listing company's or salesperson's Web sites or promoted with tie-ins between the local MLS and the Internet or on national real estate sites such as Zillow or realtor.com, as long as the seller has not restricted Internet exposure.

Owners vigilantly watch the amount of exposure their listings get and are often critical of the way their listings are advertised. A salesperson may have made promises just to get the listing, or perhaps a frustrated property owner would not be satisfied with any amount of advertising for a property that hasn't yet sold. Regardless of the reason, the cause is the failure to present a well-defined marketing plan at the outset and to deliver periodic follow-up reports that demonstrate performance.

Brochures and Flyers

A brochure can be useful for marketing a listing. However, because of the expense involved, the truly elaborate ones are typically produced only for unique, boutique, or high-priced properties. A lesser version is a flyer, which is a nice supplement to the information that is provided in an MLS feature sheet. Flyers are useful for other companies' salespeople as well as for prospective purchasers and tenants. Again, management should monitor the content of brochures and flyers to ensure it doesn't create legal problems.

Open Houses

Open houses have been another standard tool of the trade, though they have their critics. The customs in the local marketplace, the company's measured results, the price of the property, and the salesperson's feelings about their effectiveness all factor into the decision to include an open house in a listing's marketing plan.

Open houses appeal to people's natural curiosity. Some owners don't want their properties to be fodder for that curiosity, while others see an open house as just another way that could possibly produce the one sought-after buyer. Owners sometimes measure the attentiveness of salespeople by their willingness to conduct open houses.

Salespeople have mixed views on the subject as well. Some contend that open houses aren't worth the effort, especially when no one shows up, and jeopardize their personal safety and lead to commission disputes between listing and selling agents in the process. Other salespeople have a more pragmatic view and hold open houses to appease sellers. Some studies suggest that open houses are better for self-promotion, benefitting the salesperson more than the seller.

Open houses are joint projects between the owner and the salesperson, and require careful planning and execution, regardless of whether they are conducted for other salespeople or the public. The critical, maybe event mystical, part of open houses is picking the right day and time. A weekday evening during daylight savings time may work in some areas but not in others, or a decorated holiday tour of the company's listings may work. Owners hesitate to authorize open houses when they expect to be inconvenienced, especially if no one shows up, and are sometimes uneasy about opening their homes to strangers.

Safety of the salesperson. Unfortunately, real estate salespeople have been victims of violent crimes while on the job. The company should insist that salespeople faithfully observe basic personal safety rules—their whereabouts are always known and they have the ability to summon help if necessary and an escape plan at the property. There's also safety in numbers, which is an argument for using several hosts, especially if the structure is large. Sign-in/sign-out registers, although not foolproof for identifying those with questionable motives, just might encourage such a person to leave.

Safety of the seller. No one should be allowed to freely wander through a property unattended. Although sellers should be encouraged to tuck away valuables, this does not guarantee that the owner's belongings are secure. Nor does the salespeople's presence, for that matter, but they must be vigilant observers.

Think about the artful thief whose hands are quicker than the eye or an unscrupulous visitor who's casing the premises for future reference and establish procedures to handle suspicious situations. At the conclusion of the open house, the salesperson should account for every visitor (the reason for sign-out entries) to be sure no one is still lurking in or around the property.

Safety of the visitor. Open houses can create liability for the company and the seller because people attend as invitees of both the owner and the brokerage firm. Salespeople must be alert to conditions that could jeopardize public (the visitors) safety to protect the interests of all concerned.

The company should insist that salespeople inspect properties for hazards and take precautionary steps (posting signs or colored tape, or verbally warning visitors). Although this case set a precedent in New Jersey, it also provided evidence that could be used by courts elsewhere.

Yard Signs

Yard signs are site-specific ads as well as institutional advertising. Although signs are the subject of ongoing controversy in some municipalities and are not permitted on certain properties (such as condominiums), yard signs are eye catching and often come with "take-one" boxes for flyers or digital connections to audio or visual information about the property.

■ THE COMPANY'S IMAGE

Everything a company does and says affects its brand and its relationship with the public. Unfortunately, a few missteps hurt public relations more than many good steps help, but such is the nature of business. The company's attentiveness to public relations plays a major role in its ability to generate business. In a word, this means reputation.

Marketing specialists do look at the company's reputation. As much as the marketing plan needs to match the business plan, there may be image-making efforts that will enhance other marketing efforts. Perhaps the company could do a better job of demonstrating its business philosophy, concern for community, or any number of other company ideals that foster goodwill with the public.

Companies enhance their community stature by doing things like underwriting charity fundraisers and youth sports teams to volunteering to fix up or repair someone's home. Within their own institutions, companies enhance their reputations with their attentiveness to customer satisfaction. While the company can't give away the store, so to speak, the little extra effort, or money if that's what it takes, returns invaluable goodwill.

All the best marketing plans and goodwill efforts won't undo the damage done by overly aggressive or illegal business practices. Consumers have grown increasingly intolerant of activities they see as the business community's chase for the almighty dollar at their expense.

Today's consumers have spoken—they want to be left alone—and they have the backing of a number of laws that sales businesses have to navigate when promoting their services.

Sales materials or brochures that are personally distributed to people's homes cannot be placed in a mailbox or other receptacle intended for use by the U.S. Postal Service. The offender can be subjected to the amount of first-class postage for the entire postal route in which the material was hand delivered, can be fined, or can jeopardize the company's bulk-mail permit.

Direct marketing by door-to-door and telephone solicitation can affect goodwill and run afoul of a number of laws as well.

One is the law of agency. The relationship a consumer has already established with another broker cannot be disrupted. The company needs a strict policy that its salespeople will not engage in discussions about future agency relationships with another broker's client unless invited to do so.

General solicitations to a geographic area or group, which may include individuals who are already clients of other firms, are not unethical. But targeting solicitations to another broker's client that promote the same services that are already being provided by the other licensee is a problem.

Telephone Consumer Protection Act. Telephone solicitation poses another problem. As of January 1, 2005, they are required to search the do-not-call registry every 31 days and eliminate from their call lists the phone numbers of registered consumers. This is one of a number of regulations that support the Telephone Consumer Protection Act that was passed in 1991, which governs the use of telephone lines for commercial solicitation and advertisement.

The legislation is intended to protect telephone subscribers who do not wish to receive unsolicited, live "cold call," autodialed, prerecorded, or artificial voice messages and fax machine solicitations.

Contacts with emergency lines to 911, healthcare facilities, physicians, poison-control, and fire or law enforcement are prohibited. Also prohibited are contacts with telephone lines in hospitals, healthcare facilities, and retirement home guest or patient rooms as well as paging services, cellular telephones, or any other service for which the consumer is charged a fee. (The law does not protect against solicitations by certain not-for-profit enterprises, and political candidates and parties.)

According to the procedures in the regulations, the soliciting company

- may not telephone a residence before 8 AM or after 9 PM;
- must identify the business name and telephone number and the name of the person making the call;
- must adopt a written policy and maintain a do-not-call list of residences requesting that they not be called;

- must advise and train all personnel and independent contractors engaged in any aspect of telephone solicitation regarding the do-not-call list maintenance and procedures;
- must share the do-not-call list with an affiliated entity (one that a consumer reasonably would expect to be affiliated with the soliciting company based on the company's name);
- may not use an automatic telephone dialing system in such a way that two or more telephone lines of a multiple-line business are engaged simultaneously; and
- may not use a telephone, computer, or other electronic/mechanical fax machine device to send unsolicited advertisements to another telephone, computer, or electronic/mechanical receiver.

The law allows calls to "existing customers," who are defined as people with whom the salesperson has done business in the past 18 months. A cold call is permitted to a FSBO (for sale by owner) who is registered on the do-not-call list if the salesperson has an actual buyer for the property, but not to solicit the listing.

The company's lawyer can help draft written policies and procedures that comply with the Telephone Consumer Protection Act. If the company has established written policies regarding these procedures, they may be used for defending alleged violations.

Be sure that the company and sales staff faithfully observe the provisions of recent federal (and perhaps state) "do-not-call list" legislation. A case in Pennsylvania resulted in $34,000 in penalties for violation of that state's law. For more information, go to *www.donotcall.gov*.

Note that some state laws are more restrictive than the federal law. The company and its sales staff must also comply with spam and fax laws.

Harassment. Salespeople must use common sense about how aggressively they pursue prospective customers and clients. If people feel harassed, the net effect is they have been alienated. Unfavorable comments spread faster than the favorable ones, so not only has one potential customer been turned off but so have many others. Also be sure that any local solicitation ordinances, along with permit requirements, are observed.

Blockbusting/panic selling. Any discussion of solicitation would be incomplete without a mention of blockbusting and panic selling. This consists of frequent efforts to sell real estate in a neighborhood by generating fear that people in protected classes are moving into or out of a neighborhood. The fair housing laws further define these actions as ones that include representations that real estate values are declining because of these transactions, which in fact have nothing to do with the intrinsic value of the real estate. Blockbusting or panic selling violates the fair housing laws.

A final comment about company image brings us back to a few other pitfalls that management needs to be aware of.

- If you're going to promote yourself as an expert, remember that consumers have grown weary and wary of the hollow representations that are occasionally made in this business. Claims need to be substantiated.
- Targeting a message to the wrong audience is not only a waste of time and money but also can damage reputations. Have you ever received a mailing and wondered why? Perhaps it was addressed to a party who has long since moved from your address, or its subject matter was totally irrelevant to you. Whether it's this activity or others, carelessness raises questions about attentiveness to details.
- Do you claim to be "Number One"? Number one in what? We're all number one in something, but unless you're specific, this claim can be misleading. Do you mean sales volume, market position, or number of offices? Can you substantiate this claim? (State license law may speak to these issues as well.) A point to ponder—what are the actual *benefits* to a consumer for doing business with number one?
- Use care when making comparisons between you and the competition. False or misleading statements about competitors are unethical. Knocking the competition looks desperate or unprofessional, neither of which will enhance reputations.
- Be *truthful* and *realistic* in your claims. Stating that you provide a "free service" when the service is contingent on some business ben-

efit to you (like a listing or a commission) is not only unethical but also a flagrant misrepresentation. Offers of premiums, prizes, or merchandise discounts may be regulated by your state's licensing laws.

- Do you have an affiliation with a professional organization or trade group? The industry tirelessly promotes its organizations and professional designations, and also vigilantly monitors unauthorized use of its trademarks, trade names, or insignia, and designations. Unauthorized use may also violate state license law.
- Promote the company's equal opportunity service, regardless of a consumer's race, color, religion, sex, familial status, handicap, or national origin. Display the equal opportunity slogan and logo in all printed material and publications. When using pictorial or graphic representations of people in a community, neighborhood, or housing development, be sure that the human models represent a cross section of the population.
- Selective use of media (broadcast, print, or electronic) could lead someone to conclude that your services are available only to certain populations. Publications whose audience profile is a population protected by the fair housing laws can be used only as long as publications that have general circulation are also used.
- Can you select publications that target specific audiences by, for example, nationality, language, or religion? Yes, provided you also advertise in a publication with general circulation. For example, if you are fluent in another language, you may want to use this skill to assist individuals who speak that language. You are permitted to advertise in a foreign language or nationality publication as long as you also advertise in a publication that reaches the general population.

CONCLUSION

What people see about a company is what drives business for the company, which makes marketing a core activity for every organization, not an expendable accessory. There is no one right marketing plan for everyone, only the one that delivers the messages in the venues that suit the individual company and its audience. Marketing plans have changed dramatically so that they reach the contemporary consumer. No doubt, the media business of today will be a different one tomorrow, simply because of technology. Even e-mail that has been a staple for the past decade is being surpassed by more spontaneous, interactive formats. Marketing is all about engagement, not just creating visibility.

■ DISCUSSION EXERCISES

What marketing strategies have been most effective in promoting your firm in your area? What did you try that didn't prove to be very effective? What techniques have you found to be most effective for capturing leads from Web sites?

What marketing strategies have you found to be most effective in promoting your listings? What ways have you found to control the cost of advertising listings?

What, if any, legal problems have you observed in the way companies and listings have been promoted in your area?

IN CONCLUSION OF UNIT III

The purpose of organizing is to properly equip a company so that it can conduct business efficiently and effectively. Every part of a company's structure—from its ownership, affiliations, and physical facilities to its business policies, alignment of its financial resources, and marketing plan—contributes to that operation. With all of that in place, the company has the systems that enable the people who provide the company's service to do their jobs.

■ THE SCENARIO

Having read this unit, what is your analysis of the following scenario?

The managers of the sales offices were each given a budget for their respective offices. The revenue from the salespeople's activities must cover the office's expenses for overhead (rent, telephone and communications, computers, and other equipment), advertising, salaries for clerical staff, and compensation for the manager as well as the salespeople and legal advisers. In addition, each office shares in the cost of the company's central administration. These include the company's accounting, marketing, relocation, and training departments. Essentially, each sales office is expected to operate as its own profit center while also supporting the company's overhead.

Taking the assignment to heart, Sally decides that if she is responsible for her office's meeting all of these expenses and must also turn a profit, she must make some changes. The first thing she does is goes shopping. The antiquated copy machine is replaced with a lease on a new, more cost-efficient and effective model. The outdated telephone system is replaced with one that is equipped with voicemail to minimize the time the secretary devotes to answering the phone and provide remote message access for the salespeople.

Next, Sally decides to institute a new advertising policy. Each salesperson is entitled to five listing ads per month at office expense. Additional ads must be paid for by the salesperson, though Sally has the right to review their content.

Finally, Sally looks at transaction revenue. She decides to set up a schedule of fees for services. Because the company provides both buyer-agency and services for selling properties, she identifies selected tasks that the salespeople perform for sellers and buyers. She then implements a fee-for-service menu of options that the salespeople can offer. Sally's notion is that charging for individual services rather than depending solely on full-service commissions would enhance revenue.

Sally feels very proud of herself because after the first quarter of the year, office revenue was ahead of projections and expenses were under budget. Her contentment, however, is short-lived.

When the office managers gathered with the broker and the heads of the administrative departments for a first-quarter review, Sally was asked to discuss what she had done to produce her results. It was then she learned that she had grossly overstepped her bounds. Office equipment must be requisitioned through headquarters because the company has a master contract with a vendor to provide all copier machines and supplies. The company also wanted the entire organization to be using the same phone system. Sally's fee-for-service menu was attacked because the company did not have any such policy to offer services under this pricing structure. About the only thing Sally did "right" was to exercise her authority over her office's advertising policy.

In a decentralized organization, one would think that the managers have total authority to run their departments or offices as they see fit, as long as they produce the results needed for the good of the whole. Apparently, that's what Sally thought, too. So, what pieces are missing here?

■ THE ANALYSIS

The discussions in this third unit should shed some light on Sally's situation in the scenario.

Obviously, the things Sally did produced positive results, at least in terms of efficiency and financial benefit for her office. Senior management could learn from this, that the company could make some changes and the organization as a whole would very likely benefit. The companywide financial impact, however, would have to be looked at more closely. In any event, Sally's office essentially became a pilot program, even though senior management hadn't planned on test-driving new procedures, especially testing marketplace reaction to a different fee structure.

The way Sally exercised authority, however, gets to the heart of organizational systems. Clear lines of authority are established to create order. Obviously, there was disorder, though the fault is not known. If senior management had not clearly communicated to subordinate managers the scope of their authority, then senior management is at fault and should take steps to correct that. If the subordinate manager (Sally) took it upon herself to fix things she thought senior management was negligent in addressing, then she's at fault. Better, she should have gone to the seniors with her observations.

Even in decentralized organizations, there are unified systems that intend to create efficiencies for all the business units. Centralized or bulk purchasing usually achieves cost efficiencies. The notion that every office has to endure the headaches of a lousy copy machine or an antiquated phone system simply because all of them do suggests that the system is managing the company instead of the company managing the system.

Because the business units function as individual profit centers, the company could direct unit managers to plan equipment upgrades in their budgeting processes. Senior management must also then be prepared to tolerate slimmer or neutral net profit from the units.

■ THE SUMMARY

Depending on whether you are the broker/owner, a senior manager in a large organization, a sales manager, or a department manager, your involvement in the various decisions and tasks involved in the organizing function of management will probably be different. As a guide for understanding where you participate in the process, the following summary is provided.

- Structuring the ownership, business affiliations, and human resources:
  - The broker/owner must decide the most suitable legal structure for the ownership and, perhaps with the assistance of senior management, decide the business affiliations for the company, chart the organization, and make preliminary decisions about the manpower requirements.
  - Other levels of management need to be familiar with the decisions that the broker/owner and senior management make and understand specifically where their authority or chain of command fits within the entire organization.
- Structuring the business systems, which include the company's physical facilities and communications and information systems:
  - The ultimate responsibility for deciding the location of offices and the design of the company's communications and information systems rests with the owners and, perhaps, senior management.
  - Lower levels of management may be invited to provide input into these decisions.
  - Depending on the scope of authority, a sales or department manager may be authorized to purchase office equipment and furnishings, and design the physical layout of the office.
- Structuring the finances of the organization:
  - The development of the general operating budget, including the compensation programs, is the responsibility of the broker/owner and senior management. They may, however, solicit input from other managers.
  - Lower levels of management are normally responsible for the budgets for their departments or offices.

- Developing policies and procedures for the company:
  - The broker/owner decides the general business philosophy and ethics for the organization.
  - All levels of management are typically involved in developing the policies and procedures to define the rules people are expected to follow in the general conduct of business.
- Marketing and advertising programs:
  - The chain of command in the organization determines the management level at which the major decisions about the company's general marketing plan are made and the level that is responsible for individual marketing strategies.

UNIT IV
STAFFING AND DIRECTING

An organization's business plan, and systems and facilities structures are hollow halls without people. The business management functions explored so far are designed primarily for the benefit of the organization's people. Planning gives them direction, guiding management's decisions and telling people what they need to be doing. Organizing gives order to the institution and assembles the necessary provisions so people can work effectively and efficiently.

Now comes the heart of the organization, the people who actually do the company's work. Managing the company's human resources is part of the job for any manager who supervises people. Most of all, the job is about motivating and inspiring the people the manager supervises. This is the staffing and directing function of management. In a real estate company, human resource management is a primary job, especially for managers of sales offices.

Human resource management involves

- recruiting, selecting, and hiring the appropriate personnel;
- creating a workplace environment that fosters professional development; and
- coaching performance and removing barriers that inhibit personal accomplishments and the ability of the company to accomplish its goals.

A multitude of issues and related tasks fall under these headings, ranging from processes that help management make legal hiring decisions and administer compensation (and perhaps benefit) programs to minimizing turnover, retaining valued personnel, and making prudent termination decisions.

Depending on the organization's departmental structure and hierarchy, a company's human resource policies and procedures may be directed by a human resource (HR) department or by senior management. But the person who is directly responsible for administering those policies and who has the greatest effect on the daily life of a company's worker is the immediate manager or supervisor. This is where that person's interpersonal skills (think back to Unit One) will make or break the relationship between the worker and the company.

The chapters in this unit are devoted to the activities that are necessary to assemble, develop, and retain staff and create an environment in which they can be productive.

13

CHAPTER THIRTEEN

THE PRACTICAL AND LEGAL REALITIES OF STAFFING

How do you decide which people to hire?
How much should they get paid?

Should the sales staff be employees or independent contractors?

While building a sales force is management's primary staffing activity in a real estate company, today's companies are generally supported by a number of administrative, secretarial, and clerical personnel as well. As organizations grow and become more diverse, they require more people with more specialized or diverse skills. And they need more managers, too.

The company's staffing requirements are determined by the organizational process that looks at the work that needs to be done and the job positions that are needed to do it (Chapter 8). Now all of this must be converted to specific talent.

The practical matter of staffing is that a company needs the best people it can hire, who have the credentials needed to do the jobs, and a plan to compensate them in ways that fairly convert their value to the company into pay. A company has just so much money to go around, so the company has to get the best talent it can afford. The legal reality of staffing is that a company must do this in ways that treat people fairly and equally in their respective job classifications.

■ PERSONNEL POSITIONS

Employment positions are typically characterized as full-time, exempt or nonexempt (a distinction that will be unraveled shortly), and contingent positions. The latter are the temporary, part-time, or leased (on loan) workers and independent contractors (ICs), who are consultants and special-service contract workers.

The scope and permanence of the work drive decisions about whether full-time employees or contingent workers are needed to fill the positions. A real estate company whose salespeople are independent contractors and the staple of that company's workforce would not consider them contingent workers, though.

Clerical and Administrative Support Positions

These include receptionists, secretaries, transaction coordinators, data entry and computer-support personnel, bookkeepers, and others who are trained specifically to handle paper and process, the behind-the-scenes support a company needs to operate. Typically, these are full-time and part-time or temporary employees.

Let's begin with the receptionist, the person who makes the first impression for the company. Some companies put the floor-duty salesperson in this seat, but that person's primary job is to sell, not to entertain visitors, direct them to the person with whom they have an appointment, or go searching for documents they stopped by to pick up. Though some companies see any face-to-face meeting as a sales opportunity (hence the salesperson in the receptionist seat), a person who's trained to handle receptionist and other clerical duties is a far more suitable host or hostess.

Secretaries and other clerical personnel provide essential services, but the company must be clear about whether their primary responsibility is to expedite paper and processes for the company or for the salespeople. If the salespeople think a secretary works at their beck and call to perform clerical tasks and the company expects a secretary to be handling company correspondence and other business, somebody's work isn't getting the priority it should. The secretary is then put in an untenable position.

Transaction coordinators are clerical personnel (hired by the company or a separate transaction-coordinating company) that are responsible for orchestrating the flow of documents between the time a sales contract is signed and escrow or title closes. Companies hire these workers to relieve salespeople of those chores and provide some quality assurance that transactions will proceed smoothly to settlement. These clerical personnel are the company's hires, not the salespeople's.

Data entry and computer support personnel are responsible for the high-tech data management functions in today's companies, although a company may outsource some of its computer support to a consultant. Bookkeepers support the company's financial management systems, though they may also be responsible for other clerical functions as well.

Personal Assistants

Personal assistants play an increasingly important role in today's real estate business, handling non-sales-related tasks for the salespeople. But incorporating those assistants within the company structure requires answers to some very important questions.

- Does the assistant work for the salesperson or the company?
- What are the specific tasks an assistant will perform?
- Must the assistant be licensed to perform these tasks?
- Is the assistant an employee or an independent contractor?
- Who pays the assistant?
- Who is responsible for withholding income tax and Social Security and paying statutory benefits such as workers' compensation and unemployment compensation for an employee?
- Who is responsible if the assistant violates the law?
- Who is liable if the assistant is injured at the company's workplace or while performing duties off-site?

Clearly, a personal assistant who is hired by the company becomes the company's employee (or IC), and the company is solely responsible for compensating and supervising the individual, particularly to ensure activities comply with real estate license law.

However, even if the personal assistant is hired by a salesperson, the company can still be responsible for the assistant's conduct, especially if the person's activities violate license law. The company must establish policies that define conduct for a salesperson's employee with respect to permissible tasks and use of office space, supplies, equipment, and other company resources.

Managerial Positions

Depending on the internal structure of the organization, there may be designated work groups that are responsible for activities such as training, marketing and advertising, recruiting, and accounting. These departments can be staffed as they would be in any corporation, though a familiarity with real estate may be helpful in some cases. These positions are typically full-time employees. Sales office managers are also part of the management team, typically as employees as opposed to contract workers.

Sales Force

The centerpiece of a real estate company's staff is its sales force. Assembling a sales force that is effective and cost-efficient involves several basic employment decisions.

- How many salespeople does the company need?
- Are they full-time or part-time personnel?
- Are the salespeople experienced or newly licensed?
- Are they employees or independent contractors?

The size of a sales force. Some companies accumulate licensees while others employ a small, highly skilled staff. The former group sees the size of the market share they can control being related to the number of salespeople they hire. Consequently, they plan for large sales staffs, expecting to control a larger share of the market. The latter group sees a smaller sales staff as more professional, more cost-efficient, and more easily supervised. If that's a staff of top producers, they'll control a sizable share of the market anyway.

Regardless of staffing philosophy, the reality is any given market can sustain only a finite number of salespeople competing for a finite amount of business. A company needs achievable staffing goals that are also financially feasible. That feasibility is a function of cost, revenue, and the break-even point.

Basically, what does a salesperson cost the company (both in direct costs like compensation and in indirect costs of managerial time, training, advertising, and the like) in relation to the revenue the person generates? Without a handle on these numbers, management can't determine the profit benefit of the current sales staff, let alone a new hire. And a new hire is more likely to function at the break-even (or deficit) point before becoming a profit benefit.

Companies sometimes use *desk cost,* which is simply a rule-of-thumb calculation that divides expenses by the number of salespeople. If expenses are $20,000 and there are two salespeople, the desk cost for each is $10,000 annually. If there are four salespeople, the desk cost is $5,000 for each one. On a 50–50 split, for example, each of the four salespeople does not begin to earn a profit until each has brought in a total of $10,000 gross commissions. This, too, is a break-even calculation, so there's no profit figured into the equation.

A major caveat to using the desk cost calculation is it doesn't accurately portray break-even in today's real estate company. Typically, commission splits vary from salesperson to salesperson, and often the salesperson's share is significantly higher than the company's. If à-la-carte menus of services are offered, there are more variables to complicate the math. Consequently, desk cost doesn't reflect the true cost of sales staff and isn't particularly useful for determining the number of salespeople needed.

Many more companies are learning to work more profitably with more streamlined sales staffs, primarily because of these financial revelations. The ability of managers to supervise the sales staff (one that expands beyond 30 people is more difficult) and the size of the available pool of talent the company desires (and can reasonably expect to attract) also factor into the staffing decisions.

The full-time versus part-time decision. An employee can be designated as full-time or part-time within the context of the number of hours worked per week. There's no such distinction for an independent contractor (IC). Because ICs are service-for-hire workers, their employment is a function of the services they render. The IC determines how much time is needed to perform the services the person has contracted to provide.

With that said, many real estate companies refer to their IC salespeople as being full-time or part-time. That's a vague (and not necessarily appropriate) characterization unless the IC contracts define the distinction—perhaps that a full-time salesperson is one who has no other employment or outside commitments and a part-time salesperson is one who does. But these definitions don't accommodate the salespeople who are good producers but have other careers, or the ones who fall within the full-time definition, but produce little. Better (and safer from an IC contract point of view) to categorize employment by production.

Regardless of whether a salesperson is an employee or an IC, production can be achieved by a full- and/or a part-time sales force. Sometimes full-time/part-time decisions are strictly philosophical, arising from notions that full-time people are more professional, more knowledgeable, or more committed and part-time people are less so. Although these perceptions may be justified in some cases, they are not universally applicable. Furthermore, some companies view part-time people as a unique asset because of their network of contacts in business and the community. However, part-timers can feel like second-class citizens unless managers provide the same degree of support they do for full-time salespeople.

As a practical matter, salespeople may need their current jobs to survive financially, support their real estate careers and provide for their families, and preserve hospitalization or other benefits for a period of time. Although some managers feel the best way to start a career is to jump in with both feet, this is unrealistic in many cases and could discourage an otherwise suitable hire.

Experienced versus newly licensed sales force. Both have their advantages and disadvantages. The obvious benefit of experienced salespeople is they have a customer base and the skills to make a productive contribution immediately. But experienced salespeople can be expensive to recruit. Top producers command top dollar and top amenities in the workplace. While it's tempting to try buying talent with generous compensation arrangements, that strategy will backfire if these people are treated more favorably than current, equally desirable salespeople. Resentment could result in the departure of others on the sales staff.

New licensees require considerable indoctrination, training, and supervision to get them started, which is a significant investment of time and money, and most don't begin producing for several months. All the while, they create expenses. Although their production will increase eventually (if they turn out to be successful), it usually takes several years to get established and about five years before people start earning a good living. Of course, there are always the individual rapid-fire success stories, but studies of median gross personal income show a dramatic jump from less than $20,000 during the first one- to five-year period to the mid-$40,000s in the next six- to ten-year period.

There are advantages, however, to building a sales staff with newly licensed people. The major one is they've not acquired any habits in the real estate business, so they don't have any bad habits to break. It's relatively easy to train a newly licensed salesperson in the company's way of doing business, which is sometimes a difficult retraining process for experienced people. As long as the company retains the newly licensed people who become solid producers, they can provide a solid revenue base while the company nurtures more newly licensed salespeople.

Real estate companies are often just trading talent among themselves. And sometimes they are trading personnel problems as well. Not every salesperson is suitable for your company. The one who blames the company (rather than himself or herself) for lack of success is not likely to do any better in another company. On the other hand, a company may be giving talent a chance to flourish in ways that were not otherwise possible. Different work environments, management styles, and business philosophies suit different people. Some people are simply disruptive influences anywhere they work, though.

Regardless of how attractive and competitive the company's services are, the company is not likely to attract top producers who are content where they're currently working. On the other hand, they know their worth, and if they feel they are being used to support the company and receive little reward or recognition in return, they will go elsewhere to work (and they will leave you if that happens in your company).

Employee versus independent contractor. The employee-salesperson model, the one most commonly used in the corporate world, looks like this—a company evaluates business potential in target markets and sales territories and assigns salespeople to selected territories based on workload or call-rate capacity. Generally, the salespeople are required to make certain quotas, by contacts and closings. Compensation is salary, commission, bonus, or a combination thereof, complete with required withholding and statutory workers' comp and unemployment benefits. Often employees also receive fringe benefits and are reimbursed some or all of their travel, entertainment, communications, and other out-of-office business expense.

The IC model, on the other hand, says that the salesperson earns commission according to rates stated in the contract and is responsible for all of his or her business expenses. In a real estate company, that often also includes a share of the company's expenses. The employing company/broker is responsible for the IC's conduct in accord with real estate license law, but otherwise ICs are free to work wherever and however they choose (within the jurisdictional limits of their licenses). The IC contract typically states some mutually agreed-on amount of production.

From a company's point of view, the employee model has a number of advantages, despite the cost (like statutory benefits and administration of tax withholding). In a word, control. There is no freewheeling marketing and selling (as with an IC), but rather a shorter leash with which to manage and supervise specific tasks and hold people accountable. The payback to the company is presumably better production and better quality service.

The IC model is traditional in the real estate industry, originally because it's a less expensive way for a company to field a sales staff and supports the notion that the sales staff would work harder as independent business people. The IC incurs a considerable amount of expense and the company reaps the majority of the income benefit, without any obligations for tax withholding or statutory benefits. This saves costs for the company, and the IC gets the income tax deduction for expenses.

Within the IC model, there are two classifications—**statutory independent contractors** (described in the federal tax code as statutory nonemployees) and **common-law independent contractors**. Federal tax law prescribes a three-part test for a salesperson to be considered a statutory independent contractor—(1) a properly issued real estate license; (2) a written IC agreement with the company/broker; and (3) substantially all of the compensation must be based on output or production, not hours worked. Statutory nonemployee or IC status is established when all three requirements are satisfied, at least for federal tax purposes.

Common-law independent contractors, on the other hand, do not meet the three-part test per se, but by appearances and conduct may be considered ICs as defined by court law. The missing part of the test is typically a written IC agreement. This leaves the IC versus employee determination to be decided by the manner in which the salesperson is supervised, the degree of control the company exercises over the activities, and the manner in which the person is compensated.

The distinction between statutory and common law ICs is especially significant where state laws vary with federal law. The salesperson could be an IC for federal tax purposes but considered an employee by the state, which then requires withholding for taxes and payment of unemployment and workers' compensation.

As a real estate company's cost of doing business increases, the advantages and disadvantages of the two models become less significant. Although the majority of real estate companies use the IC model, companies do choose to go the employee route, buying into the added employee costs to gain greater control over the sales activities. Generally, these companies have smaller sales forces and are more selective about the salespeople they hire. Often those salespeople feel like they are part of a finely tuned sales organization.

A way out of the full-time/part-time dilemma. In some parts of the country, real estate companies set up separate subsidiaries called *license-in-referral organizations (LIFROs)*. These are licensed brokerage firms that hire licensed salespeople, but these people don't actually engage in any sales activities. Instead, they provide business leads (referrals) that the LIFRO then refers to the affiliated brokerage firm. LIFROs are a way to attract or retain salespeople who don't meet a company's full-time criteria but can contribute by referring business.

LIFROs normally exist where the licensing laws prohibit the payment of a referral fee to people who don't have a real estate license. A referral company is a legal conduit through which licensees can receive these fees when they are collected from the conventional brokerage firm. LIFROs have also been formed to avoid membership assessments by industry organizations for people who are licensed but act only as referral agents.

Job Qualifications

Before the company jumps on the recruiting bandwagon to fill any personnel positions, management needs another set of marching orders—the job description and the qualifications for the position. The job description (which was developed in the previous unit) describes the role and responsibilities of the position. The qualifications describe the knowledge, skill sets, experience, and personal characteristics that are necessary to perform that job and are a business necessity for the company. The equal employment opportunity laws require criteria that are associated with *job relatedness* and *business necessity*.

How do you know what qualifications are necessary? Use a *job analysis*, which is a process of analyzing all of the activities a job entails and determining what a person needs to know or be able to do. If the company hasn't prepared its own, HR resources (on the Internet) can provide sample analyses for various staff and clerical positions, and real estate industry resources have similar ones for salespeople. All of these can be refined to suit the individual company. A job analysis serves as the benchmark for matching work and qualifications, which is a strictly job-performance-based exercise.

One of the most useful ways to convert qualifications to a hiring guide is with a *candidate profile*. This says "here are the absolute essential or minimum qualifications (knowledge, skill sets, and so forth) to perform the job, and here are the ones that would be helpful or nice to have." The more thought given to whom the company needs to hire, the more efficiently management can screen candidates. Generally, the first cut is based on the minimum qualifications, so think about the kind of candidate that may be eliminated (or slip through) at that point.

■ COMPENSATION MANAGEMENT

Pay is a significant factor in a company's ability to recruit, motivate, and retain personnel. Today's real estate company has more hourly-wage and salaried workers, not just straight commission people, and more variations in personnel positions (managerial, administrative, clerical, as well as sales), all of which require thinking about pay in a new light. People's perception that the company's pay is inappropriate can seriously compromise a company's staffing efforts.

Compensation planning and administration is a function of the company's philosophy about paying people, the position of the jobs within the organization, and the accompanying qualifications and expertise or experience level of the people in those jobs.

People need to feel they are being fairly compensated for their efforts and must also be able to earn a decent living. The company needs affordable compensation programs so it can stay in business. These are not necessarily opposing desires, but they are certainly ones that require some careful planning to satisfy.

Compensation plans reflect a company's philosophy about pay. The *entitlement* philosophy says that pay should increase with seniority or length of service to the company, without regard to changes in the industry or economy. The *performance* philosophy says that pay is solely a function of the outcomes of a person's performance, with the result that pay can go up and down, perhaps dramatically.

Both philosophies are impractical in their purest forms. A company can't endure the inflexible financial commitment of entitlement or administer a pure performance-based system accurately and fairly. In the real world, pay plans are variations on the themes of these philosophies.

The point of compensation is to *reward people for their value to the company*. The purpose of a compensation plan is to convert that value to pay. How much are people worth? Many of them are worth far more than the company can afford to pay, but as long as people feel they are being fairly rewarded and have a rich environment in which to work, the company has made a satisfactory statement. Most companies use a traditional compensation model to convert value to pay. The process involves

1. Analyzing the importance of job positions in the company, the level of responsibility, and the sophistication of expertise (knowledge, skills, and abilities) required, all of which are revealed in job descriptions and job qualifications
2. Analyzing the pay structures of other similar organizations for similar jobs, as revealed from compensation surveys
3. Developing a pay structure for the organization, using job evaluation and survey data to classify jobs and pay grades (or ranges of pay) within the organization
4. Developing pay structures for individual positions, including a process to use performance appraisals to evaluate individuals
5. Institutionalizing the company's compensation program with communication, implementation, and monitoring

The goal of this process is to align pay with the work people do, align the company's pay with the marketplace, and develop an affordable pay structure that the company can administer fairly.

Pay Plans

Pay comes in various forms. *Wages*, which are hourly rates of pay; *salaries*, which are characterized as annual rates of compensation; and *variable pay* plans, which are singular or combinations of base salary, commission, bonuses, or other benefit incentives. A real estate company has a number of personnel positions, not just the sales force, for which it needs a pay plan.

As much discretion as a company has to devise its own policies and pay plans, a company doesn't necessarily have free rein to do as it chooses. Pay practices have to be grounded in a firm legal foundation, particularly to ensure that *equal work gets equal pay* in compliance with employment laws.

Designing compliant pay plans isn't easy, and small business owners, especially, are often overwhelmed by the task. (Some operate under the misguided notion that the laws don't apply to them.) Adding to the task is that state and federal laws constantly change, raising and lowering thresholds for required compliance, increasing minimum wages, and altering job classifications and rules for pay. A company can't design pay plans and forget them. The simplest way to make sense of a very complicated maze is to say that every company needs the advice and counsel of skilled labor law specialists.

State labor and wage-and-hour laws may apply, and perhaps the Federal Labor Standards Act (FLSA) as well. Pay attention to provisions regarding the employment of minors, minimum wage laws, and rules for overtime pay. Generally, full-time hourly workers are considered to be working a 40-hour week. Additional hours are considered overtime and must be compensated at one-and-a-half times the hourly rate for each hour of overtime.

Exempt versus nonexempt workers. One of the most baffling and, therefore, challenging compliance issues comes from the FLSA (a state law may be similar) and regulations about which workers must be paid for working overtime. This is where the exempt and nonexempt distinction applies.

The laws are very complex and should be investigated thoroughly, but generally salaried executives, managers, and administrative and outside sales personnel are *exempt*. In other words, work is performed for the stated salary (without overtime pay) regardless of the number of hours or workdays devoted to the job. *Nonexempt* salaried workers, like clerical personnel and laborers, are not exempt from overtime rules and must be compensated accordingly.

Changes in FLSA regulations in 2004 attempted to resolve some of the confusion about which workers are exempt and nonexempt, and who must receive overtime pay. This meant looking at employees in a new light because some who were previously exempt were not any longer, and vice versa. Three tests must be met to be considered *exempt*.

1. **Salary level test.** Employees making more than $455/week, which translates to a yearly salary of $23,660 (increased from $8,060), are considered *exempt*. The effect of raising the threshold for exempt workers is that many more workers are entitled to overtime pay. The regulations also created a "highly compensated" exempt status for people earning more than $100,000 per year (including commissions and nondiscretionary income and bonuses) who regularly

perform exempt duties defined in the job basis test for executive or administrative or professional positions. The status of workers that fall between the two salary thresholds is more challenging to decipher, which makes the next two tests exceedingly important.

2. **Salary basis test.** The worker must regularly receive a predetermined amount of compensation that cannot be reduced or "docked" because of variations in the quality or quantity of work performed. The regulations, however, provide seven exceptions to the "no dock" rule that protect the exempt status, although pay is deducted.

3. **Job basis test.** This defines the duties that entitle executive, administrative, and professional positions to exempt status. The executive must customarily direct the work of two or more employees and have the authority (or influence) to hire and fire others. The administrative position qualifies if the primary duty is to perform office or nonmanual work related to the management or general business operations of the employer, and to exercise discretion and independent judgment over matters of significance. Professional positions must perform work requiring advanced knowledge in a field of science or learning that is predominately intellectual and perform work that requires invention, imagination, originality, or talent in a recognized field of artistic or creative endeavor.

Clearly, there are a lot of regulatory words and meaning behind this three-test summary, but it provides a starting point and further testimony to the need for expert assistance, including for today's typical real estate company.

Variable pay plans link compensation with performance in some fashion. These plans are suitable for salespeople and executives, managers, and other professionals where individual performance or production, or contribution to organizational accomplishments can be measured. For employees (as opposed to ICs) there is a base pay, but the incentive in these pay plans is the reward for past performance or accomplishments, with the expectation that greater accomplishments will be forthcoming in the future.

The theory behind variable pay is that people are motivated by money, which means bonuses, overrides, and higher commission splits are suitable incentives. These also provide recognition and when pay is tied to organizational accomplishments, people feel they are stakeholders in the company, which fosters commitment. Companies can also demonstrate worth with benefits like expense accounts, profit-sharing or stock-purchasing programs, and pension plans.

Pay is a package comprising wage, salary, or variable pay and incentives plus other benefits a company may be required to provide (unemployment compensation and workers' compensation) or discretionary fringes like health care or life insurance, profit-sharing, and retirement plans. Some workers consider required withholding for income taxes and Social Security from employee wages to be a benefit.

Equity

Equity is the perceived fairness of what a person gets paid in relation to what a person does. People measure fairness in comparison with what others in the organization do and get paid (*internal equity*) and what people in other companies do and get paid (*external equity*). All of this is a function of perception as well as fact.

Consequently, equity arises from how well the company aligns pay with work, aligns pay with the competition, and communicates to its workers exactly what the company's pay policies and structures are, all of which are part of the company's compensation management process.

In theory, a company can pay people whatever it wants to or can afford. However, people (especially salespeople) go shopping for the best deal and if a company can't provide that deal in terms of money and work environment, then the company is not in a strong position to recruit or retain personnel. Industry surveys (the most current are available on the Internet), particularly those that are broken down by region and firm size, provide a starting point for evaluating market pay. Clerical, administrative, and managerial pay can be evaluated similarly.

A company can fix its pay levels to fall at the bottom, middle, or highest range in comparison with other companies.

- The bottom range says that 75 percent of the companies pay more. A company may choose this strategy when it's short of funds or the labor market is flush, but the likelihood is that the company will experience greater turnover.

- The highest range says that the company is near the top 25 percent compared with other companies. This is an aggressive strategy that is very attractive for recruiting and retaining top personnel and increasing productivity. But the company must be very selective in its hiring and vigilant about monitoring personnel performance to gain maximum financial benefit.
- The middle range pegs the company in the mid-market, with 50 percent of the companies paying more and 50 percent paying less. This is a moderate strategy that has neither enormous competitive advantage nor disadvantage, but it keeps the company in the running and is the strategy many companies use, particularly because it's more affordable than the highest sector.

From an internal perspective, equity means that all people who work in the *same class of jobs* are compensated at the same pay scale. While the golden goose (the sales force) is valuable, other positions are also valuable, and pay must be commensurately aligned with the level of responsibility in the organization. Managerial positions are especially vulnerable to the equity comparison in this respect.

Secrecy is a major enemy to equity. Companies can foster an atmosphere of fairness by publishing pay policies and wage, salary, and commission scales (not what each person makes). People need to see where their pay falls within the big scheme of things and exactly how pay, performance, and promotions through pay are evaluated. People may not necessarily like what they see, but they are far more content when they see a fair rationale for compensation.

Justice

Like other organizational policies and procedures, compensation policies must be faithfully, consistently, and even-handedly administered. Justice arises from the perception (again) that people are being treated fairly, that the rules management has laid out are being equally applied to each person in the same class of jobs.

One of the reasons pay is categorized in ranges is so people in the same job classification can be compensated according to performance, experience, or seniority (if that's a company policy). This means that individuals' pay can be different, depending on performance, expertise, or seniority, but pay must fall within the set range for that job classification.

Pay is periodically adjusted, commonly on an annual basis, though a new hire's pay may be reviewed after an initial three- or six-month period. Management needs specific, stated procedures (that it faithfully follows) for reviewing personnel and increasing, decreasing, or sustaining pay. Performance reviews are the typically stated platform for assessing personnel. Company procedures need to state how performance will be evaluated so people know what is expected of them ahead of time.

Any time management favors some personnel over others with similar experience or production (or bends the rules for recruiting purposes), management is suspect. While the favored party may be happy, the rest of the company's workforce can feel they too may be victimized by (or can manipulate) management—so much for justice. Furthermore, the company is ripe for accusations that equal employment laws have been violated.

Sales Compensation

Sales forces are typically compensated with

- straight salary, though that is usually done only for a short-term base period.
- straight commission, which is a sell-to-earn plan.
- salary and bonuses, which include base salary plus a range of bonuses or other performance incentives, including expense accounts, profit sharing, and the like (for employees). The larger the difference between the base and the bonus, the more incentive-dependent the pay.

Straight commission doesn't provide great financial security, especially when sales don't occur at regular intervals. The gap between checks can be bridged with a draw (advance against future commission), the expectation being that the bookkeeping will come out even as commissions earned cover pay that has been advanced. The possibility of a deficit always exists, though.

Draws are not particularly desirable forms of pay (especially when they are routinely paid to an unproductive salesperson) because they can be construed as unplanned salary. That's not so problematic for the employee-salesperson but can become a significant issue for an IC, especially if there's a deficit.

The rationale behind the real estate industry's traditional IC, straight-commission model is the expectation that salespeople will be motivated to work harder and make more money. That harder work is often rewarded with a graduated commission split, with a larger share of the gross being the salesperson's pay.

This is a worthy incentive only as long as the company doesn't play numbers games by deducting a variety of company expenses from the salesperson's share. A split that appears attractive on the surface could in reality mean the salesperson earns less. Baiting salespeople with such programs can result in their switching to the competition.

This IC, straight-commission model is clearly performance-based, but it also assumes that money is an enduring motivator, which is not necessarily the case once the salesperson pays a child's tuition for the term or has earned enough to vacation or visit the grandchildren. Often workplace conditions and benefits like healthcare, retirement, or profit-sharing plans mean more. Unless the salespeople are employees, fringe benefits must be structured meticulously to preserve the IC status.

Another challenge to the straight-commission plan is that today's real estate industry is no longer a straight-commission business. With more and more companies adopting alternate pricing models, company revenue is an increasingly complex mix of fees collected for a variety of services. The bookkeeping alone is a burdensome task using the traditional split methodology.

From a performance-based perspective, the question arises whether all fees earned for services are equally valuable to the company. Differentiating between those the company values more and applying a different split to them only adds to the mathematical nightmares. Because the salesperson's job is to provide service, the salesperson is better compensated for the effort of delivering those services plus a bonus (rather than a split) on fees generated in excess of a base amount. This is a great argument in favor of paying a base salary to an employee-salesperson plus a bonus.

Managerial Compensation

Structuring appropriate compensation for supervisory and managerial personnel, senior management, and even executives is more challenging. By the definition of their responsibilities, their activities contribute indirectly to the productivity of the organization. This is not to say that their roles are less important than the people who directly generate revenue (the sales force), but it's more difficult to quantify the relationship between managerial effectiveness and company performance.

Companies address this by holding managers accountable for certain performance objectives, standards, or outcomes within the company and then compensating according to the results. Pay is linked to the scope of responsibility and the position in the organization's hierarchy. The higher the position, the greater the responsibility and scope of authority and therefore the higher pay. The value to the organization conversion is based on the premise that all that happens can ultimately be credited to or blamed on leadership.

In effect, companies pay managerial personnel for exercising their judgment as they make decisions and discharge their responsibilities. Experience (gained within and/or outside the organization) and sometimes seniority factor into pay, especially for senior managers. Companies are often willing to pay dearly for their proven track records (and presumably good judgment), the expectation being that their value to the company is worth the pay. Though people often question the value of some senior executives to warrant the seemingly outrageous amounts of pay they receive.

A flaw in an accountability-based compensation plan for managers in lower levels of the organization is they have less or little control over all the variables that affect the performance outcomes of the office or department they supervise. If they don't have the authority to select or hire the personnel they supervise, that only exacerbates the situation.

A sales office manager depends on the skills and abilities of others and, therefore, has no direct control over revenue, but yet is accountable for achieving revenue objectives. If that manager's sales staff is less skilled or effective than other sales managers', the manager has more potential performance deficits to supervise. Often greater effort is required to supervise the less-skillful or less-experienced sales force. If the manager's pay is based solely on office performance without consideration for these variables, then pay is not fair or equitable in comparison with other managers doing similar jobs.

Real estate sales managers look at equity and justice in pay the same way any other worker does. This says that a company's pay policies for sales managers must be devised following the process described earlier. These are best designed as employee (as opposed to IC) positions because of the level of control and accountability that accompanies these supervisory roles.

Sales manager pay can be structured as straight salary or as variable pay, a base salary plus a bonus or an override on the percentage of gross commission (before salespeople's shares are deducted) or on net profit of the office. The latter is an incentive for the manager who has authority for financial decisions to manage expenses. The net profit calculation, though, is affected by the commission splits of the individual salespeople. An office of top producers with top splits leaves less for the company, and the net profit doesn't look as good as the gross volume would.

To fairly compensate the manager, override percentages need to be structured with this in mind.

The debate over full-time managers and selling managers arises again when it comes to devising pay plans. There may be some financial realities (especially for a start-up or cash-strapped company) that require a manager to also sell. However, this should not take the place of fair compensation for the supervisory job the company expects the manager to do.

■ LEGALITIES OF EMPLOYMENT

In addition to laws referenced earlier, a number of other laws affect personnel policies and procedures and the workplace environment. The way companies recruit, select and hire, promote, and terminate people and the social and physical environment in which they work are all subject to an ever-expanding body of law, particularly as courts further interpret the laws.

Lest one say that the way out from under all of this is to employ ICs, the fact is the laws don't distinguish between ICs and employees. The applicability of some laws, however, does differ, depending on the number of workers a company has and other distinctions that an attorney skilled in employment law can interpret for the company.

Equal Employment Practices

Most companies with at least 15 employees are covered by the employment discrimination laws that are enforced by the federal Equal Employment Opportunity Commission (EEOC). The laws apply to employment practices related to hiring, firing, promotion, harassment, training, wages and benefits. Although race, gender, age, and disability continue to represent the highest number of job discrimination complaints, no class is immune from employment discrimination, especially in today's more culturally diverse workplace.

As the workforce ages, companies attempt to reduce the number of high-salaried workers and the long-term costs of their retirement benefits, with the result being a rash of age discrimination complaints, often accompanied by accusations that employers fabricated reasons to terminate employment. Though any time the economy heads south and companies trim their workforces, the number of discrimination complaints increases.

When the economy starts to pick up, employers often look for less expensive ways to restore their workforces, which also makes it difficult for the 40-year-and-older worker to regain employment.

The latest attempt to address age discrimination as well as to bolster employment is the Reasonable Factors Other than Age regulation that was adopted by the EEOC in March 2012. The rule attempts to strike a balance between protecting older workers from discrimination and preserving the employer's ability to make reasonable business decisions.

The rule prohibits policies and procedures that have the effect of harming older workers in favor of younger ones, unless the employer can show the practices are based on some reasonable factor other than age. The rule applies to private employers with 20 or more employees, among other employers.

A number of other employment laws are designed to protect against discrimination in the workplace. Among these are Title VII of the Civil Rights Act of 1964, the Civil Rights Act of 1991, the Age Discrimination in Employment Act, and the Americans with Disabilities Act (ADA). In addition, there is the Equal Pay Act of 1963, the Pregnancy Discrimination Act of 1978, and the Family and Medical Leave Act of 1993. Most states and some cities or municipalities have their own employment laws as well, some of which are similar to and others more restrictive than federal law.

The best advice is not to devise any employment policy or procedure until all of the laws are investigated. The purpose of equal employment laws is to prevent the employer from basing employment decisions on factors that are unrelated to the actual performance of a job. This means that virtually every human resource management activity *must scrupulously guard against any conduct* that, in purpose or effect, treats people differently because of their race, color, religion, sex or gender, national origin, age, marital status, or disability.

Job application forms and job screening and interview procedures, selection and hiring procedures, training, advancement, pay, and termination of employment as well as recruitment, advertising, tenure, layoff, leave, fringe benefits, and responsiveness to conflicts in the workplace are all potential places for allegations of discrimination. Even when a company declares suitable equal opportunity policies and procedures, lax or inconsistent enforcement can also raise questions of discrimination.

Like complaints of discrimination in housing, allegations of employment discrimination are time-consuming to defend, even if no grounds are found, and costly if a company is found guilty. The public relations fallout in an industry that supports equal housing opportunities can be especially damaging.

While information is essential for a manager to properly manage personnel, there is certain information that is *patently irrelevant* and should not in any way be explored in application forms, job interviews or counseling sessions, or captured in personnel records. One of the virtues of the job qualifications discussed earlier is they are clearly job based. Use those as a guide to avoid wandering into territory that could violate the law. Avoid all inquiries that relate to the protected classes and discussions that could be construed to tread into those areas, such as

- Citizenship and origin of name or maiden name
- Physical abilities, or limitations or disabilities
- Education and experience that are not a requirement for the job (arbitrary qualifications could effectively be discriminatory)
- Family matters (spouse, marriage or pending prospect, and children or pregnancy can lead to gender discrimination; ages of children can reveal worker's age)
- Feelings about working with people (either in the workplace or consumers) who are older/younger, or another gender, race, nationality, etc.
- Availability to work on Saturday or Sunday (can be a religious issue)
- Childhood background (place where grew up and the like; can reveal nationality, race, etc.)

Anti-Harassment Policies

Cultural diversity in the workplace plus growing intolerance of certain gender-related conduct creates an environment in which managers must manage not only uncomfortable and offensive but also illegal behavior. In addition to the equal employment laws previously referenced, there are numerous state and local laws prohibiting discrimination based on gender or sexual orientation.

Harassment is generally considered to be behavior or conduct that is hostile or demeans, humiliates, embarrasses, intimidates, or threatens a person. Management's zero-tolerance of inappropriate behavior is not only a requirement of the law but simply the right thing to do.

The company needs to publish an anti-harassment policy that clearly defines behavior that is not tolerated and establish a nonthreatening, open-door policy so that an offended person can bring the matter to management's attention without fear of reprisal. To support the policy, management needs a declared process to resolve the issue. Generally, this involves

- appointing a member of staff who is the point person to investigate complaints.
- developing a plan to handle the individual complaint, including identifying the key people involved and the situations that need to be explored.
- interviewing the person who lodged the complaint, complete with reassurance that the person was right in stepping forward and that the person's job is not in jeopardy by doing so.
- informing the accused person of the complaint, complete with reassurance that the accused's side of the story is part of the investigation.
- interviewing the accused and any witnesses.
- developing an appropriate resolution, which may include adjusting working conditions to separate the parties involved.

Document all that transpires. A company is defenseless without good records in the event of future misconduct. Typically, companies adopt procedures for warnings, followed by periods of mandatory leave, and then dismissal for repeat offenders.

Safety in the Workplace

The company has valuable human resources that need to be protected. People also deserve healthful working conditions and the Occupational Safety and Health Act of 1970 says so, too. The law covers ergonomics, lighting, and equipment layout as well as exposure to hazardous substances, substance abuse, and workplace air quality, which is where smoking issues fall. Certainly, these are legal issues that management must be attentive to, but there's also the practical matter that the more pleasant the working conditions, the better people perform.

■ CONCLUSION

The foundation of the staffing function is the company's personnel policies and procedures. These guide virtually every event in human resource management. The discussions relating to personnel positions, requirements for jobs, compensation management, and the legal issues that surround all of these topics provide a platform on which to further develop lawful and practical policies and procedures for recruiting, selecting, hiring, and supervising personnel.

■ DISCUSSION EXERCISES

Select a job position in your company and develop an appropriate candidate profile for that position. How does what you developed compare with what currently exists? How did you arrive at the qualifications you've selected as appropriate?

Identify the pros and cons of hiring a sales staff of employees versus independent contractors. If you hire a salesperson as an employee, how would you structure the job and compensation?

Discuss your perceptions of pay (either as a salesperson or a manager) and the strengths or weaknesses in the way compensation is administered in your company, based on what you've learned in this chapter.

What do you consider the most challenging legal issues in today's world of employment law? Why?

14

CHAPTER FOURTEEN

RECRUITING, SELECTING, AND HIRING THE STAFF

Why do people leave your company?
How does that affect recruiting and hiring new personnel?

How do you decide which salespeople to hire?

The job market is a market on the move, not just because companies lay off and people have to look elsewhere for work but because the market churns. People quit to take jobs with other companies, they retire, and they leave the job market for other reasons. Those departures open up positions for people who've been unemployed, for new entries into the workforce, and for those who've been working with other companies. And as new hires move on over time, the cycle continues.

Companies essentially trade talent. That pool of talent is larger or smaller, depending on the economy at the time. But even when that pool is large, the specific talent a company needs may not be available or available at the price the company wants to pay. Just because a person needs a job and the company has a position to fill doesn't necessarily make a match that suits both the company and the worker.

The objective in recruiting, selecting, and hiring is to pick the right person for the position. That right person, however, is one who feels he or she has picked the right position in the right company as well. Any discussion about recruiting, selecting, and hiring staff is premature without first looking at whether the company is in the position to be the employer of choice.

■ EMPLOYER OF CHOICE

The most trusted companies are in the best position to be that employer of choice. Back to the company's policies and practices that demonstrate concern for others, which for the worker translates to concern for "me," and commitment. This then translates to delivering on the promises the company makes to its workers. A compassionate place to work, a fair and honest competitor, and an institution of integrity commands a following.

Turnover is a strong indicator of a company's following. Although people leave for a variety of voluntary and involuntary reasons, the company bears some responsibility in all cases. Companies make poor hiring decisions and over sell jobs to capture prime recruits, which then turn out to be problems that could have been avoided. Even when people leave for better opportunities (the churning effect), the company needs to consider what's lacking in opportunities or attractive alternatives that would give it a competitive advantage.

We think about the power of a company's brand and reputation in the marketplace, but those also give the company power as an employer. Any company that thinks even clerical workers, let alone salespeople, don't pay attention to a company's reputation is missing an important point, especially today. The company and its principal players are an open book on the Internet, and you can be sure that potential workers are searching. Although it would be nice to think that some internal business would stay within the company, that's not the real world of hyper-spontaneous communications.

Note that employer of choice is not all about money. Certainly, a company is conspicuously unattractive without a fair and just compensation plan (back to the previous chapter), and workers have to be able to trust the company to deliver the money as promised (and not play games with pay).

But there's a lot more to trust about the way a company treats its workforce, in the company's personnel relations and the honor and integrity of its managers. With at-will contract workers (the ICs), that's all the clout the company has to retain a valued resource.

Companies can't afford to invest in new hires, only for them to leave. Staffing is an expensive proposition in management's time and company's money to recruit, select, and hire personnel and then indoctrinate and train them. Departures cost mightily in exit procedures and lost production while the company spends more money to hire and train replacements. The right hire is one the company can *retain*.

■ EMPLOYMENT PROCESS

The employment process is a series of methodical steps intended to produce intelligent hiring decisions. The previous chapter's discussions about employment laws, job performance-based qualifications, and compensation management are centerpieces of that process, regardless of whether the company is hiring an employee or an independent contractor.

Although some steps in the process are more involved when the job position involves significant responsibility or specialized skills, the general framework is the same for any position. The process begins with *recruiting*. This step gathers potential applicants and follows with *prescreening*, which is normally an application and preliminary interview or conversation. Then *formal interviews* are conducted and follow with *selection*, which is when the candidates are evaluated. And finally, the *hiring* step when an offer of employment is extended.

Each step is a filtering process, with the object being to narrow the field of contenders and identify the most suitable candidate for the position. (See Figure 14.1.)

Recruiting

Recruiting is simply the process of assembling a *pool of candidates* or *applicants* for consideration. That process is all about networking to generate candidates. Obviously, the larger the pool, the greater the choices the company has. But the request for applications or the job posting has to be

FIGURE 14.1
Employment Process

Step	Activity	Purpose
Recruiting	Generate a pool of candidates	Gather applicants for consideration
Prescreening	Application and preliminary interview	Gather preliminary information to determine whether to pursue the next step (Decision Point 1)
Formal Interview	Formal job interview(s)	Gather sufficient information to make a decision whether to hire an applicant (Decision Point 2)
Selection	Review information gathered about an applicant	Determine whether applicant is suitable for the position (Decision Point 3)
Hire	Make job offer and establish personnel file	Ensure new hire and company are properly prepared to begin a working relationship

sufficiently explanatory, at least with a brief description of key credentials, so as not to waste people's time.

Companies often have policies that job opportunities must be offered to current workers before soliciting applicants from outside the organization, which means that job postings must be communicated so that everyone in the organization is aware of the available position. These hire-from-within policies are consistent with protocols that create opportunities for advancement and professional development.

A company's current workers, including their managers, are also good recruiting ambassadors. Their first-hand experience with the company lends credibility to the process but they also have a vested interest in the company team. Good people want to be associated with other good workers and often know someone (who may know someone else) who would be an asset to the organization.

The major external recruiting tool today is the Internet, with employment and trade association Web sites as well as the company's own site. In fact, some sites are set up to collect applications and résumés and perhaps even prescreen the applications before the company sees them. Temporary placement agencies are also helpful, even if the position is not intended to be temporary because talent is often looking for full-time placement. (Tactics for recruiting salespeople will be discussed later in the chapter.)

Prescreening

The purpose of prescreening is to decide whether an applicant meets the minimum requirements for the position as outlined in the candidate profile. This is a quick weed-out step, from which management develops a short list of applicants for further consideration. (Decision Point 1)

Prescreening can be done with an application form, a résumé, a short phone or videoconference conversation, a brief face-to-face meeting, and replies to a series of questions on the company's Web site. Any one or several of these methods can be used, as long as they are applied uniformly so that all applicants have an equal opportunity to be considered. The object is to be fair and efficient.

An application gathers basic personal information such as name, phone number, address, education and experience (that are applicable to the job position), former employers, license information (if applicable), and references. Frequently, there are also several questions that require brief written answers, which are useful for evaluating communication skills as well as for the content of the response.

Résumés can also provide a good overview of a candidate, with much of the same information typically gathered on applications as well, and may be the "first cut" screening tool of choice. Sorting a large number of résumés can be overwhelming but can be done quickly by starting to read at the end where the less flattering information is usually buried.

The qualifier about résumés is that the required attributes may not be readily apparent unless the résumé is prepared in response to a specific job posting. Résumés can also suffer from being overstated or understated, which can make the difference between an applicant making the first cut and falling out of the running. Wise managers set aside the rejected résumés that are worth a second look if the first round of contenders does not produce a suitable hire.

A preliminary interview or conversation is an informal exchange of information for both management and the applicant. (The applicant is narrowing the field as well.) While it's permissible to tell a short story about the company, the purpose of the exchange is to learn about the applicant. Although these are informal exchanges in person or via digital means, the conversation must focus on topics that are clearly job-related and not wander into areas that could violate employment laws.

Formal Interviews

The candidates who survive the prescreening step move on to the formal interview step. Formal or structured interviews are face-to-face, two-way exchanges and, depending on the job position or the number of candidates, can involve several interviews before narrowing the field once again. (Decision Point 2)

The list of candidates may be as long or short as management desires, depending on the quality of the applicants and their suitability for the position. It's possible that no candidates are suitable. If that's the case, go back to the recruiting step rather than waste time with candidates who don't meet minimum qualifications.

A formal interview is also the forum for discussing the specific job description. One of the most common complaints is that the job didn't turn out to be as it was represented. The company needs to present a realistic preview of what the job entails and must also be careful not to convey any message that could be interpreted as a commitment or binding contract of employment.

Conducting a good and legally proper employment interview requires some skill, which means learning to explore the right topics in the right ways to gain useful information. For an interview to be productive, the interviewer needs a plan.

Prepare the interview. After reviewing the applications and notes from preliminary interviews, plan the topics to explore and prepare a script for the interview. A script enhances the quality of information that can be gathered but also keeps the interview on the track of job-related conversations and provides a uniform basis for evaluating multiple candidates. A script also helps the interviewer run a professional interview (which impresses candidates) and concentrate on listening instead of thinking about what to ask next. The interview generally consists of the following elements.

- **Introduction**—This is the icebreaker that puts the candidate at ease. An opening question could be something like, "How did you become interested in our firm?" or "What do you know about our company?" Observe appearance and the ease with which the candidate communicates.

Then set the stage for what follows by saying, "Certainly it's in your interest as well as ours to get to know one another. First, I'd like to get information about you, then I'll be happy to answer any questions you have about the company and the job position." Then tackle the list of scripted topics that relate to the items below.

- **Work experience**—In addition to topics introduced in the application or résumé that the candidate wants to further discuss, this is a time for the interviewer to explore—"What have you done best? Less well? What were your major accomplishments? What were the most difficult problems you've encountered in your jobs? How did you handle them? In what ways are you most effective with people? Why have you changed jobs (if this is applicable)? What are you looking for in a career, and what are your goals and aspirations?"

  These reveal skills and competence, motivation, attitude about work and employers, interpersonal skills, initiative, and problem-solving ability.

- **Education**—In addition to any particular education the candidate wishes to highlight, explore—"What were your special accomplishments? How did you choose the course of study? How has what you learned related to your career? How do you feel about additional education, or what would you like to study next?"

  These reveal the level of accomplishment, professional interests, and potential for growth and development.

- **Job-related skills and professional assets**—Explain the job and then give the candidate the opportunity to sell himself or herself with answers to—"What do you think are your major assets or best qualities for the job? What strengths do others usually see in you? Why are you a good person for this company to hire? What are your shortcomings or areas that need improvement? What qualities do you want to develop further? What training or additional experience do you need or would you like for the job?"

  These reveal a candidate's job skills and suitability for the position as well as any professional development that may be required.

- **Closing**—The interview concludes with the interviewer summarizing the discussion and saying, "I've enjoyed talking to you and you've given me a lot of valuable information to help make a decision. Before you leave, do you have any further questions about the job, our company, or anything else we've discussed?" Finally, close with a "thank you" and tell the candidate what happens next.

  This indicates what the interviewer has learned and because candidates are narrowing the field as well, this gives them an opportunity to resolve any lingering issues.

Conducting interviews. By their very nature, employment interviews are stressful. A one-on-one interview is less stressful, though, than panel interviews, in which the candidate meets with a group of people, or serial interviews, in which the candidate is passed from one person to another, each of whom has a separate interview agenda. Simulation or audition interviews are the most stressful, putting the candidate on the spot with a skill demonstration or problem-solving exercise. The choice of interview styles typically depends on the nature of the position being filled.

The best information is gathered in structured interviews when people feel at ease and can be candid. The use of first names (if that's acceptable company practice), comfortable seating (without the interviewer stationed behind a desk), and a private setting that is free of interruptions create an atmosphere in which conversation can flow freely.

Work through the script in a conversational way, and keep the following in mind.

- Don't talk too much (notice there's no company commercial in the script) and listen beyond the words that are spoken. Ask open-ended questions (who, what, where, how, when) to encourage the candidate to talk.
- Play down any unfavorable information. Don't disagree; otherwise the applicant will try to retreat and say what the person thinks the interviewer wants to hear.
- Don't telegraph the correct answer with a statement such as, "We are looking for highly motivated people. How would you describe

yourself?" There's little point in asking that question because the candidate has already been told the answer.

- Watch, listen, and take notes. The interviewer should be able to learn what is needed in about 45 minutes.
- Above all, avoid questions or topics of conversation (discussed in the previous chapter) that could violate employment laws.

The conclusion of interviews can be awkward. The interviewer is often preoccupied by all that's transpired, and the candidates typically want to know their fate as soon as possible (unless they've learned enough to tell the interviewer they're no longer interested). Conclude with a simple "we'll contact you in (a time period) with our decision" or "we'll be making decisions about second interviews by (date)" (if second interviews will be conducted). Tell a candidate who's not likely to still be in the running to feel free to interview elsewhere. (Candidates rely on the company to determine whether they are suited for the job.)

A formal interview is not intended to conclude with a job offer, but there may be times when the interviewer feels that such a step is appropriate (provided the person has authority to extend an offer of employment).

Selection

Don't hire quota. Hire quality. The purpose of the entire process is to select the best match for the job and the organization. Although the interviewer forms some impressions during the interviews, selection is not a rush-to-judgment exercise, but the final filtering step of the employment process. (Decision Point 3)

The company needs an objective process for evaluating candidates based on the information gathered in the formal interview. This is typically done by establishing job-specific criteria (based on the job analysis of the position) and perhaps also criteria related to general characteristics that predict job performance. Those can be drawn from studies of personal characteristics of people who perform the job within the company or from industry profiles for certain jobs (such as attributes commonly attributed to successful managers or real estate salespeople).

These criteria become the platform for evaluation. One way to evaluate is with a *rating system* in which each candidate is scored on each criterion, perhaps on a scale of five to one (one being least favorable). Those scores are tallied, with the totals providing a quantitative view of each candidate that can be used to rank hiring preferences, or to determine that none of the candidates is suitable.

An additional issue to consider is whether an individual can fill the job immediately without training or ramp-up time. An axiom in human resource management is that a bad selection can't be fixed with training. On the other hand, the company doesn't want to miss prime talent that could do the job very well with a little training or practice.

Companies generally also check the candidates' business and personal references and often include those in their rating systems, as well. If the most recent employer is not mentioned, that's not necessarily a disqualifier but does raise a question that should be explored with the applicant. Prior business relationships can end acrimoniously but that's not necessarily a sign of future problems. (The licensing conduct of a salesperson should also be explored.)

More companies today are also checking job applicants online, especially on social media sites. Beware that not everything you see is necessarily a good indicator of an applicant's character or general behavior.

Company protocol may include other steps in the selection process as well. Because those steps involve time and expense, companies generally use scores from the interviews and references as the first cut before proceeding with other tactics. Guidance of an attorney is advised when pursuing any of the following steps.

- **Job tests and assessments.** These include knowledge and skill tests and personality assessments, such as Myers-Briggs or Minnesota Multiphasic Personality Inventory. Tests must be job-skill related or reliable predictors of performance. Otherwise, they can be construed as an unfair or unlawful way to eliminate applicants. Not everyone performs well on tests and some tests are biased in ways that are discriminatory. Companies often avoid the legal landmines by using job tests as a management tool after an individual is hired.

- **Credit checks.** Credits checks performed by a third-party consumer reporting agency (CRA) provide information about character, general reputation, and lifestyle as well as the customary credit information. The Fair Credit Reporting Act (FCRA) strictly controls the manner in which information is used for employment purposes, which includes promotion and termination as well as hiring.

  The company must notify (and receive authorization from) the individual before the report is ordered and provide a summary of rights prescribed by FCRA. If the company uses any adverse information for employment decisions, certain notices and explanations of rights (including the right to dispute the accuracy of the report) must be provided to the candidate/employee. Appropriate forms and instructions are provided by the CRA. Failure to comply with the FCRA can result in a civil penalty up to $1,000 and possibly punitive damages.

  Despite all of this said about credit checks, companies have to be exceedingly careful because *a number of states have passed laws that limit the practice of checking the credit history of job applicants.* This trend gained considerable traction in the wake of the recession, which left many workers with tattered credit histories that could bar them from future employment.

- **Criminal background checks and drug testing.** These are more customary than not in today's workplace but are appropriate only as long as they are standard operating procedure for all prospective hires and, in the case of drug testing, performed by credible third-party enterprises. Some companies do criminal-background checks in addition to the checks a state may require for real estate licensure.

  Because of the disproportionate number of arrests and convictions among people in the protected classes, denying employment based on a criminal conviction is permissible by EEOC regulations *only* if the illegal activity is relevant to the job a person would be doing and the procedure is consistent with business necessity.

Ultimately, the selection step concludes with a hiring decision. It's possible that several candidates are highly appealing, in which case they are ranked in the order in which the company will extend a job offer.

Hiring

The person who hires is also the one who usually fires. The hiring person should be totally committed to the person who is finally selected to minimize the likelihood of having to do an about-face and show that person to the door. And the new hire also should be committed to the company. Hiring generally consists of two steps—(1) the offer and acceptance of the job and (2) the formal employment paperwork.

The first step begins with the formal offer of employment for a specifically defined job and the conditions of employment. The compensation package and rules of engagement (start date, probationary period, vacation, etc.) are also part of the offer. For salespeople, the offer would also address insurance requirements, MLS and franchise fees, and the like.

The specific job may not be exactly the one discussed in prior phases of the employment process. The job may have expanded to take advantage of the individual's specific skills or abilities or contracted to get a highly attractive hire, with the expectation that the person will grow into the position and assume the job's original level of responsibilities in the future. Occasionally, the job description is permanently altered along with the description of another position so the two complement one another.

The selected hire must then accept the offer. This is not necessarily a simple or on-the-spot "yes." At the very least, the new hire will likely ask questions to clarify the offer, but it's not uncommon for negotiations to ensue. The compensation package is usually the major subject of debate, sometimes because the selected hire simply can't live with the money, but often because initial offers are known to be low-ball offers.

If the original offer is the final offer, then say so. Otherwise, be prepared to give and take, which may be over something that doesn't mean as much to the company as it does to the selected hire. Once the parties come to terms, they shake hands and put it all in writing.

This brings us to the second step of the hiring process—the paperwork. Some companies see the handshake as the employment contract, but that, like any other verbal contract, is subject to faulty memories, misinterpretations, and a host of potentially defenseless possibilities.

Unless the company's legal counsel supports this way of doing business (rarely), the best use of counsel is to draft a suitable written document (or a form that can be completed) that the parties will sign. Most important, the terms and conditions must be consistent with the company's employment policies and procedures for a full-time, part-time, or contingent worker (the consultant and special service positions).

The most prevalent special service position in a real estate company (if sales personnel are independent contractors) is the salesperson. In this case, the employment contract is the independent contractor agreement, which would also satisfy one of the three federal tax law requirements for statutory nonemployees. (See the discussion in Chapter 13.) The contract must comply with prevailing federal and state law (including any statutory benefits the company must pay) and spell out the company's IC employment policies, including elective benefit programs the IC may be able to buy into. A sample form that can be used as a model for preparing an IC agreement appears at the end of this chapter (see Figure 14.2).

Noncompete covenants. One of the more controversial conditions of employment in today's business world is a *covenant not to compete*. While moving from one employer to another can be very enriching for employees, companies can lose valuable business and talent in the process. Noncompete clauses in employment contracts intend to diminish negative impacts by imposing certain restrictions on a worker's future employment. However, the clauses may or may not be enforceable depending on whether the courts deem the time and place (geography) restrictions to be reasonable.

Standards of reasonableness vary from locale to locale as courts look at the nature of work involved and the level of competition in the particular geographic area. Those standards (evidenced by local court decisions) are best assessed by legal counsel before any covenant is drafted. Only very limited covenants in time and geography will likely be upheld for IC salespeople. More restrictive conditions for managerial or other key positions may survive. Or the company may see enforceability as more costly or difficult than it's worth and choose not to use noncompete covenants.

Enthusiasm for beginning a new job can cloud the realities of conditions imposed on its end. It's surprising how many people are unaware until they leave a company to go elsewhere that their options about where that is or what they can do are limited. A selected hire may be subject to noncompete conditions from the previous affiliation, which puts an entirely new (and perhaps unexpected) spin on the job the selected hire may be able to do (if anything). Difficulties such as this have made more people aware of noncompete conditions, so an employer can have more problems getting a selected hired to sign on under these conditions. Some new hires will patently refuse to do so.

Additional paperwork associated with hiring includes W-4 forms for employees or W-9 forms for others and information for unemployment and workers' compensation and any fringe benefits (i.e., hospitalization). If the new hire is a salesperson, the appropriate license forms must also be completed. Each new hire should be given (and sign a receipt for) copies of the employee handbook and the company's procedural manuals.

In essence, the process assembles a *personnel file*, which includes a variety of other information the company attorney may recommend (and avoids information that should not be retained), along with the original employment application. Because the hiring decision has already been made, certain personal information can be gathered, though it becomes part of a *confidential* file and cannot be used in management's later decision making. Several examples include closest family members for contact in an emergency, a copy of a driver's license, and citizenship information so that the company has proof the new hire is authorized to work in the country.

■ RECRUITING SALESPEOPLE

A brokerage company is only one of several in the area all competing to recruit the top producers and newly licensed salespeople. And those people are out comparison shopping, looking at how all the companies stack up against one another. A company is recruiting, and the salespeople are selecting.

The earlier discussion about the brand name of the company as a potential employer is very apropos when the time comes to recruit salespeople. They want a workplace where they can get maximum support so they can be most productive. This doesn't mean just good clerical and technology support and appealing marketing and commission programs, but an environment that is energizing, rather than somber, tension filled, or contentious. The responsibility for creating that environment falls squarely on the managers who supervise that workplace.

Don't confuse recruiting with selection. Even though recruiting salespeople is highly competitive, a company must *qualify* the people it selects. Recruiting salespeople is like prospecting for customers, meaning that the sales manager will make many contacts before making a contract, or in this case, selecting the right person to hire—the "hire quality, not quota" mantra.

Quota figures into recruiting only to the extent that management must analyze the company's recruiting history to determine the effectiveness of various recruiting strategies and the number of contacts that were needed for the company to select the most suitable salespeople. Unless the plan is to reduce the sales force, management also needs to look at the *annual rate of attrition* to determine the number of people that have to be brought on board each year to maintain, let alone expand, the sales staff.

The end result of these analyses plus the factors explored in the sales force discussion in the previous chapter give management its marching orders for developing a suitable recruiting and hiring plan for the year. Unfortunately, many managers see recruiting as something to do in their spare time (which never materializes). Or they embark on an aggressive campaign only after they lose a number of salespeople. A company's cash flow and profitability can't withstand long periods of drought between departure and rehire. In that sense, recruiting is, again, like prospecting for customers—an ongoing activity.

There are many ways to network with potential salespeople. Some of them are more likely to reach unlicensed prospects while others will reach either newly licensed or experienced agents. And some ways take longer to generate a pool of candidates than others.

Recruiting Experienced Talent

Obviously, the place to find experienced talent is the competition, the most vulnerable companies (unfortunately) being those around which rumors of pending changes and discontent circulate. Interestingly, real estate companies seem to have a double standard about recruiting—"It's okay for me to recruit your salespeople, just you stay away from mine." Before soliciting people in another company's office, think about the chain of events that could negatively affect yours.

Recruit a manager. Because good sales managers often develop a loyal following of good salespeople, some companies see recruiting a manager as a good way to also attract experienced sales talent. However, this strategy may not work as intended if the manager's contract prohibits soliciting or recruiting salespeople from the former company for a period of time after the manager departs. The result would be no recruits and perhaps a costly legal battle with the manager's previous employer over a disputed nonsolicitation clause.

Network the industry. The most desirable way to get experienced salespeople is for them to initiate the contact. The visibility and professional stature of the manager are strong draws for that contact. A presence where salespeople gather, meet, or do business creates opportunities for them to become acquainted with the manager and for the manager to converse with them. Any overture is an opportunity to tell the company's story and perhaps plant a seed that will be beneficial eventually. Respect people's allegiances, though. Knocking the competition or soliciting at every closing or open house will turn people off.

Mobilize ambassadors. Current salespeople are also great ambassadors. Good salespeople like to work with others who are as dedicated and hard-working as they are. The real estate business is one of unique relationships. Salespeople are fierce competitors who also frequently cooperate with one another. When they see others in action, they can identify those who would be an asset to the company. Some companies offer enticements like bonuses or prizes for salespeople who recruit others to join the firm.

Recruiting Unlicensed Talent

One of the most pressing questions for prospective licensees is "How do I select the right broker?" Frequently, they are advised to

- interview with a variety of companies—several small, medium, and large, some with franchise affiliation and others that are independent—and attend career nights;

- talk to friends in the business to get the practitioners' perspectives on various companies; and
- talk to people who recently have done business with real estate companies to find out what they have to say about various firms.

A company who desires newly licensed people wants to be in the running for consideration in this list. (And you may have noticed that managers scramble over one another trying to lure this talent, even while people are still taking their prelicense classes.)

The pool of possible new talent extends beyond the classroom, to virtually anywhere managers and salespeople meet people. Real estate is a popular topic of conversation, and those conversations can reveal interests and attitudes that may very well be those of a future real estate licensee. Don't overlook past customers and clients, too. The company could even establish a bonus or shared commission program to compensate the salespeople for recruiting this talent as well.

Select advertising media and tailor the message in the same way as any other advertising, that is, identify the target audience and promote the message where that audience is likely to see it. Today, that place is online—the company's Web site, social media sites, and even in blog commentary. Companies often have standing career opportunities messages on their own sites but can also ramp-up the messaging to coincide with schedules of real estate classes or take advantage of other opportunities.

Be careful about advertising overly attractive enticements (a luxury car, a trip, or the promise of earning exorbitant amounts of money). Because consumers also see recruiting ads, they may think twice about paying the price for the company's services if they think it has large sums of money to pay salespeople.

Be sure that the language in the ad is not discriminatory. The phrase "experienced salespeople only" could have that effect if a housewife has been home raising her children or a minority person has not had the opportunity to gain experience. Phrases such as "equal employment opportunity," "previous training not necessary," or "experienced or inexperienced invited" make a public statement that the company provides hiring opportunities to everyone.

Recruiting Brochures

A recruiting brochure is intended to make an impression on people who contemplate working for the company in the same way sales brochures make impressions on consumers. A recruiting brochure (paper or electronic medium) is a tangible memory minder that is also an important companion to other recruiting strategies. Follow the suggestions for preparing a sales brochure in Chapter 12, and the result will be a similarly appealing professional statement about a career with the company. Content should also include answers to the typical questions people have about the industry and a brokerage company. (Think back on your own experience for a guide.) A self-evaluation exercise is also a helpful inclusion.

Career Seminars

People attend seminars with a variety of motives, ranging from curiosity about the business or just toying with the notion of a career to seriously looking for an employer. From the company's point of view, seminars are an opportunity to explain the real estate business and showcase the company in the process. The expectation is that the program will stir sufficient interest to entice a number of attendees to pursue the matter with the company.

Just as people have various motives for attending, seminars are conducted for a variety of reasons as well.

- Local educational institutions may sponsor seminars so that their students can explore career options and begin planning what they will do when their course work is finished.
- Educational institutions may use seminars to stimulate interest in the industry as a way to get people enrolled in their classes. Companies appear as a public service and showcase their career opportunities in the process.
- A franchise may conduct a seminar to promote the franchise's advantages for the salespeople. Member companies showcase themselves as well as provide testimonials.
- A company may sponsor its own seminar. In the previously mentioned formats, the company contributes to the program agenda developed by someone else. In a company-sponsored program, the company controls the agenda for its specific purpose.

Attendees sometimes see company-sponsored seminars as nothing more than glitzy commercials, masquerading as career nights. A program billed as a *career* seminar should be delivered as such. Explain real estate careers, presenting a completely objective discussion of the options. Then explain how the company fits into the picture. If the intent is to conduct a *recruiting* seminar, plan and promote an opportunity for people to learn why the company is a superior place to work. Promote advantages, but don't knock the competition.

One of the major criticisms of these seminars is that people feel they weren't given realistic information about how much money they will make and the amount of effort (and length of time) it takes to turn a fledgling job into a very profitable career. Showcasing success stories is one thing, but the extraordinary tales can be deceiving. The reality is that 20 percent of the industry's sales agents typically make less than $10,000.

The goal of career programs is to generate a pool of people to interview. Because the percentage of people attending a seminar who have the desire or ability to become real estate salespeople may be small, the audience needs to be large enough to justify the preparation time and expense. National companies and franchises provide guidance and support materials for these events, or the following information can be used as a guide.

- Select a central location that is convenient for the people the company wants to attract. If the purpose of the program is to recruit for the company, the office showcases the actual work site, but this is appropriate only if there is a suitable professional conference or meeting room. An off-site facility is better for a true career (as opposed to a recruiting) program.
- Select a facility that can accommodate a range of group sizes. Hotels and conference centers provide a professional atmosphere and the flexibility to adjust seating as reservations or attendance requires.
- Promote the career seminar with flyers and press releases, advertising, and Web site postings to announce the event at least seven days in advance. Request reservations and provide a telephone number or e-mail address. Designate a person to handle contacts, distribute tickets, and follow up contacts a day or two before the program to verify attendance.

- Confirm the room arrangements. The virtue of reservations is they help gauge the number of people attending. Add 10 percent to accommodate people without reservations, but be prepared for no-shows as well. If the room is too large, people get the feeling that the event is not worth attending.
- Arrange for projectors, screens, sound systems, registration tables, and a podium. Be prepared to cope with potential (that invariably turn out to be real) problems with malfunctioning equipment. Also be sure the atmosphere is comfortable; minimize distracting noise and erratic temperatures.
- Plan refreshments. A beverage and light snack are an icebreaker and create an opportunity to mingle with the attendees before and after the program. Name tags are also a nice touch.
- Prepare literature. A packet for each guest should include general information about real estate careers and specific information about the company, including its career brochure.
- Plan and conduct the program. In a recruiting seminar, showcase the company's services for consumers and services for the sales staff. Invite a few people from the company to speak about their special areas of responsibility or expertise. A career seminar should also include a brief discussion of real estate ownership, its economic importance, and interesting market statistics.
- End with a question-and-answer period and an invitation for attendees to contact the company's recruiter or a sales manager.
- Follow up with thank-you notes, emails, or telephone calls to attendees.
- Plan the next career seminar. When these events are conducted on a regular basis, the company gets more mileage out of advertising and planning expenses. School directors and previous attendees also know when to expect the event and can refer others to a program.

Licensing Courses

Brokerage companies and franchises often operate real estate schools as a way to recruit salespeople for their companies. But the students pay to be educated. Before deciding to open a real estate school, investigate state laws and procedures for operating a proprietary school. Providing quality education requires specialized expertise, and running a school may be a more significant (and expensive) undertaking than is warranted just to create a pool of recruits.

To protect the educational integrity of the classroom, some state licensing authorities prohibit solicitation of students or the dissemination of class rosters. Even if state law permits these activities, some educational institutions prohibit them to protect the confidentiality of their students. Consider that if you recruit a prospective licensee and refer that person to an educational institution, you'd be upset if another broker or the instructor tried to scoop that recruit from you.

Because of their industry expertise, managers are often invited to be real estate instructors. This is a good opportunity to share that expertise, though managers often underestimate the time and skill required to prepare and instruct an educationally sound program. If the purpose for teaching is to recruit students or gather student rosters, consider the earlier point about scooping other brokers' referrals to the institution. Even if the educational institution does not have a policy about its instructors recruiting students, remember that the entire class is expecting to learn. An instructor who favors some students (as potential hires) over others can disrupt the educational process.

Trial Training Sessions

Because training and professional development are important to recruits, give them a preview of what the company does with a trial training session. This can be promoted via a Web site or e-mail to the real estate schools. The audience will likely include members of the public who are curious about the business as well as people in various stages of licensure.

Scholarships

Scholarship programs for prelicense or degree courses benefit deserving students and provide considerable public relations benefit to the company. It's important, however, that the company not be directly involved in actually selecting the recipients.

The company can commit the funding and also set guidelines for the award (merit or financial need). Then the educational institution should take over and screen applicants and select the recipients. Any deeper involvement can tarnish the company's public relations, particularly with applicants who are not awarded a scholarship. The company can reenter the process by participating in an award ceremony. In return for the company's generosity, the recipient may consider it for possible employment.

Direct Mail

Direct mail is less common today because of the popularity of online and digital communications. But some companies do occasionally do mailings and have found that postcards with sharp graphics and a concise message are more appealing to today's sound bite–focused, quick-sorting consumer than an envelope packed with paper, which is likely to get tossed in the trash without even being opened. As postage rates rise, a postcard is also cheaper to mail. Sharp and concise, though, means that postcards must be really engaging or creative to prompt a phone call or visit to the Web site.

A rule of thumb is that mass mailings generally produce about a 2 percent response rate. Keep this in mind when investigating costs of print and postage (bulk rate is preferable) and mail-house service if the mailing is not prepared in-house. This may not be a worthwhile expenditure, but if it produces one qualified prospect to interview for every ten respondents, then it is useful.

■ SELECTING SALESPEOPLE

The process of prescreening candidates, conducting formal interviews, and then selecting sales staff is no different than it is for any other personnel position. Keep several additional points in mind when selecting sales staff.

- Prelicense courses are designed to a minimum level of proficiency for licensees to protect the public interest. The courses are *not* designed to develop successful business and selling skills or to identify suitable personality traits. A license could be just as easily a license to fail. A company can minimize this possibility by hiring people who are suitable for the business and providing professional training.
- One of the attractions for IC salespeople is the ability to control their daily work as well as their income. This feature also contributes to failure. Human beings by nature are not particularly disciplined. People rely on others to create structure, or they have to make a conscientious effort to create it for themselves. Unless people can

plan, prioritize, and manage their time and activities well, they will not succeed in an unstructured environment.

- Salespeople must also be able to withstand pressure while maintaining their composure, cope with rejection without feeling demoralized, and empathize with their customers and clients without losing their objectivity or letting their own self-serving interests interfere.

Many people with different personalities match the profiles that are commonly suggested for salespeople. Typically, companies look for traits that other successful people possess. But those may not be so significant, given differences in individual personalities. What is important is how well people can adapt their personal skills to the situation. Selection is a judgment call. No one will always make perfect selections. Every manager, on occasion, has been surprised that the least likely person turns out to be a superstar and the most likely person to succeed quickly falls by the wayside.

■ CONCLUSION

The future of the company rests in the hands of the people it hires. Therefore, it's incumbent on the manager to make the right personnel choices, from identifying the skills and attributes that are needed for a position to developing a pool of talent from which to make the right selection. Selecting a new salesperson involves more than just spending 20 minutes with anyone who is interested in selling real estate and then making a job offer. Selection errors consume far too many company resources and make victims of people who deserve better treatment. A methodical selection process provides the information needed to make appropriate choices, which benefits both the company and the candidates.

■ DISCUSSION EXERCISES

Discuss how brand-worthy your company is as an attractive employer. What are its recruiting strengths and weaknesses?

What salesperson recruiting techniques do you think are most effective in your area?

If you've had experience conducting employment interviews, discuss ways to conduct a successful interview. As an interviewee, discuss your experiences during employment interviews.

What aspect of the employment process do you find most challenging and what have you done (or could you do) to make hiring easier, more effective, or more efficient?

FIGURE 14.2
Sample Independent Contractor Agreement

REALTOR®

NEW JERSEY ASSOCIATION OF REALTORS® STANDARD FORM OF BROKER-SALESPERSON INDEPENDENT CONTRACTOR AGREEMENT

EQUAL HOUSING OPPORTUNITY

THIS AGREEMENT, is made and entered into this ________day of ____________________, 20______, by and between ____ (hereinafter referred to as the "Broker"), having its principal office at ____, ____, and ____ (hereinafter referred to as the "Salesperson"), residing at____ ____

WITNESSETH:

WHEREAS, Broker is engaged in business as a real estate broker trading as ____, with its principal office at ____, and as such is duly licensed to engage in activities including, but not limited to, selling, offering for sale, buying, offering to buy, listing and soliciting prospective purchasers, and negotiating loans on real estate, leasing or offering to lease, and negotiating the sale, purchase or exchange of leases, renting or placing for rent, or managing real estate or improvements thereon for another or others; and

WHEREAS, Broker has and does enjoy the goodwill of the public, and has a reputation for fair and honorable dealing with the public; and

WHEREAS, Broker maintains an office in the State of New Jersey equipped with furnishings, listings, prospect lists and other equipment necessary, helpful, and incidental to serving the public as a real estate broker; and

WHEREAS, Salesperson is duly licensed by the State of New Jersey as a real estate salesperson; and

WHEREAS, it is deemed to be to the mutual advantage of Broker and Salesperson to enter into this Agreement; and

WHEREAS, Salesperson acknowledges that he has not performed any acts on behalf of Broker nor has he been authorized to act on behalf of Broker; and

WHEREAS, the parties acknowledge that they deem it desirable to enter into an agreement in compliance with the provisions of N.J.A.C. 11:5-4.1;

NOW, THEREFORE, in consideration of the foregoing premises and the mutual covenants herein contained, it is mutually covenanted and agreed by and between the parties hereto as follows:

1. **SERVICES.** Salesperson agrees to proceed diligently, faithfully, legally, and with his best efforts to sell, lease, or rent any and all real estate listed with Broker, except for any listings which are placed by Broker exclusively with another salesperson(s), and to solicit additional listings and customers for Broker, and otherwise to promote the business of serving the public in real estate transactions, and for the mutual benefit of the parties hereto.

2. **OFFICE SPACE.** Broker agrees to provide Salesperson with work space and other facilities at its office presently maintained at __ ____, or at such other location as determined by Broker at which Broker may maintain an office. The items furnished pursuant to this Paragraph 2 shall be for the convenience of the Salesperson.

3. **RULES AND REGULATIONS.** Salesperson and Broker agree to conduct business and regulate habits and working hours in a manner which will maintain and increase the goodwill, business, profits, and reputation of Broker and Salesperson, and the parties agree to conform to and abide by all laws, rules and regulations, and codes of ethics that are binding on, or applicable to, real estate broker and real estate salespeople. Salesperson and Broker shall be governed by the Code of Ethics of the NATIONAL ASSOCIATION OF REALTORS®, the real estate laws of the State of New Jersey, the Constitution and By-Laws of the ____________________ ____________________ Board/Association of Realtors®, the rules and regulations of any Multiple Listing Service with which Broker now or in the future may be affiliated with, and any further modifications or additions to any of the foregoing. Salesperson acknowledges that it is his responsibility to familiarize himself with all current Code of Ethics, the Local Board/Association By-Laws, the rules and regulations of any Multiple Listing Service with which Broker is now affiliated, the Rules and Regulations of the Real Estate Commission and the License Law of the State of New Jersey. Broker agrees to maintain copies of all the foregoing and to make the same available to Salesperson. Salesperson agrees also to abide by the rules, regulations, policies and standards promulgated by Broker.

NJAR® Form-134-7/12 Page 1 of 5

FIGURE 14.2
Sample Independent Contractor Agreement (Cont.)

4. **LICENSING AND ASSOCIATION MEMBERSHIP.** Salesperson represents that he is duly licensed by the State of New Jersey as a real estate salesperson. Salesperson acknowledges that Broker is a member of the ______________________ ______________________ Board/Association of Realtors®, the New Jersey Association of REALTORS® and the NATIONAL ASSOCIATION OF REALTORS®, and as a result thereof, Broker is subject to the rules and regulations of those organizations. Salesperson agrees to be subject to and act in accordance with said rules and regulations. If Broker requires Salesperson to become a member of any real estate organization, then Salesperson agrees that he shall become a member thereof and shall pay all applicable fees and dues required to maintain said membership. As a result of Broker being a member of the aforesaid groups, Broker and Salesperson agree to abide by all applicable rules, regulations and standards of such organizations, including, but without limitation, those pertaining to ethics, conduct and procedure.

5. **COMPENSATION.** Salesperson's sole compensation from Broker shall be in the form of commissions. The commissions for services rendered in the sale, rental, or leasing of any real estate and the method of payment, shall be determined exclusively by Broker. Commissions, when earned and collected by Broker, shall be divided between Broker and Salesperson after deduction of all expenses and co-brokerage commissions in accord with the Salesperson's Commission Schedule attached to this Agreement as Schedule A which is an outline of compensation to be paid by Broker to Salesperson during the Salesperson's affiliation with Broker.

6. **MULTIPLE SALESPEOPLE.** In the event that two (2) or more salespeople under contract with Broker participate in a sale and claim a commission thereon, then and in that event the amount of commissions allocable to each salesperson shall be divided in accordance with a written agreement among said salespeople. In the event that the salespeople shall be unable to agree, the dispute shall be submitted to and be determined by Broker, in his sole discretion.

7. **RESPONSIBILITY OF BROKER FOR COMMISSIONS.** In no event shall Broker be liable to Salesperson for any commissions not collected, nor shall Salesperson be personally liable for any commissions not collected. It is agreed that commissions collected shall be deposited with the Broker and subsequently divided and distributed in accordance with the terms of this Agreement.

8. **DIVISION AND DISTRIBUTION OF COMMISSIONS.** The division and distribution of the earned commissions as provided for in this Agreement which may be paid to or collected by the Broker, but from which Salesperson is due certain commissions, shall take place as soon as practicable after collection and receipt of such commissions, but in no event more than ten (10) business days after receipt by the Broker, or as soon thereafter as such funds have cleared the Broker's bank.

9. **RESPONSIBILITY FOR EXPENSES.** Unless otherwise agreed in writing, Broker shall not be liable to Salesperson for any expenses incurred by Salesperson or for any of his acts, nor shall Salesperson be liable to Broker for Broker's office help or expenses, or for any of Broker's acts other than as specifically provided for herein.

10. **ADVANCES.** Broker may from time to time and in his sole discretion make advances to Salesperson on account of future commissions; it being expressly agreed, however, that such advances are temporary loans by Broker for the accommodation of Salesperson which are due and payable on demand or as otherwise agreed to by the Broker, and are not compensation. Upon notice to Salesperson, Broker shall have the right to charge interest on any and all advances made to Salesperson, either at the time of making the advance or thereafter, at a rate chosen by Broker in his sole discretion, but not in excess of the maximum rate permitted by law. Upon receipt of payment of commissions, Broker shall credit the account of Salesperson (first toward interest, if any, and then toward principal) with the portion of such commissions due Salesperson. If at any time, the advances made to Salesperson together with interest thereon, if any, exceed the credits to his account for his share of commissions collected, then such excess shall be owing by Salesperson to Broker and shall be due and payable upon demand. After such demand, interest at the maximum rate permitted by law shall accrue upon the amount due Broker, notwithstanding the fact that any or all of the advances made to Salesperson have initially been interest free or at a reduced rate of interest.

11. **REAL ESTATE LICENSES, BONDS, DUES AND FEES.** Salesperson agrees to pay the cost of maintaining his real estate license, dues for membership in the NATIONAL ASSOCIATION OF REALTORS®, the New Jersey Association of REALTORS®, the local Board/Association of REALTORS® and other dues and fees related to the rendering of services by Salesperson as a real estate salesperson.

12. **AUTHORITY TO CONTRACT.** Salesperson shall have no authority to bind, obligate, or commit Broker by any promise or representation, either verbally or in writing, unless specifically authorized in writing by Broker in a particular transaction. However, Salesperson shall be and is hereby authorized to execute listing agreements for and on behalf of Broker as his agent subject to Broker's office policy.

13. **CONTROVERSIES WITH OTHERS.** In the event any transaction in which Salesperson is involved results in a dispute, litigation or legal expense, Salesperson shall cooperate fully with Broker. Broker and Salesperson shall share the payment of all judgments, awards, settlement and other expenses connected therewith, in the same proportion as they normally would share the commission resulting from such transaction if there were no dispute or litigation. It is the policy to avoid litigation wherever possible, and Broker, within

FIGURE 14.2

Sample Independent Contractor Agreement (Cont.)

his sole discretion may determine whether or not any litigation or dispute shall be prosecuted, defended, compromised or settled, and the terms and conditions of any compromise or settlement, or whether or not legal expense shall be incurred. Salesperson shall not have the right to directly or indirectly compel Broker to institute or prosecute litigation against any third party for collection of commissions, nor shall Salesperson have any cause of action against Broker for its failure to do so. In the event a commission is paid to Broker in which Salesperson is entitled to share, but another real estate broker disputes or may dispute the right of Broker to receive all or any portion of such commission, Salesperson agrees that Broker may hold said commission in trust until such dispute is resolved or sufficient time has passed to indicate to Broker in his sole and absolute judgment that no action or proceeding will be commenced by such other real estate broker regarding the subject commission. In the event Broker shall pay any commission to Salesperson and thereafter, either during or subsequent to termination of this Agreement, Broker shall become obligated, either by way of final judicial determination, arbitration award or good faith negotiation, to repay all or any part of such commission to others, Salesperson agrees to reimburse Broker his pro rata share thereof. In any such instance, Broker agrees to keep Salesperson reasonably informed of any proceeding.

14. **OWNERSHIP OF LISTINGS.** Salesperson agrees that any and all listings of property, and all actions taken in connection with the real estate business and in accordance with the terms of this Agreement shall be taken by Salesperson in the name of Broker. In the event Salesperson receives a listing, it shall be filed with Broker no later than twenty four (24) hours after receipt of same by Salesperson. Broker agrees, but is not obligated, to generally make available to Salesperson all current listings maintained by its office. However, all listings shall be and remain the separate and exclusive property of Broker unless otherwise agreed to in writing by the parties hereto.

15. **DOCUMENTS.** Broker and Salesperson agree that all documents generated by and relating to services performed by either of them in accordance with this Agreement, including, but without limitation, all correspondence received, copies of all correspondence written, plats, listing information, memoranda, files, photographs, reports, legal opinions, accounting information, any and all other instruments, documents or information of any nature whatsoever concerning transactions handled by Broker or by Salesperson or jointly are and shall remain the exclusive property of the Broker.

16. **COMMUNICATIONS.** Broker shall determine and approve all correspondence from the Broker's office pertaining to transactions being handled, in whole or in part, by the Salesperson.

17. **FORMS AND CONTRACTS.** Broker shall determine and approve the forms to be used and the contents of all completed contracts and other completed forms before they are presented to third parties for signature.

18. **INDEPENDENT CONTRACTOR.** This Agreement does not constitute employment of Salesperson by Broker and Broker and Salesperson acknowledge that Salesperson's duties under this Agreement shall be performed by him in his capacity as an independent contractor. Nothing contained in this Agreement shall constitute Broker and Salesperson as joint ventures or partners and neither shall be liable for any obligation incurred by the other party to this Agreement, except as provided herein. The Salesperson shall not be treated as an employee for Federal, State or local tax purposes with respect to services performed in accordance with the terms of this Agreement. Effective as of the date of this Agreement, Broker will not (i) withhold any Federal, State, or local income or FICA taxes from Salesperson's commissions; (ii) pay any FICA or Federal and State unemployment insurance on Salesperson's behalf; or (iii) include Salesperson in any of its retirement, pension, or profit sharing plans. Salesperson shall be required to pay all Federal, State, and local income and self-employment taxes on his income, as required by law, and to file all applicable estimated and final returns and forms in connection therewith.

19. **NOTICE OF TERMINATION.** This Agreement, and the relationship created hereby may be terminated by either party hereto with or without cause, at anytime upon three (3) days written notice. However, this Agreement shall immediately terminate upon Salesperson's death. Except as otherwise provided for herein, the rights of the parties hereto to any commissions which were accrued and earned prior to the termination of this Agreement shall not be divested by the termination of this Agreement.

20. **SERVICES TO BE PERFORMED SUBSEQUENT TO TERMINATION.** Upon termination of this Agreement, all negotiations commenced by Salesperson during the term of this Agreement shall continue to be handled through Broker and with such assistance by Salesperson as is determined by Broker. The Salesperson agrees to be compensated for such services in accordance with Schedule B attached hereto.

21. **LIST OF PROSPECTS.** Upon termination of this Agreement. Salesperson shall furnish Broker with a complete list of all prospects, leads and foreseeable transactions developed by Salesperson, or upon which Salesperson shall have been engaged with respect to any transaction completed subsequent to termination of this Agreement in which Salesperson has rendered assistance in accordance with the terms of this Agreement. Except as expressly provided for in Paragraph 20 of this Agreement, Salesperson shall not be compensated in respect of any transaction completed subsequent to termination of this agreement unless agreed to in writing by the Broker.

22. **DUTY OF NON-DISCLOSURE.** Salesperson agrees that upon termination of this Agreement, he will not furnish to any person, firm, company, corporation, partnership, joint venture, or any other entity engaged in the real estate business, any information as to Broker or its business, including, but not limited to, Broker's clients, customers, properties, prices,

NJAR® Form-134-7/12 Page 3 of 5

FIGURE 14.2

Sample Independent Contractor Agreement (Cont.)

terms of negotiations, nor policies or relationships with prospects, clients and customers. Salesperson, shall not, after termination of this Agreement, remove from the files or from the office of the Broker, any information pertaining to the Broker's business, including, but not limited to, any maps, books, publications, card records, investor or prospect lists, or any other material, files or data, and it is expressly agreed that the aforementioned records and information are the property of Broker.

23. **COMPENSATION SUBSEQUENT TO TERMINATION.** Upon termination of this Agreement, Salesperson shall be compensated only in accordance with the appended Schedule B.

24. **ESCROW DEPOSIT.** All contracts of sale shall be accompanied by an escrow deposit in an amount as determined by Broker. Salesperson will, at all times, require purchaser or prospective purchasers, to put up such escrow deposit unless a higher or lower sum shall be mutually agreed to by Broker and Salesperson. Salesperson is expressly prohibited from accepting a smaller escrow deposit, a post-dated check, or agreeing not to deposit an escrow check, unless such action has been expressly authorized by Broker.

25. **AUTOMOBILE.** Salesperson agrees to furnish his own automobile, pay all expenses in connection with the operation and maintenance of said automobile, and that Broker shall have no responsibility therefore. Salesperson agrees to carry throughout the terms of this Agreement public liability insurance upon his automobile with minimum limits not less than ____________________ ($____________________) for each person and ____________________ ($____________________) for each accident, and property damage insurance with a minimum limit of not less than ____________________ $____________________). Upon request, Salesperson agrees to furnish to Broker certificates certifying as to such insurance prepared by the insurance company.

26. **ASSIGNABILITY AND BINDING EFFECT.** This Agreement is personal to the parties hereto and may not be assigned, sold or otherwise conveyed by either of them.

27. **NOTICE.** Any and all notices, or any other communication provided for herein shall be in writing and shall be personally delivered or mailed by registered or certified mail, return receipt requested prepaid postage, which shall be addressed to the parties at the addresses indicated herein, or to such different address as such party may have fixed. Any such notice shall be effective upon receipt, if personally delivered, or three (3) business days after mailing.

28. **GOVERNING LAW.** This Agreement shall be subject to and governed by the laws of the State of New Jersey, including the conflicts of laws, irrespective of the fact that Salesperson may be or become a resident of a different state.

29. **WAIVER OF BREACH.** The waiver by the Broker of a breach of any provision of this Agreement by the Salesperson shall not operate or be construed as a waiver of any subsequent breach by the Salesperson.

30. **ENTIRE AGREEMENT.** This Agreement constitutes the entire agreement between the parties and contains all of the agreement between the parties with respect to the subject matter hereof; this Agreement supersedes any and all other agreements, either oral or in writing between the parties hereto with respect to the subject matter hereof.

31. **GENDER.** When used in this Agreement, the masculine shall be deemed to include the feminine.

32. **SEPARABILITY.** If any provision of this Agreement is invalid or unenforceable in any jurisdiction, the other provisions herein shall remain in full force and effect such jurisdiction and shall be liberally construed in order to effectuate the purpose and intent of this Agreement, and the invalidity or unenforceability of any provision of this Agreement in any jurisdiction shall not affect the durability or enforceability of any such provision in any other jurisdiction.

33. **MODIFICATION.** This Agreement may not be modified or amended except by an instrument in writing signed by the parties hereto. Any modification to this Agreement between the parties after the date of the Agreement shall be of no effect unless such modification is in writing and is signed by both Broker and Salesperson.

34. **PARAGRAPH HEADINGS.** The paragraph headings contained in this Agreement are for reference purposes only and shall not affect in any way the meaning or interpretation of this Agreement.

35. **SURVIVAL OF PROVISIONS.** The provisions of this Agreement shall survive the termination of the Salesperson's services under this Agreement.

36. **COPY RECEIVED.** Salesperson acknowledges receipt of a fully executed copy of this Agreement, duly signed by Broker and Salesperson.

FIGURE 14.2

Sample Independent Contractor Agreement (Cont.)

IN WITNESS WHEREOF, the undersigned have set their hands and seals, or if a corporation, has caused this Agreement to be signed and sealed by its duly authorized corporate officer, the day and year first above written.

WITNESS:

______________________________ ______________________________
(Broker)

WITNESS:

______________________________ ______________________________
(Salesperson)

FIGURE 14.2
Sample Independent Contractor Agreement (Cont.)

SCHEDULE A

SALESPERSON'S COMMISSION SCHEDULE WHILE AFFILIATED WITH BROKER

Salesperson shall be entitled to receive the following percentage as his portion of the commission earned by Broker as a result of closed sales, listings, rentals, leases, after deducting all expenses and co-brokerage commissions:

SALES TRANSACTIONS

1. ________% for written listings produced by Salesperson.
2. ________% for written listings produced and sold by Salesperson.
3. ________% for selling property listed by co-operating broker.

RENTAL/LEASE TRANSACTIONS

1. ________% for written listings produced by Salesperson.
2. ________% for written listings resulting in a signed lease agreement.
3. ________% for signed lease agreement listed by co-operating broker.

ADDITIONAL PROVISIONS (IF ANY):

NJAR® Form 134- 07/12

FIGURE 14.2
Sample Independent Contractor Agreement (Cont.)

SCHEDULE B

SALESPERSON'S COMMISSION SCHEDULE AFTER TERMINATION OF AFFILIATION WITH BROKER

The rate of compensation to be paid by Broker to Salesperson pertaining to transactions which close and on renewals which occur subsequent to the termination of Salesperson's affiliation with Broker is as follows:

1. AS TO SALES TRANSACTIONS

A. Listings

As to written listings which have been produced by Salesperson prior to the date of termination, Salesperson shall be entitled to receive the following percentage of his portion of the commission pursuant to Schedule A for each such transaction, upon collection by Broker.

(I) ________% if a contract of sale has been executed by all parties and all contingencies contained therein have been satisfied as of such date;

(II) ________% if a contract of sale has been executed by all parties but any contingencies contained therein have not been satisfied as of such date;

(III) ________% if a contract of sale has not been executed by all parties as of such date.

In the event a listing originally produced by Salesperson expires, and is renewed after such termination date, Salesperson shall be entitled to receive ________% of his portion of the commission for any such transaction upon collection in full by Broker.

B. Sales

As to transaction in which a prospective purchaser has been produced by Salesperson prior to the date of termination, Salesperson shall be entitled to receive the following percentage of his portion of the commission pursuant to Schedule A for any such transaction, upon collection by Broker:

(I) ________% if the title has closed, but the commission has not been collected as of such date;

(II) ________% if a contract of sale has been executed by all parties and all contingencies contained therein have been satisfied as of such date;

(III) ________% if a contract of sale has been executed by all parties but any contingencies contained therein have not been satisfied as of such date;

(IV) ________% if a contract of sale has not been executed by all parties as of such date; but thereafter a contract is executed by all parties.

2. AS TO RENTAL TRANSACTIONS

A. Listings

As to written listings which have been produced by Salesperson prior to the date of termination, Salesperson shall be entitled to receive the following percentage of his portion of the commission pursuant to Schedule A in any such transaction upon collection by Broker:

(I) ________% if a lease agreement has been executed by all parties as of such date, but the commission has not yet been received;

(II) ________% if a lease agreement has not been executed by all parties as of such date, but thereafter, a lease agreement is executed by all parties.

B. Leases

As to rental transactions in which Salesperson has produced a prospective lessee prior to the date of termination, Salesperson shall be entitled to receive the following percentage of his portion of the commission pursuant to Schedule A upon collection by Broker:

(I) ________% if a lease agreement has been executed by all parties as of such date, but the commission has not yet been received;

(II) ________% if a lease agreement has not been executed by all parties as of such date, but thereafter, a lease agreement is executed by all parties.

FIGURE 14.2
Sample Independent Contractor Agreement (Cont.)

ADDITIONAL PROVISIONS (IF ANY):

NJAR® Form 134B- 7/12 Page 2 of 2

CHAPTER FIFTEEN 15

PROFESSIONAL DEVELOPMENT

What should a company do to indoctrinate people to the organization?

What can a company do to nurture people's professional skills?

Once people are hired, the job of a manager really begins. This is when the manager's ability to provide leadership, cultivate talent, and create a stimulating work environment is tested. The manager's focus at this point is to facilitate the professional growth of the people who do the organization's work. This is the directing function of management.

Directing is not a matter of barking orders but the function that creates a job-rich environment, one that invests in professional development and engages people in the organization. Today's companies provide a variety of opportunities for their workforces, not just in the one-on-one time with the managers but with programs that give people the opportunity to both learn and contribute to the development of their co-workers and the company team.

■ INDOCTRINATION

The introduction people get to the company during the selection and hiring process is basically a brief overview. The next step is to open the rest of the book and tell people about where they've come to work and help them become an integral part of the company's team.

Indoctrination is not a one-time event or a single program but a process that begins the first day a new hire steps into the office and continues for several weeks or months while the newcomer gets acquainted with the organization and learns what's expected. No one, including the IC salesperson, should just show up unannounced and have to fend for themselves.

The newcomer deserves a chance to get off on the right foot, especially in the office where the person will be working. The manager's job is to pave the way by informing the existing staff about the pending new arrival, making workspace preparations, and being the welcoming host. That job includes explaining the unwritten practices and subtleties of the office culture (who cleans the coffeepot or changes the printer toner kinds of things), the omissions that can otherwise turn the first weeks on the job into really bad experiences.

The company needs the relationship to get off on the right foot as well. The newcomer creates new social dynamics, which means the manager is responsible for rebuilding the team. The sooner the newcomer becomes a contributing member of that team, the sooner the company benefits from its hiring decision.

Orientation Programs

Orientation programs are the more formal part of indoctrination that give people the information they need to know about how the company works. The program can be conducted in a group setting if a number of people join the company at the same time. Or the broker and the immediate supervisor can present the orientation story to the new hire one-on-one. Regardless of the format, the substance is essentially the same.

- **An introduction to the company.** This includes a brief history of the company, its philosophy of doing business, and a general outline of the work that the company does. People need to see the big picture of the company and its various departments and offices so they know how the company operates and where their positions fit into that picture.

How to work in the organization is covered with an explanation of the company's policies and procedures, daily office procedures, benefit and compensation programs, and professional development opportunities.

The introduction to the company part of the orientation program is meaningful to any new hire, regardless of the job the person will be doing.

- **The specific procedures that apply to the person's job.** For a salesperson, this part of orientation explains how the salespeople are expected to serve the company's customers and clients and all of the procedures for handling the various aspects of a real estate transaction. This includes internal procedures for handling paperwork and depositing money or escrow funds, fiscal matters concerning negotiations of fees and cooperative transactions and the way the sales staff works together, and how the support staff functions.

  Similar information is tailored to the specific responsibilities and tasks associated with any other job position.

Although this is a fairly comprehensive story to tell, it intends to avoid the "I was never told that" kind of problems that could arise later on. Granted, there is a learning curve that managers must patiently coach people through until they are more familiar with the company's way of doing business. But orientation sows the seeds that make a manager's job easier.

Orientation should include an introduction of the upper echelon of the company. These are the individuals for whom people really work, and new hires deserve an opportunity to put names to faces. The broker and representatives of senior management should at the very least make a cameo appearance. Orientation is often one of the few occasions that people see senior management, especially in sizable or diverse organizations.

Assessing New Hires

Just as a new person needs to learn about the company, the manager needs to learn more about the new hire. Companies do this with pre-employment interviews, which are meetings with the manager or immediate supervisor before the new hire's first official day on the job, and job-skill or personality assessments (rather than incorporating them in the hiring selection process).

The purpose is to evaluate talent and identify education and training that will be beneficial. Obviously, assessments are tailored to the skills required for the specific position (e.g., mathematical or computer skills). For salespeople, interactive programs such as the simulation-based Success Profiler can be used to do this.

Because of cultural or verbal bias or the lack of correlation between tests and a person's potential for success in the job, some assessment instruments are more valid than others. Regardless of the instrument used, the supervisor should *manage the person, not the data.*

Business Plans

Every new hire needs to know early on what management expects and how performance will be reviewed. Just as the manager has reciprocal discussions with each worker to develop performance criteria and a plan of action for their jobs each year (see the next chapter), the manager does likewise with the newcomer. Obviously, the expectations must allow for ramp-up time and perhaps additional training, but the end product is a business plan with specific criteria and an understanding of the procedures used to monitor and evaluate performance.

For salespeople, the typical business plan also includes a plan for promoting their affiliation with the company. Marketing programs in some companies include the promotion of their salespeople, perhaps also with announcements the salesperson can distribute to a network of contacts. Salespeople may develop their own self-promotion material as well.

■ PROFESSIONAL COMPETENCE

Like many things a company does, developing professional competence is a process. It begins with indoctrination and continues with a variety of things managers do to inspire the people and the formal programs the company provides. People typically think of training programs in such areas as management development and sales proficiency, but the process can also include mentoring and job-shifting programs.

Companies invest mightily in professional development, but they also have to make wise decisions about those expenditures. Just as companies tend to assemble bloated workforces, they tend to assemble more training and development programs than the companies can afford, especially when they get sold on every new program or training idea that comes along with "a proven way to produce outstanding results."

Results are definitely the key to making wise programmatic decisions, but not every company realizes the same results from the same expenditures. Programs have to suit the business needs of the company and its workers. The company also has to be realistic about the results of its expenditures. Some efforts take time to produce quantifiable dollars and others contribute indirectly to the bottom line, with such benefits as workplace satisfaction, advancement opportunities, and minimal turnover.

Another part of the results equation is the company has to correctly identify business needs that can be addressed with training and needs that can be addressed only by managerial oversight or by changing company systems or processes. *Training doesn't fix everything.*

Training Programs

Training is the general name companies give to programs intended to raise the level of engagement of their workers. Although a company can provide purely knowledge-based educational sessions, training typically has a blended-learning focus, which concentrates on developing skills or behaviors. This happens when people

- become motivated to adopt certain behavior;
- learn to process information and experiences;
- transfer learning into application, develop skills; and
- receive support and reinforcement from their managers or supervisors.

The distinction between education and training is that education builds knowledge and training develops skill by converting that knowledge into action. The courses required for initial licensure are a good example of the difference. For the most part, they are knowledge-based programs that don't ordinarily develop the actual skills needed to apply that knowledge in daily practice.

Unfortunately, brokers or managers sometimes tell their salespeople to "forget what you learned in school. I'll teach you what you really need to know." But this overlooks one very important fact—salespeople need a wide range of both knowledge *and* skill to be successful.

The how-to of training programs involves the answers to

- **Who should be trained?** The answer is everyone in the organization deserves training opportunities, from senior managers to the lowest position in the organization. Although the emphasis in real estate companies is generally on sales training, managers deserve management development and administrative and clerical personnel deserve the opportunity to develop skills for their jobs as well. Training also creates opportunities for advancement.
- **What should be taught?** This answer depends on what people need. Certainly, some training topics are beneficial for everyone but others are more job-specific. Some training is remedial (which renews proficiency) and other training is innovative, developing new techniques or strategies to suit contemporary practices or recent legal developments.

  Effective training is based on a job-skills analysis, the same analysis that was used to develop position qualifications for hiring (see Chapter 13). An analysis answers the "how do you know people need to know this?" question so the company can make the best use of training money and time for both the attendees and the people doing the training.

  The obvious benefit is that enhanced proficiency means enhanced productivity. But companies also benefit when skill development supports the company's business philosophy and minimizes risk.
- **How should a program be developed?** This answer depends on the subject matter, the expertise available to develop the curriculum, and the economics involved. In-house talent (a training director or department) may have the expertise to develop curriculum and supporting learning exercises and conduct training sessions.

Supporting an in-house department can be expensive, especially to attract exemplary training talent. But the virtue of in-house programming is the company can tailor the curriculum to suit the specific needs of its workforce and the company's way of doing business.

Training can also be outsourced, either in whole or part. A company may rely solely on resources outside the company or may incorporate outside resources or purchased programs in their in-house programming for selected topics. Outside resources such as private schools, collegiate institutions, or industry organizations may be a more economical solution, especially if the company doesn't have sufficient ongoing need, and are suitable for certain topics.

But outside resources and packaged programs (the pre-prepared kinds of programs) aren't company specific and are only a good fit if the curriculum suits workers' needs, and the company supplements the programming to suit its organization. Rarely can a company just buy a program "off the shelf" and use it as-is.

An alternative is to engage training consultants to develop company-specific curriculum and either deliver the training or train in-house personnel to conduct the program. Or professional trainers (i.e., national speakers) can be engaged to deliver their programs, often with additional advice about how to institutionalize the curriculum within the company. An outside expert sometimes carries a more powerful message for certain topics.

- **How should training be delivered?** This answer consists of two issues—who conducts the training and the forum for the training sessions. The presenter and the developer of the program may be one in the same but often that's not the case, which means the presenter must learn the material and prepare the presentation. This may involve a train-the-trainer type of program to help the presenter (which may be the office manager) conduct an effective program.

  The classic training forum is a classroom setting, which appeals to the learning mindset developed early in childhood. But that requires a setting that is conducive to learning and student participation, be that a formal training room or conference facility.

  Today, training is just as likely to be delivered via video conferencing or Web-based seminars, which still provides the benefit of group interaction but isn't as conducive as a classroom setting for skill development. Or training can be a self-directed, independent learning program delivered online, otherwise known as distance learning. The choice of forum depends to a large degree on the primary purpose of the training (informational or skill) and the subject matter.

- **How should training be evaluated?** The key to effective training is what happens next—outside the classroom or after the program. Companies enhance the effect with clearly defined objectives relating the value of the training, what people will learn, and how they will apply that learning and impact the company's business.

  Training sessions often begin with participants writing goals about what they want or expect to be able to do at the conclusion of the session. Then they are asked to critique the experience, relative to the goals they sought to achieve, and to write an action plan for how they will use what they have learned.

  Although formal exams can be used to gauge effectiveness, systematic surveying (especially when a program involves multiple sessions) indicates the likelihood that the training will effect new behaviors. An action plan of what needs to be done, by when and with whom, increases that likelihood. Behavior rarely changes immediately and managers must be patient while people program (or reprogram) themselves and incorporate new behaviors in their jobs.

Managers as trainers. Managers play a vital role in what happens afterward. One of the major failures of training is that, like a motivational program, it doesn't have a lasting effect without follow-through. People need their manager's support in implementing their post-training plans, including the feedback that motivates them to use newly acquired skills.

Although the manager may, in fact, play a formal role as trainer (often a necessity when the manager *is* the training program for a single trainee), the manager more likely plays a supporting role with one-on-one sessions and group-centered exercises such as staff meetings devoted to specific topics covered in the formal training programs.

Some companies provide train-the-trainer programs to help managers lead those group exercises and fulfill their post-training responsibilities. Figure 15.1 provides some practical rules to assist that function. Whether the manager is leading classroom instruction, conducting educational business meetings, or working one-on-one with people, the manager is still teaching adults. This requires strategies that suit the way adults learn—the *andragogy* of the adult learner.

- Adults are very time-and-benefit-oriented. They want their time to be respected (begin and end punctually) and the content to be substantive and worthwhile. They grow impatient quickly with disorganization and long-windedness.
- Most adults are not accustomed to being in a classroom or subordinate to an instructor, especially if the instructor is younger than they are. Adults are more likely to be anxious over their performance and need to feel respected. It's important to minimize intimidation and the potential for embarrassment.
- It is possible to "teach an old dog new tricks," but the older the adult, the slower the process. It takes patience and a little extra time to help adults adopt new behaviors. When working with a variety of age groups, this will be particularly evident.
- Adults, especially those over age 50, experience changes in visual, auditory, and motor skills. And some of those changes are different for men and women. Everything, from the level of lighting, amount of glare, and size and color of print-type, to the frequency and volume of sounds and speech, is affected. Because the over-50 age group is growing, learning more about these issues has relevance to everything a company does.
- Adults have learned to think and analyze. They are less likely to accept facts without explanation and rationale. "Just do it because I say so" may work with children (well, some children) because they are conditioned to follow authority. But adults are more inclined to question and filter information. They also respond to stimulating and thought-provoking exercises.
- Adults have many life experiences from which to draw. They integrate new information by relating it to their experiences and finding correlations. Stimulating them to recall experiences helps them as well as others in the group to learn.

Effective sales training. Sales training over the years has been built around the modeling approach "just give me the words" or scripted training. The presumption is the script provides fail-safe, proven comebacks to effectively handle any situation that could arise. The flaw in the modeling approach is that people focus on the memorized lines (and have to try remembering all of them and sound natural delivering them) and don't learn to listen, size up situations, and think on their feet.

FIGURE 15.1
Rules for Trainers

Do

Project a personal interest in each student as a unique person.
Respect the student. Be tactful, fair, and objective.
Praise the students' accomplishments.
Set a good example by your appearance.
Demonstrate the competency students should achieve with quality examples and exhibits.
Relate the subject matter to real-life situations. The more relevant the subject appears to the students, the more interested and motivated they will be to learn.
Project a positive attitude and enthusiasm toward the subject to emphasize how it is important in the students' business.
Display integrity: "We don't cut corners, lie, cheat, or misrepresent at any time in any form."
Be modest and don't brag about yourself or your personal accomplishments.
Be prepared for each class. Follow a predetermined and logical outline.
Maintain student interest by planning a variety of learning activities.
Create a fast-paced and exciting rhythm with lectures, discussions, projects and case studies, videos, group sessions, or other techniques.
Use tone and volume of voice and physical mannerisms to keep student interest, but don't let them distract from the subject.
Create opportunities for students to share their personal knowledge and experience, but don't let anyone monopolize the discussion.
Use lecture and dialogue rather than straight lecture in classroom presentations.
Reinforce key points by summarizing periodically during the class session.
Use humor occasionally, but be sure that it will not be offensive to anyone.
Use theatrical devices or drama occasionally if they make a point, but don't threaten your credibility by appearing unprofessional. People should remember the point, not the method.
Strive to improve yourself. Use classroom evaluations to analyze your effectiveness.
Avoid rambling, illogical, or unproductive discussions.
Avoid telling the students: rather, show them what you mean. Remember that you make a stronger impression when you appeal to several senses.
Avoid gossip and don't slander the competition.
Avoid making promises that can't be fulfilled or exaggerating potential earnings.

While this training strategy can give the novice a few comebacks to get started, the person really hasn't learned much else. Sales training is most effective when

- selling is approached as a business that is a continuum of certain professional, ethical, and legal behaviors, not merely signatures on contracts. Signatures are simply the end result of sales.
- salespeople learn to build relationships. Learning to relate to people as individuals helps salespeople to be effective at delivering personalized services. Selling is all about the people; the product or service is simply the article of trade.
- salespeople are encouraged to develop the professional expertise that complements or builds upon their individual strengths. Not everyone has the temperament, talent, or aptitude to excel at both listing and selling, and people should not be faulted for that. Training can't fit people into molds in which they don't fit.
- training is institutionalized, which means that training is not a specific, formal learning session (or sessions) but a workplace culture that fosters or supports the behaviors that are the subjects of formal sessions (which is primarily a job for the manager or immediate supervisor).
- training appeals to what the salespeople think they need to hear as well as what management thinks they need. The company needs to sell benefits (yes, in training, too) so that people feel their time is well spent. Otherwise, they will simply go through the motions and not "tune in." Management should also periodically ask what the salespeople think they need.
- program objectives are clearly defined, along with specific behavior the trainees are expected to adopt at the conclusion of the program. This tells how the program should be designed (content, forum, presentation and handout materials, learning exercises, and so on).

The content of sales-training programs falls into several general areas.

- Basic real estate information, including economic trends and changes in demographics and lifestyles, environmental issues, construction, and property development
- Sales and listing strategies, including sales techniques directly related to activities that enhance services and produce revenue
- Company policy issues, including new programs, services, sales tools, policy changes, or issues that need to be clarified because of recurring problems or disputes
- Legal and risk-reduction issues, including recent litigation that affects real estate transactions and ownership and changes in federal, state, and local laws and ordinances
- Motivational subjects, including kickoff campaigns for new programs and the new year's objectives
- Personal development, including time management, personal business plans and goal setting, and technology skills

One size doesn't fit all for veterans and newly licensed salespeople. Training for newly licensed associates suits their novice state, though pacing the delivery of information for them is challenging. The tendency is to overload them with everything they'll ever need to know so they're prepared to handle any situation.

But until salespeople have some field experience, much of the information they're exposed to isn't relevant. It's more effective to develop some very specific skills they can practice for awhile. Then bring them back into the training room or the manager's meetings to develop more skills. Dedicating sessions to novices also precludes their being dissuaded by the skeptical (or cynical) views that some veterans are inclined to freely share.

Training for veterans is often retraining to sharpen stale skills or align skills with contemporary practices (and laws) and help people integrate the company's sales practices into their methods. Sessions comprising solely experienced people help them build rapport with one another and also acknowledge their seasoned expertise.

Sales managers need to attend training sessions from time to time as well. They are at a great disadvantage when they don't know what's being taught, which can also lead to conflicting directives to their salespeople. The managers' critique of the program also helps develop content that suits the needs of the sales staff.

Mentoring Programs

Another path to professional competence is a mentoring program. Mentoring is essentially one-on-one, on-the-job training, typically to complement (rather than replace) formal training programs. Although everyone gets on-the-job training to some extent simply from the experience of "doing," mentoring programs forge working relationships that help the inexperienced learn from the voices of experience.

Managers play a mentoring role, just because that's one of their jobs. Sometimes that involves directing certain assignments and other times the manager actually accompanies the salesperson in the field. The salesperson learns the ropes of real-life situations from the manager while the manager learns about the salesperson's skills and the frustrations the sales staff encounters in daily practice. These are also good rapport-building opportunities.

Colleagues create their own mentoring relationships, simply by gravitating to one another out of respect for talent and willingness to help a colleague. These informal relationships usually develop because someone takes another person "under their wing."

Companies can formalize these relationships by creating official mentoring programs. These pair designated colleagues to work together as mentor and mentee. Unlike shadowing programs in which a trainee learns by following and observing another worker, mentoring programs focus on engaging the mentee in various activities. Mentors benefit from the opportunity to make a contribution, earn respect, and prove their competence, which can be a stepping stone for advancement or promotion as well.

Mentoring programs are typically used in sales and managerial positions but can be used in other positions as well. This kind of program eliminates boss-subordinate dynamics but has its own set of dynamics unless the collaboration is properly structured.

- **Recruit the right people to be mentors.** They need outstanding skills and professional business practices and the aptitude (and attitude) for a training role. They also have to be people the company can trust to use their position responsibly. Mentoring programs create more problems than they solve if the mentors manipulate mentees to make themselves look good or sabotage the mentees' standing with their managers or supervisors. A team player is much more suitable than the office malcontent or personality problem (which could create an additional personnel problem).
- **Train the mentors.** The company is essentially delegating training responsibilities, which means the mentors need to know the what-and-how of their assignment. This involves learning to delegate meaningful activities, provide feedback to the mentees and their managers, and handle situations that arise in these relationships. The mentor also has to learn how to manage the responsibilities of both mentoring and the person's customary job. People who volunteer are more likely to be willing to take on the additional responsibilities.
- **Pick the right people to mentor.** As desirable as mentoring programs are, not everyone plays well in these relationships. People have to be willing to forge partnerships and accept the guidance of their mentors. Good mentees are also people the company can trust not to take advantage of or sabotage their mentors. The objective is to help mentees gain proficiency, not for them to use the mentors to do their jobs.
- **Match a pair that meshes.** The more the mentor and the mentee have in common, the better they will work together. Similar personalities, values, and work habits go a long way to forging harmonious relationships. The object of the pairing is to create a positive relationship in which people can learn and share with one another and foster good skills.
- **Train the pair at the outset.** Many mentoring problems can be avoided by clearly communicating expectations to both parties, gaining their commitment to the relationship, and discussing conflict

management. Establish guidelines about the frequency and nature of the tasks the pair will work on together.

- **Establish an end-time.** Although people may develop an enduring camaraderie, the formal relationship is not intended to last forever. People need to know (ahead of time) what the timeframe is (typically a few months) so there won't be any misunderstandings or hurt feelings when the mentor resumes the primary job and the mentee moves on after learning all the mentor has to offer.
- **Monitor the mentoring.** The manager or coordinator of the mentoring program should receive periodic feedback from both parties and be available to resolve issues that arise between them. If the relationship isn't working, both parties need to know they are free to speak up. Better to end the relationship and match people with different partners than to waste people's time in an unproductive or dysfunctional relationship.

Mentoring programs give mentees the opportunity to see various work strategies in action as well as to receive one-on-one attention. The programs can also inspire mentors to step up their game. The relationships strengthen the team atmosphere in the office and enhance retention. But the downside is the bond that forms could be the one that loses both parties if one of them decides to leave the company.

Lest mentoring programs look like a free way to develop professional competence, the fact is the mentor makes a significant commitment to the assignment and is entitled to proper compensation (perhaps with a shared commission arrangement if the parties are salespeople). The specific duties and obligation of the assignment, time period of service as well as compensation arrangements are typically spelled out in a mentor agreement. This also becomes evidence of the mentor's commitment to serve.

Reverse mentoring. Conventional mentoring typically assigns older or more experienced workers to mentor the younger ones. But an innovative way to do mentoring is to turn the ranks upside down and give the younger workers an opportunity to mentor their superiors. This reverse mentoring is a growing trend in business as a way of giving managers and senior executives a fresh perspective, a chance to bridge generation gaps and see what the younger workers see.

Although some older workers bristle at the notion of being mentored by someone younger or less experienced, reverse mentoring builds trust and loyalty and gives the Gen Y workers a sense of purpose, especially when they can speak the language they know best—technology. That's where the generation gap is most evident and where the older generations can easily learn a lot about marketing and communicating in the contemporary business world.

The Gen Y worker is a huge asset as a mentor in a real estate company where the managerial ranks are largely populated by older workers, and the Internet and digital media are central in today's business. Gen Y is also an asset in training salespeople to sell to that generation.

Cross Training

Companies are far more resilient and adaptable when people are trained in multiple disciplines. Cross training is also the quintessential investment in professional competence by giving people an opportunity to grow beyond the jobs they currently do.

The business community has traditionally used job rotations or job-shifting assignments to familiarize senior executives with different departments or sectors of their companies. The obvious benefit is that trained talent is available to fill vacancies, but the company's decision makers also gain a holistic view of the organization.

Those same benefits (and more) can be realized at every level of the organization. Cross-training programs foster teamwork across specialties and departments, as well as help people develop new skills. This strategy not only gives people a chance to test-drive other jobs but also enhances morale and retention. The company also learns where people fit best into the organization and develops a pool of diverse talent, especially for promotion.

Cross training is an ideal way for real estate companies to give salespeople an opportunity to explore management and learn about the organization. Sales managers can also learn to do other jobs. Back to the strengths discussion in Chapter 3 and the manager (and the company) may find a position that is a better match for those strengths.

■ ENGAGEMENT IN THE ORGANIZATION

Another way companies invest in professional development is by creating cultures that respect the value of talent and engage people in collaborative efforts, such as discussed in Chapter 3 about participatory environment. Companies do this with such efforts as mentoring and cross training programs, but any group-centered activity, regardless of the number of people involved, can foster teamwork, stimulate ideas, and ultimately enhance the way people work.

The manager is the key to constructive group-centered activities, with all the skills the manager learns about getting things done through other people and communicating effectively (recall Chapters 3 and 4). People generally think about informational and training forums, which are the common purpose for business meetings. But people can be engaged in more participatory activities, either virtually or in a central physical site.

Problem-Identification Meetings

A problem-identification meeting does just that, identifies problems. The singular purpose is to create a forum to gather information. Periodic meetings (perhaps several times a year) give people a chance to air concerns with the company or the business, but managers can also convene meetings around problems they think need to be discussed.

No problem can be solved before first determining there's actually a problem and clearly defining what the problem is. This prevents flawed assumptions and the rush-to-judgment to fix something that isn't broken. The group-think can resolve an issue when people hear one another's viewpoints, in effect, talking one another out of a problem, or can reveal information that gets to the heart of a problem.

These meetings work well when the purpose is clearly announced and people come prepared to discuss the issue the manager is putting on the table or issues they want to raise. The manager can set parameters (a specific company issue or one in the industry) or state that any topic is welcome.

Meetings that are singularly focused can be managed by keeping conversation on topic. When the meeting's purpose is to give people a chance to air general concerns, the rules of engagement are especially important so the meeting doesn't become an unruly gripe session or a shouting match.

Passion, though, can be a good thing. The key to success is to set rules of engagement at the outset.

- Everyone will have an opportunity to speak.
- Participants will have a certain amount of time to talk.
- Conversation will be limited to descriptors and analysis of the problem(s) and will not delve into solutions.
- The meeting will end at a pre-stated time, if not before.

The manager's job is to create a relaxed risk-free setting and then sit back, listen, take notes, and maintain order. The manager must maintain a non-judgmental climate that welcomes everyone's viewpoints (don't try to argue someone into a change of mind). Generally, people feel freer to express themselves in a group (as opposed to one-on-one with the manager). An alternative is to gather written submissions and then log them anonymously on a flipchart or whiteboard for the group to see.

The final step before the meeting concludes is to prioritize the issues and gain consensus about which ones should be addressed first. It's not uncommon that many of the issues are interrelated, so major problems are relatively easy to identify.

Perhaps the most important part of a problem-solving meeting is what happens after it's over. People welcome the opportunity to speak up, but they do so because they expect to get someone's attention. Don't ask what people think if you aren't going to listen to what they have to say.

Issues that fall under the manager's responsibility are ones the manager must do something about. Others must be referred to the appropriate people in the organization. In either case, people deserve feedback or status reports, especially if they're not going to participate in developing solutions.

Brainstorming Meetings

Brainstorming is a problem-solving exercise, similar to part of the classic decision making model (recall Chapter 4) that generates ideas and analyzes alternatives. Brainstorming gives talent a chance to shine as people "noodle" a specific topic or problem, perhaps one that came out of a problem-identification meeting. Think about the managing diversity discussion in Chapter 3 when forming a brainstorming group so that exercise is most effective.

Brainstorming meetings can be very energizing and enjoyable. Define the issue and then just let the creative energies flow. With many minds engaged, an issue gets analyzed from a variety of perspectives. While it's particularly valuable to involve people who are affected by or most familiar with the subject, others who aren't as close to the subject can offer a fresh perspective. One person's idea spurs others, with variations and refinements. The quality and creativity of the dialogue can be quite impressive.

The manager's job is to list the possible solutions on a flipchart or board and keep the group focused on the most important rule: no criticism of the solutions is permitted. Keep the group moving at a fast pace. When they've exhausted all the possibilities, take a break or close the meeting. If that's the end of the exercise, the participants need to be told what management intends to do with all the suggestions and who will make a decision (and when).

Decision-Making Meetings

These are the participatory decision-making exercises that were discussed in Chapter 4. Decision-making meetings are the next logical step after a brainstorming session or can focus on a different issue presented by management. It's important to clearly state at the outset whether the group's assignment is to make a decision or make a recommendation for management's consideration so people know exactly what will happen with the end product of the meeting.

Generally, these meetings follow the classic decision-making model, involving no more than 15 participants. (Any larger and it's difficult to reach consensus.) Depending on the nature of the issue, the manager can act as an impartial moderator or participate in the discussions as an equal with the others, in which case the manager has to guard against dominating the process. In either case, the manager is responsible for keeping the group focused on the outcome—a decision or recommendation.

The meeting ends with everyone reaching a conclusion they can all live with, even if everyone doesn't fully agree. That may be the course of action that has the fewest undesirable consequences. The goal is to arrive at *consensus*, not make decisions by majority vote. When the minority loses, the people who don't favor the decision aren't likely to support its implementation.

In highly monolithic organizations, decision making, even about relatively insignificant matters, is rarely entrusted to anyone other than senior management or the broker/owner. If this is the culture in your organization, you're not likely to be conducting brainstorming or decision-making meetings.

Attitude and Recognition

Not all group-centric exercises are intensely work-centered. In fact, a great element of team building is the light-hearted, celebratory time and the time to recognize accomplishments (recall the commentary about praise in Chapter 3). When the company has had a banner year, everyone in the company (down to the receptionist) should be recognized for their contributions. If it's the beginning of a new year, a rally can mobilize everyone around the company's objectives and financial goals. Or the company can just have fun with a social or athletic event.

Companywide events build camaraderie and foster commitment to the company. All of the staff (management, support, and administrative personnel, as well as salespeople) play on the same team and should be included in these events. If you manage an office for a large company that doesn't have such an event, hold one just for your office.

Meetings of this nature should be upbeat and if the event is worthy of grand celebration, it should be held offsite with great fanfare. People should look forward to participating, rather than feel they are attending a command performance. An important part of the affair is the informal, social time before and after the program. In large organizations, this is one of the few times everyone gets to "rub elbows" with senior management.

Many of the people attending have nothing in common, except that they work for the company, and will have a much better time if the program gives them something to talk about or a fun project to work on together that's unrelated to business. The point is to relax and have fun, which also shows the company cares.

Retreats

Another forum for fostering camaraderie and engaging people professionally and socially is a retreat. While these events involve considerable planning and expense on the part of the company and commitment of time on the part of the people who attend, they offer benefits far beyond the program agenda.

Despite the fact that management is attempting to build a team, the reality is that today's mobile salespeople rarely see one another aside from an occasional staff meeting. A retreat is a prime opportunity to draw all of them and the administrative staff together with the additional benefit of the after-hours brainstorming people commonly do at professional meetings.

One of a meeting planner's greatest challenges is to gather a captive audience without the distractions of telephones, appointments, and office business. Those distractions can be eliminated by convening a meeting off-site at a conference facility with perhaps an overnight stay. Once people are totally immersed in the meeting, it's surprising how much they can accomplish, especially in brainstorming and decision making. Give people a problem today and by tomorrow they'll have a solution, including a plan for implementation.

A retreat can serve a variety of purposes—wrap up last year and kick off the new year; develop a strategic plan; strategize the design of a new system, service, or department; develop a business plan for the year; or conduct management or sales training.

The purpose of the retreat will determine who attends and the length of the time for the program. Assemble the entire organization for an educational forum or motivational rally (a mini-convention for the company), or assemble only management or certain department personnel. Planning the facilities, the program, food service, and other accommodations for a retreat is a major undertaking. But it's worth the effort to accomplish more in a shorter period of time than is possible in other forums.

■ ADDITIONAL OPPORTUNITIES

The discussion to this point has focused on the internal environment the company creates to empower people to do their jobs. But there are a number of opportunities outside the organization for people to enhance their competency as well. In fact, a company that is committed to professional development encourages people to seek these opportunities and often grants paid days off and/or subsidizes registration or tuition costs for employees to attend professional programs.

People gain as much from associating with other professionals with similar interests as they do from the actual education and training program. There are organizations and councils for brokers and managers, educators and trainers, marketing and advertising specialists, accountants, secretaries, professional women, and business owners. People should be encouraged to explore opportunities beyond forums that focus on real estate.

The obvious forums include colleges, universities, real estate schools, and professional organizations, but there are also self-training opportunities available online and through correspondence courses. Professional organizations conduct seminars, training programs, and more intense courses related to their members' activities, including designation programs.

The National Association of REALTORS® research group reports that salespeople who have designations from its institutes, societies, and councils earn more money. Most every real estate activity has related designations or organizations, including residential sales, buyer-agency, appraising, property management, nonresidential brokerage and management, counseling, and investment and international brokerage.

■ CONCLUSION

When people feel satisfied with their jobs, the place in which they work, and the progress they are making toward their career goals, they can be more productive for the company. Professional development is about creating opportunities for people both to gain proficiency in the skills they need for their jobs and to influence their quality of life at work. The company that supports continuous learning opportunities is also able to retain key talent. Exposing the company's personnel to a broad range of business education and professional associations adds a dimension to the organization as well as to the individual jobs people do.

■ DISCUSSION EXERCISES

What are the most important things a new hire should know about your company that should be included in an orientation program?

From your experiences in training programs, what would you like to see your company do in the programs it conducts for new salespeople? For experienced salespeople?

Discuss your experiences with mentoring programs and with cross-training programs. What worked, and didn't work, well?

From your experiences with sales meetings, either as a participant in a sales meeting or the person in charge of one, describe one of the best and one of the worst meetings. What happened that made the good one good and what made the other one bad?

CHAPTER SIXTEEN

16

COACHING PERFORMANCE

How does the manager contribute to performance? And evaluate performance?

How does the manager affect the retention of personnel?

Managers inspire and motivate people in a variety of ways, but none is more important than the individual attention they give to each person they supervise. The job is captured as coaching because, like an athletic coach, the manager is responsible for cultivating performance from each of the "team players." This often also means that the manager is counselor, problem solver, and negotiator as well.

In the parlance of human resources management, this part of a manager's job is characterized as "people are a lot of work." But if a manager isn't willing to take on that work, there's no reason to have a manager. The manager is also the only one who can remove obstacles within the company that hinder people's performance. (The systems don't run people; people run the systems.)

Coaching is another way to deliver training and foster professional development, which is crucial to retaining good personnel and reducing turnover.

But the manager's job is also about the elements of personnel management that affect continuing employment decisions and hold people accountable for doing the jobs for which they've been hired. When the time comes to evaluate performance, think about this—the performance of a worker is directly related to the performance of the manager.

■ MANAGING EMPLOYEES AND INDEPENDENT CONTRACTORS

Managers in today's real estate companies typically supervise both employees and independent contractors. It's important to understand the difference in the amount of control the company can exercise over people's activities. Managing those differences is particularly significant for preserving an IC relationship.

Step out of the real estate business and think about the working relationship that exists between employers and a large portion of this country's workforce. The company prescribes the number of hours that people work, allotments for vacation and personal days, meetings they are required to attend, and just about every other activity employees are expected to perform. This is a very structured environment that gives the company considerable control over the methods employees use to perform their jobs, even in a participatory work culture.

Independent contractors, on the other hand, work in a much less structured environment. An IC agreement is a service-for-hire contract in which the company engages the IC to achieve certain outcomes or objectives. The independent contractor controls the methods used to accomplish these objectives. A written contract (similar to the one in Chapter 14) defines the responsibilities of the IC and the company, but the contract cannot unduly restrict the independent contractor's methods.

The end result of an IC agreement is that management can't impose but can recommend, suggest, or encourage certain behavior. The IC controls conference and vacation schedules, daily activities (the number of sales calls, listing presentations, or open houses), and the properties and buyers the IC services. One of the situations currently blurring the IC-employee line is the practice of pressuring salespeople to do business with (or refer business to) the company's affiliated business enterprise.

The company can't have life both ways. It can't enjoy the financial benefits of hiring ICs while managing them as employees. One of the outgrowths of the recent economic recovery is the high number of jobs (50 percent by some estimates) that have gone to contractors or consultants. The U.S. Department of Labor and the Internal Revenue Service suggests that thousands of companies are calling workers ICs who are really full-time employees. This has led to an increase in IRS audits and some states proposing higher fines and criminal sanctions for companies that misclassify workers to cut costs.

Real estate industry outsiders look at the practice of staffing the core of a company's business with ICs as a rather odd way to run a company. IC implies that workers are temporary, on board only as long as the contracts are in force, which is a challenging way to sustain operations and revenue. ICs are also considered organizational outsiders, yet in real estate companies ICs are an integral part of the company in much the same way employees are.

The real estate workplace model is an anomaly (though traditionally it has been a successful one) that poses unique management challenges for companies whose sales force is IC. Sustaining the company's operations and revenue means assembling a stable army of independent workers and corralling that independence so the company's services can be delivered in an effective and professional manner and achieve the company's goals.

The key is an effective (not controlling) manager who is engaged with the sales force and constantly strives to foster their professional growth. Some managers give up, feeling that ICs are so independent there's little point in trying to supervise them at all. But the end result of that mindset is scattered or sporadic attempts by salespeople who receive little guidance or support. Managing ICs really requires the most astute people-management skills.

■ PERFORMANCE MANAGEMENT

The goal of human resource management is to forge a *psychological contract* between the company and the individual workers, a key factor in the relationship between the company and both employees and ICs. The contract arises from the company's providing compensation, career enhancement, and quality in work life. And the worker's contributing his or her skill, reasonable time and effort, and extra effort when needed. The basis of a psychological contract is commitment, with both the company and the worker making a commitment to one another.

In this sense, performance is a two-way street. The company must uphold its end of the bargain by providing the leadership and supportive, energized work environment that attracted people to it as the employer of choice. The workforce is obligated to discharge the responsibilities of the jobs for which they have been hired.

The two-way street becomes one way, though, as the company is ultimately responsible for workforce performance (back to the company's part of the bargain). That includes removing such barriers as inefficient company procedures, conflicts among workers, deficiencies in skills or abilities, or ineffective leadership that hinder performance. Interestingly, a major barrier is the failure to articulate exactly what that performance should be.

Performance management consists of identifying performance criteria and then using that criteria to encourage, evaluate, and reward performance. Performance criteria are the basis for management's coaching and professional development efforts, advancement and pay decisions, and disciplinary actions or termination decisions.

Performance Criteria

People need to know what's expected of them. Just as companies prepare business plans to direct company performance, the company's personnel need similar direction so they know what they're supposed to do. This is not a matter of handing a person a job description and saying, "Here, do this," or waving an IC agreement and saying, "Produce this much." A job needs to be broken down into specific outcomes or benchmarks—the performance criteria.

Performance criteria generally have results-oriented and behavior-related components that are tied to a position's job description (including necessary skills and abilities) and the company's business strategies and priorities. The criteria must focus on the most important aspects of a job and then be linked with measurable outcomes so the person knows the standards for satisfactory performance.

Although the production of a certain number of sales units is easily measured, behavior-related components can also be quantified numerically (the number of "highly satisfied" customer feedback reports, the number of courses or seminars completed, and so on). The important thing is to make the criteria fit the responsibilities of the position and eliminate variables that affect performance but which the individual can't control.

Performance standards must be developed for everyone in the organization, from the maintenance staff to the top executives and everyone in between. Typically, there are criteria for all personnel in the same job category plus specific criteria for individuals.

The *process* of developing standards is as important as the end result, that being the written words. (Yes, put all of this in writing.) Criteria are developed during one-on-one discussions between worker and supervisor (such as salesperson and sales manager). This is generally a conversation at year-end in preparation for the coming year. Keep several things in mind about the process.

- Discussion of past performance is an opportunity to praise, listen to frustrations, and identify skill enhancements or competencies that can be incorporated in the coming year's performance standards.
- Targets for future performance must be realistic. High performance standards are desirable for professional growth and organizational accomplishments, but arbitrary or overstated outcomes set up a person to fail. Targets must be tailored to the capacity, experience, and skills of each person.
- The process of developing standards is a reciprocal discussion or two-way process, which also creates an opportunity to achieve buy-in. Workers often have good ideas about what they can or should be doing and will support a plan they have an opportunity to influence.

Several things become very evident as performance standards are developed. Some people are high or overachievers and will work toward commensurately high accomplishments, while others are focused on basic food and shelter or just want to still have a job next year. Others are hesitant to set their sights at any point out of fear of failure, feeling that if nothing's said then any performance is a plus. The manager's job is to help resolve those underlying concerns so that collective efforts achieve the company's goals.

People want direction and a fair shot at proving themselves, but setting performance standards can be intimidating. They represent written commitments for which people will be held accountable. This also means shortcomings will be exposed, a risk some people readily accept but one that threatens others, especially when they can't control all the factors that affect their performance. Performance standards are only as constructive as management's willingness to foster a supportive work environment. (Here's where a manager's performance is reflected in that of a worker's.)

Personal Business Plans

A personal business plan is a holistic approach to performance that incorporates job performance standards and professional accomplishments in a plan that resembles the structure of a company's business plan. Goals are converted to specific, measurable targets that are supported with strategies and benchmarked with timeframes for achievement. Personal business plans are powerful tools for salespeople to self-direct and for management to coach performance. Managerial personnel often also prepare personal business plans.

Personal plans are developed one-on-one as part of the performance standards discussion. The process and rules for developing performance standards apply to personal business plans as well. (*Professional Real Estate Development* by Patrick Keigher and Joyce Emory is useful for developing personal business plans.) This is a team effort, with the manager providing guidance so the company's issues are addressed as each salesperson's personal plan is developed. If the salesperson is an IC, mutual agreement over performance standards is essential.

From a production standpoint, the manager can identify what needs to be accomplished based on the company's business plans and budgets. In the example in Figure 16.1, the total amount of revenue the office expects for the year is $350,500. Notice that for two quarters of the year, the example shows actual production in the previous year and the goals that ten salespeople are expected to reach in the coming year as the responsibility for the $350,500 is distributed.

FIGURE 16.1
Annual Office Production Goals, 2011–2012

Name	1st Quarter 2006 Actual	1st Quarter 2007 Goal	2nd Quarter 2006 Actual	2nd Quarter 2007 Goal	Total Year 2006 Actual	Total Year 2007 Goal
FORD	5,000	7,500	5,800	9,000	24,000	30,000
SMITH	8,000	8,000	4,700	5,500	29,000	35,000
ADAIN	5,000	8,000	6,000	8,000	30,000	37,500
DINKEL	7,500	11,000	8,000	10,000	34,000	40,000
FRANKS	5,500	6,000	4,200	6,000	26,900	30,000
RIGGS	9,500	10,000	9,500	10,000	48,000	50,000
KEAST	13,000	12,000	0	10,000	39,800	60,000
JONES	2,100	2,000	4,000	4,000	8,100	18,000
COSTA	5,500	6,000	3,300	6,120	25,600	24,000
BOWERS	0	6,000	3,000	6,000	13,000	24,000
COMPANY	10,766	130,500		127,500	278,300	350,500

Personal plans convert these production goals into individual accomplishments. Any number of other goals can also be developed in a salesperson's plan, ranging from improving customer services or the transaction fall-through rate to obtaining an industry designation. Plans help people prioritize activities so they can focus on those that directly relate to achieving their goals. The manager's role is to support the implementation of a person's plan.

Performance Feedback

People need to know how they're doing, or perhaps just as important is they deserve to know. Providing feedback is the essence of management's coaching job, the motivation and encouragement that help workers thrive. The important point is *not to wait until the end of the year to talk to people about what they should have been doing during the year*.

Performance feedback is essentially a periodic performance review, with the performance standards providing the script or talking points. The object is not to formally grade performance but rather to gauge how people are doing, praise their progress, help solve their problems, and identify adjustments that may be needed (including by management) so people can reach their targets by year-end.

Performance feedback is one way of advancing the psychological commitment people make to the company. The company's part of the contract is advanced with support and encouragement and its willingness to remove obstacles or at least tell people what's practical and impractical for management to do.

The when and how of providing feedback is where generational differences often collide. Gen Ys expect frequent feedback and candid advice and counsel from their managers, often in digital exchanges. Older generations are geared to more formal and less frequent performance discussions. Younger generations are more vocal about their demand for feedback, and older workers are less likely to initiate inquiry. Gen Y and Boomer managers view their feedback jobs differently as well, but this is another time managers need to learn how to manage multiple generations (recall Chapter 3).

Quarterly performance conversations, typically one-on-one, will suit many workers but managers shouldn't overlook the less formal, more spontaneous opportunities to coach, tutor, and teach. Performance feedback is also important for updating criteria if company priorities or quantitative measures change during the year.

Performance Incentives

Some people can thrive simply on self-satisfaction, but people deserve the company's acknowledgment of their efforts. Incentives are ways for companies to recognize performance and encourage people to keep going. Because people's motives for working and responses to recognition differ, companies generally employ a variety of incentives to reward and inspire people.

Incentives need to contribute to the quality of life in the workplace. The downside of some incentives is they can have the opposite effect. Incentives that single out certain people can damage the team spirit companies try to build. Some incentives are so predictable that people come to expect them, which means they are no longer incentives.

Job-performance-based pay. Money is typically seen as a powerful incentive, which is the reason for job-performance-based, variable pay plans (recall the compensation discussion in Chapter 13). The assumption is that a reward for past performance is also an incentive to perform well in the future. The major downside to performance-based pay is that people may work harder with good purpose than is often reflected in their paychecks.

Any incentive must be fairly administered, but that's especially important for performance-based pay. The company has an unequivocal obligation to ensure that this type of pay is properly benchmarked to performance. Not only can the company make or break its reputation as an employer of choice when paychecks are handed out, but most important is the company is in a very vulnerable position with respect to equal employment laws unless it can defend its pay decisions.

Defensible evidence requires stated performance standards and fair, objective methods of evaluating performance. Numerically defined targets, benchmarked timeframes, or other quantitative figures are easiest to assess. But not all job-based targets or professional achievements are as easily captured numerically, which means the evidentiary burden falls on the description of the standards and the rating system used to assess performance.

Status. The purpose of status incentives is to reward or inspire initiative or to give special skills or abilities an opportunity to shine. The company can do this in a variety of ways.

- Assign a salesperson with exceptional skills to be a mentor or partner for a newly licensed salesperson.
- Ask a person with good writing skills or a background in publishing to be the editor of the company's newsletter.
- Assign someone to oversee staff in the manager's absence.

- Invite someone to make a presentation at a company meeting.
- Assign a person to chair a special-project task force or a problem-solving project.

These incentives are an effective way to foster professional growth, but they can disenfranchise equally skillful or deserving people unless management makes such opportunities part of the workplace routine. Management must also guard against violating equal employment laws when selecting people for these opportunities.

Some special assignments deserve compensation. One of the gripes people have is the tendency of companies to pile on responsibilities without giving people commensurate job titles or additional compensation. Status incentives are intended to encourage people to take initiative and develop recognition-worthy skills. The shining stars who are singled out as well as others the company is trying to inspire won't be flattered by the opportunity if they feel they're being used.

Pick people wisely. Some people will help themselves to more than the company intended once given the opportunity. The person who is just waiting to be sales manager may not be willing to relinquish the position or could undermine the manager's authority once the temporary assignment is over. A good idea could fuel office politics and power plays that could disrupt office harmony. Be very clear about the details of the assignment and the limits of authority.

Contests. Contests intend to increase production with valuable recognition or reward to the victors. Not all companies agree on the value of sales contests, and indeed, there are some ways contests can backfire.

Good-natured, spirited competition can turn into a managerial nightmare if people try to win at any cost. Unless the contest is structured properly and the manager is prepared to manage the situation, the contest can create controversy over sales leads, an increased number of disgruntled sellers or buyers, or more overpriced listings than the company wants to advertise.

As companies try to foster team building and more salespeople are structuring their own sales teams, the playing field for contests changes. Pitting individual salespeople against one another can destroy the close-knit crew in a sales office and, unless all the salespeople are assigned to teams, production outcomes are not comparable.

Production contests tend to be biased, with the top producers typically being the same people who always win. The message to others is their contributions aren't valuable so there's little reason for them trying to compete. Contests must be structured so that people with differing levels of experience or expertise can compete on similar levels.

Finally, there's the prize and the debate over whether the prize or the recognition is the incentive. Winning is recognition. A prize needs to be valuable (which usually also means costly), but it may not be universally appealing unless the company is willing to trade cash for equivalent value (the Caribbean or Hawaiian vacation for cash). An inexpensive or unique prize (the pressure cooker) has humorous value and while fun is good for reducing tension and building camaraderie, that's a different goal than a true sales contest.

Awards. Awards to the listing leader, the sales leader, or the outstanding customer-service person are typical, be they a nameplate added to a plaque in the reception area or a trophy. While these are useful ways to recognize accomplishments, awards are so common that they suffer the predictability downside (the same people always win) and are little incentive unless they are also showcased for marketing purposes or backed up with a monetary award.

Award programs can polarize the sales force into the "outstandings" and the "also-rans." The "outstandings" compete with one another, trading a trophy back and forth. The "also-rans" don't even bother trying. Eventually awards become meaningless or even embarrassing for the person who constantly wins. This is not to suggest that the leader-of-the-month award should necessarily be eliminated, but consider other programs as well.

Negative incentives. Some managers see fear, embarrassment, reprimand, and criticism as performance incentives, thinking that if an experience is sufficiently unpleasant, people will strive to avoid similar unpleasantness in the future. Yelling at a salesperson who hasn't had a listing in three months, and doing so in front of the entire staff, certainly lets everyone know what the manager thinks. But it's insulting to be the subject of ridicule, as if the salesperson isn't already aware of the listing deficiency.

Negative incentives do more harm than good. At best, they work only momentarily. The subject salesperson may get out of the office in a hurry, perhaps to find a listing but more likely just to get out of the line of fire. Relationships suffer, including the manager's relationship with others in the office, and create an antagonistic atmosphere that takes far more time to repair than it took to create. Certainly, this does not provide the quality of life in the workplace and the respected leadership people want.

■ PERFORMANCE APPRAISALS

Performance appraisals, also known as *performance evaluations* and *performance reviews*, consist of a two-step process of rating each individual's performance and then communicating that information. Performance appraisals are generally formal, year-end activities that provide information for administrative purposes (such as compensation, advancement, and termination decisions) and for assessing personal development (identifying strengths, weaknesses, and professional development). The outcomes of one year's appraisal are then used to formulate performance standards for the next year.

The basis of performance evaluations is the performance standards that were developed earlier in the year. The legal reality of evaluations is they must be clearly job-performance based, not personality or character assessments, and must be fairly and equitably administered for each person. Otherwise, the company can have significant legal exposure when personnel decisions are made. The practical reality is evaluations provide much useful information for

- merit or performance adjustments in wages, salaries, and variable pay.
- identifying candidates for promotion (or demotion) to other positions in the company or for termination.
- identifying situations in which a person's skills are better suited for a different job in the company.

- determining whether management's expectations of people are unrealistic, which will be obvious if everyone is performing poorly in certain areas.
- determining job descriptions that may need to be revised based on changes in the marketplace, in the company's business plan, and in jobs of other personnel.
- determining the effectiveness of training programs, hiring procedures, and company policies and procedures, including revisions that may be necessary.

The practice of doing formal performance reviews is a long-standing tradition in the business world, but it's also controversial. The manager-subordinate team can turn into a "me-versus-you" relationship and a one-sided report card that is tainted with political or subjective evaluations, which can also vary considerably from manager to manager. Although this sounds like a royal indictment of performance reviews, it makes the point that the company can significantly damage relationships with an ill-conceived performance review process.

Rating Performance

The first step of a formal review is to rate performance. Rating is a process of using a formal methodology to evaluate actual performance in relationship to the standards that were benchmarked as satisfactory performance. Some rating methods are more quantitative than others, but the commonality is they provide objective strategies for preparing a "report card." Regardless of the method, the same one should be used companywide, or at least for the same classes of jobs. Sample performance evaluations and self-evaluation instruments that can be suitably tailored are available on the Internet.

One way to assess performance is with a *rating scale*, which assigns numerical values to various levels of performance. These quantitative measures are used to rate each performance standard, with the total values providing an assessment of overall performance.

- **A scale of 1 to 5.** This is a very straightforward method of assigning numerical values: a 3 is satisfactory, a 5 is the highest, and a 4 falls in between; a 2 is something less than satisfactory but not as deficient as a 1. This scale is sometimes seen as the easiest to use, though requires refinements in the definitions for each value. Does a satisfactory 3 mean an individual did what was expected and a higher value means excelling beyond that point? Or does a 3 mean acceptable progress toward reaching a target, which would be a 5?

- **A scale of 1 to 10.** This provides a wider range of quantitative values: satisfactory is a 5 or 6 and a 10 is the highest. This scale provides a more precise assessment of performance, but it is more difficult to use and defend. Values can be grouped at the low, mid, and high points, but the differences between each number are less easy to distinguish. What's the measurable difference between a 6 or a 7, or a 7 and an 8?

An alternative method for evaluating performance is with *descriptive* ratings. The most desirable is "below expectations," "meeting expectations," "exceeding expectations," and "outstanding." The relationship between the terminology and performance is readily apparent, which makes this process easy for people to understand and for managers to use (eliminating arguments over a rating of 6 instead of 7).

After each standard is evaluated, overall performance is evaluated similarly. This descriptive method is preferable to the less defensible and more subjective "outstanding," "good," "fair," "needs improvement," or "poor" assessments. Does "good" mean a person met the standard for performance, which is a good thing? Or is "fair" satisfactory or OK?

As straightforward as these methods sound, rating requires some careful contemplation to fairly assess performance. A number of variables can skew the outcomes, ranging from defects in the descriptions of standards at the outset to the manager's inexperience with the rating process. Some managers are just generally harsher graders than others (just like school teachers). Many variables are correctable over time to make the rating process evenhanded. But subjectivity is the most troublesome variable to eliminate.

- The star employee or producer has a lousy year. The tendency is to overlook this year's performance because of past activities, but unless this year doesn't count for everyone, the evaluation is not evenhanded. The people who did do well or improve this year will resent the lack of acknowledgment.

- Managers often have better relationships with some people than others, and some personalities are more likable or abrasive than others. These are personality issues, not performance issues and can't be allowed to affect ratings. Managers tend to overlook people's weaknesses that are similar to theirs and overly critical of people whose weaknesses they don't have. Perfectionists tend to be overly critical of everyone. Criticism isn't part of performance.
- A worker's performance is also a grade for the manager. Ratings can reflect self interests or personal agenda in an attempt to justify the manager's existence or make manager look good to superiors.
- Using ratings to contrive ways to promote a favorite worker or demote or terminate a problem one when performance doesn't truly warrant favorable or unfavorable ratings is not only the epitome of subjectivity but also creates significant legal problems.

An increasing number of companies are trying to remove subjective variables by focusing more on quantified targets. The virtue of those metrics is that performance is relatively easy to evaluate using a *1-2-3 rating scale*: 3 means a target was reached, 2 gives the worker credit for almost reaching the target, and 1 is obviously not near the target that was expected. The aggregate scores demonstrate overall performance. Of course, this type of evaluation model is fair only if the specific targets are defined when performance criteria are developed at the outset.

One of the most interesting ways to evaluate performance is to ask people to do *self-evaluations* using the same rating methodology used by the managers. Sometimes people are far more critical of their performance than the manager is. Self-evaluations also reveal what matters most to people about their performance and provides information the manager may not have known.

Often several open-ended questions are included so people can express their thoughts about job satisfaction, pay, and the like. Although this is a good opportunity to gather information, managers must guard against letting the responses influence their evaluation of performance.

Generally, a self-evaluation is submitted to the supervising manager, who then compares the individual's ratings with ratings the manager has already formulated. In some companies, the self-evaluation starts the process and the manager uses that assessment as the basis of his or her review.

Performance Interviews

The second step of a formal review is the meeting. The purpose of a performance interview is for the manager and the worker to engage in a reciprocal discussion of the performance evaluation. The outcome of the meeting is mutual understanding of the evaluation and a plan for the coming year.

Although people may have some trepidation, these are not intended to be confrontational or interrogation sessions. If the manager has done his or her job during the year, there shouldn't be any great surprises. Performance reviews are not simply "report card" conferences but an extension of the relationship-building managers do with their workers.

- Follow the performance standards "script." It's essential to keep these interviews on track to make efficient use of time. These meetings generally take about an hour.
- As each of the performance standards is addressed, compare the assessments and learn from different perspectives.
- Don't dominate the meeting. It's the other person's forum to speak his or her mind as much as it is the manager's.
- Don't criticize! If the meeting is seen as the manager's opportunity to beat up on the interviewee, there won't be any constructive two-way exchange. The person will just bluff through the meeting until it's over.
- Don't dwell on faults. This is the time to praise accomplishments as well as develop solutions when someone is straying off track.
- Performance standards for the coming year are not necessarily limited to refinements of the current year's "script." This is an opportunity to frame targets for new accomplishments or realign responsibilities to support the company's work plan for the coming year as well.
- Take notes and stay focused on information that is relevant to a person's job description so as not to stray into topics that could cause legal problems.

Because performance ratings and interviews have legal significance, managers should follow the advice of the company's attorney about the appropriate way to conduct and document these activities and the records that should be committed to personnel files.

■ RETENTION

Presumably the work environment that attracts recruits to the company is the environment that also retains them, but that means the company must follow through with its part of the psychological commitment. Valuable lessons can be learned about how well the company manages that environment from the people who do leave.

The keys to retention, regardless of the personnel position, are

- realistic job previews,
- good hiring selections,
- positive employer-employee relations, and
- opportunities for career enhancement.

All of these are management's responsibility, which essentially makes management responsible for retention and turnover. Although no one can fully anticipate what the working relationship will be, people arrive on the job expecting the relationship will turn out to be positive.

The relationship gets off on the wrong foot if people have been misled with overly flattering portrayals of work life or guarded representations of the job they will be doing. However, even candor at the outset won't retain a worker unless management follows through with a job-enriching place to work.

Employee Relations

Employee relations is about quality of life with the company—the "keep them happy and they will work" mantra.

The most striking example of how well this plays has been showcased by a privately held corporation that operates in a campus-like facility, complete with tennis courts, fully equipped exercise facilities and spa, dining facilities with live piano music, and onsite childcare that parents can visit throughout the day. Employees are provided meals, healthcare, and assorted other benefits as well as maximum flextime work hours. This is the ultimate model of an employee- and family-friendly workplace.

When asked why the company treats employees so well, the CEO commented because this is the right way and it works. People are happy, healthy, relaxed, and highly productive. The company has a major investment in its employees, but the company also has low absenteeism and loses very few of its hires.

Certainly, this model is the exception, but there are elements of this model that are fairly common in today's workplace. Companies are more family-friendly than once was the case, more concerned about the general welfare and health and safety of their workers, and more attentive to employee concerns. In short, today's workplace is far more compassionate.

Although companies do a variety of things to enhance employee relations and their psychological commitment to the workers, one of the common themes is the interaction between managers and workers. Looking at this from the worker point of view, people want to know they are valued and respected and have the support of their managers. This is true for all workers but especially the Gen Ys.

Managers can be coaches in a formal sense, being actively engaged in goal setting and prescribing, nudging, and cheering the steps along the way. Most commonly, though, managers do that to some extent with all of their workers, which is a little different than the scope of services provided by professional business coaches (someone a manager can think about hiring for his or her personal career).

But all managers can be accessible and learn to listen. We've repeatedly observed that people have good ideas about what the company can do and how to solve their daily problems. If the manager is one of those problems, people need to be able to say that too. Candor is good for an organization, but one of the most frequent criticisms of managers is the workers' inability to get their ears.

The voices that often get the manager's attention are the top-performing, positive, or energetic workers, but everyone deserves the manager's ear. Then there are the one or two bad apples that spoil the workplace for everyone with their laziness, incompetence, or difficult personalities.

They are management's hiring mistakes that hopefully would have been avoided but once on board, fall into the keep-your-enemies-closer category, unless management is willing to remove the destructive personality from the workplace. One toxic personality can have a greater negative effect in the workplace than dozens of positive personalities can overcome.

Another very useful and simple way to enhance employee relations is by periodically conducting an *employee survey*. A survey requires some careful planning to elicit useful information, but it's invaluable for finding out what people think about

- compensation policies.
- workplace environment and morale.
- business ethics.
- potential for advancement.
- fairness or evenhandedness in the way management treats people.
- opportunities for professional development.
- general satisfaction with the company, management, and their careers.

Surveys are essentially management's report cards. Even if there are things that the company cannot afford to do (like better pay or better benefits), there are things that management can say and do to enhance understanding and improve the work environment.

Problem Solving

Ask managers in any real estate office how they spend most of their time and they'll say solving problems and resolving conflict. Problems may be issues between the manager and a person he or she supervises or issues among workers. In either case, the manager's objective is to resolve the situation in a mutually satisfactory manner. Sometimes this involves a disciplinary meeting and other times the manager has to put on the counselor hat.

Management's problem. Recall the discussion in Chapter 3 about assessing behavior and the lessons about ways that managers can effectively address problem behavior. In a real estate office, the most common problems involve real estate transactions and breaches of company policies and procedures. But there are also morale issues (jealousy, commission disputes, personality conflicts, and cliques) that can turn a once positive, energized environment into an unappealing place to work (which is turnover in the making). In the most serious sense, the company could face litigation over employee discrimination and harassment.

■ **CASE IN POINT** The morning you discover that a salesperson has lost an earnest money check begins by hauling the person into your office. You slam the door and wave the company's policy and procedures manual under the person's nose. You vent: "Don't you know any better than to be so careless? See what the manual says you're supposed to do with the check. Don't you know how much trouble we can all be in? What if the buyer backs out and we don't have the deposit in our account? I'll take that money out of your next commission check! Now, get out of my office and don't ever let that happen again!" Okay! Problem identified; problem solved.

In this scenario, the manager identified what happened (the check got lost) and some of the difficulties that could result, but was the problem identified? Maybe the check was simply filed incorrectly by the secretary. But there was no discussion so the manager doesn't really know what happened. The poor salesperson didn't get in a word edgewise (which may have been better than getting into a shouting match). The manager presented a solution, but it certainly was an ill-conceived one. This encounter missed the mark in a number of ways.

Identifying problem behavior is a necessary part of a manager's job. But managers need to approach this task with a purposeful, constructive plan. Serving notice that a person's conduct was unacceptable is only part of the process. The manager needs a solution or a course of action that corrects the situation and prevents it from occurring again. That solution must be acceptable to both the manager and the offender, and if several people are offenders, each one must commit to the resolution.

Disciplinary meetings. Problem-solving meetings involving unacceptable behavior are essentially disciplinary meetings. Because they can be the prelude to employment decisions that can have significant (and possibly legal) consequences, disciplinary meetings must be developed in a methodical manner.

- **Identify the problem before scheduling a meeting.** It's obvious that something happened, but the first step is to determine exactly what and identify the appropriate person with whom to address the problem.
- **Study the problem before confronting the person.** This slows you down long enough to gather the facts and describe the situation correctly.
- **Describe the problem for the person from your point of view.** ("As I understand it . . .") Presenting the problem in a descriptive fashion helps the person understand exactly the behavior that is observed. Don't be judgmental or accusatory or try to speculate why. Just provide a factual description.
- **Gather information from the person.** Ask questions. There may be information about what happened that you don't have. The meeting may end at this point if you learn that you misinterpreted the event. Be fair and give the person a chance to share some observations.
- **Keep the meeting objective.** This sounds difficult, but the purpose of the meeting is not to prove who's right or wrong, to pass judgment on a person's character, or to clobber a person's self-esteem. Minimize tension and defensiveness. "Yes, you did" and "no, I didn't" won't resolve anything.
- **Don't sugarcoat the problem.** This is not a meeting to praise and then sneak the problem into the agenda. The person needs to know precisely the point of the problem.
- **Agree that a problem exists.** The manager may be the only one who thinks there's a problem. Before the issue can be resolved, the offender must agree that this is an issue that needs attention.
- **Develop mutually acceptable alternatives as possible solutions.** The person must participate in this process. The manager is asking the person to change behavior, which means that a solution that is acceptable to the person is more likely to work. However, the man-

ager has the right to veto alternatives that are unacceptable from the company's point of view. The manager must also be willing to contribute to the solution.

- **Agree on a course of action.** This includes the timeframe within which the corrective action will occur. Both of you must select the same course of action from the list of alternative solutions.
- **Agree on a follow-up meeting.** This occurs at the end of the established timeframe to ensure that the problem is resolved.
- **Conclude the meeting once you have agreement.** Don't drag it out and cloud the issue.
- **Focus on one problem at a time.** It's tempting to unload and find fault with everything a person does. But this is not a gripe session. It's a problem-solving meeting.
- **Acknowledge the change.** A manager's job is to praise as much as it is to correct problems, so be sure to recognize the steps the person takes to correct the problem.
- **Document the proceedings.** Follow the advice of the company attorney as to proper documentation. A disciplinary meeting may be a prelude to more demonstrative discipline or eventual termination. Documentation is critical for the company to defend its actions.

Using this as a guide, how would you handle the scenario of the lost earnest money check?

The employee's problem. The manager may be gliding through the day, feeling that everything is under control. It may not be readily apparent that trouble is brewing, but it's best to be watchful of group dynamics.

- Do people hush as you stroll through the office?
- Is there a clique that huddled together over lunch, particularly after you announced a new office procedure?
- Is there a heated exchange in the back room or by the water cooler?

People must feel free to raise their concerns and the sooner the better. They may need a little encouragement like, "I notice that you seem to be . . . Would you like to talk?" or "How can I help?" The manager has to be willing to listen and accept the fact that he or she may be the cause of a problem.

Give the person an opportunity to describe the problem without interfering or getting defensive. This can be a very emotional or delicate conversation for the person. If the problem is you, don't argue. If the problem is someone else in the office, don't take sides, make excuses, or defend the other person. If the problem is outside the office (with someone in another office, a customer, or the person's private life), listen.

If the manager is the source of the problem, the manager is responsible for the solution. The conversation needs to end with a description of what the manager intends to do to resolve the issue and a commitment to follow through on that course of action. Managers only make matters worse if they just placate people to get them out of the office or don't take their concerns seriously.

If the problem is someone other than the manager, the manager has to decide whether to intervene (the manager takes responsibility for the problem) or to help the person find ways to deal with the situation (the person owns the problem).

■ **CASE IN POINT** The manager's dilemma is similar to that of a parent confronted with two children picking on one another. One child comes with a long tale about what his brother did to him. It could be the child just wanted to air his frustrations, and he's totally content to run off and forget the matter or handle the situation himself. Maybe he wants you to go tell his brother off. But this means taking sides (one boy must be right and the other must be wrong) with the risk being that one person is alienated in the process of satisfying the other. Another point to consider is that maybe the reason his brother lashed out is totally justified. Intervention may be condoning unacceptable behavior.

Take this analogy back to the office and put a worker in the child's place. It's possible that all the person wants to do is vent frustrations or use the manager as a sounding board and doesn't expect the manager to take any action. Or the person may be asking for help. If that's the case, then the manager needs to be clear about what help is being requested.

If person A asks the manager to intervene in a problem with person B, remember that there are at least two sides to the story. Rather than risk a relationship with both people, it's best to help A find a solution first. Depending on the nature of the problem, the manager may decide to have a conversation with B to investigate whether there are also other problems that need to be addressed. B has to be approached objectively so that B doesn't feel like the target of A's anger or ridicule. Don't betray confidences.

If it's appropriate for the manager to be the negotiator and arbitrator, then the manager has to get out of the middle and help A and B find a solution that is acceptable to both of them.

■ RESIGNATION AND TERMINATION

A common law doctrine of employment is *employment-at-will* (EAW). This says employers have the right to hire, fire, demote, and promote whomever they choose, and employees have the right to quit whenever they want.

However, at-will is not nearly as simple as it sounds. At-will carries with it a *covenant of fairness and good faith* between the employer and the at-will employee. This means that if the employer breaches the covenant with unreasonable behavior, the employee can seek legal recourse.

Employment is established by either express (written) or implied contract, which arises from an employee doing the job. Long service and lack of job-performance criticism implies continued employment, which gives the dismissed employee recourse under EAW.

Independent contractor agreements are typically at-will. Generally, very clearly stated language proclaims that the contract is at-will. This attempts to insulate the employer from claims of wrongful discharge. However, the carefully crafted words won't do much good if the actual practices are contradictory.

The bottom line is that the company door is not as free-swinging as at-will implies. The scales are tipped today in the employee's favor as a result of years of employers abusing at-will doctrine. That prompted a variety of equal employment laws that are also founded on the principle of fairness.

Resignation

The best a company can do to prevent people from resigning is to uphold its psychological commitment. But once an employee has decided to leave (the "will" of the employee is to quit), it's probably too late to convince the person to stay. That's not to say the manager shouldn't explore the reason for leaving and where the person is going, however.

- If the person wants to change specialties or job position, there may be a different role or new opportunity within the company that will appeal to someone the company wants to retain.
- If the person wants to change companies (a lateral move into a similar job), there may be an internal problem that can be resolved. On the other hand, the company may be losing personnel because of deep-seated management problems or is losing its competitive edge over other employers. These situations definitely require attention but can't be quickly remedied to retain one desirable worker.

Salespeople are more likely to leave because they're dissatisfied with the company's management of personnel (or lack thereof) than because of the company's commission split. Although conflicts with others in the office and conflicts with managers cause dissatisfaction, top producers are most irked by the failure to terminate poorly producing salespeople. Feelings of resentment grow when top producers think they're carrying more than their fair share of the responsibility for the company's revenue or are held to higher standards of performance than other salespeople are.

To determine if a salesperson is producing a profit, establish the minimum average production (MAP) needed from each person. Begin with the desk cost and add a percentage that represents the minimum profit. Divide that figure by the number of salespeople. The result is the MAP, which can then be compared with actual production.

Some people consistently fall below the MAP, some are average or above, and others exceed the MAP by a wide margin. The MAP calculation can also reveal that "average" is not especially lucrative. For an interesting comparison, divide the sum of desk cost plus profit by a smaller number of salespeople and then look at where salespeople fall. The result will reveal whether the sales staff is right-sized with the right personnel and how vulnerable the company is to losing its top producers.

As much as the manager may not want to lose personnel, it's important to avoid getting into a bargaining position. If there are legitimate changes the company can make, that's fine, but playing favorites to keep people is as bad as playing favorites while they're working. That upsets both fair pay practices and morale.

Sometimes the person does management a favor by volunteering to leave. If this is the office malcontent or poorest performer, the manager is off the hook for not having addressed that problem sooner. If a person is truly miserable, do that person (as well as the company) a favor and let him or her go. Sometimes people are just discouraged for the day. (How many times do salespeople "quit" when the business gets frustrating?) Rather than accepting a hasty decision, help the person over the hurdle before taking action.

Finally, graciously send the person on the way. The company that is truly compassionate and committed to professional development supports people's decisions to move on to new job opportunities. And don't permanently close the door.

Today's companies commonly welcome workers back with open arms. Good people are hard to find and they can hit the ground running when they return, which makes exceeding good financial sense for both the company and the company's business. Gone are the days that a departed worker is persona non grata.

Termination

When the "will" of the company is to terminate an at-will employee, the process must be handled in such a way that the company doesn't breach the covenant of fairness and good faith. Any time management must tell someone to leave is difficult, but some times are more complicated than others.

Layoffs are the most straightforward terminations and generally the least problematic from a legal point of view. People lose their jobs because the company no longer has jobs for them to do. Although there are instances when companies suddenly announce that a person's services are no longer needed, layoffs are typically planned with enough foresight to provide workers advanced notice and perhaps severance pay.

A company can get into trouble, however, if a termination is represented as a layoff when the real motive is to fire someone without justifying the cause. The "laid-off" person may have legal recourse.

The practical reality of layoffs is they temporarily affect morale in the remaining workforce, especially if management doesn't take steps to reassure people that their jobs are secure.

Sometimes a termination is the most compassionate way out of a relationship that just isn't working. There are occasions when a person is simply not a good fit, not because of poor job performance but because, despite everyone's best efforts, the company and the employee haven't managed to work well together. The person's skills and the job (or any job in the company) may not mesh, or there may be personality conflicts that can't be resolved.

When the time finally comes that the manager says that "it's not your fault, but this isn't working," the employee is generally given the option of resigning in lieu of being terminated. The situation must be presented strictly for what it is, not masquerade as poor performance or a layoff. The company should be supportive with generous advance notice, severance pay, and an offer to help secure a position elsewhere.

The most challenging terminations involve decisions to fire a worker. Any termination represents failure, but the hardest to confront is employee behavior or performance because the problem is as much management's failure to do its job as the employee's failure.

Companies often hesitate to terminate out of fear of lawsuits and even duck the issue entirely by shuffling their problems from department to department or office to office. Guilt, fear of lost friendship, or pressures from senior management can turn an obvious termination decision into unwarranted job security for the worker. But employment laws were established to protect workers from abusive and unfair labor practices, not to prevent a warranted termination. The greater harm is done when companies establish personnel policies that they selectively or don't enforce.

Common reasons for showing people to the door include lack of productivity, violation of laws or company policies and procedures, or because the employee is a serious personnel problem. Often companies are hesitant to let salespeople go, that one lost is a loss of a transaction. But there's little point in expecting performance and then doing nothing when people don't measure up.

Termination is the absolute final step of the disciplinary process. This process involves a series of steps for handling personnel problems fairly and in good faith, with the possibility that the matter can be resolved along the way and never even reach the point of termination.

If that is the final outcome, however, no one should be surprised. The slippery slope out the door is not a direct shot, except in egregious situations like theft or embezzlement. Even in these cases, it's safer to suspend a person temporarily (rather than terminating) and then get direction from legal counsel. A fundamental rule of problem resolution is—never fire in a huff!

EAW case law provides considerable guidance for developing defensible disciplinary and termination policies and procedures (a job for the company's attorney), which then must be published in the company's policy and procedures manual and employee handbook. Published statements tell people (including independent contractors) about their rights and recourse and also aid the company's defense if an employee alleges wrongful discharge, which means that managers must also follow the published rules. Disciplinary and termination procedures generally include a series of steps.

- Investigate and document evidence of the behavior. A performance review or appraisal is a start. Because a manager can misinterpret behavior, further evidence is needed to verify whether accusations are justified. Investigation must be a fair and impartial inquiry, and all subsequent actions must be applied even-handedly. (The employer would do the same for any worker in a similar situation.)
- Communicate concerns to the person and describe the behavior. Also inform the person that the situation is serious enough to warrant termination. This is known as a *warning*.

- Develop a plan for corrective action, document the plan, and provide the support and assistance necessary to help the person correct the situation. This may be the end of the matter, but documentation should be retained so that if subsequent behavior warrants more serious action, the company has defensible evidence.
- Depending on the employment laws that govern the company (a factor of number of workers and state law), the company may be required to accept a rebuttal or explanation of the event from the employee's point of view, which is made part of the personnel file.
- Subsequent misbehavior is handled following the same procedure as in the first event and may be disposed of with a *second warning* or perhaps a *suspension* for several days.
- Behavior that finally warrants termination is communicated to the person along with the decision to terminate. This should be done privately and confidentially with a clear description of the reason for termination. Remain calm, firm, and professional. The chances are the person being terminated won't, but that's to be expected.
- Resolve the details for departure, including the date of departure and the way pending business is to be handled. Sometimes companies usher people out the door within the hour, though that's not practical, humane, or necessary unless the person's job position is such that the company is vulnerable to theft or sabotage.
- Protect the firm. Secure the facilities (change locks) and systems (change computer access codes and passwords), and take other actions the attorney recommends.

The company attorney is the best adviser, but the heads-up conclusion to this discussion is that disciplinary and termination actions create great liability for the company. The point can't be repeated often enough about the importance of just cause, due process, and documentation.

Without warnings (documented), evidence of the conduct (documented), and fair and even-handed application of rules and penalties, the company is particularly vulnerable. The company also has to be able to prove that a disciplinary or termination action was not taken in retaliation for a worker's having filed a legally protected complaint.

Exit Interviews

One final and very important step is an exit interview, regardless of whether people leave voluntarily or involuntarily. This step rarely gets the attention it deserves, but it provides extremely useful information for the company to evaluate its operations and personnel management procedures. Because people who leave the company can be either its greatest advocates or greatest adversaries, one final conversation is an opportunity to promote the former and defuse the latter.

An exit interview is a debriefing session and a time to bring closure to the relationship. Regardless of whether the person resigns or is terminated, there are likely to be loose ends of business to tie up. But most of all, the session provides an opportunity for the manager to listen to what the person has to say about the association with the company and the way the resignation or termination was handled. This meeting is usually conducted several days after the employee's last day of work, by which time some of the stress of decision day has worn off.

Despite the rationale for exit interviews, converting good management practice into productive action is not so easy. Because of legal liability, the one time that managers are especially diligent about following employment procedures is when people leave. The result is people often get more attention during disciplinary interviews and termination, or when they speak up and resign, than they do at any time while they are working. Then, the time comes when they're finally out of the company and management wants another meeting. Some people will be very cooperative.

For others, exit interviews are not especially popular, so much as to think "now that I'm out of here, you want to hear what I have to say?" Some people will speak frankly and tell the former supervisor or the human resources manager exactly what they think about the company. The manager may hear more candor than he or she bargained for, but the forum is created to get feedback.

Others will be very hesitant to speak their minds out of fear they could hurt their professional reputations or quash favorable job references in the future. Those exit interviews won't yield much helpful information unless the manager can establish a level of trust.

Obviously, some interviews will go better than others. But in all cases, it's important to strive for calm constructive conversation, not argue or be defensive (opinions aren't likely to change at this point anyway), and end the interview professionally with best wishes.

Then, sit back and learn from the experience.

■ CONCLUSION

The notion that work isn't supposed to be enjoyable or that the workplace isn't supposed to be pleasant (after all, this is work) says little about the way today's companies operate. Despite all the difficult personnel decisions managers make and all the legal issues that are part of the process, the most rewarding part of a manager's job is watching people thrive under the manager's direction. While some of those directions come in the form of formal performance standards and are faced in performance reviews, the coach, teacher, and counselor part of the job is as energizing for the manager as it is for the people being supervised.

■ DISCUSSION EXERCISES

List at least three things you as the manager can do to help energize and empower your salespeople to be productive and develop professionally.

Discuss your experiences (positive and negative) either with conducting performance reviews or with being reviewed.

Select a problem that you are currently dealing with in your office and discuss how you plan to handle it.

Critique the experiences you've had with terminating a worker (or being terminated). What was done well? What should have been done differently?

IN CONCLUSION OF UNIT IV

The staffing and directing functions of management are essentially human resource management functions. The organization is prepared to conduct business by recruiting, selecting, and hiring the appropriate personnel, who must now have a workplace environment that is supportive. That means a workplace that fosters professional competency and is free of the barriers that distract or inhibit performance. The responsibility for creating this environment falls squarely on the shoulders of the manager and tests the manager's ability to be a leader, a teacher, a counselor, a negotiator, and an arbitrator.

■ THE SCENARIO

Having read this unit, what is your analysis of the following scenario?

Dale, who is the manager of a single-office brokerage company, came to work one Monday morning after agonizing all weekend, trying to come up with some answers for that morning's meeting with his broker. This once productive and congenial office seemed to be crumbling around him, and Friday afternoon's announcement by two more of his salespeople that they were leaving felt like the final blow. Dale's broker told him that come Monday morning he better have a plan to turn things around and stop the hemorrhaging of the office's bottom line.

Dale was fairly certain that the broker wanted to hear a plan for hiring more salespeople. While that would certainly be appropriate, Dale also knew there was more to the story that needed to be told. The more he analyzed the state of affairs in recent months, the more troubled he was by a number of situations that had gotten out of hand.

First, there is the office secretary. She is really a very good "Girl Friday," the sole staff person who acts as bookkeeper, telephone answerer, transaction coordinator, and personal secretary for Dale and, on occasion, the broker, whose primary activity is real estate development. At one time, she was a licensed salesperson in the office but because of changes in her personal life, she needed a job with regular working hours and benefits. Dale thought she would be an asset to his office because in addition to having broad clerical skills, she was familiar with the real estate business and the company's operation. Now, after a year and a half, Dale is contending with a secretary who thinks she is the sales manager.

Then, there is the high turnover in the sales staff. This situation had become increasingly problematic in the past six months. Dale was hired three years ago to manage the brokerage business so that the broker could devote more time to his other endeavor. Dale was previously a sales trainer with another real estate company, so when he came on board he instituted a training program and revamped the commission plan. The company successfully recruited salespeople, mostly newly licensed, and succeeded in retaining a core staff of about 15 highly talented, productive people.

That is, until recently. Now down to seven after Friday's announcements, with rumblings that another salesperson might leave as well, the broker's answer is just "hire more." Does the broker have the right solution? Or are there other steps Dale should recommend at his meeting with the broker?

■ THE ANALYSIS

The discussions in this fourth unit should shed some light on Dale's situation. His dilemmas are not atypical, as many sales managers have faced similar situations.

Dale's office problems are a lot easier to avoid than they are to quick-fix. It's very likely that hiring a few people immediately, assuming there is ready, experienced talent willing to step into the firm now, will have, at best, short-term benefit. Even at that, new hires need some settling-in time with a new company, so Dale's office won't feel the benefit of their production for a few months.

Recruiting will be difficult for Dale anyway. He may be able to encourage a few people to come to the company on the strength of his personal reputation as a good trainer. But the professional grapevine has probably worked over the problems in that office, perhaps to the point that the word is worse than reality.

The first thing Dale should do Monday morning is talk to the salesperson who's rumored to be the next one leaving. What Dale needs to hear firsthand is the reasons for the discontent. The conversation may demonstrate management's attentiveness to the situation and could be a move that could retain the wavering salesperson. Even if the person's beyond retention and does leave, Dale still has some helpful information.

Of course, Dale should have been gathering information all along. Better observation of behavior in the workplace, periodic one-on-one meetings with the salespeople, and an exit interview when the first person took off would have given Dale the heads-up so that he could have nipped the problems in the bud months ago.

One could assume that one of the problems is the secretary but that may be a premature leap to a conclusion. Girl Friday may have taken it upon herself to be sales manager because the salespeople found her to be a better leader than Dale is. If that's the case, Dale should have wised up to that fact a while ago. On the other hand, Girl Friday could be one of those people who, once given a little authority (considering all the hats she wore), simply takes on more. Clearly, the lines of authority are blurred, in any case, and Dale needs to get that straight with Girl Friday.

Otherwise, Dale needs a plan to get to the root of the problems. The first step should be talking one-on-one with the salespeople who are still on board. The point of the meetings is to assess what people think about the company as a place to work and to learn how Dale and the company can support their work. Until this is known, anything else is pure speculation about the secretary, the company's commission plans or services, or Dale.

■ THE SUMMARY

Whether you are the broker/owner, a senior manager in a large organization, a sales manager, or a department manager, your involvement in the various human resources activities will differ. As a guide for understanding your role(s), the following summary is provided.

- Recruiting, selecting, and hiring the appropriate staff
  - The broker/owner(s), and possibly senior management, have previously determined the overall manpower requirements for the organization in the organizing function.
  - The broker/owner is normally responsible for selecting and hiring senior management. The broker may also prefer to be an active recruiter for salespeople, depending on the size of the organization and the amount of other responsibilities that have been assigned to the sales manager.
  - Either senior management or the broker/owner selects and hires office or sales managers.
  - Sales and department managers are normally responsible for recruiting and selecting the staff whom they supervise. The procedures in the organization will dictate whether the manager or someone higher in the organization has the ultimate authority to hire.
- Creating opportunities for the staff to develop professional competency
  - The broker/owner(s) and possibly senior management are normally responsible for making decisions about the nature of the professional development the company provides and committing the necessary financial resources.
  - The department manager, specifically the training director, and the sales managers are actively involved in assessing training needs and developing the orientation and training programs.
  - The sales manager is responsible for supporting training and the professional development of the staff in group functions such as sales meetings and in one-on-one involvement with the sales-

people. In small organizations, the sales manager also may be the trainer.

- Coaching people to accomplish the company's as well as their own goals
  - Anyone who directly supervises people is responsible for coaching their performance, conducting performance reviews, and handling problems, conflicts, or other issues that directly affect the performance of the people who work for them. In small organizations, the broker/owner may also be the sales manager.
  - Depending on the procedures in the organization, the person who supervises an individual may have the authority to terminate a worker. In some organizations this person may need the approval of an individual at a higher level in the organization to do so.

UNIT V
CONTROLLING THE ORGANIZATION

Once a company opens its doors for business and starts all the wheels into motion, the organization takes on a life of its own. It becomes an institution propelled by people, processes, and systems, all churning under the sheer force of their own momentum, the result being that many things are happening in a company at one time, regardless of its size.

Although the functions of management (planning, organizing, staffing, and directing) have been captured in this business management discussion under orderly headings, the real world is that managers' jobs are not so orderly that they can dispense with one and turn the page to the next management function. Managers are occupied to some degree by all of these responsibilities all the time, simply because of the magnitude of the various systems, processes, and people the company has empowered.

It's easy for management to get caught up in the day-to-day details and lose sight of the big picture. The general health and well-being of the organization depends on managers to monitor the aspects of the operation for which they are responsible and keep the organization on a prosperous course. Although most organizations won't stray so far off course that they will run aground in one year, it's easier (and wiser) to keep nudging a company in the right direction than it is to shift to a new course in a short period of time.

The controlling function of management does just that, makes sure that the resources of the organization are channeled in the right direction. Management does this by

- critiquing operations and
- managing risk.

The purpose of controlling the organization is to protect assets so the company has the resources to promote growth. The controlling function assesses vulnerabilities and mobilizes efforts to neutralize those vulnerabilities and direct resources in the most effective ways. This is not something management does at the end of the year by looking at the latest financial report but rather is a series of procedures that enable management to periodically assess the company's performance.

If management relies only on the accountant to report financial status and the lawyer to bail the company out of trouble, that intervention will be too little too late. It's far more prudent to detect problems early and take corrective action before the minus sign appears on the income statement or litigation arises.

CHAPTER SEVENTEEN 17

CRITIQUING OPERATIONS

When times get tough, what costs do you cut?

Are your customers and clients satisfied with your service? How do you know?

In the game analogy, critiquing company operations is akin to analyzing team performance and making adjustments that improve the likelihood of a winning season. The "win" for the company is that it meets (or exceeds) performance projections by the end of the year.

To analyze company performance, managers need information. For the most part, that information comes from reports and statistics that give them the quantitative evidence needed to accurately assess the company's activities. Today much of that information resides in the computer's database and with the variety of commercially available software, most aspects of the company's operation can be easily evaluated.

However, talk of computers and databases is somewhat of a cart-before-the-horse exercise, because management must first develop procedures to collect information. Typically, information is gathered with the forms or reports that are the customary routine in the workplace. The success or failure of these procedures, though, is a function of how well they are designed.

Management needs the cooperation of everyone in the organization to gather accurate information, so ease and efficiency are critical.

Once gathered, the information must be used. Time and money are too precious to bog down the organization with busywork. If the information is worth gathering, it's worth using. Information tells powerful stories that need to be read periodically throughout the year. Is the organization taking all the steps necessary to maximize income? Are expenses under control and as effective and productive as possible? And because the future of the company depends on its reputation with consumers, what does the company's customer service report look like?

■ MANAGEMENT OF INFORMATION

Business enterprises become repositories of huge amounts of information, often because of legal and regulatory requirements. One of management's responsibilities is to ensure that paperwork as well as data collection and retention procedures satisfy those requirements (especially relevant to real estate license law). Guidance of legal counsel and an accountant is valuable for identifying bank statements, compensation records, legal correspondence, tax returns and other records that should be retained.

Lurking in those files is a vast amount of information that is very useful for critiquing the company's activities. The information that usually comes to mind is the financial data that can be assembled from general ledgers, accounts payable, accounts receivable, payroll records, and commission records plus various budgets. But there's a lot of other information that can reveal the health or well-being of the organization.

The value of information is only as good as the data that are assembled. When the company selects software and powers up its computer system, decisions are made about what management wants to learn from the data. The object of data collection is to gather information that is

- accurate,
- complete, and
- timely.

Missing, inaccurate, or stale information skews the picture and can cause management to get in a frenzy over bad news that really isn't all that serious or to rejoice over good news that really isn't that rosy. In either case, faulty information can cause faulty course corrections (or no corrections) for the organization.

The information that is important to management is typically inconsequential to the people management counts on to complete reports. Report forms must be easy and efficient to use (keep paperwork reduction in mind), and procedures, including timeframes, for completing the documents must be established. Making the disbursement of a commission check dependent on a transaction file being completed (or some other conditional action) is one way to get people to cooperate.

A number of people, including salespeople and support staff, are likely to be handling documents, money, files, and computer input. An *office procedures manual* should be developed to

- manage the flow of information and paper, including *what*, *where*, *how*, *when*, and *by whom* forms, reports, documents, and data that's processed.
- specify who has access to what data and files to ensure that accuracy and confidentiality are protected. Procedures should specify what must remain onsite, what is permitted offsite (including in the salespeople's possession), and what information can be released (and by whom) to outsiders. Because of the increasing number of incidents of identity theft, it's important to ensure that personal information is securely protected.
- maintain and retain data, files, and records as required by law.

Transaction or Service Files

Transaction files should be sufficiently complete to comply with license law—including contracts, disclosures, closing cost statements and escrow documents, and evidence that documents have been properly delivered to the signatories. These files must be retained for the time period required by law.

The company may also require other documents, reports, or correspondence to be included in transaction files. Documentation is essential defense in the event of litigation but as a practical matter, the files provide information for solving problems and resolving controversies so that matters don't rise to the point of litigation.

Because state license law is usually quite specific about the way escrow funds (hand money, earnest money, or binder deposits) must be handled, transaction files should include a paper trail (like transmittal forms) to trace funds from the time they are received by the salesperson through each step along the way until funds are deposited (either by the company or a cooperating broker) and then released.

All of this documentation puts the company on sound legal footing, but transaction files also provide a lot of information about the organization's listing and sales activities. If the company is using transaction management software, the salespeople or support staff can easily assemble this information.

Listing activities. Managers can monitor the effectiveness of the company's listing activities as well as the performance of individual salespeople by studying listing contracts and gathering answers to the following questions:

- How long are listings on the market?
- What's the difference between the listing and the actual selling price?
- How many listings terminated or expired?
- What is the source of the listing contacts?
- Where are the listings located?

A comparative analysis of length of time on the market, terminated or expired listings, and differences between listing and actually selling prices over time can indicate economic trends or consumer behaviors in the marketplace. But the statistics can also indicate efficiencies or deficiencies in the company's or an individual salesperson's marketing efforts or pricing practices. The source of contacts and location of listings are useful gauges of the company's advertising and geographic influence, which is especially relevant for those related to organizational objectives.

The numbers that raise immediate red flags are listings that sit on the market longer than the norm, large numbers of listings that don't sell, and wide disparities between listing and sales prices. An occasional errant number can be chalked up to a unique circumstance but generally these issues increase promotional costs (and in the case of unsold listings, not produce any offsetting income) and damage customer relations.

Sales and closing activities. When the pending sales files are compared with the closed transaction files, management can learn how well buyers and sellers are being serviced and the effect of marketplace conditions on the company's business. One of the most significant pieces of information is the cause of contracts that don't proceed to settlement. In many cases, the manager knows the stories intimately because these are problem transactions the manager had to help nurture and defuse along the way.

- Were buyers not properly qualified?
- Are appraisals coming in low?
- Are there problems with home inspection reports?
- Are new lending procedures, certain types of mortgage loans, or lenders a problem?
- Did buyers feel deceived, or were there misrepresentations?
- Are contracts being lost because contingencies aren't being satisfied?
- Were there defects in the way contracts were prepared?
- Are new closing regulations or settlement procedures a problem?
- How well were transactions prepared for settlement?

A seemingly smooth transaction can suddenly explode at settlement only because a minute but important detail was overlooked. If the company doesn't have a transaction coordinator on staff, all of these details become the salespeople's responsibilities. Monitoring settlements identifies tasks that are overlooked and procedures that are needed to correct problems. This is the final step in the transaction when the company's public relations are on the line.

Once transactions close, managers have valuable information about the sources of buyers; the productivity of a referral or relocation network affiliation; the in-house versus cooperating-broker transactions; transactions in which a buyer was a client or a customer (depending on the company's policies); and trends in market values, financing, and the pace of the market.

License Records

Good license management procedures are critically important for the company to provide its real estate services. No one should be permitted to perform activities for which a real estate license is required until that license has been properly issued. There are procedures for license applications, renewals, transfers, and departing licensees, as well as license requirements for the company's real estate offices.

Although a staff person could be assigned the responsibility of tending to the paperwork, the broker is ultimately responsible for seeing that all requirements are satisfied. The broker also should review the license records periodically to ensure that the company is in compliance with all of the requirements.

Personnel Records

Individual personnel files provide a history of the workers' affiliation with the company, which serves both a legal and management purpose. The files typically include personal data, employment applications, employment or independent contractor agreements, compensation records, performance reviews, and other records or information recommended by the company lawyer. Because this is very personal information, the company also needs to limit access to those files to protect confidentiality.

Closely related to this subject are the company's referral rotation procedures. One of the greatest sources of controversy in a real estate office is the distribution of referrals and leads. The company should have clear procedures (that are publicized and followed) for distributing and tracking referrals. Keep a master ledger as these assignments are made, and also record them in each salesperson's file so that authoritative documentation is available.

■ MANAGING WITH INFORMATION

Typically, senior management reviews the balance sheet, cash flow statement, and income statement, comparing the actual figures against the budget each month. Office managers, division managers, and other staff people usually are responsible for doing likewise, particularly as the reports relate to their areas of responsibility.

Monthly review shows trends in the flow of money and production activity, which is essential information for monitoring the company's financial condition and taking corrective actions as warranted. If there are major deviations from income or expense projections, these may be events the company anticipated and for which contingency plans were prepared. Otherwise, the discussions later in this chapter about income and expenses will be particularly useful.

Managing with information also means using what management learns to periodically review (perhaps quarterly) the company's business plan for the year. While a budget intends to keep the financial resources on track, the business plan intends to keep all of the company's activities focused. By looking at the year's goals in comparison with year-to-date company performance, management can see which efforts are on track and those that need to be enhanced.

Although critiquing the organization is a management function, the company's workforce (especially the salespeople) can provide a lot of useful insight. Feedback gathered during quarterly performance reviews can elicit suggestions as to ways the company can work more cost-efficiently and effectively. These are also good topics for engaging people in problem-solving and brainstorming meetings.

■ MAXIMIZING INCOME

Maximizing income is a prudent management activity, whether the company is meeting projections or needs to take corrective steps to get back on track. Even if the company is ahead of projections, the market can suddenly deteriorate and take the company's income along with it.

Business Sectors

One way to maximize income is to direct manpower, money, and marketing to sectors of the company's business that are performing well or where maximum opportunities exist. Conventional wisdom says that directing resources to underperforming sectors is desirable only if opportunities are underutilized.

Companies with multiple business units (such as brokerage and mortgage and/or settlement services) can make diversification work by shifting emphasis to or increasing performance targets for those endeavors (and overcome lagging production in other sectors). Or a company can become more diversified and create a new unit to capture a business opportunity.

But even companies that are solely brokerage-oriented can shift emphasis and concentrate on certain property sectors or buyer profiles, depending on market opportunities. This strategy benefitted brokerage companies in the recent economic slowdown, with some concentrating on sectors of buyers less affected by the financial crisis and others concentrating on foreclosures.

Pricing Strategies

A company can also shift pricing strategies to maximize income. Some companies cut prices to gain volume and scale, expecting that income will increase significantly. The reality is this strategy works for very few companies and is often financially disastrous. An alternative is to set price based on performance. By doing a superior job of meeting the consumers' needs, the company can command higher prices. However, this pricing model works only if the company can come up with an improved value proposition.

Real estate companies have learned they get into trouble with RESPA by charging extra fees that don't deliver added value or benefit (recall the discussion in Chapter 10). In effect, RESPA made a statement about performance-based pricing. This also says companies have to think beyond long-standing pricing formulas that don't suit contemporary reality.

We know that antitrust and license laws stand behind the consumer's right to choices (and negotiation) and prevent price-fixing practices (hence, no "going rates"). The conundrum for individual companies is to devise pricing strategies that suit their businesses and also appeal in the marketplace.

In this regard, companies get stuck in the herd mentality of how everyone else structures their prices and "average" pricing, which means some people who negotiate the same rate of commission overpay—the seller whose property sold in three days—and others underpay—the seller whose property sold in three months. Companies hesitate to change pricing strategies out of fear they'll price themselves out of the market or will no longer be competitive. But if they deliver on the superior value proposition, they can charge higher prices.

But consumers won't pay the price (any price), or recommend that others pay the price, if they don't see value in the company's services. And value is measured by customer satisfaction. Companies often pledge to deliver quality service with the belief that the better the quality, the better the income. That also minimizes the cost associated with each transaction because resources can be devoted to new business instead of problems associated with transactions already logged on the books.

Quality Service Standards

Without satisfied customers, companies don't have loyal customers, the image, or reputation that fosters future business. Recognizing this fact, customer satisfaction is a major priority in most business enterprises. Merchants that consumers frequently patronize for their daily needs have more opportunities to satisfy their customers and develop loyalty. But developing loyal relationships with real estate consumers is more difficult simply because people don't frequently patronize real estate services. This says that a company has to give it its best shot when it has the opportunity.

That best shot comes when quality service is delivered. But the company has to define what constitutes quality service or set standards so that everyone, especially the salespeople, knows what is expected. (They have as much at stake in their success as the company has.) The standards reflect the company's philosophy of doing business and the nature of the services it provides. Most importantly, quality service standards must become a priority in the company. (Recall the discussion in Chapter 11 about institutionalizing those standards in a company's operations.)

Quality service standards are not only internal but external statements of the company's value proposition to its customers and clients. The most obvious standards for a real estate company relate to services provided to buyers and sellers, depending on the market segments the company serves. But quality service also includes servicing complaints and solving problems.

The National Association of REALTORS® periodically surveys buyers and sellers, and publishes a report (the most current of which is available from NAR's research division). The *Profile of Buyers and Sellers* is useful for determining who the consumers are, what they want, and the ways in which real estate professionals can improve their products and services for these consumers. One of the consistent themes in these reports is the importance of satisfaction with a salesperson in deciding to use the same salesperson in the future and to refer family, friends, and other real estate professionals.

Servicing sellers. For the company that lists property or provides other marketing services for sellers, standards should make statements about how the company delivers these services, especially to address the sellers' most common complaints.

- Salespeople don't return phone calls or answer e-mails.
- Salespeople don't communicate with sellers frequently enough.
- Sellers don't know what the salespeople are doing to get the property sold.
- Salespeople make promises when the properties are listed that aren't fulfilled.
- The property took too long to sell or the salesperson wasn't creative or aggressive enough to get it sold.
- The settlement didn't go smoothly.

Converting these lessons into standards says sellers should be provided an explanation of the listing-to-sales process and what the company and the salesperson intend to do throughout, including the marketing plan. The better the communications, the fewer the problems. A comparative market analysis and a discussion about contemporary market conditions go a long way toward avoiding unrealistic expectations about prices and the time within which a property will sell.

Factor into this the fact that buyers are using the Internet to avoid paying too much for a property and, consequently, deal from a much stronger negotiating position after logging on to research comparable sales prices and the property's original sale price, mortgage balance, and property taxes. The buyer can also learn when properties are actually selling far below the listing price, which may not be information a seller (or seller's agent) is pleased to have known.

Service standards can incorporate such items as home warranty programs, referral or relocation services, or discount or cross-marketing programs that the company provides. For risk-management purposes, service standards should also address contract preparation and consumer protection issues such as agency, property, and lead-based paint disclosures.

Servicing buyers. Customer service standards for buyers are developed in a similar fashion, considering the services the company provides and the factors that influence buyers' choices of property and the kind of professional assistance they desire.

Quality service standards for buyers would also address agency disclosure and contract procedures, standards for preparing and negotiating sales agreements, and assisting the buyer through the transaction to settlement. These could include mortgage financing, home inspections or warranties, insurance, title and settlement services, and services such as referral, relocation, and cross-marketing programs. Consumer protection and risk-management procedures, including procedures for documenting the showings, conversations, and negotiations with a buyer, should also be addressed.

Quality Control

Quality service standards are empty public relations words unless the company institutes quality control measures. This can be done by monitoring information in the transaction files and incorporating quality service standards in the criteria used for performance reviews. While the most obvious are the salespeople's criteria, everyone involved in any aspect of customer service should be accountable for doing their part.

Customer feedback. The company's perception and the public's perception of the company can differ, so it's important to get feedback from outside the organization. This can be done using toll-free phone numbers or Web site comment forms. Companies can also engage the services of commercial enterprises that develop quality service programs and surveys, such as QSC (*www.qualityservice.org*), or use NAR's survey service. Regardless of the form, the point is to do a *customer service survey*. No one should conclude business with the company without an opportunity to critique the experience.

There is some amount of squirm factor in conducting surveys because they should be a critique in every sense of the word, not just a make-the-company-feel-good exercise. Keep several things in mind about surveying.

- Survey questions must be short and easy to complete. Several yes/no queries, several scaled queries (met expectations, exceeded expectations, below expectations, etc.), and one or two open-ended questions should be adequate.
- Truly meaningful feedback is gathered when questions are framed around known weaknesses, as well as strengths, and are worded in ways that elicit the most candid responses, not just what the company wants to hear.
- Gather only information that the company plans to act on; otherwise, don't waste people's time.
- Develop a plan for reviewing the surveys and acting on the information. Customers appreciate the opportunity to speak their minds, but they become dissatisfied when the company doesn't pay attention to what they say.

In addition to a critique of services, gather suggestions for enhancements that can be considered for future planning.

Don't overlook the buyer who terminated a buyer agency agreement or the seller who terminated a listing or whose listing expired. Their critiques reveal corrective steps that are needed as well as the sentiments they are broadcasting to the community. Simply the act of soliciting opinions can help defuse negative feelings. Better to see those in a survey than vented on social media sites.

Professional competency. One final comment about quality control—at some point management has to look closely at the competency of the salespeople and the managers. Critiques are meaningless unless the company acts on what it learns. These lessons can be factored into performance criteria, coaching activities with the salespeople and other personnel, and the company's professional development and training programs.

Problem Solving

Customer relations problems generally arise from miscommunications or misunderstandings. But there are times when someone makes a serious mistake or the company institutes procedures that do more to create irate customers than to improve company operations. In the scheme of the customer-is-always-right, customers at least have the right to get someone to listen to their concerns.

A major consumer complaint is the inability to find someone to actually speak with. Companies set up convoluted telephone trees that only increase frustration and turn the moderately disgruntled into patently outraged callers. Although the salespeople need to do their part in handling problems, the sales manager is usually the first customer-relations stop in a real estate company.

The way managers handle these situations will be a win-win for the company and the consumer. Or someone will be the loser. The goal is to resolve the problem so that everyone feels at least satisfied, if not victorious. Early intervention and good give-and-take with the manager can diffuse many situations before they evolve into formal courses of action.

Sometimes people just want to vent, and there are times when the disgruntled person demands the attention of company superiors. This often puts the sales manager squarely in the middle between the salesperson and the disgruntled caller and, on occasion, between the salesperson and senior management.

Until the matter is resolved with the consumer, the company, the manager, and the salesperson must present a united front and not disparage one another in front of outsiders. Before plunging headlong into the situation, the manager has to get all the facts straight and talk with the salesperson involved. Managers must, however, be forthright and acknowledge mistakes. If the issue is suspected to involve legal issues, everyone must avoid making comments without legal advice.

Once the matter is resolved, then internal issues can be addressed. Digressions from company policy should be handled one-on-one with the individual salesperson, and solutions should be developed to prevent problems from arising again.

■ MINIMIZING EXPENSES

Minimizing expenses does not necessarily mean trimming or eliminating valuable services for the customers or sales staff. As a practical matter, there's a limit to how much expense a company can cut before its business is seriously harmed. A company does need to make the most efficient use of its resources, but that means making wise decisions about where to cut and where to spend. Expense management is essential throughout the year, not just when the company hemorrhages from overspending or the market suddenly changes and income declines.

Significant cutbacks generally mean significant change. Change is always a hard sell so it's best to make everyone part of the solution. The workforce often has good ideas about the best places to spend money and cut costs, and if the choice is job-versus-no-job, people are more likely to cope with cutbacks, even if they're not especially pleased.

Personnel Costs

Personnel costs can be sizable, and business enterprises do tend to become job heavy over time, or to hold on to poor performers. But as tempting as it can be to cut staff when the year and the money aren't coming out even, personnel decisions require a methodical rather than a knee-jerk approach so the organization can still work effectively.

One of the first cuts companies often consider is the receptionist. With today's mobile and digital communications, telephone answering is less demanding and other administrative work can be assigned to other positions. But not everyone agrees this is a good position to cut. Eliminating the first-person contact with the company and the live voice at the other end of the phone can negatively affect company image and customer relations.

Administrative and supervisory positions are other places companies look for economies. Technology is a big help in doing more with less, with Web-based tools and virtual workers who can perform administrative tasks off site. Responsibilities can also be distributed among other workers, which allows for the elimination of positions (including sales office managers who manage several offices). Or a full-time position can be converted to a part-time one.

Companies often look at the cost of individual workers. In one company, people who filled four positions were targeted for dismissal. These were long-term workers with compensation and benefit packages associated with experience and longevity. The dismissals would have terminated good performers but would also have affected females and racial minorities as well as people over the age of 40, in some cases, all of the above—a careless notion that the company reconsidered, fortunately.

Clearly, managing personnel costs is challenging. But companies can make wise decisions by keeping several things in mind.

- People don't have to be let go, especially if that means losing prime talent. They can be reassigned to busy sectors of the company where there is more work for them to do.
- Eliminating a position may be a long-term savings but with an immediate cost because the person who is laid off receives severance pay, which can be sizable depending on the position's level of responsibility. An alternative is to relocate the worker to another position.
- Benefits can be adjusted, but those often mean as much to employees as wages and salaries. If the choice is a higher deductible for healthcare insurance or a higher out-of-pocket co-payment, let the workers decide which one is preferable. Or perhaps they'll decide to forego some other benefit.
- Overtime can be costly. Although the company has to pay nonexempt workers for overtime, the company can restrict the number of overtime hours they work (as long as the company's work gets done).
- Payroll can be trimmed with pay freezes, furlough policies (which require workers to take a certain number of days off without pay), or reductions in pay, which is effectively what happens when more company costs are shifted to the salespeople. Any of these is an

option as long as the company doesn't upset pay equity or lose valuable talent.

- Outsourcing can be cheaper than salary and benefits. Companies that provide payroll management, benefits administration, or records management services are likely to be more cost-efficient than supporting in-house departments or personnel. This is particularly attractive to small business owners who don't have the time or expertise to devote to certain administrative tasks.

Marketing and Advertising

The objective in minimizing the expense of marketing and advertising is to reduce the cost of contact. That's different than cutting marketing plans when times get tough. In fact, a sure fire way to cut business (and income) is to cut the company's visibility.

A McGraw-Hill Research study during the recent recession revealed that companies that maintained or increased their marketing expenditures averaged significantly higher sales growth than companies that decreased or eliminated spending. Even during a tough economy, there are consumers who are looking for buying opportunities, and the beneficiaries are the companies that maintained their visibility.

Regardless of the times, companies need to manage marketing and advertising costs (which can be as much as 25 percent of the company's budget) with an eye for what does and doesn't work for promoting the company's brand and generating business. Make the strategies that work be most cost efficient, which gets to be a more pressing issue as the end of the budget year approaches. This is another data-driven exercise, a task that benefits from the help of public relations or marketing experts, and the company's Web site manager.

The primary data with which to evaluate marketing are collected from consumers, though the quality of that data can be skewed by their perceptions. A consumer may indicate that a friend referred the person, but the decision to contact the company may have been reinforced by the Web site or an advertisement. Nonetheless, the company needs procedures to gather data about the source of initial inquiries and the source of contact that actually resulted in a transaction.

Web site statistics, response logs, and advertising registers tell the source of contact, which are then analyzed to determine the per-contact cost (compare the number of contacts with the cost of the medium). Even more important is the cost of contact that converts to a contract, which indicates whether advertising is reaching the actual purchasing audience and whether salespeople are making the most of those contacts. Several months of statistics also reveal the seasonal effect on the volume of contacts, which is helpful for gauging potential income at different times of the year.

Companies put a lot of stock in the power of the Internet and their Web sites to draw business. That power, however, may not be nearly as commanding as the company expects or yield the desired results, depending on how well the Web site performs. Even the most compelling sites lose their visual appeal and effectiveness over time as visitors' search patterns and interests change.

Does the site load quickly? Is it easy to navigate? Are the pages visually appealing or are they too hard to read? Are they loaded with annoying graphics or effects? Do pages tell visitors what they want to know? Are links (especially ones that are paid for) helping or hurting, and are there new ones that should be considered? Does the site provide good interactive features? If all the answers are not readily apparent, ask visitors to critique the site or call on a professional to help.

Is the site capturing the attention of the search engines? Software is available for purchase and download that provides a variety of tools to optimize site content, keywords, and metatags and improve search engine rankings. Or perhaps the time has come to consider paying for site placement. If the Web site is producing traffic but not producing business, then look at the in-house procedures that are supposed to support the interactive features of the site. Are visitors getting prompt responses, and are the salespeople following through on those contacts? Is there a better procedure for capturing and distributing leads?

Cost-per-contact efficiencies can also be achieved by looking at how money is spent in other areas. Does the company really need more printed brochures or will a digital version suffice? Can the company renegotiate contracts with the media, printers, or other suppliers? Although the company should always be looking for the best deal it can get, those businesses are additionally motivated to make a deal in recessionary times to hold on to your business when other companies are discontinuing theirs.

Is the company making the most of messaging opportunities? It doesn't cost anything to include the company's signature on e-mails and other digital communications. And it costs very little to add the company's signature to invoices, envelopes, and other correspondence.

The time may also come to retool the distribution of advertising and promotional costs between the company and the salespeople. The salespeople may be happy to participate if this means preserving or adding exposure. (Don't suddenly burden them with all of the advertising costs, though.) Engage the salespeople in solutions. Not only are they likely to have good suggestions, but their participation in the decision also quells dissatisfaction.

Cost of Sales

The cost of sales on the income statement includes all of the costs for commissions and referral and franchise fees that are associated with the sales transactions. Before cutting commissions to control costs, remember the rationale for setting the pay schedules in the first place. Track referral and franchise fees over the long run to determine if there is sufficient added benefit to warrant the expenditure. Also consider the effect of "after the fact" fees charged by the referral company in transactions when its client began working with the real estate company without the benefit of the referral.

Pay attention to the number of in-house versus cooperating sales. Depending on commission arrangements with the salespeople and other brokers, one way to minimize costs is to encourage the salespeople to sell the company's listings. This strategy is only feasible, however, as long as it doesn't conflict with agency laws or compromise the quality of service provided to customers and clients. No one should be pushed into a property simply because of a company's profit motive.

Economies in the Office

The little things add up! Ask the utility companies to do energy audits if the company is paying utilities. Insist that the person responsible for stocking office supplies comparison shops to locate the most cost-efficient vendor. Even if a staff person has to do the pickup and delivery, the cost savings could be worth the company time. Buy in bulk, provided the stock has a long shelf life, and discourage waste by not making all of the stock readily available.

Look at the company's printing bill. Even with technology, businesses are still paper heavy. The question to answer is whether the paper, forms, and promotional materials (or anything else on the printing bill) are most suitably produced outside or whether the same quality can be produced in-house at less cost.

Although it's cheaper to fax than it is to use postal mail, the most favored tools today are virtual faxes and e-mails with attachments for business documents and promotional materials. E-mail and text messaging are the most popular mediums for brief or routine communications. Thanks to competition among telephone and Internet service providers, discounts, incentives, and packages of phone and Internet services can provide considerable savings.

Even though electronic communication is more cost efficient than the alternatives, the company can't do business without a good telephone system. But phone bills can rack up more expense than is necessary or even legitimate, especially with charges for duplicate or incomplete calls or pirated access to the account.

One of the best tools for monitoring telephone bills is a log of long distance calls that includes the name and number of the person called, the purpose of the call, and the person who initiated the call so that legitimate charges can be identified and illegitimate ones can be successfully argued for credit.

Comparing the log and the bills also reveals who within the company needs to be cautioned about the length of their calls. Although personal use of the company phone is less of a problem since people have personal cell phones, the company does need to have (and enforce) a personal-use policy. Even when reimbursement is expected, collection can become a problem.

Postal mail is still a business necessity, and even though fewer pieces are mailed, the bill doesn't necessarily get smaller as postage rates rise. However, there are ways to economize.

- Put a scale in the office or, better yet, check out the postal service's *www.stamps.com* (or a similar service). The service is an efficient computer-based solution for weighing, paying, and shipping, which is especially desirable for an office or small business. Companies often overspend on mailings that are lighter than the weight of one first-class stamp (include a promotional piece to make up the difference) or with two first-class stamps when less postage will do.
- Use second-day rather than overnight delivery when possible, and compare prices and services of various carriers. Some delivery services are helpful in planning the most cost-effective way to send a parcel. Encourage people to pack wisely; a fraction of an ounce can push delivery cost into the next price category. It's also cheaper to fax the forgotten form than to send a second overnight letter.
- Don't scrimp on details that could cost money later. If proof that notice was served on a certain date is needed, get it. Certified mail isn't nearly as expensive as the legal problems that could arise in the future.
- If the company does bulk mailing, consider the services of a mail house. That may be more cost-effective than the cost of staff time devoted to stuffing envelopes or folding flyers. Be sure to follow the procedures required for bulk mail permits and plan mailings well ahead of time to ensure timely arrival, especially if they contain time-sensitive information.

Use paper wisely. Don't skimp on the quality of the paper stock and graphics on the company letterhead, but don't use them for memos or scratch paper. Buy cheaper paper for this purpose, and scatter scratch pads generously around the office. Test recycled paper in the computer printer or copier machine. It's cheaper stock and a cost savings, as long as the quality of the printed product is not compromised.

The cost of duplicating keys for listings and rental units can add up. The cost of inconvenience and emergency locksmith services (because of misplaced or lost keys) can be even greater. If the company duplicates a large number of keys, the purchase of key-cutting equipment, or even certifying someone on staff as a locksmith, may be more cost-efficient. This could be a big plus for the company that does property management as well as sales.

Keep track of yard signs and lockboxes. Use a log to identify locations where these items are being used and the people who checked them out. Missing tools are as aggravating as they are expensive to replace.

Don't overlook economies that can be achieved by renegotiating the lease on the office space. Depending on the economic climate and the terms of the original contract, the property owner may be willing to restructure the terms to hold on to a tenant.

Manage Cash

Perhaps managing cash sounds like an odd strategy for a discussion about minimizing expenses and will sound even more peculiar at the mention of spending money. But that's exactly what real estate companies should do so they can weather slumps in the economy or the housing market. A cash flow analysis (see Chapter 10) can be used to determine how much working capital is needed for a minimum of six months, but companies can relieve pressures on that working capital by making cash count during the good times.

Companies can do this by buying ahead, not on a reckless spending spree, but by making prudent purchases now so as not to drain monthly cash later. Possibilities include computer and other equipment upgrades that have been deferred or would eliminate leases, consumables (paper products, office supplies, and promotional literature), and insurance premiums. Also, secure a line of credit. Credit is much easier and cheaper to obtain before lenders get skittish over sagging markets.

■ LOOKING INTO THE FUTURE

The information gathered about the organization while critiquing this year's activities is critical when charting its course for the future. If all of this looks familiar, that's because it's the same kind of data that is part of the situational analysis that supports business plans. We've come full circle from the planning discussion in Chapter 2; now to prepare next year's plan.

As the contemporary environment in which a company does business changes, and the company proceeds through its life cycles, the path to profitability changes as well. The company may choose a path that grows the organization vertically or horizontally. Vertical growth increases capacity in current core services. Horizontal growth increases the scope or number of services or target markets the company serves. (See Figure 17.1.)

FIGURE 17.1
Growth of an Organization

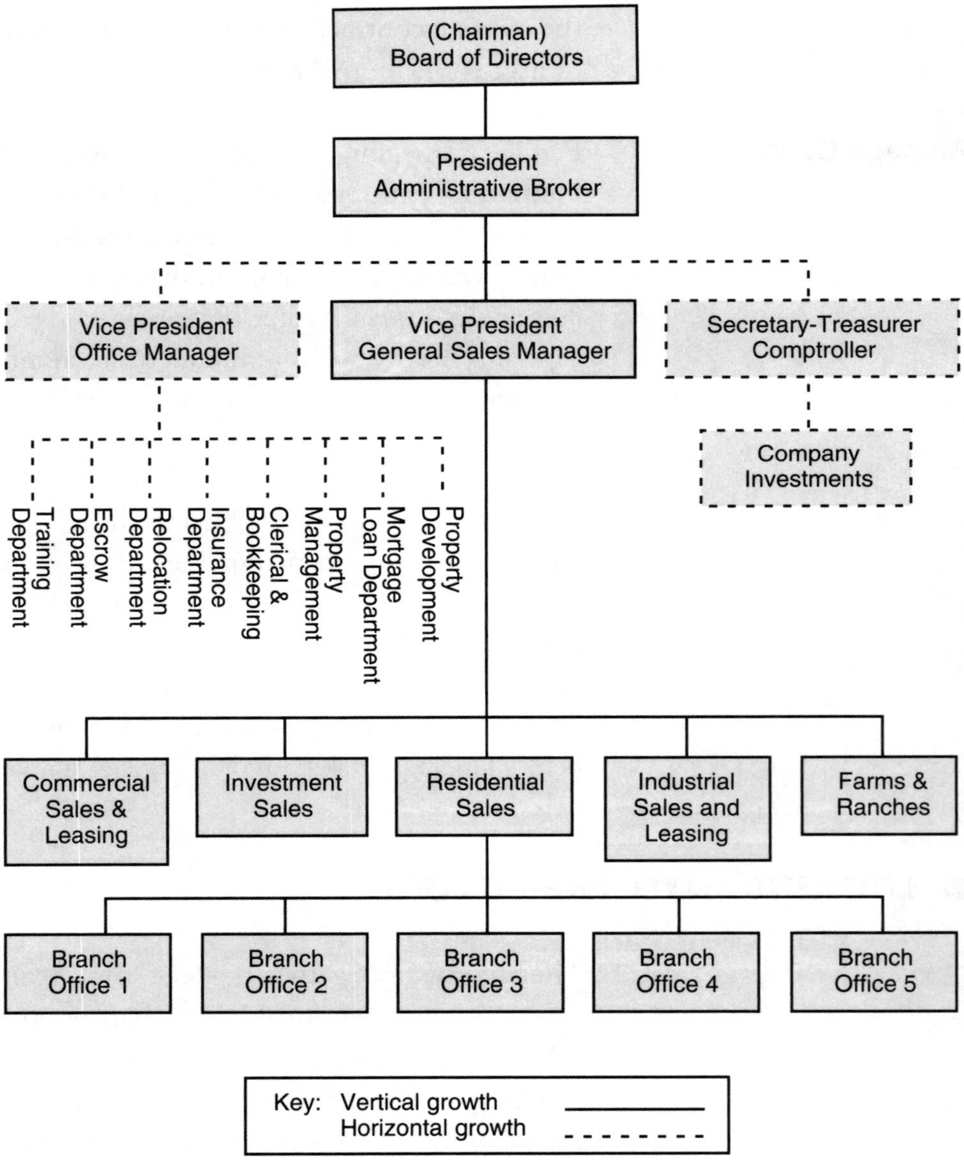

Growing the Enterprise

Seemingly, every business enterprise is seeking growth. In corporate-sector theory, companies must generate profits that grow faster than returns available elsewhere to attract investors (shareholders). The universal imperative is that companies must grow to attract and retain talent. Otherwise, talent will go elsewhere, and that is where greater opportunities exist. Greater opportunities are powered by greater profits.

Often managers see cutting expenses as the path to greater profits. While systematically monitoring expenses will certainly improve the profit picture and keep the organization humming, rare is the company that grows significantly simply by cutting costs. Meaningful growth is achieved with strategic moves that increase a company's power in the marketplace. The range of options for doing that is vast. Narrowing those options and choosing the right path to growth is what separates success from the strategic moves that tank.

Most business strategists agree that the best (and least risky) first step is to grow vertically by capitalizing on the power of the company's current products and/or services. But the company has to determine which products or services have the potential for maximum growth and profit. What's the growth potential in the marketplace and how will competition affect the company's ability to grow in that market? What efforts produce a lot of income but, because of costs in money and manpower, produce little profit in return? Are existing customers satisfied or likely to defect? Are they good referral ambassadors?

While sounding a lot like a strategic analysis, the singular focus of this exercise is on growing profit. The answers are used to direct money and manpower to sectors of the operation that have the greatest potential for profit and to convert streams of revenue into profitable endeavors. Although cost-cutting tactics may be in order, the path to profit from an existing revenue stream may require that a product or service (or the way it is delivered) be restructured. Otherwise, that aspect of the business is eliminated so resources can be redirected.

A company may sell off an underperforming or less profitable venture or one that no longer fits its growth strategy. This is the get-smaller-to-grow-larger strategy. Business units of a company are salable commodities, just as any product or service is. As real estate companies that sit under the umbrellas of corporate holding companies know firsthand, business units get moved around on the corporate chessboard as companies redirect their resources or gain infusions of capital for growing other business units.

The risk, of course, is betting on the right units to keep and the ones to shed. Decisions are based on past performance, presuming that business units will continue to perform for the company in like manner in the future. The challenge is to correctly forecast the growth potential (or lack thereof) of business units in the future marketplace. The underperformer can be poised for flight in a different market environment; conversely, the golden goose can lose its profit luster. Missed forecasts can result in temporary (though possibly severe) setbacks for several years as new growth tactics are devised.

The riskiest growth strategies are ventures into new markets. These are the horizontal growth patterns that develop new revenue streams either internally or by acquisition. Growing profit out of new revenue can be treacherous while a company learns new markets. Overestimating revenue potential and underestimating costs can lead to a net profit that doesn't meet expectations.

Companies also can spend a great deal of capital or incur a great deal of debt to get into new ventures. Picking the right acquisitions can be as tricky as picking target markets or services with good capacity for growth. Although the majority of growth companies use acquisitions at some point, the most skillful tend to test their acuity in new markets with small acquisitions of compatible or related businesses.

What percentage of growth should a company strive for? The answer depends on the industry sector and prevailing economic conditions that affect the sector's market, the desired pace of growth (aggressive or long-term), the amount of available money (or credit), and the degree of risk company leadership can tolerate. However, doing nothing can be risky, too. Some companies aggressively grow profit while opportunities exist to insulate themselves from future risk. The reality is that no company sustains growth indefinitely (see life cycles in Chapter 8).

■ CONCLUSION

Critiquing operations involves monitoring all aspects of the business and making adjustments where necessary. Ultimately, the goal is to ensure that there is a business to manage next year. There's nothing quite so exhilarating as to see the company exceed expectations. And there's nothing quite so unnerving as to discover that the company is struggling, especially if this is the firm's first year in business and reserves are dwindling. The information management learns about the company can be used to either praise progress or remedy faults. Controlling should not restrict the organization, but rather should inspire the company to grow by directing resources to the most profitable activities.

■ DISCUSSION EXERCISES

Discuss transaction management software that you use; share transaction tracking forms that you use or design a tracking system for your office.

Discuss ways to economize on expenditures in your company, office, or department.

What are your experiences with customer service surveys? With outside resources that provide surveys?

What effect have efforts of your company or your office to control costs of sales had on the sales staff?

18

CHAPTER EIGHTEEN

MANAGING RISK

What poses the greatest risks for your company?

What can you do to protect the company from these risks?

Risk begins at the time you make up your mind to go into business and sign the partnership, corporation, and loan papers. It sits on the slippery doorstep of the office, in the seat of the first employment interview, and at your feet with the first employee you let go.

Step outside the office on a listing presentation or into a property with a buyer, the conference room to negotiate a sales contract, or a local eatery for lunch with fellow brokers, and you're in the riskiest arenas of the real estate business. Add more salespeople, several employees, and a lot more buyers and sellers to the mix and the risk increases exponentially.

This is not to suggest one should be intimidated by risk, but rather to say that risk is a given in the business world. Virtually every business enterprise and profession has had to learn how to insulate itself from threats to their enterprises and navigate an increasingly litigious environment. Our nation's court dockets are choked with lawsuits, and that's not likely to change any time soon. But litigation is only one of the bolts of lightning that can rock an organization.

■ PROTECTING THE INSTITUTION

There's a sense of comfort or complacency that settles in when a company is making money, or at least keeping its head above water, and manages to put out the daily brushfires. It's not uncommon for managers to feel that they're managing the company just fine, as long as the money and the brushfires are under control. While these are not unimportant activities, there's more to consider about the health and well-being of the institution.

Protecting the Brand

Call it brand, name, or goodwill, this is the company's image and reputation in the marketplace. While a company's product or service is associated with that brand, the name the organization attains gives it stature. Though it's an intangible asset (distinguished here from the value of projected earnings when a company is sold), brand has enormous effect on a company's position in the marketplace and its future.

A company works hard to establish an identity and credibility when it first opens its doors. As the company proceeds through its life stages and touches more people, the company can continually enhance its reputation and demonstrate its trustworthiness. But that's also when the way the company manages its finances, handles customers, and treats workers has the powerful potential to damage that reputation.

That reputation is even more on the line today—online. Thanks to blogs and social networks, people can freely express themselves, name names, and post photos. All of that gets memorialized for the world to see, often with the company being none the wiser that its brand is at stake. (Though there are services that can scrutinize reputations on the Internet and help repair any damage.)

The reputation of the institution rarely rises or falls on singular events (even recent corporate scandals were tips on bigger icebergs). However, many good deeds are easily overshadowed by a few missteps in which consumers, investors, or people who work for the company feel their trust has been violated. Once the company's reputation declines, the organization is more suspect on all fronts.

Value the integrity of the institution. Demonstrate that with conscientious-to-a-fault customer service and fair, honest dealings with the people who work for the company and with other professionals in the industry. These are not lofty ideals, but the ways an institution proves its trustworthiness and earns respect.

Protecting the License

Any business enterprise that requires a government permit or license for a part or all of its operation is vulnerable if that privilege is suspended or revoked. Certainly, a real estate company is vulnerable in this regard, and perhaps more so than other enterprises.

Although the worst-case scenario of the principal broker sitting in jail for fraud or drug trafficking would be a major disruption, the company's license is far more likely to be affected by something one of the licensees affiliated with the company does. This falls under a very simple, though powerful, license law statement that says the broker is responsible for the actions of his or her underlying licensees. The phraseology may differ from state to state, but the effect is that the broker is ultimately responsible for supervising and exercising control over all licensed activities.

The risk to the company increases with each licensee who works for the company. It's rare that a real estate company says, "we can't hire any more licensees because we can't keep track of them." (Maybe it should.) Certainly, the more licensees a company employs, the better skilled its managers need to be. Unfortunately, the larger the sales staff, the greater the likelihood that the manager knows less about what licensees do.

The company is also vulnerable when its business philosophy pushes the envelope to "make the deal" or the salespeople are more focused on the deal and less on how they made it (all points that have been made in earlier chapters). If that's the way of the company, then the company has to face the fact that the broker's exposure and the risk of sanctions are increased if the way to the deal violates the law.

At the very least, allegations of violations distract valuable time and resources from other activities during the investigation and defense stages of the enforcement process. Depending on the nature and severity of the transgression, the principal broker (and if there's a company license, the company as well) can be fined, or the license can be suspended or revoked. Although a fine obviously has financial implications, the other two possibilities can seriously threaten the very existence of the institution.

The most apparent conclusion to all of this is that a company needs to take proactive, preventive steps. Some companies establish zero tolerance policies, refusing to hire anyone whose license has previously been sanctioned or who has a criminal past (more stringently investigated than criminal background checks by licensing authorities). The caveat about using criminal conviction and arrest records in hiring decisions, however, is they could have the effect of disparately treating minority groups.

Companies can also put some grit behind the grin of their policies and procedures and employee handbooks. Pledges to observe all license laws, internal procedures to support those laws, and well-crafted company codes of ethics are meaningless unless the company institutionalizes procedures to sanction those who digress. The company shouldn't wait for the enforcement agency to make a routine inspection or sit in silent hope of dodging official notice that someone has filed a complaint.

The front line managers, the sales managers, are the company's most critical defense. They must be diligent (which isn't easy with the mobility of today's workforce) about investigating how people conduct the company's business. Customer service and transaction reports and one-on-one conversations with salespeople are useful ways to gather this information. The most important thing, however, is that management takes its responsibility for supervising licensed activities seriously.

Planning Succession

What happens if an owner or the broker of the company dies? Or wants to retire or sell the business? What happens if any member of the management team suddenly departs by virtue of a better offer elsewhere, a change in career, retirement, temporary disability, or terminal illness?

Succession planning is the equivalent of writing a will, which business owners typically think they'll get around to "someday." That someday needs to be sooner than they think because succession takes time to orchestrate—to prepare someone to take over and to make suitable financial arrangements. The smaller the company, the more vulnerable it is when a principal owner dies or wants to retire.

State license laws often provide a transitioning process to protect client funds and draw the business to an orderly close if the principal broker dies and hasn't designated a licensed successor. But that's a poor substitute for preparing a suitable replacement to take the helm and planning the distribution of ownership and other financial matters to keep the business running.

As important as estate and tax planning are for safeguarding the company, its future really rises or falls on the designated successor, especially in a closely held or family business. A business owner's child makes a good heir-apparent only if the person is trained in all aspects of the business, not just in the job the child is currently doing (back to succession takes time to orchestrate). If the owner has several children, they all must support the parent's choice for the company to succeed and preserve family harmony in the process. Sometimes the business is simply better off in the hands of someone outside the family.

The survival rate of family businesses into the second generation in this country is the lowest in the world. Legacy and tradition are not as important as they are elsewhere, but more significant is that owners have to inspire passion for the family business. And that training has to start early.

The business needs that same preparation if the owner wants to retire or sell, as well. The owner often transfers responsibilities gradually as he or she phases out of that role, which makes for a smooth and orderly transition. But the buyout or financial arrangement is generally a transitioning process as well, sometimes a lengthy one considering the economic and tax implications for all concerned.

Although the owner is a key player in the stability of the institution, the company can flounder with any disruption in the leadership or managerial ranks. Responsibilities can be temporarily assigned if the vacancy is not permanent or divided until a suitable replacement is found. Better still is a plan for identifying suitable replacements before they are needed.

There's an axiom in management that says people should always be grooming their replacements. That's just good business but also gives talent within the company an opportunity to grow.

While senior managers are responsible for grooming successors for their positions, they also need to be looking at every position in the organization with an eye for talent that is waiting in the wings or that could be nurtured as replacements. Each sales office manager should be doing likewise, as well.

The people who take on temporary assignments during vacations or other absences of their superiors, or the companies that have job shifting or cross training programs, provide readily available talent—not just when the unexpected happens but during the normal course of attrition. Although the uniqueness of an individual is irreplaceable, other talent is available that can do a job, maybe differently or maybe even better.

Cyber Security

The obvious statement about cyber security is the company needs strong computer and data security with active firewalls, updated patches to software programs, and current antivirus and antispyware software. And be especially wary (stop banking and other online activities) if the computer system starts to run slowly or behave unusually.

That's a relatively effective defensive posture as long as the company institutionalizes aggressive security-management procedures and protects all of its data portals, including those in their workers' smart phones, tablets, notebooks, and laptops. But few companies truly understand how vulnerable they are to intrusion until it happens.

The headline grabbers are the large corporations, banks, and healthcare and government institutions whose customer databases are breached. But small companies are even more vulnerable because their technology and security procedures are typically less sophisticated. Most intrusions are random attacks, generally by hackers that deliver malicious payloads through Web site vulnerabilities and scam e-mails. But some hackers are much more purposeful, instigating what are known as APTs (advanced persistent threats).

Hackers carefully choose their targets (ones that have or have access to sensitive information) and then wait for the right moment to strike, generally with a new code that isn't likely to be detected by security software. They search the Internet, especially social networking sites, and use job and other personal information people reveal to identify targets and write emails they are likely to open. Once people do, the hacker is in and can root around the company's files (or use that "in" to access another company's system), and steal workplace data.

Identity theft is estimated by the Federal Trade Commission to claim about ten million victims a year. Any employee's portal in any company is a possible gateway to that information, which could become part of the estimated 15,000 stolen accounts that are posted in hacker chat rooms each month. But hackers aren't the only threat. Anyone who knows where to look on the Internet can find files with names, social security numbers, and other personal information.

The company's own identity is vulnerable as well. All it takes is one click-before-you-think to open an email that grabs a user name and password, and a hacker can highjack the company's bank account and make wireless transfers. In the world of cybercrime, these are known as corporate account takeovers.

Corporate accounts are particularly attractive because banks don't often do as much to protect business accounts from online fraud as they do for consumer accounts (which is required by the federal Electronic Funds Transfer Act). Although consumers are promptly notified of suspicious activity and have limited liability for monetary loss, businesses are typically unaware of fraudulent activity until the monthly statement is posted or the account is drained. Unless the company has insurance for wireless fraud or deals with a bank that provides security for its corporate customers, the company is out of luck (and money).

Cyber security is not just about the hackers. They just take advantage of the open doors and are usually several steps ahead of the "good guys" who write the software upgrades to close those doors to the company's infrastructure or system. Although no strategy is fool proof, companies can be more proactive about protecting that infrastructure and the company data.

- **Use diagnostic tools that find the weak spots in the infrastructure.** Vulnerability management or vulnerability assessment software reveals where the company's system is insecure, including the loopholes that aren't closed with software patches, antivirus and antispyware programs, and scanning procedures.
- **Protect individual files from unauthorized use.** Encrypt data, build strong access controls (including frequently changed passwords), and block the transfer of data from secure to unsecured devices and

Internet sites. Limit the personnel who have access to particularly sensitive and confidential information.

- **Purge data.** Minimize the potential for identity theft by disposing of personal information in a secure manner once it's no longer needed (shred paper documents and securely remove computer files). Also, securely dispose of hard drives, printers, and portable devices to prevent people with the know-how from reconstructing data imprints.
- **Limit hardware portals.** An increasing number of systems no longer have CD ports, but they do have USB ports. The company can require the use of secure flash drives from a particular manufacturer and install software that recognizes only those devices. However, any portable medium can corrupt or infect the system unless it's scanned for malicious software as well.
- **Use only secure wireless networks.** Although the company can do its part in-house by guarding and changing passwords, the company data the workforce exposes on public and unsecured networks each time people connect mobile devices to the Internet is particularly vulnerable.
- **Monitor internal as well as outside traffic.** Although the company can't spend enough to detect every risk, it can narrow the time between the malicious act and detection to minimize the damage. Network traffic logs show the Web sites that company computers tried to reach and the user passwords that accessed sensitive files, which can identify employee data theft as well.
- **Monitor the postings.** With all the online social media conversations, not just the company's but all the workers' (especially the salespeople's) as well, comments can easily reveal information that can violate privacy laws or compromise the company's data. A company-wide social media policy should address security as well as legal issues.

The company can do its part for cyber security, but everyone else has to do their part, too. People have to think-before-you-click on any suspicious e-mail and not open emails that appear to come from a friend or one who doesn't usually respond to a social media posting (the APT threat). And guard the company data and identity information that reside in mobile devices. Because they aren't typically owned or issued by the real estate company, the company doesn't have the ability to track or disable a device that has been compromised or misplaced.

Companies can make their data more secure with policies and procedures that address the way people manage cyber security on personal devices, including a requirement to report any data breach or lost or stolen device to senior management. The description of confidential information and the timing of the event are essential for notifying people whose identity has been compromised as required by data security laws.

Workplace Fraud

Troubled economies often drive people to do desperate things. But even without a poor economy, companies are easy targets for employee embezzlement, wire fraud, and theft of data, especially to support lavish lifestyles or pay extraordinary bills. In real estate companies, client funds are also at risk.

The financial loss can reach millions of dollars before anyone is the wiser, and online banking makes the take even easier. The wealth of accessible data that can be traded for cash, particularly the identity of high-worth customers, also makes fraud easier.

The procedures a company puts in place to limit access to sensitive files, including financial accounts, and the checks-and-balances in best accounting practices (see Chapter 10) not only protect the institution but also protect people from themselves. This is also an argument in favor of investigating the background of the people the company hires.

Natural Disasters

Even the most healthy and enduring institutions are no match for Mother Nature. That should be a statement of the obvious, but the reality is unspeakably cruel for victims of vicious storms, rising waters, or ravaging flames. No pictures are as poignant as the people stranded on rooftops along the Gulf shores without any means of communicating their plight, let alone rescuing their businesses or livelihoods. Several years ago this would have sounded like editorial drama. Instead, it speaks to the increasingly commonplace fact of life on our changing planet.

Adversity teaches powerful lessons about the proactive steps needed to keep business enterprises running in the aftermath of disaster. Hazard and business interruption insurance (which is also becoming more expensive and less inclusive) goes only so far in arming the enterprise with the tools to move forward.

The best way to assemble those tools is to stand in the office and imagine how the business would function if that office were an empty shell. Although equipment can be replaced, the files, data, and even contact lists that reside in computers, cabinets, and drawers (and in staff belongings) are irreplaceable. Yes, they can be reconstructed, but even that process requires some usable fragments of information.

Clearly, the most proactive step is to assemble a contingency file, including insurance policies, that resides off-site. A great deal of the most critical information is likely to reside in a backup of the company's database already, but critical documents (copies of applicable licenses, leases, and the like) need to be scanned into files created specifically for emergency purposes. Even if the data are not up-to-the-minute current, there will be enough threads to begin pulling operations back together. The contingency file needs to include the answers to several questions.

- Who should be contacted first, and how would they be reached? (Secondary contacts should also be included in case the first-line contact doesn't work.)
- What information about the company, its financial accounts, and its pending business would be needed immediately?
- What evidence (inventories, photos, purchase receipts, etc.) would be needed to prove loss, especially for insurance?
- Who are the vendors, contractors, and other professionals with whom the company customarily does business? How would they be contacted?
- What archived records would be the most critical in the event of tax or regulatory audits or litigation?

There are a lot of details in the answers to these questions. Some time is involved in contemplating and collecting all the important pieces of information but waiting until after the fact is too late. A final comment is that a company also has to be prepared for hitches in logistics, especially the lack of communications and major utilities.

■ RISK MANAGEMENT CULTURE

Risk management means different things to different people. To some it means keep dousing the brushfires. To others it means keep the organization's vulnerabilities hidden, that if no one knows where the vulnerabilities are, the company will be OK (or at least the responsible manager won't look bad). Then there are those who chalk up risk as an inevitable fact of life and budget for the cost of bailing the company out of problems.

Although a company can prepare financially (especially for lawsuits) by setting aside reserves in a litigation fund or, as many more do, purchasing liability insurance, the company is managing on hope—hope that the costs won't exceed the financial resources. But there are better ways to protect the company and in so doing, direct the company's financial resources to productive endeavors.

A risk management culture is an environment that makes risk management a priority in everything the company does and infuses responsibility for managing risk in everyone in the organization from the most senior to the lowest positions in the company. This is a *proactive* environment that builds offensive strategies by identifying potential threats or anticipating crises and assembling procedures to eliminate or minimize risk to the organization.

The how-to of risk management involves a series of steps similar to any problem-solving process (identifying, analyzing, evaluating, and handling). Typically, someone in senior management (or the owner of a sole proprietorship) is the risk management officer and is responsible for convening people within the organization to periodically assess operations from a risk management perspective and preparing additional offenses as necessary.

Because many risks involve matters of law, the company's legal counsel should be involved in the process as well. Often the real estate industry's professional organizations have legal hot lines that can also be helpful resources, especially for ways to handle certain risks.

Identify Risk

The assessment of risk looks into all the chambers of the company's operations at every level of the organization. Risk arises primarily because of ignorance, carelessness, or breach of a company policy or procedure. Although not all vulnerabilities pose the same level of risk, there are a number of things management should be looking for in its information systems, workplace relations, and external or public relations. Many involve practices that are simply a function of the real estate business.

- **Advertising.** Risks abound in what is said and how the company's services, listings, sales and production results, and employment opportunities are portrayed. State licensing law requirements for advertising are a particular concern (such as names, phone numbers, and often license numbers in communications and promotional materials). Accuracy of data in MLS listings is also an issue. Equal employment and housing laws are also a concern, as is the company's brand and reputation.

- **Agency relationships.** These are the law of agency issues that affect the way customers versus clients are serviced, beginning with legal requirements for disclosing relationships to the way salespeople handle fiduciary (or nonagency) responsibilities during a transaction. A company is also vulnerable with respect to practices involving relationships with other brokers and the relationships they have with their clients. Breach of fiduciary duty, dual agency, agency disclosure, and buyer representations are major sources of recent civil litigation.

- **Antitrust.** These are issues that create vulnerability under federal and, perhaps, state antitrust laws. Price fixing, group boycotting, territorial assignments, and tying agreements are all practices specifically prohibited. Company fee and commission policies, and the way they are represented by the salespeople, must avoid any appearance of price fixing.

- **Conduct of sales staff.** Legal liability as well as company image and reputation are at stake in every activity anyone undertakes on behalf of the company, including Internet and digital postings and promotional pieces prepared and distributed by the salespeople. Not only should all of these issues be addressed in policies and procedures, but the company also has to look at how are they enforced and how the managers supervise the salespeople's activities.

- **Cultural diversity.** These are issues that relate to cultural awareness in the workplace and the marketplace and people's attentiveness to legal rights and appropriate behaviors with respect to race, ethnicity, gender, and the like. These are management as well as customer-service issues.

- **Disability.** Practices that fail to enable people with disabilities to access the company's services and facilities and the failure to properly accommodate these people in the workforce violate the Americans with Disabilities Act and perhaps similar state laws.

- **Document management.** Many of the documents created become documents that must be stored (electronically or in hard copy) for certain periods of time to satisfy requirements of various laws as well as to provide evidence in the event of litigation. There are also legal as well as business reasons for disposing of documents containing confidential and proprietary information in a secure manner, either in-house (typically by shredding) or by a contracted records-destruction vendor.

- **Employee-at-will and equal employment laws.** These are issues that arise from a number of employment laws that affect recruitment, hiring, training, advancement, discipline, and firing practices as well as pregnancy, family and medical leave, military service considerations, and wage and salary laws. Practices that target older workers (persons age 40 or older) and terminate any worker without just cause and due process in accordance with employment-at-will (EAW) also create vulnerability.

- **Fair housing.** These are practices relating to federal, state, and local laws that, by intent or effect, discriminate against people seeking housing for sale or rent because of their race, color, religion, sex, handicap, familial status, national origin, and perhaps others as defined by state or local law. Failure to display equal opportunity notices as prescribed by a law is also a violation.

- **Financial management.** Vulnerabilities lie in the way client funds are handled (license law issue) and financial obligations (debt payments or tax filings) and accounting procedures are managed. Are company assets (money and equipment) vulnerable to tampering or misappropriation? Has an independent audit been conducted recently?

- **Harassment.** A workplace environment that tolerates offensive behavior (including the jokesters and people who can't keep their hands to themselves) or fails to respond to allegations of harassment is vulnerable under equal employment laws, with sexual harassment being the most common issue. Offensive behavior with customers and clients is also problematic.
- **Internet.** The vulnerability of the company's database to invasion or paralysis can cause major disruption in business. The misuse of intellectual property (whether by downloading, copying, publishing, posting, or hyperlinking) either by the company or its staff infringes on copyright, trademark, or business method patents. A company that fails to protect its intellectual property also loses valuable assets.
- **Personal identity.** Risk lurks in any form, document, or file (and even the copier machine) where a Social Security number, driver's license number, credit card number, or financial account information is recorded for any person (company personnel and contractors, as well as customers and clients). If, in fact, that information is necessary, it must be scrupulously protected and disposed of in a secure manner. Data security laws affect the manner in which data can be shared and require that consumers be notified of certain events.
- **Personal injury.** This deals with the liability for (or loss the company could incur from) an injury of a consumer, affiliated contractor (especially a salesperson), or employee. In the real estate business, the most likely event involves automobile accidents; slip-and-fall injuries account for the largest percentage of other accidents. Although personal injury claims can be managed with insurance, the more prudent course is to identify and attempt to mitigate potential for injury (including in the company's listings).
- **Property conditions.** These are the issues that relate to the real estate that is the subject of transactions, particularly conditions that statutory or case law has determined are material to a purchaser's decision. Vulnerability can lurk in misrepresentations or fraud, failure to meet the legal requirements for disclosure of property conditions, and the

advice or recommendations salespeople provide relative to professional inspections or curative measures. Vulnerability can also arise in the way environmental conditions are handled, including requirements of the Residential Lead-Based Paint Hazard Reduction Act.

- **RESPA.** These issues relate to practices governed by the Real Estate Settlement Procedures Act, including disclosures of settlement charges and affiliated business arrangements (AfBAs) and payments of kickbacks and prohibited referral fees.

- **Social media.** Blogging and social networking pose liability ranging from licensing, fair housing, and antitrust laws to copyright infringement. Media sites also have their own terms of use, take-down policies, and decency standards. The company needs a social media policy (which is also enforced) that addresses these issues as well as practices for monitoring the company's sites and postings.

- **Solicitations.** Telephone solicitations and promotional faxes and e-mails are all suspect if procedures and practices do not meticulously follow the laws that are designed to protect consumers from unwanted solicitations. Are current do-not-call lists readily available to the sales staff?

- **Workplace safety.** In addition to OSHA (safe workplace laws), civil actions could arise if workers or visitors to the place of business are injured on the premises. The company must also be vigilant about dangerous or threatening behavior.

A company can be vulnerable in any of these areas because of inadequate policies or procedures. Frequently, however, the organization has protective mechanisms that, for a variety of reasons, fail to work the way they were intended. In many cases, this happens because management falls short on its enforcement responsibilities or allows people to bend or ignore the rules.

Analyze Risk

This step in the process analyzes the discoveries in the prior step. The purpose is twofold. One is to determine how the threat occurs. By understanding why it happens, possible solutions to prevent it become evident.

The other purpose is to determine the level of financial, legal, or public relations risk to the organization. This helps management prioritize its efforts and close the most risky loopholes first. Certainly, routine patterns or practices that are related to matters of law and recent litigation deserve attention and guidance from legal counsel.

The analysis process also tests the organization's level of tolerance for risk. That tolerance gets tested with each issue managers confront and perhaps also reveals how committed the organization is to fostering a proactive risk management culture. An issue that would cause many sleepless nights for managers in one organization could get a ho-hum response in others. Even within the same management team, not everyone has the same tolerance level. Some are more immune to risk and others are far more unnerved, which also means that the team has to achieve consensus.

Evaluate Alternatives

This step identifies ways the company can protect itself. What processes, systems, or tools should be created or enhanced? A range of possibilities may exist, or perhaps there's only one logical solution. Even if the risk is something the organization can't do anything about, the organization can be proactive by planning suitable defensive strategies ahead of time.

Solutions can come in the form of more diligent oversight of company procedures and staff behavior, new or revised procedures, enhanced training of staff, better attentiveness to customer service, or perhaps allocation of financial resources to undertake a major initiative. Or a solution could involve a combination of these alternatives.

One of management's most useful tools is the company's policies and procedures manual, which can become clear written evidence about how processes are to work and people are to behave. However, the company is defenseless in the event of litigation if it fails to enforce policies or purposely engages in practices that contradict the stated policies and procedures.

One of the greatest vulnerabilities for a real estate company involves the transaction itself, particularly the way the salespeople conduct themselves.

- **Sales training.** A well-trained staff is one of a company's most powerful risk management assets, but training is more than how to sell and make money. Training should form a basis for ethical and legal conduct (the legal liability and risk reduction issues) and foster patterns of behavior in which consumer rights and laws are faithfully observed, absent the shortcuts that sometimes tempt salespeople (things like getting the disclosure forms signed after the fact or filling in the rest of the contact blanks after they're signed).

- **Discover, disclose, document.** The attentiveness of the salespeople to any property condition that could materially affect a consumer's decision is also effective risk management. A vigilant posture involves a process in which salespeople observe (within the limits of their expertise) and facilitate professional inspections to discover and disclose defects or environmental conditions, and then *document* the disclosures that have been made.

  Documentation may be a legally required disclosure form, a professional report, acknowledgment of conditions in a sales contract or lease agreement, and/or a trail of notes and correspondence in the transaction file that document conversations between the salesperson and the consumer. In fact, any notes, including telephone and appointment logs, can close a window on risk, especially in the event of litigation.

- **Customer satisfaction.** Attentiveness to customer service goes a long way toward insulating the company. Establishing quality service standards should contribute greatly, especially when those standards include educating buyers and sellers about the "rules of the game" when they begin working with the company. Minimizing violated expectations and educating consumers about certain laws, like fair housing, agency, and environmental and property disclosures, will avoid problems later on.

  Although no one can prevent people from pursuing their legal rights, many times these actions can be averted with management's attention to a customer complaint and attempt to resolve the differences. Yes, there are those disgruntled people who will feel no justice unless they see the broker in court, but from the company's point of view that should be the court of last resort.

Handling a Risk

This is the step in which management decides on the most suitable course of action, implements it, and then follows up to ensure that the risk has been contained.

The most critical part of this process is assigning someone the responsibility for managing the risk. That person, generally a member of the management team, becomes accountable for directing company activities in the design of the process or procedure and then seeing that it is implemented.

Additional Offense

At the risk (pardon the pun) of sounding redundant, the importance of a lawyer and accountant can't be overemphasized. One of the most valuable lines in the company budget is their monthly retainer and the roles they play at management meetings and company events.

The company pays these people to keep it out of trouble. Will you take their advice, even if they don't tell you what you want to hear? Are you going to search until you find someone to give you the answer you want? Or are you going to ignore the professionals' advice entirely? Second opinions can be useful, but ducking the facts can be risky business. Lawyers and accountants can't defend indefensible actions.

Their retainer fees are valuable risk management fees, but there are also times when billable hours are involved. Define which services will be performed for the retainer and the services that the company will pay for as billable hours. Also, clarify exactly which company personnel are permitted to contact these advisers and for what purposes. Otherwise, the company could exceed the services covered by a retainer and be very surprised by the amount of the legal and accounting bills.

The real estate industry's professional organizations monitor laws and court decisions that affect industry practices and provide valuable analyses. They also have good resource information for developing risk reduction policies, including such issues as social media, privacy laws, and agency. Complete texts of the laws are also available on the Internet.

Another valuable resource is the relationship the company develops with government regulators and fair housing agencies. Unfortunately, some people see them as adversaries who should be avoided. However, these agencies are very useful for clarifying and interpreting their laws and answering specific questions. Better to ask ahead of time and keep the company out of trouble. These resources willingly help because that lightens their enforcement workload as well.

A final thought is that the object of risk management is to protect the organization, not to bog it down in procedures and paperwork. The virtue of a risk management culture is that as people behave in ways that are attentive to risk, the practice becomes second nature. Then there's less risk, and attending to new threats that come along can be handled rather matter-of-factly.

■ DEFENSE IN RISK MANAGEMENT

A very important point about a risk management culture is it also creates procedures and processes that help the organization present a suitable defense should that become necessary.

Regardless of how attentive management is to protecting the institution, a fact of business life is that even the best intentions will not prevent an allegation of misconduct.

Dealing with allegations can be as distracting as winding up in a formal legal proceeding. Considerable financial and human resources are devoted to jumping through the hoops erected by regulatory agencies and the court system. The good news is the matter may be dropped or resolved during that process. Otherwise, the company has a longer journey and expends more resources until a final verdict is reached.

Documentation

Once again, the power of information empowers management, in this case to defend the organization. But the company loses its most persuasive ammunition if the information it needs is lost or wasn't captured in the first place. There's no way to anticipate when the seemingly innocuous note or record will be the most critical piece of information.

The documentation and record-keeping procedures that are part of a proactive risk management culture become the power for the defense. The company's legal counsel is invaluable for recommending defensible documentation procedures. But that also means that the company has to instill procedures that gain the cooperation of everyone to make them work.

Insurance

Insurance is the part of a risk management defense that intends to shield the company from financial impacts. While the cost of insurance can be considerable, it's a critical cost of doing business that small companies often overlook or give little consideration. Insurance is an investment of financial resources that can pay even greater dividends if the need arises, especially if the company is targeted for its "deep pockets."

The National Association of Insurance Commissioners has a good online resource to help business owners learn about insuring their enterprises. Policies can vary but there are several types of coverage to consider.

- **Workers' compensation**. The purpose is to protect people against loss of income due to injuries sustained on the job. Workers' compensation insurance is a statutory requirement for employees and, depending on state law, may also be required for independent contractors. In addition, the company may consider offering disability insurance to employees to cover loss due to any illness or injury, whether it is job-related or not.
- **Property casualty and liability**. Standard commercial coverage protects the business property (and contents) for the same reasons people get homeowner's policies for private residences. Fire and personal injury on the premises are the most common concerns, but policies may cover other events, depending on inclusions/exclusions for damage caused by natural events.
- **Employee practices liability**. The purpose is to protect the company from such work-related issues as sexual harassment, discrimination, and wrongful discipline or termination. As with any insurance, the ability to get coverage and the premiums involved are affected by the company's past history of employment practices.
- **Computer fraud**. Policies vary but the intention is to cover liability arising from breaches of the company's data systems, which can also include loss from fraudulent electronic transfers.
- **Business interruption**. This helps businesses pay expenses when it can't operate. Any company that has lived through the aftermath of a fire, flood, or other natural disaster can attest to the financial disaster that also looms without insurance.
- **Errors and omissions**. The company's E&O insurance covers certain claims against *the company* because of the professional actions

of their workers, including their salespeople. Licensees should also have their own coverage (a requirement for licensees in some states), or the company could offer a group policy in which the salespeople can participate. E&O insurance includes the legal defense against a claim as well as damage awards for insurable events. Those rarely include violations of the law, however.

- **Automobile liability.** This covers the company's liability for accidents while workers, especially the salespeople, are engaged in company business. This coverage is normally contingent on the salespeople proving they carry adequate liability insurance themselves, typically at least $300,000 per person, $500,000 per accident, and $100,000 for property damage.

The company's insurance agent or carrier can structure the most affordable way to tie all of the coverage together. A risk assessment is often required before polices are issued, but that provides good proactive strategies that will benefit the company in any case.

Dispute Resolution

The legal system in this country is designed to ensure that justice is served by giving everyone his or her day in court and an opportunity to be heard. Nevertheless, the system is stressed to its limits, particularly with civil matters. Often people must cool their heels for years before they are heard, and incur sizable legal bills in the process.

Mediation and arbitration are alternatives for resolving disputes in a speedy, affordable manner. These methods are used to resolve many types of disputes, and real estate is no exception. Mediation is a forum in which the parties meet with an impartial mediator and negotiate a resolution to their dispute. Arbitration involves an arbitrator (or panel of arbitrators) who takes testimony from both sides as would be done in court and then renders a decision. In most jurisdictions this decision is as binding as any court decision would be.

Although these alternatives are very beneficial for buyers and sellers, the real estate company also benefits because it's frequently named as a party in their disputes. There are organizations throughout the country that are sanctioned by the legal community to provide mediation and arbitration services. Some provide only mediation or only arbitration, and others provide both. Sales agreements often include language that requires the parties to resolve disputes over specific matters in this manner.

Arbitration Between Brokers

Buyers and sellers are not the only ones who find themselves in disputes. Controversies between brokerage companies arise, particularly over commissions. Professional real estate organizations frequently offer their members an arbitration forum in which these matters can be settled. Again, the advantage is a speedier, less-costly way to resolve these controversies. (Note, too, that these organizations provide forums for ethics complaints as well.)

■ CONCLUSION

The purpose of risk management is to be attentive to threats to the organization. All of management's efforts to monitor activities to keep the organization on course are insufficient to truly insulate the institution from risks that are inherent in doing business. A risk management culture infuses the organization and its systems, processes, and people with vigilance to risk. An organization manages risk, not just in the way it attempts to avoid the indiscretions that create vulnerability but also in the ways it prepares to defend itself should the need arise.

■ DISCUSSION EXERCISES

What procedures has your company adopted to manage the risks that are prevalent in your practice?

Discuss the general circumstances of closed legal cases of which you are aware (from personal experience or professional readings), the final rulings, and possible ways that the litigation could have been avoided.

What procedures has your company instituted to protect the personal information of customers and clients? The workforce?

What issues do you anticipate will pose the greatest liability within the next five years?

IN CONCLUSION OF UNIT V

The control function of management should protect, preserve, and promote the growth of the company. This should empower the organization to pursue its goals and not restrict or burden the operations. Because certain events can inhibit the company's progress, especially risks that could divert the firm's resources into litigation, it's important to be proactive in establishing procedures and monitoring activities to facilitate the way business is conducted. The things you learn about the company in the process are useful as you revisit the management functions and begin planning for the future.

■ THE SCENARIO

Having read this unit, what is your analysis of the following scenario?

The first phone call of the day to the broker brought news from the company's attorney. (Well, from the broker's point of view, these calls were just all part of doing business, so better that than a panicked alert from the chief financial officer. Anything was fixable as long as the company had money.) Several issues were pending on the attorney's desk, some of which could be disposed of relatively easily. Others, however, were more ominous.

The company had completed a business planning session several weeks ago and decided that on January 1 it would implement several new policies. In order to maximize revenue and minimize expenditures, the company would no longer accept listings on properties valued less than $40,000 and would enter into buyer-agency agreements only with prospective purchasers who were qualified to purchase properties valued at $40,000 or more. The company's customary concierge services would be offered only to buyers who purchased properties valued at $500,000 or higher. The company also would require buyers who had houses to sell to enter into listing agreements with the company before their offers could be presented to the company's client-sellers.

By the middle of the next year, the formation of a title abstract and settlement company will be completed. This will enable the company's salespeople to offer buyers and sellers a neat package of services. The fee structure is still under discussion, though the intention is to quote a packaged fee for title and settlement services, which will also include an amount to be paid to the real estate salesperson involved in the transaction.

In the meantime, several company procedures need to be resolved. After the business planning session, the office managers were instructed to go back to their offices and scrutinize several procedures. Their assignment was to make sure that personnel files contain proper documentation and that transaction files contain the required paperwork. They were also instructed to review the company's business policies and procedures manual and go over it with their salespeople and support staff. It seems that the company has been notified that a former employee is pursuing legal action for wrongful termination. The attorney has also had received a letter, though no formal legal action has been taken yet, from a salesperson alleging sexual harassment.

In addition, the company has had an increasing number of cases in which the attorney has had to unravel disputes over escrow or hand money and property conditions, apparently the result of careless procedures or inappropriate representations by salespeople. Fortunately, formal legal action has been averted. However, because of the increased amount of time devoted to these matters, the attorney is proposing that his compensation and the scope of his retainer be restructured. The company is contemplating assessing each sales office a prorated share of the attorney's retainer and/or charging hourly fees for out-of-the-ordinary services to the offending office.

■ THE ANALYSIS

The scenario in the introduction of this unit says several things about the company. One is that the broker seems to be doing the right thing in keeping legal counsel in the loop, but one would also hope counsel knows about several things that were discussed at the recent business planning meeting.

Although it's likely that financial motives are behind the benchmark of $40,000 for listings and buyer-agency contracts, there is a distinct possibility that this policy could violate the fair housing laws, having the effect of denying persons in the protected classes the company's services. So much for equal opportunity in housing. The benchmark for concierge services, however, would not have fair housing implications.

Presumably, legal counsel is involved in developing the corporate structures that will affiliate the brokerage company with a title abstract and settlement company. Affiliated business associations are a subject of RESPA and pending regulation. Unless disclosure procedures and referral payments are structured appropriately, the companies have some problems.

As a practical matter, a bone of contention among salespeople has been the force or requirement (however it is employed) to recommend the services of an affiliated company to a consumer when the terms are less favorable than can be obtained elsewhere. This is not to say that the company should not embark on such a venture, and in fact, it has appeal to the seamless-service-oriented consumer, but the company should be aware of the consequences, particularly if the consumer is the client.

With respect to files and procedures, the good news is that the company has embarked on a system-wide investigation to ensure that all is in order. The bad news could be that this effort is too late to properly defend a wrongful termination and a sexual harassment case.

It appears that the company needs to take some steps to increase attentiveness to hand money and property condition issues. Fortunately, the issues have been resolved and in fact, most companies can tell of numerous experiences in this same vein. However, it's only a matter of time when resolution won't be enough to avert legal action.

With respect to counsel's fees, the company has several choices. Assessing the offices a share of the expense would be appropriate, especially if the assessment was divided according to the past year's use so as not to overburden offices that have fewer occasions to use the services. The retainer could be restructured to minimize hourly fees, and, although this may result in a larger retainer fee, retainers are usually less in the long run than hourly rates. In any event, the company can take steps through training and other risk management oversight activities.

■ THE SUMMARY

Depending on whether you are the broker/owner, a senior manager in a large organization, a sales manager, or a department manager, your involvement in the various activities that are associated with the control function of management may be different. As a guide for understanding your roles, the following summary is provided.

- Critiquing the operations
  - — The broker/owner and senior management are normally involved in evaluating all aspects of the organization's activities.
  - — Lower levels of management are most involved in monitoring the activities for which they are directly responsible, though they also may have access to reports of other aspects of the company to see how their areas of responsibility affect the big picture.
- Managing risk
  - — Although the broker/owner and senior management are normally responsible for establishing policies, a proactive risk management program must involve everyone who works for the company so that risk management permeates the entire organization.

FINAL THOUGHTS

Customarily, nonfiction books or manuals end with a bibliography. But we're breaking with tradition to say that the Internet does a far better job than we can at opening the door to the vast resources available. Although several authors are mentioned in this book, they are but a few of the many people who have wise things to say about running a business and managing people.

As with any introductory book, *Real Estate Brokerage: A Management Guide* provides an overview, otherwise known as the "101 course." Each of the chapters, even sections within chapters, deserves an entire book, and in fact, many are already written. Explore Amazon, Barnes and Noble, or simply "Google" or "Bing" any topic, from business planning or business writing to leadership development or motivating a sales force, and you can add considerably to our "101 course."

Also explore industry resources. Numerous newsletters and blogs as well as publications are circulated by industry analysts, the National Association of REALTORS®, and this publisher—resources that explore the hot topics of the day and contemporary practices.

Another part of the business management story is the fluid nature of laws and regulations. Certainly, real estate licensing laws change (and vary from state to state). But once you cross the threshold into management, you enter a larger world of local, state, and federal law that affects business operations, employment, and numerous other company practices—all of which are best guided by the latest versions of the laws (also available on the Internet).

A final comment is that one of the great things about management is that it isn't an exact science. Yes, there are certain timeless principles and personal skills that are inarguably cast. But beyond that, management is an art.

This is the creative part of business management that gives managers the opportunity to explore endless possibilities and make choices that achieve the most desirable outcomes.

We started in Chapter One by saying there are no magic answers, only some that are better than others. It all depends on the situation. We conclude by saying that good managers are the key to finding the best answers to suit their situations.

GLOSSARY

Accounts payable Liabilities that represent amounts owed to creditors, usually for goods or services that were purchased.

Accounts receivable Claims against debtors, usually for goods or services that were delivered to the debtors.

Agency A relationship in which one person (the principal or client) delegates authority to another (the agent) to act on behalf of the principal in certain business transactions. This creates a fiduciary relationship, which imposes certain responsibilities on the agent who acts in this capacity.

Agency contracts Written agreements that create an agency relationship between a principal and an agent. These include listing agreements such as an open listing, an exclusive agency and an exclusive-right-to-sell agreement, and buyer agency contracts (i.e., open agreements, exclusive agency buyer agency agreements, exclusive buyer agency contracts).

Agent A person authorized to act on behalf of the principal and who has fiduciary responsibilities to the principal. In a real estate transaction, the broker is normally considered to be the agent of the principal or client.

Affinity programs Enticements such as coupons, discounts, and points used in marketing programs to attract consumers by giving them increased purchasing power for a wide range of products and services. Also known as cross marketing programs.

Americans with Disabilities Act (ADA) A federal law enacted to eliminate discrimination against people with disabilities in employment, public accommodations, government services, public transportation, and communications.

Andragogy The process by which adults learn, which distinguishes the adult learning process from the child's. It recognizes differences in approaching and processing new information.

Antitrust laws Federal and state laws enacted for the purpose of fostering competition and preventing anticompetitive practices. Antitrust violations include price fixing, certain types of boycotts, allocations of markets, and tying agreements.

Arbitration A nonjudicial proceeding in which a third party determines the resolution of a dispute between parties. The determinations of the arbitrator can be as enforceable as a decision rendered in court.

Autocratic style Management style in which the manager dominates the organization and makes all decisions, but in a more humanistic or benevolent manner than the dictatorial manager. In the autocratic style of management, there is greater concern for people, which enables them to feel more secure and comfortable. The atmosphere is more relaxed. *See also* dictatorial style; laissez-faire style; participative style.

Balance sheet A financial statement that itemizes assets, liabilities, and net worth.

Blockbusting *See* panic selling.

Brainstorming A group discussion held for the purpose of having participants generate a variety of ideas relating to a selected issue or solutions to a specific problem. Management uses brainstorming to encourage people to participate in the organization and utilizes their creativity and talents, rather than making unilateral decisions without the benefit of staff input.

Branch office A secondary office or place of business of a brokerage firm, normally required to be registered, licensed, and supervised according to the real estate licensing laws of the state.

Brand The company's market identity, the asset that is developed by its name recognition and reputation in the marketplace.

Broker A party, being a person, a corporation or a partnership, that is properly licensed as a broker under the real estate licensing laws within the jurisdiction where the individual or entity serves as a special agent to others in the brokerage of real property.

Brokerage The specialty in the real estate business that is concerned with bringing parties together in the sale, lease, or exchange of real property.

Budget A statement of estimated income and expenses; a forecast to guide the financial operations of a business.

Business plan A long-range blueprint, typically covering three to five years, that includes the mission statement, general objectives, goals, and strategies of the company.

Buyer's broker A broker who represents a buyer in a fiduciary capacity in a real estate transaction.

Caveat emptor The Latin term meaning "let the buyer beware," denoting that a buyer purchases at his or her own risk. This ancient doctrine is replaced today by a more consumer-oriented approach; that is, the seller or the seller's agent has a duty to disclose any factors that might influence a buyer's decision.

Certificate of occupancy A certificate or permit issued by a government authority indicating that the building is fit for use or occupancy according to the laws that the authority enforces.

Chain of command The hierarchy of authority, which normally begins with upper levels of management and filters down to lower levels of management.

Clayton Antitrust Act A federal statute that prohibits price discrimination, exclusive dealing arrangements, and interlocking directives.

Client The person who employs an agent to perform certain activities on his or her behalf, also known as the principal under the law of agency.

Client trust account An account set up by a broker in which clients' monies are segregated from the broker's general business accounts. Individual states' real estate licensing laws prescribe specific requirements for the manner in which these accounts must be administered. Also known as earnest money or escrow accounts in some states.

Closing The consummation of a real estate transaction in which the seller delivers title to the buyer in exchange for payment of the purchase price by the buyer.

Code of ethics A standard of ethical conduct, normally committed to writing. Any organization can establish a code of conduct for its members, such as the code of ethics of the National Association of REALTORS® and other professional organizations.

Commingling Mixing or mingling monies; for example, depositing client funds in the broker's personal or business account. Licensees who do this are subject to disciplinary action by the regulatory body that enforces a state's real estate license laws. Some states' laws do permit brokers to deposit a small amount of business or personal funds in trust accounts to cover fees or other deposit requirements of a bank or savings institution.

Common-law independent contractor An individual who does not meet the three-part test in the federal tax code but may be considered an independent contractor by court law, based on the manner in which the person is supervised, the degree of control the company exercises over the activities, and the manner in which the person is compensated.

Company dollar Funds remaining from gross income after the cost of sales has been deducted. The cost of sales includes the commissions paid to the salespeople and other brokers cooperating in transactions, overrides to the manager, and sales fees such as MLS, franchise, and referral or relocation fees.

Comparative market analysis A value analysis of a seller's property compared with other similar properties and their sales prices to arrive at an anticipated sale price for the subject property.

Comprehensive Environmental Response Compensation and Liability Act A federal law that imposes liability on owners, lenders, occupants, and operators for correcting environmental problems on a property. Superfund statutes establish a fund to clean hazardous waste sites and respond to spills and releases on properties.

Computerized loan originations (CLOs) Automated systems that enable a purchaser/borrower to locate a lender, submit a mortgage application, and obtain a conditional loan commitment right in the real estate office. With CLOs, consumers can comparison shop the various mortgage lenders and all of their loan products. CLOs must comply with the requirements of the Real Estate Settlement Procedures Act. *See also* Real Estate Settlement Procedures Act (RESPA).

Conciliation agreement A settlement or compromise agreement. Under the fair housing laws a respondent in a discrimination complaint can agree to a settlement rather than having the case resolved by judicial proceedings.

Consumer price index A statistical measure prepared by the Bureau of Labor and Statistics that indicates changes in the prices of consumer goods.

Contingency A provision in a contract that requires the completion of certain acts or requires certain events to happen before the contract is binding.

Contingency plans Alternative goals and strategies that a company can implement in case certain events happen. These may be events that could affect a company's operations but have not yet occurred (and may never occur) when the company develops its business plan. Contingency plans provide a course for the organization to follow if these situations arise.

Contract A legally enforceable agreement between competent parties who agree to perform or refrain from performing certain acts for a consideration.

Controlled business arrangements (CBAs) Networks of interrelated companies that offer real estate services associated with a real estate transaction. They offer convenience to consumers and enhance the broker's service because the broker has control over all phases of the transaction.

Cooperating broker A broker who assists another broker to complete a real estate transaction. The cooperating broker may act as a subagent of the other broker's principal, as the agent of his or her own principal, or have no fiduciary obligation to anyone in a transaction.

Corporation A legal entity created under a state's law that is an association of one or more individuals and has the capacity to act as an individual. A corporation is usually governed by a board of directors elected by the shareholders.

Cost of sales Commissions paid to the salespeople, to other brokers cooperating in real estate transactions, overrides to the manager, and sales fees such as MLS, franchise, and referral or relocation fees. Also included are transaction fees, which are monies brokers are collecting separate from commissions to cover administrative costs associated with processing sales transactions.

Cross-marketing programs Enticements, such as coupons, discounts, and points, used in marketing programs to attract consumers by giving them increased purchasing power for a wide range of products and services. Also known as affinity programs.

Customer service surveys A tool to find out what customers and clients think about the services that the company and its personnel provide. Information gathered from these surveys enables the company to monitor and improve the quality of its services where necessary.

Decentralized organization An organization in which there are fewer levels of management and authority, giving each level greater authority and control over the activities of its departments or divisions.

Demographics The profile of the population in an area, considering such characteristics as age, education, income, employment, and household structure.

Desk cost Reflects the amount of the company's expenses that can be attributed to each salesperson who works for the brokerage firm. It is calculated by dividing the expenses of the firm by the number of salespeople and can be used as a guide to determine the amount of expense each salesperson's production should cover.

Dictatorial style Management style in which the manager has absolute and total control over all decisions. Nothing is delegated, only orders are issued, and there is little interaction with the people being supervised and little concern for them as human beings or for their capabilities. *See also* autocratic style; laissez-faire style; participative style.

Discrimination Making a distinction against or in favor of a person because of the group or class of people with whom the person is identified. Illegal discrimination is the failure to treat people equally under the fair housing or equal opportunity laws because of the group with which they are identified.

Disparate impact The fact that an action has a significant impact on people in a protected class. This determines that the action is discriminatory, that is, the effect of an action is discriminatory without regard to the intent of the action.

Dispute resolution Mediation and arbitration services for resolving disputes; a speedy and affordable alternative to resolving disputes in civil court.

Dual agency Representing two principals with opposite interests in the same transaction. State law normally specifies whether a real estate licensee is permitted to provide dual agency. In states where it is permitted, the laws require that both principals must provide written consent for the dual representation.

Earnest money A cash deposit made by a prospective buyer as evidence of good faith to perform on a sales contract. It is also known as deposit money, hand money, or a binder.

Earnest money account *See* client trust account.

Employee A person who works under the supervision and control of another. For income tax purposes, an independent contractor is distinguished from an employee. *See also* independent contractor.

Equal employment opportunity laws Laws that provide for equal employment for all qualified individuals regardless of their race, color, religion, sex, age, disability, marital or family status, or nationality.

Equity with the competition The comparison of a company's compensation or commission program in relation to competitors' programs.

Ethics A system of moral principles, or rules and standards of conduct. *See also* code of ethics.

Exclusive agency A written listing agreement that gives an agent the sole right to sell or lease a property within a specified time period, with the exception that the owner can sell or lease the property himself or herself without being liable to the agent for compensation.

Exclusive agency buyer agency The buyer contracts with a sole agent for locating a property that meets certain specifications, with the exception that the buyer is relieved of any obligation to the agent if the buyer locates the property without the assistance of the agent or another broker.

Exclusive buyer agency The buyer contracts with a sole agent for locating a property that meets certain specifications. The buyer owes 100 percent loyalty to the agent and is obligated for a commission, whether the buyer, the agent, or another broker locates the property.

Exclusive listing A written listing in which an owner of a property contracts with a sole agent to sell or lease a property. It may be an exclusive agency or an exclusive-right-to-sell agreement.

Exclusive-right-to-sell A written listing giving an agent the sole right to sell or lease a property within a specified time period. The owner is liable to the agent for a commission whether the agent, the owner, or another broker sells or leases the property.

Facilitator A person who assists a buyer or seller to reach an agreement in a real estate transaction. A facilitator does not represent or have fiduciary obligations to either party.

Federal Fair Housing Act Title VIII of the Civil Rights Act of 1964, as amended. It protects people against discrimination in housing because of their race, color, religion, sex, handicap, familial status, or national origin.

Federal Trade Commission (FTC) A federal agency responsible for investigating and eliminating unfair and deceptive trade practices and unfair methods of competition.

Fictitious business name (FBN) A business name, other than the name of a person, under which the business is registered to conduct business.

Foreign Investment in Real Property Tax Act (FIRPTA) A federal law that subjects nonresident aliens and foreign corporations to U.S. income tax on their gains from the disposition of an interest in real property.

Franchise The formal privilege or contractual right to conduct a business using a designated trade name and the operating procedures of the company that owns the franchise.

Fraud An intentional deceptive act or statement with which one person attempts to gain an unfair advantage over another. It may be either a misstatement or silence about a defect.

General objectives Major aspirational objectives an organization intends to accomplish to fulfill its mission.

General partnership A form of business organization in which two or more owners engage in business. All of the general partners share full liability for the debts of the business.

Goals The end results that a company wants to achieve. Goals break down the aspirational or futuristic nature of the general objectives into specific, measurable, short-term accomplishments and show how the organization intends to achieve its general objectives.

Gross income The total income derived from doing business before any costs or expenses are deducted.

Group boycotting An antitrust violation in which two or more competitors band together to exert pressure on another competitor for the purpose of eliminating competition. It may involve withholding goods, services, or patronage that are essential to the competitor's economic survival or dealing only on unfavorable terms with the competitor. Group boycotting is a per se offense if it is done for the express purpose of reducing or eliminating competition.

Hazardous substance Any material that poses a threat to the environment or to public health.

Hazardous waste Materials that are dangerous to handle and dispose of, such as radioactive materials, certain chemicals, explosives, or biological waste.

Home officing A term in business referring to the practice of people working primarily from their homes. This is an increasingly popular trend in business, made possible by technology.

Horizontal growth Organizational growth strategy that increases the scope of services or business sectors. The organization's activities become more diverse as opposed to growing monolithically. *See* vertical growth.

Human resources The people or personnel of an organization.

Income statement *See* profit and loss statement.

Independent contractor A person retained to perform certain acts or achieve certain results without control or direction of another regarding the methods or processes used to accomplish the results. The two classifications of independent contractors are statutory independent contractors (known as statutory nonemployees in the federal tax code) and common-law independent contractors.

Intellectual property Assets that are original works; this refers to the product of an individual's creative efforts, such as manuscripts and art. With the emergence of the Internet, intellectual property has gained new meaning as individuals create Web sites and display their wares, including listings.

Internal equity A comparison of compensation plans within a company that prescribes that all people who work in the same class of jobs within an organization be paid at the same rates, and that people with greater experience or productivity, or who have specialized jobs, be compensated at higher rates.

Job description Precisely defines the responsibilities as well as the activities of a position. This ensures that both the company and the worker know exactly what a person in a specific position is expected to do.

Laissez-faire style A management style in which the manager adopts a hands-off, do-nothing approach, characterized by nonintervention and indifference. This creates a chaotic environment because the manager doesn't exercise any authority. *See also* autocratic style; dictatorial style; participative style.

Law of agency The common-law doctrine that pertains to the relationship created when one person or entity is authorized to act on legal matters for the benefit of another.

Lead poisoning Illness caused by high concentrations of lead in the body. Common sources are lead that was used in paint prior to 1978, water contamination from lead pipes, and solder containing lead.

License referral company Separate subsidiary of a brokerage company that some companies use as an alternative to accommodate licensees who do not meet their criteria for full-time salespeople, but whom the company wants to capture because of the business that these people may be able to refer to it.

Licensee A person who is issued a valid real estate license by the licensing body in the jurisdiction in which the person provides real estate services as prescribed by law.

Limited liability company (LLC) An alternative business entity with characteristics of a limited partnership and an S corporation. Investors are members rather than partners or shareholders in the business and hold membership interests rather than stock in the company. A LLC has advantages over corporations and partnerships because personal liability and taxes are different.

Limited partnership A partnership in which one person or group (known as the general partner) organizes, operates, and is responsible for the partnership venture. Other individual members are merely investors and are responsible for potential liabilities only to the extent of their original investments.

Line authority The authority given to the people who are responsible for contributing directly to the achievement of the company's objectives, such as the sales office or the property management, leasing, or new construction departments.

Listing agreement A written employment agreement between an owner of real estate and a broker that authorizes the broker to find a suitable buyer or tenant for the property. There are several types of contracts, including an open listing, an exclusive agency, and an exclusive-right-to-sell listing.

Lockbox Small, secure box affixed to a property that enables only certain authorized individuals to access its contents, usually a key to the property.

Management The activity of guiding or directing the financial and human resources of an organization. There are various management philosophies that attempt to define the way in which organizations function and managers use their authority and make decisions. The common theme in current management trends is the participative style, which emphasizes the value of people and their contribution to the organization.

Manager Individuals who are responsible for guiding or directing the financial and human resources of an organization. The prevailing theory in management today is that managers inspire, energize, and support the people they supervise rather than controlling or dominating them.

Market The geographic area in which a company does business or the specific consumers the company seeks to serve with its products or services.

Mediation An alternative to arbitration and judicial proceedings in which parties can resolve disputes between themselves using an impartial third party to moderate the proceedings and help them find a mutually acceptable resolution. If the parties are unsuccessful in mediation, they may proceed to arbitration or civil court.

Misrepresentation False statements or concealment of a material fact, that is, information deemed to be pertinent to a decision. Misrepresentations may be motivated by an attempt to deceive; though, unlike fraud, they are limited to a fact that is material to the transaction.

Mission statement States what a company's purpose is for doing business, specifically what the business does and where the organization intends to be in the future.

Monolithic organization A highly centralized operation that functions as a single (mono) unit, even though it normally consists of a number of work groups, with authority being highly controlled at the top of the organization.

Monthly operating budgets Monthly budgets constructed from the annual operating budget. By dividing the annual gross income and operating expenses by 12, the company has monthly projections to use as benchmarks for monitoring income and expenses during the year.

Multiple listing service (MLS) Information systems that provide their members with a variety of information including mortgage loan information, competitive market analysis data, sample contracts, worksheets for qualifying buyers and estimating ownership and closing costs, investment analysis, and online mapping and tax records, in addition to listing inventory.

Net income The sum arrived at after deducting the expenses of operation from gross income.

Niche marketing Services directed to specialized segments of the consumer population. Niche marketing appeals to consumers because it satisfies their demand for specialized knowledge.

Open-ended questions Questions that begin with how, what, who, when, or where, and require explanations, as opposed to closed-ended questions that can be answered only "yes" or "no." Open-ended questions solicit feedback and information in a way not possible with closed-ended questions.

Open listing A listing in which the owner of the property gives the right to sell or lease a property to a number of brokers, who then can work simultaneously to effect a sale or lease. Compensation is owed to the broker who procures a ready, willing, and able buyer or tenant.

Operating expenses Recurring fixed expenses, such as rent, dues, fees, salaries, taxes, license fees, insurance and depreciation (funding for depreciation on equipment, buildings, and automobiles the company owns), and variable expenses such as advertising and promotion, utilities, equipment, supplies, and cost of sales.

Operating strategy The methodology employed by an organization to accomplish its goals. A strategy defines how the organization plans to use its financial and human resources.

Organization chart The structure of an organization that identifies the various business units, divisions, or departments within the firm and the line of authority or chain of command for each manager of the units.

Override A method of calculating managerial compensation based on a percentage of the gross commission (before the agents' shares are deducted), a percentage of commission after the sales and listing commissions are deducted, or a percentage of the office's net profits.

Panel interview An employment interview tactic in which the job applicant is interviewed by a group of people rather than one-on-one.

Panic selling Efforts to sell real estate in a particular neighborhood by generating fear that real estate values are declining because people in a protected class are moving into or out of a neighborhood, which has nothing to do with the intrinsic value of the real estate itself. Panic selling violates the fair housing laws.

Participative style A humanistic management style in which the manager creates a democratic environment that promotes initiative and recognizes the value of the human resources. Participative management utilizes the talents and insight of people to a greater extent than is common in other styles of management. *See also* autocratic style; dictatorial style; laissez-faire style.

Performance criteria The basis on which people will be evaluated in a performance review. Criteria include production quotas and other performance-based issues that are considered to be important in the performance of a person's job.

Performance reviews An evaluation of a worker's progress in which the manager and the worker, or salesperson, can meet one-on-one and discuss a variety of issues about the job and the salesperson's career.

Per se rule Decision by the U.S. Supreme Court that identifies certain antitrust activities that cannot be defended as being reasonable under any circumstances because they are so destructive to competition that their anticompetitive effect is automatically presumed. These include activities such as price fixing, certain kinds of boycotts, territorial assignments, and tying agreements.

Personal success plans A salesperson's business plan that converts the salesperson's aspirations for success into action with specific, measurable goals and strategies to guide him or her along the way. A personal success plan is a holistic approach to defining what a person intends to accomplish as a professional salesperson, in addition to a production quota.

Policy and procedures manual A document that tells people how they are to conduct business for the company. It includes the general business philosophy and business ethics, and prescribes procedures for handling a multitude of details of the company's operations.

Polychlorinated biphenyls (PCBs) Used in the manufacture of electrical products (such as transformers, switches, voltage regulators), paints, adhesives, caulking materials, and hydraulic fluids. PCBs can cause birth defects and cancer and other diseases.

POSDC A management model that groups various activities involved in the operation of a business by functions. These functions include planning, organizing, staffing, directing, and controlling.

Profit and loss statement A detailed statement of the income and expenses of a business, commonly known as a P & L, operating statement, or income statement.

Profit center A business unit within a company that is expected to produce enough income to cover its cost of operation plus make a profit for the firm.

Radon A radioactive gas produced by the natural decay of other radioactive substances, which is suspected to be a cause of cancer.

Real Estate Settlement Procedures Act (RESPA) A federal law enacted with the goal of encouraging home ownership. It intends to protect consumers from practices that are considered abusive, as well as to see that consumers are provided with more complete information about certain lending practices and closing and settlement procedures.

Referral networks Formally structured organizations that enable a broker to refer buyers and sellers to brokers in other geographic areas or to brokers who specialize in other types of real estate services. There are independent networks as well as those connected with national franchises and corporations.

Relocation networks Formal organizations that may be part of, or in addition to, referral networks to provide relocation services. There are corporate relocation management companies, otherwise known as third-party equity contractors, who enter into agreements with large corporations to handle their employee transfers.

Residential Lead-Based Paint Hazard Reduction Act Sets forth procedures for disclosing the presence of lead-based paint in the sale of residential properties built before 1978.

S corporation A kind of corporation that allows a business to operate as a corporation but not pay corporate tax. Each shareholder is taxed on his or her individual share of the corporation's income, which avoids the double taxation feature of corporations. There are limitations on the number of shareholders and the sources of corporate income.

Salesperson A licensed individual employed by a licensed broker, either as an employee or independent contractor, to perform certain acts as defined by the real estate license laws of the state.

Serial interview An employment interview tactic in which the job applicant is passed from one person to another, each of whom has a separate interview agenda.

Sexual harassment According to the federal Equal Employment Opportunity Commission, unwelcome sexual advances, requests for sexual favors, and other verbal or physical conduct of a sexual nature when submission is either explicitly or implicitly a term or condition of a person's employment, used as the basis for employment decisions affecting a person, or has the purpose or effect of unreasonably interfering with a person's work performance or creating an intimidating, hostile, or offensive working environment.

Sherman Act An antitrust law intended to curtail large trusts, cartels, or monopolies that are perceived to threaten healthy competition and the growth of businesses. The theory is that competitive forces must be allowed to function, with the ultimate result being the lowest prices, highest quality, and greatest progress in the marketplace.

Signature The name, slogan, and graphics that create an identity for the company.

Simulation interview An employment interview tactic in which the job applicant or candidate participates in a skill demonstration or problem-solving exercise. This is also known as an audition interview.

Single agency The practice of representing either the buyer/tenant or the seller/landlord, but never both in the same transaction.

Sole ownership A method of owning a business in which one person owns the entire business and is solely responsible and liable for all activities and debts of its operation. Business may be conducted under the name of the owner or a fictitious name. Also known as a sole proprietorship.

Staff authority The authority given to the people who are responsible for support services, the work groups that provide administrative support. They contribute indirectly to the achievement of the company's objectives by providing such services as accounting, marketing and advertising, training, purchasing (materials for the operation of the business), and maintenance.

Statutory independent contractor An individual who satisfies the three-part test in federal tax code to be considered an independent contractor: (1) has a properly issued real estate license, (2) has a written independent contractor agreement with the company/broker, and (3) substantially all of the compensation must be based on output or production, not hours worked. Described in the tax code as a statutory nonemployee.

Steering The illegal practice of channeling homeseekers to particular areas or neighborhoods. When another person, such as a licensee, does this, the act has the effect of limiting a homeseeker's choices by restricting the person's ability to choose the neighborhood in which she or he will live.

Stigmatized properties Those that individuals consider to be "psychologically impacted" because certain events have occurred that people may find offensive or that provoke emotional reactions. These include events such as a suicide, murder or other felony, paranormal activities (ghosts), a lingering illness, or death.

Strategies The methodology that will be used to accomplish a specific goal or objective. Long-range planning is otherwise known as strategic planning because it provides not only goals but also the strategic methodology for accomplishing them.

Subagent An agent of a person authorized to act as the agent of the principal under the law of agency.

Succession planning The process of preparing the organization to operate efficiently and effectively despite departures of personnel. This is especially important in the event of the death, retirement, or other departure of the owner but is good business for any position, which also fosters professional growth within the company as people groom their replacements.

Target market The specific audience or consumers for the company's products or services.

Team-building The process of mobilizing the collective efforts of people to work toward the goals of the organization and at the same time satisfy themselves.

Telecommuting Using technology to conduct business from any location in which computers can be linked to the base office through the telephone network. *See* home officing; virtual office.

Telephone Consumer Protection Act FCC regulations that govern the use of telephone lines for commercial solicitation and advertisement to protect telephone subscribers who do not wish to receive unsolicited live "cold called," autodialed, prerecorded, or artificial voice messages and fax machine solicitations.

Territorial assignments An antitrust violation in which competitors agree to divide the market geographically, or by some other criterion, which destroys competition when the purpose of segregating the market is to establish power in that market.

Text telephone (TT) Typewriter-like unit that displays conversation on a screen that can be read so a person who is deaf or hearing-impaired can communicate via telephone. A TT "talks" with another text telephone or a computer. Formerly known as TDDs.

Transaction expenses *See* cost of sales.

Tying agreement An arrangement in which a party agrees to sell one product only on the condition that the buyer also purchases a different or tied product. Frequently the tied product is less desirable than the tying product. The courts have concluded that the only purpose of a tying arrangement is to extend the market power of the tying product and have declared these agreements to be per se illegal.

Urea formaldehyde A chemical used in building materials in the 1970s, particularly in insulation. Urea formaldehyde foam insulation (UFFI) has been targeted because of the formaldehyde gases that leach out of the insulation.

Variable expense budgets Specific budgets prepared to identify individual expenditures within categories of certain general variable expenses, such as advertising and promotion, utilities, equipment and supplies, and cost of sales.

Vertical growth The organizational growth strategy that increases capacity in established business sectors as opposed to growing with diversification. *See* horizontal growth.

Virtual office Refers to an office that can exist anywhere, including on the Internet, or where people can use technology.

INDEX

Notes

Notes

Notes